AFRICAN HISTORICAL DICTIONARIES
Edited by Jon Woronoff

1. *Cameroon,* by Victor T. LeVine and Roger P. Nye. 1974. Out of print. See No. 48.
2. *The Congo,* 2nd ed., by Virginia Thompson and Richard Adloff. 1984
3. *Swaziland,* by John J. Grotpeter. 1975
4. *The Gambia,* 2nd ed., by Harry A. Gailey. 1987
5. *Botswana,* by Richard P. Stevens. 1975. Out of print. See No. 44.
6. *Somalia,* by Margaret F. Castagno. 1975
7. *Benin [Dahomey],* 2nd ed., by Samuel Decalo. 1987. Out of print. See No. 61.
8. *Burundi,* by Warren Weinstein. 1976
9. *Togo,* 2nd ed., by Samuel Decalo. 1987
10. *Lesotho,* by Gordon Haliburton. 1977
11. *Mali,* 2nd ed., by Pascal James Imperato. 1986
12. *Sierra Leone,* by Cyril Patrick Foray. 1977
13. *Chad,* 2nd ed., by Samuel Decalo. 1987
14. *Upper Volta,* by Daniel Miles McFarland. 1978
15. *Tanzania,* by Laura S. Kurtz. 1978
16. *Guinea,* 3rd ed., by Thomas O'Toole and Ibrahima Bah-Lalya. 1995
17. *Sudan,* by John Voll. 1978. Out of print. See No. 53.
18. *Rhodesia / Zimbabwe,* by R. Kent Rasmussen. 1979. Out of print. See No. 46.
19. *Zambia,* by John J. Grotpeter. 1979
20. *Niger,* 2nd ed., by Samuel Decalo. 1989
21. *Equatorial Guinea,* 2nd ed., by Max Liniger-Goumaz. 1988
22. *Guinea-Bissau,* 2nd ed., by Richard Lobban and Joshua Forrest. 1988
23. *Senegal,* by Lucie G. Colvin. 1981. Out of print. See No. 65.
24. *Morocco,* by William Spencer. 1980
25. *Malawi,* by Cynthia A. Crosby. 1980. Out of print. See No. 54.
26. *Angola,* by Phyllis Martin. 1980. Out of print. See No. 52.
27. *The Central African Republic,* by Pierre Kalck. 1980. Out of print. See No. 51.
28. *Algeria,* by Alf Andrew Heggoy. 1981. Out of print. See No. 66.
29. *Kenya,* by Bethwell A. Ogot. 1981
30. *Gabon,* by David E. Gardinier. 1981. Out of print. See No. 58.
31. *Mauritania,* by Alfred G. Gerteiny. 1981
32. *Ethiopia,* by Chris Prouty and Eugene Rosenfeld. 1981. Out of print. See No. 56.
33. *Libya,* 2nd ed., by Ronald Bruce St John. 1991
34. *Mauritius,* by Lindsay Rivière. 1982. Out of print. See No. 49.
35. *Western Sahara,* by Tony Hodges. 1982. Out of print. See No. 55.

36. *Egypt,* by Joan Wucher King. 1984. Out of print. See No. 67.
37. *South Africa,* by Christopher Saunders. 1983
38. *Liberia,* by D. Elwood Dunn and Svend E. Holsoe. 1985
39. *Ghana,* by Daniel Miles McFarland. 1985. Out of print. See No. 63.
40. *Nigeria,* by Anthony Oyewole. 1987
41. *Côte d'Ivoire (The Ivory Coast),* 2nd ed., by Robert J. Mundt. 1995
42. *Cape Verde,* 2nd ed., by Richard Lobban and Marilyn Halter. 1988. Out of print. See No. 62.
43. *Zaire,* by F. Scott Bobb. 1988
44. *Botswana,* by Fred Morton, Andrew Murray, and Jeff Ramsay. 1989
45. *Tunisia,* by Kenneth J. Perkins. 1989
46. *Zimbabwe,* 2nd ed., by R. Kent Rasmussen and Steven L. Rubert. 1990
47. *Mozambique,* by Mario Azevedo. 1991
48. *Cameroon,* 2nd ed., by Mark W. DeLancey and H. Mbella Mokeba. 1990
49. *Mauritius,* 2nd ed., by Sydney Selvon. 1991
50. *Madagascar,* by Maureen Covell. 1995
51. *The Central African Republic,* 2nd ed., by Pierre Kalck; translated by Thomas O'Toole. 1992
52. *Angola,* 2nd ed., by Susan H. Broadhead. 1992
53. *Sudan,* 2nd ed., by Carolyn Fluehr-Lobban, Richard A. Lobban, Jr., and John Obert Voll. 1992
54. *Malawi,* 2nd ed., by Cynthia A. Crosby. 1993
55. *Western Sahara,* 2nd ed., by Anthony Pazzanita and Tony Hodges. 1994
56. *Ethiopia and Eritrea,* 2nd ed., by Chris Prouty and Eugene Rosenfeld. 1994
57. *Namibia,* by John J. Grotpeter. 1994
58. *Gabon,* 2nd ed., by David Gardinier. 1994
59. *Comoro Islands,* by Martin Ottenheimer and Harriet Ottenheimer. 1994
60. *Rwanda,* by Learthen Dorsey. 1994
61. *Benin,* 3rd ed., by Samuel Decalo. 1995
62. *Republic of Cape Verde,* 3rd ed., by Richard Lobban and Marlene Lopes. 1995
63. *Ghana,* 2nd ed., by David Owusu-Ansah and Daniel Miles McFarland. 1995
64. *Uganda,* by M. Louise Pirouet. 1995
65. *Senegal,* 2nd ed., by Andrew F. Clark and Lucie Colvin Phillips. 1994
66. *Algeria,* 2nd ed., by Phillip Chiviges Naylor and Alf Andrew Heggoy. 1994
67. *Egypt,* by Arthur Goldschmidt, Jr. 1994

HISTORICAL DICTIONARY OF MADAGASCAR

by
Maureen Covell

African Historical Dictionaries, No. 50

The Scarecrow Press, Inc.
Lanham, Md., & London

SCARECROW PRESS, INC.

Published in the United States of America
by Scarecrow Press, Inc.
4720 Boston Way, Lanham, Maryland 20706

4 Pleydell Gardens, Folkestone
Kent CT20 2DN, England

British Cataloging in Publication Information Available

Library of Congress Cataloging-in-Publication Data

Covell, Maureen.
Historical dictionary of Madagascar / by Maureen Covell.
p. cm. — (African historical dictionaries : no. 50)
Includes bibliographical references.
1. Madagascar—History—Dictionaries. I. Title. II. Series.
DT469.M285C69 1995 969.1'003—dc20 94–45309

ISBN 0–8108–2973–8 (cloth : alk. paper)

Printed in the United States of America

The paper used in this publication meets the minimum requirements of American National Standard for Information Sciences—Permanence of Paper for Printed Library Materials, ANSI Z39.48–1984.

CONTENTS

EDITOR'S FOREWORD

Madagascar is probably the most unique country in Africa and, for that reason alone, deserves to be better known. But there has been much less research and much less news available for this country than for most others, and we actually hear less about it today than at independence. This lack of coverage has only worsened since the Malagasy Republic became the Democratic Republic of Madagascar. We are therefore delighted that, after so many years, we have finally been able to publish a *Historical Dictionary of Madagascar.*

Like our other volumes, this one sheds light on the politics, economics, society, and culture of the country. It is even more important in telling us about today's leaders, without neglecting figures who played significant roles in earlier periods. The Bibliography, while giving readers clues as to where to find additional information, also shows that the dearth of materials in English is severe and that this book is the best place to start or renew an acquaintance with an absolutely intriguing country.

The author, who had to make greater efforts than many others, is Maureen Covell. Presently professor of political science at Simon Fraser University, her own encounter began in 1967–1969, when she did research in France and Madagascar for her dissertation on local politics in the Malagasy Republic. At that time, she had already met some of the people who are active participants in the current regime, which she explored in her recent book, *Madagascar: Politics, Economics, Society.*

Jon Woronoff
Series Editor

GUIDE TO PRONUNCIATION OF MALAGASY WORDS

Although earlier European visitors to Madagascar compiled vocabularies and even dictionaries, the first systematic transcription of Malagasy into the Latin alphabet was undertaken by missionaries from the London Missionary Society after their arrival in Antananarivo in 1822. Consonants in Malagasy have the same pronunciation as consonants in English, with some exceptions. *G* is always hard; *J* is pronounced *dz,* and *S* is softened to a sound between *s* and *sh.* When *G* and *K* are preceded by *I* or *Y,* the vowel is sounded after as well as before the consonant, giving a sound like that of *Y* in "yellow."

The pronunciation of vowels is more consistent than in English, since Radama I rejected the English practice of having one letter stand for more than one sound.

A is pronounced like the *a* in "father."
E stands for a sound between the *e* in "get" and the *e* in "very."
I is pronounced like the long *e* in "green."
O is pronounced like the double *o* in "soon."
AI is pronounced like the *i* in "like."
AO stands for a sound between the *o* of "cow" and that of "row."
Ṅ represents a sound between the *ng* of "sing" and the *ny* of "canyon."

Elision of syllables, particularly final vowels and *an* and *in* in the middle of a word, is common. Thus, for example, "Merina" is pronounced to rhyme with "cairn."

ACRONYMS AND ABBREVIATIONS

ADM	Alliance Démocratique Malgache (Malagasy Democratic Alliance)
AEOM	Association des Etudiants d'Origine Malgache (Association of Students of Malagasy Origin)
AKFM (q.v.)	Atokon'ny Kongresin'ny Fahaleovantenan'i Madagasikara (Independence Congress Party of Madagascar)
ANP	Assemblée Nationale Populaire (National People's Assembly)
AREMA (q.v.)	Avant-garde de la Révolution Malgache (Vanguard of the Malagasy Revolution)
CAR	Collectivités Autochontones Rurales (Indigenous Rural Collectivities)
CFV	Comité des Forces Vives (Committee of Active Forces)
CGT	Confédération Générale du Travail (General Confederation of Labor)
CMD	Conseil Militaire pour le Développement (Military Council for Development)
CNOE	Comité National pour l'Observation des Elections (National Election Observation Committee)

CNP	Congrès National Populaire (National Popular Congress)
CNPD	Conseil National Populaire du Développement (National People's Development Council)
COSOMA	Comité de Solidarité de Madagascar (Committee for Solidarity with Madagascar)
CRAM	Collectivité Rurale Autochtone Modernisée (Modernized Indigenous Rurale Collectivity)
CRES	Comité de Rédressement Economique et Social (Committee for Economic and Social Recovery)
CSI	Conseil Supérieur des Institutions (Higher Council of Institutions)
CSR	Conseil Suprême de la Révolution (Supreme Council of the Revolution)
DM	Directoire Militaire (Military Directorate)
DRM	Democratic Republic of Madagascar
EEM	Electricité et Eau de Madagascar (Electricity and Water [Company] of Madagascar)
FAEM	Fédération des Associations des Etudiants Malgaches (Federation of Associations of Malagasy Students)
FDM	Front Démocratique Malgache (Malagasy Democratic Front)
FFKM (q.v.)	Fikombonan'ny Fiangonana Kristiana Eto Malagasy (Council of Christian Churches of Madagascar)
FIDES	Fonds d'Investissement pour le Développement

	Economique et Social (Investment Fund for Economic and Social Development)
FISEMA	Firaisan'ny Sendika eran'i Madagasikara (Federation of Unions of Madagascar)
FJKM	Fiangonan'i Jesosy Kristy eto Madagasikara (Church of Jesus Christ in Madagascar)
FNDR	Front National pour la Défense de la Révolution (National Front for the Defense of the Revolution)
FNM	Front National Malgache (Malagasy National Front)
FRS	Forces Républicaines de Sécurité (Republic Security Forces)
GEC	Groupe d'Etudes Communistes (Group for Communist Studies)
GMP	Groupe Mobile de Police (Mobile Police Group)
HAE	Haute Autorité d'Etat (High State Authority)
IBRD	International Bank for Reconstruction and Development
ILO	International Labor Organization
JINA	Jeunesse Nationale
JIRAMA	Jiro sy Rano Malagasy (Electricity and Water of Madagascar)
KIM	Komity Iraisan'ny Mpitolona
LMS	London Missionary Society

MDRM	Mouvement Démocratique de la Rénovation Malgache (Democratic Movement for Malagasy Renewal)
MFM (q.v.)	Mpitolona ho amin'ny Fanjakan'ny Madinika
MMSM	Mouvement Militant pour le Socialisme Malgache (Militant Movement for Malagasy Socialism)
MONIMA (q.v.)	*Originally* Mouvement National pour l'Independance de Madagascar: *since 1967* Madagasikara Otronin'ny Malagasy
MORENA	Mouvement de la Rénovation Malgache (Movement for Malagasy Renewal)
OAU	Organization of African Unity
OCAM	Organization Commune Africaine et Malgache (African-Malagasy Common Organization)
OMNIS	Office Militaire Nationale pour les Industries Stratégiques (National Military Office for Strategic Industries)
OMPIRA	Office Militaire pour la Production Agricole (Military Office for Agricultural Production)
ORSTOM	Office pour la Recherche Scientifique et Téchnique d'Outre-Mer (Office for Overseas Scientific and Technical Research)
PADESM	Parti des Deshérités de Madagascar (Party of the Disinherited of Madagascar)
PDM	Parti Démocratique Malgache (Democratic Party of Madagascar)
PLC	Parti Libéral Chrétien (Christian Liberal Party)

PSD	Parti Social Démocrate (Social Democratic Party)
PSM	Parti Socialiste Malgache (Socialist Party of Madagascar)
RCM	Rassemblement Chrétien de Madagascar (Christian Assembly of Madagascar)
RNM	Rassemblement National Malgache (Malagasy National Assembly)
RPM	Rassemblement du Peuple Malgache (Assembly of the Malagasy People)
SECESS	Syndicat d'Enseignants et Chercheurs de l'Enseignement Supérieur (Union of Teachers and Researchers in Higher Education)
SECREN	Société d'Etudes de Construction et de Réparations Navales (Society for the Study of Naval Construction and Repair)
SEKRIMA	Sendika Kristiana Malagasy (Malagasy Christian Union)
SEREMA	Sendika Revolisionara Malagasy (Malagasy Revolutionary Union)
SINPA	Société d'Intérêt National de Commercialisation des Produits Agricoles (National Interest Society for the Commercialization of Agricultural Products)
SIRAMA	Siramamy Malagasy (Malagasy Sugar)
SMOTIG	Service de la Main-d'Oeuvre des Travaux d'Intérêt Général (Labor Service for Public Works)
SOMALAC	Société Malgache du Lac Alaotra (Malagasy Society for Lake Alaotra)

SOMASAK	Société Malgache de la Sakay (Malagasy Society for the Sakay)
SONACO	Société National de Commerce Extérieure (National Society for Foreign Trade)
SOSUMAV	Société Sucrière de Madagascar (Sugar Company of Madagascar)
TTS	Tanora Tonga Saina (Revolutionary Youth)
UDECMA	Union des Chrétiens de Madagascar (Union of Malagasy Christians)
UDSM	Union Démocratique et Sociale de Madagascar (Malagasy Democratic and Social Union)
UEM	Union des Etudiants Malgaches (Union of Malagasy Students)
UESM	Union des Etudiants Socialistes Malgaches (Union of Malagasy Socialist Students)
UIT	Union des Indépendants de Tananarive (Union of Independents of Tananarive)
UNAM	Union Nationale Malgache (Malagasy National Union; *originally* Union des Autochtones Malgaches, *or* Union of Malagasy Natives)
UNDD	Union Nationale pour le Développement et la Démocratie (National Union for Development and Democracy)
UNIUM	Union des Intellectuels et Universitaires Malgaches (Union of Malagasy Intellectuals and Academics)
UPM	Union des Peuples Malgaches (Union of the Peoples of Madagascar)

USM	Union Socialiste Malgache (Malagasy Socialist Union)
USDM	Union des Sociaux Démocrates de Madagascar (Social Democratic Union of Madagascar)
Vonjy	Vonjy Iray Tsy Mivaky (Popular Force for National Unity)
VVS	Vy Vato Sakelika (Iron Stone Network)
ZOAM (q.v.)	Zatovo Orin'asa Anivon'ny Madagasikara (Young Unemployed of Madagascar)
ZWAM	Zatovo Western Andevo Malagasy (Young Slave Cowboys of Madagascar)

CHRONOLOGY

c. A.D. 1?	Human settlement of Madagascar begins.
Before 1000	Islamic settlements occur along the coast and enter into the trading networks of the western Indian Ocean. On Arab maps, a large island appears off the east coast of Africa under the names Waqwaq and Komr.
15th century	The SAKALAVA* begin to form kingdoms under the MAROSERANA dynasty. MERINA kingdoms begin to form in the interior.
1500	DIOGO DIAZ sights Madagascar.
1506	TRISTAN DA CUNHA explores DIEGO-SUAREZ Bay.
late 16th century	The SAKALAVA kingdom of MENABE is established.
mid–17th century	The SAKALAVA kingdom of BOINA is established.
1642	The French attempt to found a settlement at FORT-DAUPHIN.
1645–1646	A British attempt to settle SAINT AUGUSTINE BAY fails.
1674	The French abandon FORT-DAUPHIN.

*Names and terms given in capitals may be found as entries in the Dictionary section.

1685–1730	PIRATES occupy the seas around Madagascar, and settle on ILE SAINTE-MARIE, and at ANTONGIL BAY, DIEGO-SUAREZ BAY, and SAINT AUGUSTINE BAY.
late 17th century	The BETSILEO kingdom of LALAINGINA is established.
early 18th century	The BETSILEO kingdom of ISANDRA is established.
1712	RATSIMILAHO begins construction of the BETSIMISARAKA CONFEDERATION.
1745	MAHAJANGA becomes the capital of the BOINA SAKALAVA.
1750	Queen Beti (daughter of RATSIMILAHO) signs ILE SAINTE-MARIE over to the French.
1774	COUNT BENYOWSKI attempts to found a settlement at ANTONGIL BAY.
c. 1783	ADRIANAMPOINIMERINA overthrows his uncle and becomes ruler of AMBOHIMANGA.
1786	BENYOWSKI is killed by a French expedition at ANTONGIL BAY.
c. 1793	ANDRIANAMPOINIMERINA captures ANTANANARIVO, future capital of the MERINA EMPIRE.
late 18th century	The BETSILEO kingdom of ISANDRA becomes part of the MERINA EMPIRE.
1810	ANDRIANAMPOINIMERINA dies. He is succeeded by his son, RADAMA II.

1815 The BETSILEO kingdom of LALAINGINA becomes part of the MERINA EMPIRE.

1817 The MERINA EMPIRE occupies TOAMASINA. October: RADAMA I signs a treaty of friendship with Sir ROBERT FARQUHAR, governor of MAURITIUS. It is abrogated by FARQUHAR's successor.

1819 The treaty between Great Britain and the MERINA EMPIRE is renewed.

1820 December: The first missionaries from the LONDON MISSIONARY SOCIETY arrive in ANTANANARIVO.

1824 The MERINA EMPIRE occupies MAHAJANGA. King ANDRIANATSOLY of the BOINA SAKALAVA flees.

1826 The ZANAMALATA leaders of the BETSIMISARAKA CONFEDERATION rebel against the MERINA EMPIRE and are defeated.

1828 RADAMA I dies. After internal struggles his first wife becomes Queen RANAVALONA I.

1829 Officials of the MERINA EMPIRE remove French flags from the mainland opposite the ILE SAINTE-MARIE. In retaliation the French bombard TOAMASINA.

1830 FIANARANTSOA becomes the southern capital of the MERINA EMPIRE.

1835 RANAVALONA I bans the practice of Christianity in Madagascar.

1836 The TANALA kingdom of IKONGO rebels against MERINA rule.

1837	Queen RANAVALONA sends a diplomatic mission to London and Paris.
1840	Queen TSIOMEKO negotiates a French protectorate over NOSY BE, which is ratified by the governor of REUNION, Admiral de Hell, in 1841.
1845	June: British and French ships bombard TOAMASINA.
1855	The son of Queen RANAVALONA, later RADAMA II, signs the LAMBERT CHARTER, granting territory in Madagascar to JOSEPH LAMBERT.
1861	August: Queen RANAVALONA dies and is succeeded by her son, RADAMA II. The ban on Christianity and the entry of Europeans is lifted.
1863	May 12: RADAMA II is assassinated. He is succeeded by his wife, who rules as Queen RASOHERINA. Her government denounces the LAMBERT CHARTER; France demands the payment of an indemnity to LAMBERT.
1863–1864	The MERINA EMPIRE sends a mission to Europe. It agrees to payment of an indemnity to LAMBERT. July 1864: RAINLAIARIVONY becomes prime minister of Madagascar.
1866	January: The LAMBERT CHARTER is publicly burned.
1867	The UNITED STATES and the MERINA EMPIRE sign a trade agreement.
1868	Queen RASOHERINA dies. She is succeeded by Queen RANAVALONA II.

1869 February: Queen RANAVALONA II announces her conversion to Christianity.

1878 December 27: JEAN LABORDE dies. His will leaves his property in Madagascar to two nephews.

1879 The Malagasy government refuses to recognize the LABORDE LEGACY.

1881 The UNITED STATES and the MERINA EMPIRE sign a treaty of trade and friendship.
March 29: The CODE OF 305 ARTICLES forbids the sale of Malagasy land to foreigners.
November: Flags of the MERINA are planted on the northwest coast of Madagascar. The French demand their removal.

1882 June: The French remove the MERINA flags from the northwest coast.
October: The MERINA government sends a mission to Paris.
November: Negotiations with the French government break down.
December: The French decide to send an expedition to Madagascar.

1883 The treaty between the UNITED STATES and Madagascar is promulgated.
May 16: Admiral Pierre captures MAHAJANGA.
June 10: Pierre takes TOAMASINA.
July 13: RANAVALONA II dies. She is succeeded by RANAVALONA III.
November: Negotiations begin between FRANCE and the MERINA government.

1884 March: The negotiations between FRANCE and the MERINA government break down.

1885 August: Negotiations begin again between FRANCE and the MERINA government.
December 17: A treaty between FRANCE and the MERINA EMPIRE establishes the first French PROTECTORATE. Disputes over the interpretation of the treaty begin immediately.

1890 The FRANCO-BRITISH CONVENTION exchanges British recognition of the French interpretation of its PROTECTORATE over Madagascar for French recognition of the British protectorate over Zanzibar.

1894 January: The French Chamber of Deputies accepts the principle of a conquest of Madagascar.
October: LE MYRE DE VILERS is sent to ANTANANARIVO to present an ultimatum to RAINILAIARIVONY. He arrives October 14.
October 27: LE MYRE DE VILERS rejects the MERINA counterproposals and returns to TOAMASINA.
November 16: The French Chamber of Deputies votes the credits for the invasion of Madagascar.
December 12: The second FRANCO-MALAGASY WAR begins with the occupation of TOAMASINA.

1895 January: French forces arrive at MAHAJANGA.
September 30: ANTANANARIVO is captured.
October 1: Queen RANAVALONA III signs a treaty establishing a French PROTECTORATE over Madagascar. RAINILAIARIVONY is arrested and exiled to Algiers.
November 22: The Revolt of the MENALAMBA begins with the killing of a missionary family.

1896	August 6: The ANNEXATION LAW declares Madagascar a French possession. September 26: Slavery is declared abolished. September 27: GALLIENI arrives to restore order. RANAVALONA III is removed from the throne. October 15: GALLIENI accuses the uncle of the queen, Prince Ratsimamanga, and her minister of the interior, Rainandriamampandry, of directing the MENALAMBA rising. They are executed.
1897	French forces occupy IHOSY, in BARA territory. The BARA revolt. February: RANAVALONA III is exiled to REUNION and then to Algiers. May: INSURRECTION in the south begins. June: MENALAMBA leader RABEZAVANA surrenders. August: King Toera of the MENABE SAKALAVA is killed.
1898	February: MENALAMBA leader RABOZAKA surrenders.
1899–1902	The TANALA rebel against the French. The MAHAFALY rebel against the imposition of French rule.
1900	The fortifications at DIEGO-SUAREZ Bay are begun.
1904	The INSURRECTION in the south is considered overcome. FORCED LABOR is introduced.
1912	Pastor RAVELOJAONA publishes a series of articles on Japan and the Japanese, discussing the possibility of modernization without the abandonment of national culture.

1913 The nationalist organization VY VATO SAKELIKA is formed at the BEFELATANANA Medical School.

1914 August 1: The First World War begins. Over 40,000 Malagasy are mobilized by Governor-General GARBIT to fight in the war.

1915 December 24: The leaders of VVS are arrested.

1920 In Paris JEAN RALAIMONGO founds the Ligue Française pour l'Accession des Indigènes de Madagascar aux Droits des Citoyens Français.

1921 The VVS prisoners are amnestied.

1924 DELEGATIONS ECONOMIQUES ET FINANCIERES, with some elected members, are established.

1926 The SERVICE DE LA MAIN-D'OEUVRE POUR LES TRAVAUX D'INTERET GENERAL is established.

1929 May 19: A demonstration outside the Excelsior theater in ANTANANARIVO demands independence and leads to the arrest of several nationalist figures, including JEAN RALAIMONGO.

1930 RALAIMONGO and JOSEPH RAVOAHANGY are sent to assigned residences.
December: The DECRET CAYLA gives the administration the right to arrest and detain those considered to be guilty of acts likely to create hostility to the colonial regime.

1936 RALAIMONGO and RAVOAHANGY are amnestied, and SMOTIG is abolished.

1937 The formation of trade UNIONS including Malagasy who can speak and read French is legalized.

1940 June: At the fall of France, Governor-General DE COPPET declares first for the FREE FRENCH and then for the VICHY regime. Under Vichy administrators, many of the restrictions eliminated in 1936–1937 are reintroduced.

1941 The secret society PANAMA is formed.

1942 May: The BRITISH INVASION begins.
November: The French forces surrender.

1943–1944 January 1943: Madagascar is returned to the FREE FRENCH, who call up 28,000 Malagasy.
The secret society JINA is formed.
The FREE FRENCH establish the OFFICE DU RIZ.

1945 October 21:RAVOAHANGY and RASETA are elected delegates to the first CONSTITUENT ASSEMBLY of the FOURTH FRENCH REPUBLIC.

1946 February: RASETA, RAVOAHANGY, and JACQUES RABEMANANJARA form the MOUVEMENT DEMOCRATIQUE DE LA RENOVATION MALGACHE in Paris.
April: FORCED LABOR, the INDIGENAT, and the OFFICE DU RIZ are abolished.
June 2: In elections to the second CONSTITUENT ASSEMBLY of the FOURTH FRENCH REPUBLIC, RAVOAHANGY and RASETA are reelected.
The PARTI DES DESHERITES DE MADAGASCAR is formed.
October: The constitution of the FOURTH FRENCH REPUBLIC is adopted. It makes no

provision for eventual independence for France's overseas territories.
October–November: Madagascar is divided into five provinces.
November 10: Elections to the French National Assembly are held. RASETA, RAVOAHANGY, and RABEMANANJARA are elected in the Malagasy college.

1947 Night of March 29–30: The REBELLION OF 1947 breaks out.
April–July: The parliamentary immunity of senators and deputies from the MOUVEMENT DEMOCRATIQUE DE LA RENOVATION MALGACHE is lifted and they are arrested.

1948 July 19: SAMUEL RAKOTONDRABE, accused by the French of being the ''Generalissimo'' of the REBELLION OF 1947, is executed.
July 22: The TANANARIVE TRIAL of those accused of complicity in the REBELLION OF 1947 begins.
October 4: Sentences are delivered in the TANANARIVE TRIAL. RASETA and RAVOAHANGY are sentenced to death and RABEMANANJARA to life at hard labor.

1949 July: The death sentences delivered by the TANANARIVE TRIAL are commuted to life imprisonment.

1950 September: The MDRM deputies are transferred to Corsica.

1955 September: The MDRM deputies are transferred to assigned residence in France.
November 15: The French National Assembly passes a bill providing for municipal elections with universal suffrage and a single COLLEGE SYSTEM.

1956 January 2: PHILIBERT TSIRANANA, future president of the FIRST REPUBLIC, is elected to the French National Assembly.
June 23: The LOI-CADRE is passed providing for a degree of internal autonomy for France's African colonies and for the abolition of the COLLEGE SYSTEM at the territorial level.
The province of DIEGO-SUAREZ (now ANTSERANANA) is created.
November 18: Municipal elections are held.
December: TSIRANANA creates the PARTI SOCIAL DEMOCRATE.

1957 The UNION DEMOCRATIQUE ET SOCIALE DE MADAGASCAR is created by NORBERT ZAFIMAHOVA.
March 30: Elections to the provincial assemblies are held.
May 13–19: Provincial assemblies elect delegates to the territorial assembly in ANTANANARIVO.
May 27: TSIRANANA is elected vice president of the LOI-CADRE GOVERNING COUNCIL.

1958 May 2–4: The TAMATAVE CONGRESS of parties demanding immediate independence is held.
July: MONJA JAONA creates MONIMA.
September 28: The REFERENDUM ON THE CONSTITUTION OF THE FIFTH FRENCH REPUBLIC is held. Madagascar ratifies it by 78% of the vote.
The CARTEL DES REPUBLICAINS, linking the UDSM and the PSD, is formed.
The AKFM, grouping some of the parties of the TAMATAVE CONGRESS, is formed.
October 15: A constituent assembly composed of members of the provincial assemblies meets in ANTANANARIVO to discuss the future status of the island. It votes in favor of autonomy within the French Community.

	October 15: High Commissioner ANDRE SOUCADAUX announces the abrogation of the ANNEXATION LAW of 1896.
1959	April: ZAFIMAHOVA is ousted as president of the assembly. The constituent assembly adopts a presidential constitution. May 1: TSIRANANA is elected president by the assembly. October 11: Municipal elections are held. RICHARD ANDRIAMANJATO becomes mayor of ANTANANARIVO. December: Madagascar asks for full independence.
1960	June 26: Full independence is proclaimed. The MDRM deputies return from Paris. June 27: The COOPERATION AGREEMENTS with France are signed. September 4: Elections to the new NATIONAL ASSEMBLY are held. The PSD and related lists win 104 of 107 seats and the AKFM 3, all in ANTANANARIVO.
1965	March 30: TSIRANANA is reelected president, against RASETA, with over 90% of the vote. August 8: Elections are held to the NATIONAL ASSEMBLY. The PSD wins 104 seats and the AKFM 3 seats, all in ANTANANARIVO.
1967	The regime begins to cultivate closer economic ties with South Africa.
1970	January: TSIRANANA suffers a stroke at a meeting of the ORGANISATION COMMUNE AFRICAINE ET MALGACHE in Yaoundé and is hospitalized in Paris. May: TSIRANANA returns to Madagascar. September 6: In the elections to the NATIONAL

ASSEMBLY, the PSD wins 104 seats and the AKFM the 3 seats in ANTANANARIVO it held before.

1971 February 17: TSIRANANA forms a new government and demotes his powerful minister of the interior, ANDRE RESAMPA, to the Ministry of Agriculture.
March: A strike at BEFELATANANA Medical School spreads to other parts of the university. The university is closed on March 25.
April: The government-hosted National Development days bring together the PSD, the AKFM, and representatives of other groups in ANTANANARIVO.
April 1–2: The PEASANT UPRISING in the south begins and is suppressed with many deaths. MONJA JAONA goes into hiding but is arrested on April 23 and claims sole responsibility for the uprising. By April 27, 454 have been arrested and sent to NOSY LAVA.
May: RESAMPA is ousted as secretary-general of the PSD.
May 30: A foreign embassy, understood to be that of the UNITED STATES, is accused of attempted subversion.
June 1: ANDRE RESAMPA is arrested.
October: The discovery of the ORSTOM PLOT is announced.

1972 January: Students at BEFELATANANA Medical School go on strike.
January 30: TSIRANANA is reelected president, as sole candidate, with 99.9% of the vote.
May 12–3: The FORCES REPUBLICAINES DE SECURITE stage an overnight raid on the campus of the UNIVERSITY OF MADAGASCAR and on ZOAM strongholds in ISOTRY. Over 300 are arrested and sent to NOSY LAVA. In the morning a crowd gathers in front of the Hôtel de

Ville. In the afternoon the FRS fires on the demonstrators, who counterattack.
May 14: A procession marches to the presidential palace to demand the return of the deportees and the dissolution of the FRS. It is turned back and returns to the Hôtel de Ville, which it attacks and burns to the ground.
May 15: Crowds return to the Hôtel de Ville and are joined by representatives of the CHURCHES, AKFM, and the UNIONS. Colonel RATSIMANDRAVA, head of the gendarmerie, announces to TSIRANANA that the regular armed forces will not fire on the crowd.
May 16: The deportees are returned. TSIRANANA makes a speech in which he says that if peace is not restored the FRS will return.
May 17: The crowds return to the Hôtel de Ville, demanding the resignation of TSIRANANA and the installation of a military regime. The French embassy announces that the French troops at Ivato airport will intervene only to save French lives and property.
May 18: TSIRANANA gives full powers to General RAMANANTSOA.
June 23: The new government breaks ties with South Africa and cancels the agreements it had made with the FIRST REPUBLIC.
June 26: The abolition of the head tax is announced.
September: The CONGRES NATIONAL POPULAIRE is held in ANTANANARIVO, but breaks down into quarrels between radical and conservative factions of the KOMITY IRAISAN'NY MPITOLOHA.
October 2: Diplomatic relations with the Soviet Union are established.
November 6: Diplomatic relations are established with the People's Republic of China.
November 16: Diplomatic relations are established with NORTH KOREA.

December: The MFM is officially established.
December 1972–April 1973: Anti-MALGACHIZATION riots and strokes occur in coastal cities.

1973 January: The negotiations for the revision of the COOPERATION AGREEMENTS begin.
March: The political party VONJY IRAY TSY MIVAKY is founded.
May: Madagascar withdraws from the FRANC ZONE and from the ORGANISATION COMMUNE AFRICAINE ET MALGACHE.
June 4: The new COOPERATION AGREEMENTS are signed.
October 21: The CONSEIL NATIONAL POPULAIRE DU DEVELOPPEMENT is elected. The MFM boycotts the elections.
French troops leave DIEGO-SUAREZ and Ivato.

1974 March: TSIRANANA and RESAMPA create the PARTI SOCIALISTE MALGACHE.
December 31: A coup attempt, organized by Colonel BRECHARD RAJAONARISON, is discovered. Rajaonarison and his supporters flee to ANTANAIMORO military camp outside ANTANANARIVO.

1975 January 25: RAMANANTSOA dissolves his government and is unable to form another.
February 5: RICHARD RATSIMANDRAVA becomes president.
February 11: RATSIMANDRAVA is assassinated, and three members of the GROUPE MOBILE DE POLICE are arrested at the scene.
The DIRECTOIRE MILITAIRE is formed and martial law is declared.
February 13–14: ANTANAIMORO camp is occupied and pillaged by an ANTANANARIVO mob, as is the headquarters of the PSD.
March 21: The TRIAL OF THE CENTURY, of

those suspected of complicity in RATSIMANDRAVA's assassination, begins.
April 16: ROLAND RABETAFIKA is added to the number of the accused at the TRIAL OF THE CENTURY.
May 17: Amnesty is granted to 260 of the defendants in the TRIAL OF THE CENTURY.
June 12: The cases against the remaining defendants are dismissed. The three members of the GMP found at the scene are given prison sentences.
June 15: The DIRECTOIRE MILITAIRE announces its selection of RATSIRAKA as president. He announces the formation of the DEMOCRATIC REPUBLIC OF MADAGASCAR and the NATIONALIZATION of banks, insurance companies, and the film distribution network.
June 30: The state takes 51% participation in the Société des Transports Martimes, the Société Malgache de Raffinage, and the Compagnie Marseillaise de Madagascar.
July: The NASA tracking station at Imerintotsika is closed.
December 21: A REFERENDUM ratifies the creation of the DEMOCRATIC REPUBLIC OF MADAGASCAR and the selection of RATSIRAKA as president by 94.6% of the vote. The official beginning of the republic is declared on December 30.

1976 The FRONT NATIONAL POUR LA DEFENSE DE LA REVOLUTION is created.
January 13: The CONSEIL SUPREME DE LA REVOLUTION is established.
March: The regime party of the DRM, AREMA, is established.
May 14: The FNDR accepts AREMA's application for membership.
July 26: Five years of education at the primary level is made free and compulsory.
July 30: The prime minister of the DRM, JOEL

RAKOTOMALALA, is killed in a helicopter accident. He is succeeded by JUSTIN RAKOTONIAINA on August 12.

August 21: Technical schools in ANTANANARIVO go on strike.

September 10–11: During the night there are riots, and the Palace of ANDAFIAVARATRA is burned. Two American diplomats are expelled, and the MFM is proscribed.

October 9: The FNDR accepts the applications of the AKFM and VONJY for membership.

December 20: Attacks on COMORIANS in MAHAJANGA lead to the evacuation of many of them.

December 27: The ordinance creating the DECENTRALIZED COLLECTIVITIES is published.

December 27: The FNDR accepts the application of the UNION DES CHRETIENS DE MADAGASCAR for membership. MONIMA joins without applying for membership.

December 29: The FNDR officially comes into existence. MFM leaders arrested in September are amnestied.

1977 January: A plane from South Africa lands without permission at the Manajary airport.

March 20–May 29: ELECTIONS are held in the DECENTRALIZED COLLECTIVITIES. MONJA JAONA denounces the regime for electoral fraud and calls for the annulment of the results.

May 24: An ordinance establishes the ASSEMBLEE NATIONALE POPULAIRE.

May to July: Technical schools are on strike.

June 18: MONJA JAONA leaves the FNDR.

June 30: ELECTIONS are held to the ASSEMBLEE NATIONALE POPULAIRE. MONIMA refuses to participate, as does the MFM.

July 30: MANANDAFY RAKOTONIRINA

brings the MFM into the FNDR and joins the CSR.
July 31: JUSTIN RAKOTONIAINA is replaced as prime minister by Colonel DESIRE RAKOTOARIJAONA.
August: MONIMA splits into Monima Ka Miviombio and Vondrona Socialist Monima. The latter rejoins the FNDR.
October: Three officers of the Malagasy armed forces are arrested for conspiring with South Africa against the regime.
BEFELATANANA Medical School is closed.
May: A strike in the secondary school system leads to clashes between students and ZOAM and to riots in ANTANANARIVO and the looting of INDO-PAKISTANI stores.
September 16: The army is placed on alert after mysterious plane flights, attributed to South Africa, over Madagascar.
October: RATSIRAKA announces the beginning of the ALL-OUT INVESTMENT policy, to be financed by "omnidirectional" borrowing.

1978 January: In a secret trial, the pilot and passengers of a plane from South Africa are given sentences of three years in prison for landing in Madagascar without clearance.
April: First Conference of Progressive Forces of the Indian Ocean.

1979 August: A civil servants' strike over reform of the civil service is put down by the police.

1980 Madagascar approaches the INTERNATIONAL MONETARY FUND for a loan to cover a balance-of-payments crisis.
Relations with the UNITED STATES are restored to the ambassadorial level.
March: RATSIRAKA announces the discovery of a plot to destabilize the regime and assassinate him.

October: Riots in ISOTRY.
November: MONJA JAONA is arrested in ANTANANARIVO.
December: Riots and looting of stores in ANTANANARIVO.
1980–1981: The UNIVERSITY OF MADAGASCAR is on strike.

1981 January: Madagascar approaches the INTERNATIONAL MONETARY FUND for relief from its DEBT CRISIS.
February 3–4: Riots in ANTANANARIVO lead to six deaths and to the arrests of students and professors.
March: MONJA JAONA is released from house arrest and returns to the FNDR. The first standby agreement with the INTERNATIONAL MONETARY FUND is signed.
May: Madagascar's creditors agree to reschedule the debt due between January 1981 and January 1982.
End of June, July: The strike at the university ends and those arrested in February are given conditional discharges.
September: RATSIRAKA makes a state visit to FRANCE.
November: Riots to ANTANANARIVO lead to the intervention of the army.
December: Oil exploration contracts are signed with Mobil Oil and Occidental Petroleum.
December 9–10: Riots and looting in ANTANANARIVO.

1982 January 10: RATSIRAKA announces the holding of presidential ELECTIONS and his own candidacy.
January 15: A government change ejects the members of "right AREMA" from power.
January 25: The announcement is made of a plot to kill RATSIRAKA and other members of the

government. Members of the armed forces, including five colonels, civil servants, and priests are arrested.

February 3: A cyclone leaves 60,000 without shelter in ANTANANARIVO.

February to March: Disorders occur in the northwest, especially on NOSY BE. Crowds attack government and AREMA officials for corruption, forcing many of them, including the president of the province of ANTSERANANA, to flee.

March: The return of many officials who had been forced to flee leads to more riots.

May: A clash between the gendarmerie and peasants at Bezizika in TOLIARA province leaves 200 to 300 dead.

May 17: The Malagasy franc is devalued.

June: Members of a suspected illegal VANILLA trafficking ring are arrested in ANTSERANANA province. A new agreement with the IMF is signed for financial help for a restructuring of 63 million in special drawing rights and a standby credit of 51 million. The Malagasy franc is devalued by 15%.

July 25: MONJA JAONA announces that he will run against RATSIRAKA for president.

August: RATSIRAKA attends the Tripoli summit of the ORGANIZATION OF AFRICAN UNITY and denounces those who have boycotted it over the issue of the seating of the Sahara Arab Republic, a successor to the Spanish Sahara colony, whose territory was claimed by Morocco.

November 7: In the presidential ELECTIONS, RATSIRAKA receives 80.17% of the vote, MONJA JAONA 19.83%.

November 27: MONJA JAONA demands that the High Institutional Court annul the ELECTIONS.

November: The trial of people involved in the riots at NOSY BE condemns three members of the MFM to four years on NOSY LAVA.

December: FRANCE and Madagascar begin discussions for the resumption of military cooperation.
December 14: MONJA JAONA seizes the ANTANANARIVO radio station, denounces the regime for electoral fraud, and calls for a general strike.
December 15: MONJA JAONA is arrested and dismissed from the CSR. There are riots in ANTANANARIVO, FIANARANTSOA, and coastal cities.

1983 January: The WORLD BANK names its first resident representative to Madagascar.
January 10–11: Undersecretary of state for Africa, Chester Crocker, visits Madagascar for the 100th anniversary of the US-Malagasy peace treaty.
February 27–May 29: ELECTIONS are held in the DECENTRALIZED COLLECTIVITIES.
March: RAKOTOVAO-RAZAKABOANA, leader of "right AREMA," is expelled from the AREMA political bureau.
At a meeting of the NONALIGNED MOVEMENT, Ratsiraka declares that the socialist states are the natural allies of the Third World, but attacks them for their failure to aid developing countries in the debt crisis.
April: At the meeting of the WORLD BANK consultative group for Madagascar in Paris, the minister of finance, PASCAL RAKOTOMAVO, announces new measures for the liberalization of the economy, including the end of a fixed price for RICE.
Vernon Walters, President Reagan's roving ambassador, visits Madagascar.
August 28: ELECTIONS for the ASSEMBLEE NATIONALE POPULAIRE are held. AREMA gets nearly 65% of the vote. MONJA JAONA is released from house arrest and wins a seat in ANTANANARIVO.

October 5–12: The OFFICERS' TRIAL of three military officers arrested in 1977 ends with two life sentences and one sentence of ten years imprisonment.

December 5: RATSIRAKA is promoted to admiral by the ANP.

1984 March: Following another rescheduling agreement with the IMF, the Malagasy franc is devalued by 15%.

April 9–12: A cyclone destroys 60% of the harbor installations at MAHAJANGA.

May 31: The corpse of the leader of the president's bodyguard, Colonel KAMISY, is found near gendarmerie headquarters at ANTSIRABE.

July: MONIMA holds a congress and demands the dissolution of the government and the CSR.

August: The government forbids the practice of martial arts.

September 5–8: KUNG FU groups riot and burn the former building of the Ministry of Youth.

November: The LONDON CLUB of private creditors agrees to refinance the Malagasy debt to 1990.

December 4–6: KUNG FU groups attack the strongholds of the TANORA TONGA SAINA.

December: Madagascar is elected to the Security Council of the United Nations.

The WORLD BANK consultative group approves Madagascar's investment plan.

1985 March: On the 150th anniversary of the translation of the Bible into Malagasy, RATSIRAKA declares his attachment to the lessons of the Bible.

April: The INTERNATIONAL MONETARY FUND approves a standby loan of 29.5 million in special drawing rights.

May 22–23: Madagascar's public creditors agree

to a rescheduling of debts due in 1985 and the first quarter of 1986.
Night of July 31–August 1: The army attacks the headquarters of the KUNG FU groups, killing the leader Pierre Mizael Andrianarijaona.
Another standby agreement for SDR 29.5 million is negotiated with the IMF.

1986 March: A cyclone destroys 80% of the port of TOAMASINA.
May: A standby agreement of SDR 32.7 million is negotiated with the IMF. French is reintroduced as a language of education in the secondary schools.
May: The INTERNATIONAL MONETARY FUND provides emergency relief and a standby agreement totaling SDR 32.7 million.
June: A new INVESTMENT CODE is passed.
August: The Malagasy franc is devalued by 20%.
September: The INTERNATIONAL MONETARY FUND provides further credit of SDR 30 million.
October: Madagascar's public creditors agree to a rescheduling of the debts due in 1986 and 1987.
November: There are riots in ANTANANARIVO over the proposed reform of the EDUCATION system and in TOAMASINA over food shortages and job cuts at the port. The UNIVERSITY OF MADAGASCAR begins a boycott of classes. The government postpones implementation of the reforms.

1987 February 26: Attacks on INDO-PAKISTANI traders begin in ANTSIRABE and spread to other provincial towns. Clashes with students at the UNIVERSITY OF MADAGASCAR lead to the arrest and detention of six students. Over 40 students are arrested during the strike.
March: VONJY, MONIMA, and the MFM an-

nounce the formation of the opposition ALLIANCE DEMOCRATIQUE MALGACHE, but do not leave the FNDR.

March to April: Several members of the CSR threaten to resign because of the handling of student unrest.

April: The aftermath of a football game leads to rioting in ANTANANARIVO on April 12. The government announces that classes will resume at the UNIVERSITY OF MADAGASCAR on April 27. Students attempt to block the return to classes, and clashes between striking and non-striking students lead to three deaths.

May 7: Student leader Aimée Francis, adopted son of MONJA JAONA, is arrested.

June: The Malagasy franc is devalued by 41%.

August: The INTERNATIONAL MONETARY FUND provides a credit of SDR 42.2 million. Madagascar's private creditors agree to reschedule debts coming due from 1992 to 1996.

November: A bishop's letter attacks the regime for its economic troubles and the growing gap between the rich and the poor. RATSIRAKA announces the postponement of ELECTIONS to the DECENTRALIZED COLLECTIVITIES and the ASSEMBLEE NATIONALE POPULAIRE.

December: The ASSEMBLEE NATIONALE POPULAIRE votes the budget for 1988. AREMA and the AKFM vote for the budget; VONJY, MONIMA, and the MFM vote against it.

1988 January: The WORLD BANK consultative group on Madagascar commends the government's economic policy and pledges further aid conditional on a rescheduling of debts by Madagascar's public creditors.

January 21: Finance Minister PASCAL RAKOTOMAVO announces the closure of state companies that are not working well, including the SOCIETE NATIONALE DE COMMERCE EX-

TERIEURE and the SOCIETE D'INTERET NATIONAL DE COMMERCIALISATION DES PRODUITS AGRICOLES.

February: DESIREE RAKOTOARIJAONA resigns as prime minister and is succeeded by VICTOR RAMAHATRA.

A system of IMPORT liberalization, to take effect in July, is introduced.

March: 245 members of KUNG FU groups arrested in August 1985 are tried. Eighteen members are given sentences of two years in prison; the rest are released.

August: MONIMA holds its party congress in TOLIARA. Speakers demand the resignation of the government, and MONJA JAONA announces that he will run for president.

October: Madagascar becomes the second country after Mali to benefit from debt relief under the TORONTO PLAN.

1989 January: The COMMISSION MIXTE FRANCO-MALGACHE announces the cancellation of one-third of Madagascar's debt to France. The World Bank announces aid to help those injured by the reconstruction programs.

March 3: The WORLD BANK and the INTERNATIONAL MONETARY FUND announce their support for a three-year economic development plan. The amount of the assistance is not published.

March 12: In the presidential ELECTION, RATSIRAKA is reelected with 62.6% of the vote. MANANDAFY RAKOTONIRINA receives 19.57%, JEROME RAZANABAHINY MAROJAMA 14.83%, and MONJA JAONA 2.97%.

RICHARD ANDRIAMANJATO announces his resignation from the AKFM and the formation of AKFM-Renouveau.

April 20: The ALLIANCE DEMOCRATIQUE MALGACHE holds a rally at the UNIVERSITY

OF MADAGASCAR to protest the election results. Riots in ANTANANARIVO lead to five deaths and to calls for a general strike.

April 20: MANDAFY RAKOTONIRINA is ejected from the CSR.

April 28: The visit of Pope John Paul II leads to a political truce.

May 28: ELECTIONS are held for the ASSEMBLEE NATIONALE POPULAIRE. AREMA wins 66% of the vote and 120 of 137 seats. The MFM wins 7 seats; VONJY, 4; the AKFM, 2; and MONIMA, 1.

July 25: The government announces that it is in control of the situation after a group of soldiers attempts to seize the ANTANANARIVO radio station.

August 17: The government and the CONSEIL SUPREME DE LA REVOLUTION are reshuffled. MONJA JAONA and GILBERT SAMBSON are reappointed to the CSR. The FNDR meets to discuss changes in the constitution.

The Council of Malagasy Churches (FFKM) calls for the abolition of the FNDR and the removal of references to socialism in the constitution.

September: In elections to local government institutions, AREMA maintains its dominant position.

October: The MFM calls for a constitution without references to socialism.

ANDRIAMANJATO's AKFM-Renouveau announces that it will not support the regime in the government or in the CSR.

December 21: The ANP adopts a constitutional revision abolishing the requirement that political parties belong to the FNDR, effectively ending the existence of this body.

1990 February: Reforms to the education system are announced and meet resistance.

March: The constitution is formally amended to allow the formation of parties outside the FNDR.
March 23: The revival of the PSD is announced by ANDRÉ RESAMPA.
ALBERT ZAFY, MANANDAFY RAKOTONIRINA, and RICHARD ADRIAMANJATO form the COMITE DES FORCES VIVES, uniting the opposition to the DRM and DIDIER RATSIRAKA.
Parties supporting President RATSIRAKA form the MOUVEMENT MILITANT POUR LE SOCIALISME MALAGASY (MMSM).
May 13: Armed rebels seize the radio station in ANTANANARIVO. Police put down the coup attempt, with three deaths.
August: SOUTH AFRICA opens a trade office in ANTANANARIVO and resumes air links with the island.
In recognition of its change of ideological position, the MFM changes its name to the Militant Party for the Development of Madagascar.

1991 January 31: RATSIRAKA proposes the creation of a bicameral legislature, with the CSR to be replaced by a senate.
February: RATSIRAKA reshuffles his government and removes his brother-in-law, CHRISTOPHE RAVELOSON-MAHASAMPO, as minister of defense.
April 19: SOUTH AFRICA and Madagascar sign a diplomatic agreement.
June 1: MANADAFY RAKOTONIRINA and RICHARD ANDRIAMANJATO call for a national conference to establish a new constitution.
June 10, 11, 14: Demonstrations in ANTANANARIVO call for an end to the DRM and a new constitution.
June 20: The COMITE DES FORCES VIVES announces the establishment of a provisional

onstrators in ANTSERANANA, killing eight. TOLIARA, TOAMASINA, and FIANARANTSOA provinces declare themselves federal states. Profederal forces cut the railroad line between TOAMASINA and ANTANANARIVO.

November 25: The first round of elections to the presidency of the THIRD REPUBLIC takes place. The two front-runners are ALBERT ZAFY, with 48% of the vote, and DIDIER RATSIRAKA, with 28%.

1993 February 10: Runoff elections for the presidency of the THIRD REPUBLIC are held. ALBERT ZAFY wins, with 67% of the votes cast; DIDIER RATSIRAKA has 33%.

April: In early April there are outbreaks of violence by RATSIRAKA supporters in ANTSERANANA.

June 16: Elections to the National Assembly are held. Parties supporting President ZAFY win 74 of the 138 seats.

INTRODUCTION

At once isolated and strategically located, Madagascar has long fascinated both its own population and outside observers. The island's location off the coast of Africa has involved it in the trading networks and population movements of the Indian Ocean and in contacts with the continent itself. The result is a culture that blends African and Asian (largely Indonesian) elements and a language—Malagasy—that also combines African elements with an Indonesian base. Added to the unique human culture of the island are unusual forms of plant and animal life, some of them, unfortunately, already extinct and others endangered.

Madagascar's location near important sea lanes has attracted the attention of outside powers. A millennium ago Arab traders established outposts on the island; later European powers, particularly the French and British, were rivals for influence over various Malagasy groups. In our time, the growing importance of the Mozambique Channel for the transit of oil from the Persian Gulf to Europe, as well as the overall great power rivalry in the Indian Ocean, have increased Madagascar's strategic importance. Attention from and to the outside world has not, however, diminished the importance of the internal determinants of Malagasy history and politics or the value that the Malagasy themselves give to their own history.

Geography

Madagascar lies almost entirely in the southern tropical zone between 11°57′ and 25°32′ latitude south. It is 995 miles (1,600 km) long and 360 miles (580 km) wide at the widest point. At 230,000 square miles (590,000 square kilometers), it is the fourth largest island in the world, after Greenland, New Guinea, and Borneo. The Mozambique Channel, 220 miles (350 km) wide at the narrowest point, separates it from the continent of Africa. According to geologists, the island was part of the ancient continent of Gondwanaland and separated from the African continent several million years ago. One result of this early separation was the development of unique species of both flora and fauna, while another was the lateness of human settlement. Archeological remains dating from before A.D. 1000 are rare, although more are being found, and few scholars put extensive settlement before A.D. 1.

The island itself has a variety of topography and climates. On the east is a narrow lowland coastal strip that quickly turns into a steep escarpment running the length of the island. Behind the escarpment are the Plateaux, more correctly and more currently called the Highlands since they are mountainous rather than flat. The mountains of the Highlands reach elevations of over 2,500 meters in the north (2,879 at the highest point, Tsaratanana), becoming smaller hills in the central part of the island around the capital, Antananarivo. The western slope of the Highlands ends in wide coastal plains.

These differences in topography combine with wind patterns to create a variety of climates. The eastern region has heavy rainfall and frequent cyclones. The interior has a dry season from November to March, and a rainy season from April to October. In addition, the central Highlands have a cold season, and in July and August the nights can be quite chilly, with frost recorded from time to time. The west coast, from Morombe to just north of Mahajanga, receives less rain than the east coast or Highlands, but profits from the presence of a series of rivers that provide water and alluvial deposits for agriculture. The south of the island has a desert climate with few rivers, which often disappear completely in the driest part of the year.

Population

There has been considerable controversy about the exact time of arrival of humans in Madagascar, the sources of the population, and the routes by which they reached the island. A single language—Malagasy—is spoken throughout the island, although with dialectic differences that vary in importance. The language is largely Malayo-Polynesian in vocabulary and grammar, and most sources agree that its origin lies in the Indonesian archipelago. There are important African elements in the Malagasy language, however, including most of the vocabulary having to do with cattle raising. There are also Arab elements: the names of the months are of Arab derivation; the first written form of Malagasy, collected in manuscripts known as *sorabe,* used Arabic characters. In physical appearance the population differs widely along an Indonesian-African continuum, with considerable variation often occurring within a single family. The culture of the different groups of the island also displays varying degrees of elements that have been traced to African and Indonesian, as well as Arabic and even Indian origins. A number of theories have been formulated to account for the mixture, and for the combination of unity and variety found in Malagasy culture. These theories are not without political overtones, since emphasizing African or Asian elements, unity or diversity, has its political implications.

Theories of the origin of the population of Madagascar fall into two general categories. One set of theories argues that the mixture of elements found in the population was developed over time as the proto-Malagasy migrated from the Indonesian archipelago along the northern rim of the Indian Ocean, across the southern coast of the Arabian peninsula, and down the east coast of Africa, arriving in Madagascar possibly via the Comoro Islands. The other set of theories argues that separate migrations of Indonesian, Arabic, and African stock peopled the island, although there is some debate about whether the Indonesian or African groups arrived first. The cultural unity of the Malagasy, which this set of theories considers less developed than does the first set of theories, is the result of interactions on the island itself. It is quite possible, of course, that both sets of theories are true, and that the assimilation of groups arriving separately was facilitated by a preexisting cultural blend brought by migrants who had taken the coastal route.

It is usual to divide Madagascar's population of about 10 million (in 1987) into eighteen "official" ethnic groups, and each of these groups is examined in the Dictionary. Limiting oneself to this framework, however, underestimates both the degree of unity and the degree of fragmentation of Malagasy society. The shared language, shared customs, and long-standing habits of individual and collective migration have facilitated interaction and mingling among the different groups. In addition, the groups themselves often subdivide into regional and clan units. Many never had a common political unit (e.g., the Tsimihety) or had one only briefly (e.g., the Betsimisaraka), while others seem to have been assembled from migratory fragments of other groups (e.g., the Tanala). Some were grouped together as administrative subdivisions of the indigenous nineteenth-century Merina Empire, or during the period of French occupation (e.g., the Betsileo and Bara). The eighteen "ethnic groups" should therefore be regarded as an intermediate division between the overarching Malagasy identity and smaller units rather than as the basic division of the population.

Many groups are also divided into endogamous castes. There is a basic division between the descendants of slaves and those of free individuals, and the free castes are usually divided into commoners and nobles. Within each of these categories there is often also a hierarchy of clans based on such historical factors as services once rendered to ruling groups. Most observers agree that these differences are becoming less important, particularly in the cities, as the introduction of a modern economy and the pauperization created by the debt crisis of the 1980s exercize a leveling effect at the lower ranks of society and create a new, wealth-based elite at the top.

A further division introduced into the population in modern times has been the division between non-Malagasy and Malagasy inhabitants. The non-Malagasy inhabitants include Europeans (mainly the French), Indo-Pakistanis (usually called Karany), and Chinese. The economic importance of these groups is greater than their numbers would suggest.

Summary of History

According to most theories, Madagascar was settled by people involved in the trading networks of the Indian Ocean, and the earliest archaeological remains are those of commercially oriented cities established possibly a few hundred years before A.D. 1000. The cities appear to have traded produce for manufactured goods, and some theorists argue that this demonstrates the existence of a settled agriculture that must have been preceded by a period of a hunting-and-gathering economy. Although some information about the society of these coastal cities can be gathered from the archaeological remains, little is known about the interior of the island during this period.

The cities participated first in the Arab-dominated trade of the western Indian Ocean and were later connected with the "Swahili" trading network of the East African coast. Whether conducted directly or through a series of intermediaries, this trade was far-ranging, and Chinese artifacts have been discovered in Madagascar as well as on the African coast. The trading posts were still active when the Portuguese arrived in the Indian Ocean and landed in Madagascar in 1506. By the time of the Portuguese arrival, the interior of the island had evidently been inhabited for some time. Seventeenth-century missionaries and settlers speak of already established groups in the center of the island, and the oral traditions of interior groups can be followed with some confidence back to this period.

With the arrival of the Portuguese, conditions both on the coast and in the interior appear to have changed. The Portuguese and Dutch destroyed the connection with the Arab-Swahili trading networks without being able to establish the dominance over the Indian Ocean that would have permitted them to set up their own networks. By the mid-seventeenth century it was the English and French, already rivals for the rest of the Indian Ocean, who reestablished the trading pattern. Once more, manufactured goods were traded for produce and, increasingly, weapons for slaves. Both the British and the French attempted to establish settlements in Madagascar—the British at Saint Augustine Bay in 1645–46 and the French at Fort Dauphin from 1642 to 1674.

At the same time, larger political units were beginning to form in Madagascar. The French settlers at Fort-Dauphin dealt with several "kingdoms" and heard reports of others. To the west of Fort Dauphin, along the Mozambique Channel coast, the Sakalava kingdoms of Menabe and Boina were also established. Although the Sakalava monarchs' control of their hinterland might have been rather loose, they did control the coast well enough to dominate the Malagasy side of the trade with the Europeans, and established the port of Mahajanga in the mid–eighteenth century in response to the continuing slave trade.

Also in the mid-eighteenth century, the Betsimisaraka confederation developed on the east coast. It was led by the Zanamalata, children of the pirates who had moved from the Caribbean to the seas around Madagascar at the end of the seventeenth century. By the end of the eighteenth century, the Sakalava and Betsimisaraka were mounting joint raiding expeditions on the Comoro Islands. At the same time, smaller kingdoms were being formed in the southern Highlands and their marches by such groups as the Betsileo and the Bara, but it does not appear that any of these kingdoms ever succeeded in uniting the whole of what was later considered Betsileo and Bara territory.

The most important kingdom to form was that of the Merina in the central Highlands of Madagascar, united under King Adrianampoinimerina (1787?–1810) at the end of the eighteenth century. His successor, Radama I (1810–1828), completed the conquest of Imerina and began the conquest of the rest of the island, a process that would eventually bring two-thirds of the island under at least nominal control by the Merina Empire. The Betsimisaraka and Betsileo were among the first groups to be conquered, and the Sakalava were decisively undermined, although never totally conquered.

In 1817 Radama entered into diplomatic relations with the British, who had by then replaced the French in Mauritius and the Dutch in South Africa. With diplomatic relations came assistance to train the army and the arrival of British missionaries, notably from the London Missionary Society. The missionaries transliterated Malagasy into the Latin alphabet and set up an educational system. The French, who had maintained their base at Réunion, also continued to be active in trade on both the east and west coasts. They established a trading post in the Ile Sainte-Marie on the east coast, and in 1840 occupied the island of Nosy Be on the northwest coast.

Much of the nineteenth-century history of the Merina Empire consisted of a complicated balancing act. The requirements of consolidating authoritarian rule clashed with the maintenance of popular support. It was necessary, and for some attractive, to introduce Western techniques and ways of acting to gain the international "respectability" seen as crucial to the protection of Malagasy independence, but attachment to Malagasy ways remained strong in all parts of the population. Merina rulers also attempted to balance French and British influence to avoid being taken under the domination of either power. Radama's successor, Queen Ranavalona I (1828–1861), expelled the Europeans in 1835 and attempted to reestablish the monarchy on more traditional bases, but her son, Radama II (1861–1863), reopened the country to European influence, an opening that remained after his assassination. In 1869 Queen Ranavalona II (1868–1885) and her prime minister, Rainilaiarivony, converted to Christianity.

In the end, none of the balancing acts was successful. From 1883 to 1885 a war with France was waged and ended with the imposition of a heavy indemnity on the Merina state. In 1890 Great Britain and France signed a treaty exchanging French recognition of British control of Zanzibar for British acceptance of the French claim to Madagascar. In 1895 the French invaded again, and conquered the center of the Merina monarchy at Antananarivo. Although the French occupation aroused some resistance, especially the Revolt of the Menalamba ("Red Shawls") in Imerina, and the southern uprising of 1904–1905, the conquest marked the beginning of a colonial occupation that lasted until 1958.

The Period of French Occupation

The colonial period began with the introduction of the usual administrative apparatus and the arrival of French settlers. The French presence was strongest in administrative centers, like the capital (renamed Tananarive), and in areas that were turned over to plantation agriculture, like the east and north coasts, but the colonial administration extended throughout the island. Laws like the *indigénat,* which set up a special legal system for non-French citizens, and the *corvée,* which established an obligation to furnish a certain number of days of labor to the government, as well as head and cattle taxes followed the imposition of colonial rule and facilitated control of "difficult" subjects.

Nationalist movements began in rather fragmentary ways. The first, the VVS, was centered in Tananarive, and was dismantled by the French in 1915. More widespread movements began after the First World War, with the return of the former combatants and the resentments caused by the increased exactions of the system. Such leaders as Jean Ralaimongo and Joseph Ravoahangy agitated for the granting of the rights of French citizenship to the Malagasy "subjects" and increasingly thought of independence as a possible goal. The interwar nationalist movements had the advantage of a shared language and widespread literacy, but the disadvantage of being limited largely to the cities. They were also closely watched by the French administration. A brief relaxation of political control in 1936–1937, at the time of the French Popular Front, was followed by a reimposition of controls at the outbreak of the Second World War.

After the fall of France in 1940, the governor of the island, Marcel De Coppet, declared first for the Free French and then for the Vichy regime. In response, British forces invaded the island in 1942. To the disappointment of nationalist groups, the British handed control of Madagascar back to the Free French, who treated the island as a reservoir of men and raw materials for their war effort, greatly increasing the burden of the colonial system on the population.

At the end of the war, the hopes of nationalists were once again raised. The Brazzaville Declaration, and even more the Charter of the United Nations, held out the possibility of an end to colonial rule. A political party, the Mouvement Démocratique de la Rénovation Malgache, was formed and, in spite of the opposition of an administration-supported party, the Parti des Deshérités de Madagascar, elected delegates to the constitutional congress in Paris. There they pressed for a status similar to that of Indochina, which had just been granted a large measure of autonomy. In the end, Madagascar was treated like the African colonies, with the reestablishment of colonial rule and no independence in sight. The attempts of the MDRM deputies to introduce a reconsideration of Madagascar's status in subsequent French national assemblies were equally fruitless.

The response was the rebellion of 1947, an uprising that combined the efforts of urban nationalists, returning veterans, and peasants, particularly on the east coast and eastern Highlands. The rebellion was put down, with casualities (almost all Malagasy) that have been estimated at over 50,000 and were probably closer to 100,000 out of a population of 4 million. Participants in and suspected sympathizers with the rebellion were imprisoned, shot, or barred from political life. The three MDRM deputies and other

Malagasy parliamentarians denied involvement in the revolt, but were tried and sentenced either to death or to life imprisonment, although the deputies' death sentences were later commuted to imprisonment. A state of emergency was declared that in some areas lasted until the 1956 Loi-Cadre. The result was the stunting of Malagasy political life in the post-1947 period. Political parties did not develop as they did in other French African colonies, and political discussion and activities took place via the intermediaries of the press and unions.

Political life and parties resumed when the Loi-Cadre gave France's African colonies, including Madagascar, internal autonomy. Three major parties emerged during this period. The party that became the eventual governing party, the Parti Social Démocrate, was led by Philibert Tsiranana, a former schoolteacher who became a deputy to the French National Assembly at the beginning of 1956. The party was composed largely of people with established records of loyalty to France, including some, like Tsiranana, who had been members of PADESM. Two parties took a more nationalistic position and attracted some former MDRM supporters. The AKFM was led by Richard Andriamanjato and was centered in the capital. A southern-based party, MONIMA, was led by a survivor of the 1947 repression, Monja Jaona. The two parties provided the opposition to the Tsiranana regime established in 1958, but the narrowness of their bases, and the activities, first of the colonial regime and later of the PSD government, prevented them from seriously challenging PSD control of Malagasy politics.

The First Republic

Its close relationship with the former colonial power proved to be an insurmountable handicap for the First Republic. Independence had been accompanied by the signing of a series of cooperation agreements that maintained French domination over defense, education, and the machinery of government itself. In addition, French domination of the economy continued. The regime had difficulty stimulating economic growth, in part because it controlled very few of the economic power centers and in part because of a lack of popular enthusiasm for the regime and its exhortations. In foreign policy, the Tsiranana regime followed a conservative line, and by the end of its time in power was pursuing contacts with the Republic of South Africa. The continued ties with France and the lack of economic growth aroused considerable opposition, particularly among the students of Antananarivo, who were opposed both to the ideological posture of the regime and to its failure to provide them with adequate postgraduation opportunities.

In the end, two very different revolts led to the collapse of the First Republic. On April 1, 1971, southern peasants under the leadership of MONIMA attacked government posts. This revolt was severely suppressed; its leaders, including Monja Jaona, were sent to prison. Public reaction to the suppression strained the relationship between the regime and the armed forces, particularly the gendarmerie, which felt it had been unfairly blamed for its role in putting down the rebellion. The second revolt began with student demonstrations in the capital in May 1972. These demonstrations turned into an uprising, now known as the May Revolution, led by a new group of radical and clandestine opposition figures later to form a political party called the MFM. The student revolt spread to other sectors of the Antananarivo population, and on May 15 the commander of the gendarmerie, Colonel Richard Ratsimandrava, informed Tsiranana that the armed forces would no longer defend his regime. Power was handed over to the commanding officer of the army, General Gabriel Ramanantsoa.

Ramanantsoa

Ramanantsoa's time in office lasted only from 1972 until January 1975. The period was marked by important changes in political orientation and by increasing instability. The cooperation agreements with France were renegotiated as part of a more radical stance in foreign affairs, and state marketing concerns were established as part of an attempt to gain control over the island's economy. The regime suffered from increasing corruption, however, and from personal rivalries and doctrinal quarrels among three important figures in Ramanantsoa's government: his chief assistant, army colonel Roland Rabetafika, the minister of the interior, gendarmerie colonel Richard Ratsimandrava; and the minister of foreign affairs, naval captain Didier Ratsiraka. In December 1974 a disaffected army officer, Bréchard Rajaonarison, attempted to overthrow the government. Although the coup was unsuccessful, Ramanantsoa was forced to step down and was succeeded by Ratsimandrava, whose assassination one week later led to the formation of a military directorate and another period of uncertainty. In June 1975 Didier Ratsiraka emerged as the military directorate's choice for president, and proclaimed Madagascar a "scientific socialist" state.

The Second Republic

Ratsiraka and his supporters created a regime party, AREMA (Vanguard of the Malagasy Revolution), which coexisted with several smaller parties in the FNDR, or Front National pour la Défense de la Révolution. Extensive nationalizations were carried out, a "Charter of Socialist Industry" was promulgated, and attempts were made to establish cooperatives in the countryside. Ratsiraka continued the foreign policy he had developed under the Ramanantsoa regime, stressing ties with other socialist countries, especially North Korea, supporting efforts to declare the Indian Ocean a neutral zone, and attempting to play a leading role in the Nonaligned Movement. In 1978 an "All-Out Investment Policy," designed to create an industrial base for the island's economy, was launched.

The 1980s were marked by both economic and political crises that led to increasing abandonment of the socialist direction proclaimed in the Charter of the Malagasy Revolution. The All-Out Investment Policy and the economic conditions of the early 1980s led to the accumulation of an imposing debt and recourse to the International Monetary Fund. Production of such export crops as coffee and vanilla declined, and shortages of the chief food crop—rice—led to costly import bills and a large-scale black market.

The liberalization policies undertaken as a result of the IMF agreements led to modifications of government control of the economy and foreign trade, while the need to maintain good relations with the IMF and its controlling countries led to changes in foreign policy. These included a rapprochement with France, which remained, in spite of the difficulties in Franco-Malagasy relations, Madagascar's largest creditor and most important trading partner.

Challenges to Ratsiraka's control of the political system, particularly from the youth of the capital, were also an important feature of the 1980s. In the 1982 presidential election, Ratsiraka faced a split in his own party and the opposing candidacy of Monja Jaona, and he was able to gather only a bare majority of the votes in Antananarivo. In 1985 the army was called on to destroy the headquarters of a movement of Antananarivo youth who were organized into martial arts societies under the Kung Fu label. The Kung Fu leader and several hundred of his followers were killed in the fighting. Urban unrest and insecurity in the countryside led to problems with the armed forces, and there were several attempted coups. In 1986 Guy Sibon, minister of defense and a longtime supporter of Ratsiraka, died and was replaced by Ratsiraka's brother-in-law, Christophe Raveloson-Mahasampo.

In March 1987 three member parties of the FNDR, MONIMA, the MFM, and Vonjy Iray Tsy Mivaky, announced the formation of the Alliance Démocratique Malgache. At the end of the year, their members of the Assemblée Nationale Populaire voted against the budget for 1988. In 1989 the opposition tried to unite and mobilize more forces, while Ratsiraka attempted to preserve his power and to make sufficient changes to quiet the opposition without surrendering his position as president. These measures included advancing the presidential elections of 1989.

In these elections, held on March 12, 1989, the parties of the Alliance Démocratique Malgache were not able to agree on a joint candidate, and the parties' three leaders all ran against Ratsiraka. He was elected with 62% of the vote. The results led to charges of fraud by the other candidates and to demonstrations and riots in the capital. Pressure from the opposition for change was joined by pressure from the churches, whose organization, the FFKM, announced the formation of a Committee for the Defense of Human Rights in Madagascar and began pushing for the definitive abandonment of the commitment to socialism and the dissolution of institutions of the Second Republic, such as the FNDR.

Ratsiraka continued his efforts to hold on to power by a mixture of concessions and consolidation. Leaders of the developing opposition, such as Manandafy Rakotonirina and Richard Andria-manjato (leaders of the MFM and AKFM-Renouveau, respectively), were removed from the Conseil Suprême de la Révolution while potential supporters, such as Monja Jaona and Gilbert Sambson, were reappointed. At the same time, censorship of the media was abolished, and in August 1989 the FNDR was convened for the first time since 1982, and its members were asked to submit proposals for changes in the constitution. The MFM proposed a new constitution without reference to socialism. Andriamanjato announced that his party would no longer support the government. In December parliament adopted revisions to the constitution abolishing the requirement that parties belong to the FNDR in order to have a legal existence.

This opening of the system to the possibility of multiparty politics did not satisfy the opposition, which began demanding both an end to the regime itself and the departure of Ratsiraka. Ratsiraka riposted by grouping the parties loyal to him, including AREMA, the AKFM, and UDECMA, under the label Mouvement Militant pour le Socialisme Malagasy (MMSM). The opposition began increasingly to consolidate under the label Comité des Forces Vives (''Active Forces''; in Malagasy, *Hery Velona*). Ratsiraka continued to give some concessions—the departure of his brother-in-law, Raveloson-Mahasampo, from the post of minister of defense in February 1991 was seen as a gesture to the opposition—but made it clear that he intended to remain in power.

In June 1991 Rakotonirina and Andriamanjato presented an ultimatum in the name of the Forces Vives demanding a national conference on democratization and threatening a general strike if their demands were not met. Demonstrations in the middle of June in Antananarivo, involving students and civil servants, backed up the demands. At the end of June, the Comité des Forces Vives announced the formation of a ''provisional government'' and called for a general strike. This strike, joined in the capital and other major centers, continued for two weeks and was revived sporadically thereafter. On July 22, 1991, members of the provisional government and their supporters occupied six government ministries. The government responded by arresting several of the members of the transitional government and declaring a state of emergency. At the same time, Ratsiraka made a conciliatory speech promising movement on the constitution and the appointment of a new government. The opposition demanded the release of its arrested members before it would enter into negotiations.

Ironically, the event that marked the beginning of the end of the Second Republic was the same as for the First Republic: troops loyal to the regime fired on a demonstrating crowd. On August 10, a crowd of about 400,000 marched to the presidential palace at Iavoloha. There the Presidential Guard opened fire, killing several demonstrators (estimates range from 12 to 130) and wounding Albert Zafy. As in 1971, this action led both the armed forces and the French to withdraw their support from the regime. The French government called for a compromise solution and ordered the French instructors attached to the Presidential Guard to avoid further military action, while a group of retired army officers issued a public call for Ratsiraka's resignation.

At the end of August, Ratsiraka installed a new government, led by Guy Razanamasy, with a mandate to find a formula for cooperation with the opposition. The opposition responded by appointing more members to its provisional government and calling for more demonstrations. Negotiations continued through this period, and at the end of October an agreement for a transition to the Third Republic was reached between Ratsiraka and the groups composing the MMSM, the opposition groups, the churches, and the armed forces. By the terms of the agreement, Ratsiraka would remain as president and head of the army during the transitional period, with his other powers transferred to the prime minister, Razanamasy. Zafy would become the president of the High State Authority for the transition to the Third Republic, a body to be composed of representatives of the MMSM and Forces Vives. A consultative National Committee for Economic and Social Regeneration, to be led by Manadafy Rakotonirina and Richard Adriamanjato, was also to be created.

Albert Zafy had been out of the country while the agreement was being negotiated and on his return on November 7 denounced it as leaving Ratsiraka with the crucial power of head of the armed forces. There followed a confused period of attempts to relaunch the agreement and to create a government that would satisfy the opposition without creating too much resistance from the supporters of Ratsiraka. Finally, in January 1992 acceptance of a revised agreement was announced, and a National Forum to write a new constitution began work on March 22.

The period during and after this forum was marked by preparations for the transition to the Third Republic and by attempts by

Ratsiraka and his supporters to retain some of their power. They argued for the creation of a federal system, in which the provinces rather than a central government based in Antananarivo would hold the bulk of the power. This would have protected the bases of many of the Ratsiraka forces, who came from the peripheral provinces rather than from the capital. There was also an attempt on Zafy's life on March 30, although by whom is not established. In the end, a constitution providing for a unitary state was passed.

A referendum on August 19 ratified the constitution of the Third Republic, but was disrupted by Ratsiraka supporters demanding the establishment of federalism. These demonstrations were accompanied by violence, particularly in Toamasina and Antseranana. After the constitutional referendum, the question of Ratsiraka's future centered on the issue of whether he would be allowed to run for president under the new constitution. The Ad Hoc Transitional Committee, comprised of Zafy, Rakotonirina, Andriamanjato, Razanamasy, and representatives of the churches, attempted to declare Ratsiraka ineligible. This led to demonstrations by Ratsiraka supporters in provincial cities and to unilateral declarations of federal status by several provinces. Faced with the possibility of civil war, or at least continuing unrest, the transitional committee agreed to allow Ratsiraka to run for president.

On November 25, 1992, and February 10, 1993, the first and second rounds of the presidential election were held. Ratsiraka was defeated, and Albert Zafy became the first president of the Third Republic. Legislative elections held on June 16, 1993, returned a majority of Zafy supporters to the National Assembly.

The Third Republic began with both good and bad auspices. The problems of poverty remain and the search for a solid base for the economy, which neither the First nor the Second Republics were able to create, remains, as does the problem of maintaining political stability. A maintenance of the unity that led to the overthrow of the Second Republic will be necessary if these problems are to be dealt with.

THE DICTIONARY

-A-

AD HOC TRANSITIONAL COMMITTEE. This committee was established in 1992 to manage issues arising from the transition to the Third Republic (q.v.), and was composed of the three leaders of the Comité des Forces Vives (q.v.)—Manandafy Rakotonirina (q.v.), Richard Andriamanjato (q.v.), and Albert Zafy (q.v.)—as well as the president of the FFKM (q.v.), or Council of Malagasy Churches. Its most controversial act was an attempt to prevent the president of the defunct Democratic Republic of Madagascar (q.v.), Didier Ratsiraka (q.v.), from running for the presidency of the new republic on the grounds that the constitution limited the president to two terms of office. This decision aroused violent opposition from Ratsiraka's supporters, and the committee reversed its decision.

AGRICULTURE. Agriculture is the most important economic activity in Madagascar, employing about 84% of the active population and providing over 80% of export earnings. The variety of climates across the island means that Madagascar produces a large number of different crops. The main food crop is rice (q.v.), grown both for subsistence and for export, followed by manioc and corn. Exports are dominated by coffee (q.v.), cloves, and vanilla (q.v.). Sugar (q.v.) is also produced. Cattle (q.v.) raising is important, particularly in the south of the island. *See Table 1.* Historically the agricultural sector has been plagued by poor productivity; rice imports, which began on a regular basis in 1965, are a major charge on foreign exchange, while declining production of export crops has reduced the amount available to spend on rice imports. Related to the decline in productivity has been

TABLE 1 Agricultural Production (in thousands of metric tons, 1990 estimates)

Rice (paddy)	2,400
Cassava	2,280
Sugar cane	1,970
Sweet potatoes	485
Vegetables and melons	300
Potatoes	271

Source: Food and Agriculture Organization estimates as reported in *Africa South of the Sahara, 1993.*

a decline in income for the producers in the agricultural sector, the result of population increases, the declining prices of cash crops, and government policies of price control. *See also* AGRICULTURE POLICY; AMERICAN CROPS; EXPORTS; SPICES.

AGRICULTURE POLICY. At the beginning of the colonial period, the French experimented with a variety of agricultural forms, including large-scale plantations (known as concessions) run by the island's commercial companies (q.v.), smaller plantations run by individual settlers (q.v.), and production by the Malagasy themselves. At first the Malagasy were largely used as labor on French-run plantations, but they later moved into cash-crop production and in some cases were even required to grow crops. After the Second World War, such settlement schemes as the Sakay operation were still attempted, but colonial agricultural policy increasingly concentrated its efforts on Malagasy producers, although still with an emphasis on cash crops.

French agricultural policy was criticized for its fixation on the "miracle crop"—whether luxury rice, cotton, or another—that would by itself lift Madagascar out of underdevelopment. In general, however, these crops proved to be disappointments, as did attempts to increase peasant productivity by manipulating the framework of agricultural administration. One reason for this failure was that agricultural assistance was also used as a political tool to reward supporters of the administration.

The First Republic (q.v.) continued to look for the miracle crop, although more attention was given to food crops for local consumption. The contradiction between using agricultural policy to increase productivity and using it as a tool of political patronage continued. Large-scale, regular importation of rice began in 1965.

Post-1972 attempts to gain control of agricultural activities included the creation of state companies for the collection and distribution of rice and other commodities. They included the Société d'Intérêt National de Commercialisation des Produits Agricoles (q.v.) and the Office Militaire Pour la Production Agricole (q.v.). The record of these agencies has been extremely mixed and their activities are being reduced as part of the International Monetary Fund (q.v.)–inspired liberalization of the economy. The Democratic Republic of Madagascar (q.v.) tried both to increase productivity and to give the economy a more socialistic direction. Policies included the establishment of rural credit facilities, attempts at the introduction of cooperative farming, some land reform, and the creation of some state farms. The *fokonolona* reform (q.v.) was also intended to increase productivity by changing the authoritarian relationship between the administration and the rural population. The idea of the miracle crop remained, however, (soybeans, this time), as did the use of agricultural policy for political ends. The need to seek assistance from the International Monetary Fund and the World Bank (q.v.) in the mid-1980s led to a considerable relaxation of state control. The state-run agencies charged with the collection and marketing of many commodities lost their monopolies, and private traders took their place, but the basic problems of fluctuating production of export crops and growth in rice production that does not match population growth continue. *See also* ALL-OUT INVESTMENT POLICY; DEBT CRISIS.

AKFM (Antokon'ny Kongresin'ny Fahaleovantenan'i Madagasikara, *or* "Independence Congress Party of Madagascar"). The roots of the party lie in the 1958 Tamatave Congress (q.v.), which assembled the Malagasy parties advocating immediate independence. The AKFM was formed in November 1958 from the non-Catholic participants in the congress, the Union du Peuple Malgache (q.v.), the Front National Malgache (q.v.), and the Association des Amis des Paysans. Richard Andriamanjato (q.v.) was chosen as president of the party, and Gisèle Rabesahala (q.v.) as its secretary-general. During the First Republic (q.v.) the party's bases of support lay in the capital and the province of Antananarivo, the northern part of Fianarantsoa province, and the town of Antseranana. Its leadership, drawn largely from the intelligentsia and bourgeoisie of the capital, was generally considered to have both a "pure nationalist" and a "Marxist" wing, and the party maintained links with the French Communist party and other communist parties. The AKFM also had an affiliated union movement, FISEMA.

Under the First Republic, the AKFM was the only opposition party with representation in the legislature, although administrative pressure in the countryside gradually reduced its activities to the capital. The party's leadership cherished some hopes of an eventual coalition with the regime party, the Parti Social Démocrate (q.v.), and this led it to compromises that lost it some support both to MONIMA (q.v.) and to the clandestine opposition to the First Republic that developed at the end of the 1960s. The AKFM condemned both the Peasant Rebellion of 1971 (q.v.) and, in the beginning, the May 1972 Revolution (q.v.). The party became, however, an enthusiastic supporter of the radicalization of Madagascar's foreign policy undertaken by Didier Ratsiraka (q.v.) during his tenure as foreign minister of the Ramanantsoa regime (q.v.), and it supported his candidacy for the presidency in 1975.

The AKFM was one of the strongest supporters of the Democratic Republic of Madagascar (q.v.) and did better electorally than under the First Republic, gaining eleven seats in the 1977 elections to the Assemblée Nationale Populaire (q.v.) and nine seats in the 1983 elections. In 1989, however, the party split over the continuation of support for the regime of Didier Ratsiraka. At the time of the 1989 presidential election, Andriamanjato declared his intention of running for president against Ratsiraka. The party refused to support him, and in March he announced his resignation from the AKFM, and the creation of the AKFM-Renouveau party (q.v.). This party won three seats in the May elections to the ANP, while the old AKFM won only two.

In the political crisis that led to the end of the Democratic Republic of Madagascar, the AKFM continued its support of the regime and joined other parties supporting Ratsiraka in the Mouvement Militant pour le Socialisme Malagasy (q.v.) in March 1990. The party paid for this support, however, and for its earlier failures to attract younger generations of political activists.

AKFM-RENOUVEAU (New AKFM). The AKFM-Renouveau was created in March 1989 by the former leader of the AKFM (q.v.), Richard Andriamanjato (q.v.), when the party refused to allow him to run against President Didier Ratsiraka (q.v.) in the presidential elections of that year. In the legislative elections of June 1989 it won three seats. At the end of 1989 AKFM-Renouveau declared that it would no longer support the Ratsiraka regime, and in 1990 it joined with other opposition groups to form the Comité des Forces Vives (q.v.). As a member of the opposition, it contributed members to the December 1991 government formed by Guy Razanamasy (q.v.) to begin the transition to the Third Republic (q.v.).

ALAOTRA, LAKE (17°30′S, 48°30′E). Originally the home of the Sihanaka (q.v.), Lake Alaotra is Madagascar's most important rice-growing region. Already a productive region in precolonial times, the lake was the object of development efforts during and after the colonial period, combining the draining of the swampy regions west of the lake and the extensions of irrigation in other areas. The land, originally under the control of settlers, was gradually reclaimed by the Malagasy Société Malgache du Lac Alaotra, or SOMALAC, and either farmed directly or redistributed to Malagasy farmers. Under the Democratic Republic of Madagascar (q.v.) much of the land was turned into cooperatives (q.v.).

ALBERTINI, DON IGNACE BARTHELEMY (1897–1945). Albertini was born in Corsica and studied law at the University of Paris, moving to Madagascar in 1925. There he and his wife, Lucienne, became defenders of both French and Malagasy supporters of the Malagasy nationalist movement. After his defense of the leaders of the May 19, 1929, demonstration (q.v.) in Antananarivo he was himself arrested. Although his sentence was later overturned, he continued to be harassed by the administration; during the Second World War he was detained on the order of Vichy (q.v.)-appointed Governor Cayla (q.v.). After being freed by the British invasion (q.v.), he joined the Free French (q.v.) forces in Algiers, but died before the end of the war.

ALL-OUT INVESTMENT POLICY. At the end of 1978, President Ratsiraka (q.v.) announced his government's commitment to a policy of "investissement à l'outrance," or all-out investment. He had come to the conclusion, he said, that development via modernized tropical agriculture would not be sufficient to create the socialist economy he desired or to absorb the number of young Malagasy coming into the labor market each year, a number that a World Bank (q.v.) report prepared that year estimated at a level that would double the labor force by the year 2000. A policy of borrowing to finance long-term projects designed to create an industrial economy was therefore necessary.

As developed over the next several years, the All-Out Investment Policy involved a series of projects, including a major hydroelectric installation at Andekaleka (q.v.), the construction of textile plants, a fertilizer factory at Toamasina, extension of the telecommunications system, and a major expansion of the university system through the creation of regional university centers in the provincial capitals. The policy was financed by extensive borrowing, both from official sources, led by the World Bank, and from private banks. There were, however, several flaws in the policy. Projects were decided upon often in the absence of feasibility studies or even reliable statistics. As the Malagasy economy moved into crisis in the early 1980s, the money for further projects or to complete existing ones like the Andekaleka dam, which required the construction of industries to buy its power, or for the imported raw materials needed to run projects like the fertilizer factory, was not available. The final result of the policy, combined with other economic factors, was the development of a serious debt crisis (q.v.).

ALLIANCE DEMOCRATIQUE DE MADAGASCAR. The Malagasy Democratic Alliance was formed in March 1987 by three parties belonging to the Front National pour la Défense de la Révolution (q.v.), MONIMA (q.v.), the MFM (q.v.), and Vonjy (q.v.) to provide a united front of opposition to the regime of President Didier Ratsiraka (q.v.). It was unable to agree on a joint candidate for the presidential elections of March 1989, and the leaders of its three component parties ran separately. Its strategy in the May legislative elections was also uncertain. The ADM at first urged its supporters to boycott the elections and then, after assurances of fair conduct from President Ratsiraka, agreed to run candidates, again largely separately. In the crisis leading up to the end of the Ratsiraka regime, the ADM split. MONIMA and some Vonjy supporters joined the Mouvement Militant pour le Socialisme Malagasy (q.v.), which supported the president, while the MFM and other Vonjy members jointed the opposition groups that eventually became the Comité des Forces Vives (q.v.). *See also* ELECTIONS.

AMBALAVAO (21°50′S, 46°56′E). Lying halfway between the southern capital of Fianarantsoa (q.v.) and the outpost of Ihosy (q.v.), Ambalavao was garrisoned by the troops of the Merina Empire (q.v.). During the French conquest, it also served as a center of operations for the conquest of southern Madagascar. It is currently the site of an important cattle market.

AMBANIANDRO. Literally, "Those Who Live Under the Heavens," Ambaniandro is a synonym for Merina (q.v.).

AMBOHIMANGA. It was from this village to the northeast of Antananarivo (q.v.) that Andrianampoinimerina (q.v.) embarked on his conquest of Imerina at the end of the eighteenth century. As the site of the origin of the nineteenth-century Merina monarchy (q.v.) and the site of the tombs of the royal ancestors, it was considered a holy place. Although the remains of the early Merina kings were transferred to Antananarivo in 1896, Ambohimanga is still a place of pilgrimage.

AMBOHITSIROHITRA. One of the royal palaces of the Merina Empire, Ambohitsirohitra was taken over as the headquarters of the colonial governor-general. After independence in 1960 it served as the French embassy. It was handed over to the government of Madagascar in 1975, and now serves as the presidential palace.

AMERICAN CROPS. A variety of crops from North and South America are grown in Madagascar. Some were introduced directly, and others came via the Mascarene Islands (q.v.) or Africa (q.v.). One of the most important is manioc, which was introduced in the early eighteenth century. It is widely grown, and in the southern regions of the island was used as a primary foodstuff before the spread of rice (q.v.) production. It is used as a supplement to rice in times of drought and in the period of shortage before the rice harvest. Since the colonial period manioc has been exported, mainly for the manufacture of tapioca. Corn has also been established in Madagascar for a long time and is widely cultivated, especially in the south central Highlands (q.v.) and in the southwest. Like manioc, it is used as a supplement to rice. Peanuts are grown along the west coast, and most are exported to be turned onto oil.

AMICALE DES ETUDIANTS MALGACHES COTIERS. *See* UNION DES ETUDIANTS MALGACHES.

AMNESTY. After the Tananarive trials of 1948 (q.v.) a campaign was started to secure an amnesty for those convicted of complicity in the Rebellion of 1947 (q.v.). One of the organizations working to this end was the Comité de Solidarité de Madagascar (q.v.). This campaign polarized opinion in Madagascar, and attempts to pass an amnesty bill in the French legislature were frequently opposed by Malagasy deputies and senators. A bill of amnesty was finally passed in 1958, but did not lift the sentence of exile on the MDRM deputies (q.v.). They returned to Madagascar only after the granting of full independence in 1960.

ANDAFIAVARATRA. Under the Merina monarchy (q.v.), Andafiavaratra, or ``Those from the North," was the name given to the clans, largely *hova,* or commoner, who had supported the claim to the throne of the founder of the modern monarchy, Andrianampoinimerina (q.v.). They dominated the politics of the monarchy after the death of Andrianampoinimerina's successor, Radama I (q.v.), and even more after the death in 1863 of Radama II (q.v.), the result of a coup d'état for which they were largely responsible. They engaged in mercantile as well as political activities, and occupied the top posts of the administration and army. One of the Andafiavaratra clans, the Tsimahafotsy, provided the successive prime ministers of the kingdom. The prime minister's palace in Antananarivo is called Andafiavaratra Palace (q.v.). *See also* RAHARO; RAINILAIARIVONY.

ANDEKALEKA. The Andekaleka dam was built on the Vohitra River near the border between Antananarvio and Toamasina provinces. Although attempts to finance it began in 1977, it is considered part of the All-Out Investment Policy (q.v.) begun in 1978. Financers included the World Bank (q.v.), the United States (q.v.) Agency for International Development, and the Canadian International Development Agency, as well as the Saudi Arabian and Kuwaiti development assistance agencies. The largest hydroelectric project in Madagascar, the dam was inaugurated in June 1982. The installation at Andekaleka now provides hydroelectric power for the capital and Antsirabe, two of the major industrial areas of the island. To be profitable, however, the complex needs to be expanded, and the industries that would use the power it would generate have yet to be created.

ANDEVO. A slave caste. *See also* SLAVERY; ZOAM.

ANDRA, SOSONY. Chief of police in Antananarivo, Andra was named to the AREMA political bureau in 1983.

ANDRIAMAHAZO, GILLES (1919–). Andriamahazo was born in 1919 to a Merina family living in Taolagnaro and served in the French army in the Second World War. In 1949 he was promoted from the ranks to the grade of second lieutenant and sent to training courses in France. He joined the new Malagasy army at the time of independence, and at the time of the May 1972 Revolution (q.v.) he was in charge of the Antananarivo garrison. In this capacity he participated in the decision both not to use the army to defend the regime of President Tsiranana (q.v.) and to contain popular demonstrations after the installation of the regime headed by General Gabriel Ramanantsoa (q.v.). In the Ramanantsoa regime, he was promoted to general and given the post of minister of territorial development. In the subsequent government of Richard Ratsimandrava (q.v.) he was minister without portfolio. After Ratsimandrava's assassination on February 11, 1975, as the ranking general in the armed forces (Ramanantsoa had been ousted on February 5, and would retire in March), Andriamahazo became the formal head of the Directoire Militaire (q.v.) that took power. Although Andriamahazo showed some signs of presidential aspirations, it was naval captain Didier Ratsiraka (q.v.) whom the directorate chose in June 1975 to succeed Ratsimandrava. Andriamahazo was named to the largely honorific post of president of the Comité Militaire pour le Développement (q.v.) and retired in November 1976.

ANDRIAMAHOLISON, RICHARD. A commandant in the gendarmerie in 1975, Andriamaholison served as minister of information in the weeklong government of Richard Ratsimandrava (q.v.). After Ratsimandrava's assassination, he was a representative of Antananarivo province in the Directoire Militaire (q.v.) that took power and chose Didier Ratsiraka (q.v.) as the new president. Andriamaholison returned to the gendarmerie, and in 1977 was one of three officers of the armed forces arrested and charged with conspiracy against the state. He was not tried until 1983, when he was sentenced to deportation—in effect, house arrest—in spite of his lawyers' pleas that his poor health justified clemency. An appeal of the sentence was overturned by the Supreme Court in 1987. *See also* OFFICERS' TRIAL.

ANDRIAMANELY. Andriamanely is credited with having established himself as a ruler of the Bara (q.v.) at the end of the eighteenth century. He is supposed to have been a member of a clan that came from the southeast of Bara territory during the previous century. His descendants, or Zafimanely, gradually imposed themselves as the rulers over the major Bara groups.

ANDRIAMANERISOA, NIRINA. Andriamanerisoa, a leading member of the younger generation of political figures of the Democratic Republic of Madagascar (q.v.), was named minister of agriculture in 1982. He made an unsuccessful attempt to bring order to what is considered to be one of the more difficult government ministries. In 1983 he became special presidential counselor for financial affairs, and helped draft a new investment code. He also played a role in negotiations with the International Monetary Fund (q.v.).

ANDRIAMANJATO, RICHARD (1930–). President of the AKFM (q.v.) and longtime mayor of Antananarivo, Andriamanjato was born to a noble Merina (q.v.) family. He undertook theological studies in Strasbourg in the early 1950s, and became president of the Association des Etudiants d'Origine Malgache (q.v.). He was also active in the Comité de Solidarité de Madagascar (q.v.). He returned to Madagascar in 1957 and was one of the delegates to the Tamatave Congress (q.v.) of parties demanding immediate independence for Madagascar. When the AKFM was founded in 1958, be became its first president. Andriamanjato was elected mayor of Antananarivo in 1959, and became one of three AKFM deputies in the legislature of the First Republic (q.v.). At the same time he continued to be active in the Protestant church and its educational network, and was a member of the Ecumenical Council of Protestant Churches in Geneva. In spite of frequent trips to Eastern Europe, he was usually considered to be a member of the AKFM's "pure nationalist" rather than Marxist wing.

Although at first critical of the May 1972 Revolution (q.v.), Andriamanjato later supported the Ramanantsoa regime (q.v.) that followed it, and was a member of the regime's Conseil National Populaire de Développement (q.v.). He supported the presidential candidacy of Didier Ratsiraka (q.v.) and the creation of the Democratic Republic of Madagascar (q.v.) in 1975, taking his party into the Front National Pour la Défense de la Révolution (q.v.), where he sat as the party's representative, resigning as mayor of Antananarivo so he could hold the regime post. The economic crisis of the 1980s, however, led Andriamanjato to distance himself from Ratsiraka and his regime, and at the beginning of 1989 Andriamanjato announced his intention of running against Ratsiraka in the presidential elections to be held in March of that year. This action was disavowed by the central committee of the AKFM, and at the end of March Andriamanjato announced his resignation from the party and his intention of creating AKFM-Renouveau (q.v.).

Andriamanjato then joined the groups that were calling for an end to the Democratic Republic of Madagascar. In 1991 he joined Manandafy Rakotonirina (q.v.) and Albert Zafy (q.v.) to form the Comité des Forces Vives (q.v.), which led the opposition to the regime. In the transitional institutions established under the power-sharing agreement of October 1991 (q.v.), he joined Rakotonirina in heading the 130-member Conseil de Redressement Economique et Social (q.v.).

ANDRIAMASINAVALONA. Andriamasinavalona was a Merina (q.v.) king who ruled from about 1675 to 1710. He extended the kingdom to a greater size than it had been before, but on his death divided it among his sons, leading to a period of wars among the rival kingdoms that ended with the conquests of Andrianampoinimerina (q.v.) at the end of the eighteenth century.

ANDRIAMORASATA, NORBERT SOLO. A journalist from Antananarivo, Andriamorasata founded the Union des Chrétiens de Madagascar (q.v.) in 1969, in an attempt to create a left-wing Christian party. In 1972 he attempted to run for the presidency of the First Republic (q.v.) against President Philibert Tsiranana (q.v.), but his candidacy was annulled, leaving Tsiranana the sole candidate. Andriamorasata took UDECMA into the Front National pour la Défense de la Révolution (q.v.) in 1977, and joined both the Front and the Conseil Suprême de la Révolution (q.v.). UDECMA continued its support of Ratsiraka during the crisis that led to the end of the regime, but the bulk of Christian groups supported the opposition to the regime.

ANDRIANA. Merina (q.v.) noble caste.

ANDRIANAMPOINIMERINA. Born approximately in the middle of the eighteenth century, and given the birth name of Ramboasalama, Andrianampoinimerina was the nephew of the ruler of the Merina kingdom centered on Ambohimanga (q.v.). According to legend his grandfather, Andriambelomasina, had named him to succeed his uncle, Andrianjafy (q.v.), on the latter's death. The chronicles record that the uncle was a cruel and oppressive ruler who exiled his nephew and plotted his death. Andrianampoinimerina returned, however, to take over the throne in alliance with the important Hova (q.v.) clans of the kingdom. Andrianjafy was expelled and later killed.

After consolidating his hold on Ambohimanga in approximately 1783, Andrianampoinimerina proceeded to conquer and reunite the other kingdoms of Imerina, beginning with the most important, Analamanga, which he renamed Antananarivo (q.v.). The city was permanently subdued about 1793, and turned into a second capital. The other Merina kingdoms were annexed by a mixture of wars of conquest and political marriages.

After the conquest, Andrianampoinimerina proceeded to organize the defense, economy, and administration of the kingdom. The western border was secured against the Sakalava (q.v.) who had been raiding the kingdom for slaves and tribute. The system of state-administered rice irrigation was regularized and extended, as was the system of markets. The territory of the kingdom was divided into districts, and the villages were brought under the control of the royal administration via the creation of the post of village headman, or *mpiadidy,* and roving supervisors called *vadintany.* These tasks were carried out through a system of obligatory labor. The custom of ritual payments to overlords was also regularized into a tax system.

At the level of ritual Andrianampoinimerina organized the system of the *sampy* (q.v.), or royal talismans and solidified the role of the king as mediator between the population and the spiritual world of the ancestors through ceremonies such as the *fandroana* (q.v.), or New Year's bath. After the conquest of Imerina, Nampoina, as he was also called, began extending the kingdom to the east into lands occupied by the Sihanaka (q.v.) and Bezanozano (q.v.) and to the south into Betsileo (q.v.). With the conquests came the growth of trade in slaves and guns, and the first visits of Europeans to the capital. *See also* SLAVES; SLAVE TRADE; MAYEUR, NICHOLAS.

Andrianampoinimerina is credited with inspiring the subsequent Merina attempt to conquer the rest of Madagascar, and is often quoted as claiming, ''The sea is the limit of my rice field.'' He died in approximately 1810 and was succeeded by his son, Radama I (q.v.). *See also* ANDAFIAVARATRA; MERINA MONARCHY; TANTARAN'NY ANDRIANA ETO MADAGASIKARA.

ANDRIANARAHINJAKA, LUCIEN XAVIER MICHEL (1929–). One of the central figures of the Democratic Republic of Madagascar (q.v.), Andrianarahinjaka was born in Fianarantsoa province. A professor specializing in Malagasy literature, he served as cultural counselor in the government of Gabriel Ramanantsoa (q.v.). When Didier Ratsiraka (q.v.) took power in 1975, Andrianarahinjaka was named secretary-general of the Conseil Suprême de la Révolution (q.v.). He later became counselor to the president in charge of information and ideological animation, a post from which he played a major role in the formation of the regime party, AREMA (q.v.). Andrianarahinjaka was a founding member of the party's political bureau and was one of its representatives in the Front National pour la Défense de la Révolution (q.v.). In 1977 he was elected to the presidency of the

Assemblée Nationale Populaire (q.v.), a post that he held until the institution was dissolved at the collapse of the Ratsiraka regime in 1992.

ANDRIANDAHIFOTSY (c. 1610–c. 1685). Andriandahifotsy is credited with expanding the Sakalava (q.v.) kingdom of Menabe (q.v.) to the north of its original site. His rule covered the period in which extensive trade with Europeans began, and the exchange of slaves for weapons became an important basis for the Menabe economy.

ANDRIANJAFY. Ruler of Ambohimanga (q.v.) in the late eighteenth century and uncle of Andrianampoinimerina (q.v.), Andrianjafy resented the fact that his father, Andriambelomasina, had named Andrianampoinimerina rather than his own son to succeed him. (Merina sovereigns could name successors for more than one generation, and this type of oblique succession was not uncommon.) To secure the succession for his son, Andrianjafy exiled his nephew and plotted his death. Andrianampoinimerina rallied the clans of Ambohimanga against his uncle, however, and overthrew him about 1783. Andrianjafy continued to fight to recapture his kingdom, and was killed about 1787.

ANDRIANJAKA. Andrianjaka was a Merina (q.v.) king of the early seventeenth century. He is credited with founding the current capital of Madagascar, Antananarivo (q.v.), and establishing the first royal settlement there.

ANDRIANOELISOA, THEOPHILE. A sociology professor and founding member of the political bureau of the regime party of the Democratic Republic of Madagascar (q.v.), AREMA (q.v.), Andrianoelisoa served as minister of secondary and basic education from 1977 to 1983. He was also one of the founders of the AREMA union movement, SEREMA. In 1983 Andrianoelisoa was named to the Conseil Suprême de la Révolution (q.v.).

ANDRIANTSOLY. Andriantsoly became the king of the Boina (q.v.) Sakalava (q.v.) in 1822, when the kingdom was collapsing under pressure from the expanding Merina Empire (q.v.). His capital, Mahajanga, was captured by the Merina in 1824. A convert to Islam, Andriantsoly increased the role of the Antolaotra (q.v.) in his kingdom, and with their help mounted resistance to the Merina. After an initial flight to Mayotte, in the Comoro Islands (q.v.), he returned and attacked Mahajanga, but without success. In 1831 he fled once more to Mayotte, where he became a local ruler, or sultan, while the women of the royal family established the Bemihisatra kingdom. *See also* TSIOMEKO.

ANDRY, NY "The Pillar". *Ny Andry* was the semiclandestine journal of the radical opposition to the First Republic (q.v.) in the later 1960s. Edited by, among others, Manandafy Rakotonirina (q.v.), *Ny Andry* was instrumental in politicizing the student movement of the time. *See also* MAY 1992 REVOLUTION.

ANNET, ARMAND (1888–1973). Annet succeeded Leon Cayla (q.v.) as the Vichy (q.v.) regime's governor-general in Madagascar in 1941, with instructions to control both the Malagasy nationalist movement and the Free French (q.v.) groups on the island. He originally opposed the British invasion (q.v.) of 1942, but surrendered in October of that year. After the war he was tried in France and condemned to "national degradation." Annet wrote *Aux heures troublées de l'Afrique française* to justify his position. *Further information may be found in the Bibliography following this Dictionary.*

ANNEXATION LAW. This law, which ended the French protectorate (q.v.) in Madagascar and made the island a French colony, was voted by the French National Assembly on August 6, 1896. Its passage was precipitated by the Revolt of the Menalamba (q.v.), but its main proponents, François de Mahy (q.v.) and Le Myre de Vilers (q.v.), had long been exponents of French expansion in Madagascar. Annulment of the law was a major goal of the Malagasy nationalist movement (q.v.). It was never formally repealed, but its "caducity" was announced in 1958, when Madagascar received internal autonomy.

ANTAIMORO. The Antaimoro live along the southeastern coast of Madagascar in the region of Farafangana. Their ruling groups claim to be of Arab descent, and the Antaimoro are the main possessors of the *sorabe* (q.v.), documents in Malagasy, which are written in Arabic characters. Many of Madagascar's *ombiasy* (q.v.), or diviners, are Antaimoro and practice both astrology and *sikidy,* a system of divination based on the interpretation of patterns of grains or stones. Antaimoro clans are organized into a hierarchy that includes nobles, or *anteony,* and commoners, or *ampanabaka.* At the end of the nineteenth century, after conquest by the Merina Empire (q.v.), the commoner clans revolted against the noble clans, ending many of their privileges. The Antaimoro economy is based on rice and coffee cultivation. Their population is estimated to be about 262,000.

ANTAISAKA. The Antaisaka are a group of diverse origins living in southeastern Madagascar, inland from the Antaimoro (q.v.). Their ruling groups claim descent from a prince of the Maroserana (q.v.) dynasty, while the commoners are said to be a mixture of Bara (q.v.), Sakalava (q.v.), and Tanala (q.v.). The Antaisaka have a mixed economy that includes some herding as well as the cultivation of rice and coffee. Like other southern groups they are a source of immigrants for other parts of the island, providing both migrant labor and permanent immigrants, who take up residence in the farming lands of the Malagasy middle west. Their population was estimated at about 406,000 in 1972.

ANTALAOTRA. The Antalaotra were an Islamicized group of Arab antecedents living on the west coast of Madagascar. They provided ritual specialists to several ruling groups, but were mainly active in trade and flourished with the development of the Swahili trading network that involved east Africa, Zanzibar, and the Comoro Islands (q.v.) in the eighteenth and nineteenth centuries. In the early eighteenth century their trading posts on the west coast were conquered by the Sakalava (q.v.), with whose ruling dynasties they later intermarried. Their position was strengthened by the conversion of several of these dynasties to Islam in the nineteenth century. The Merina (q.v.) conquest of Mahajanga (q.v.), however, disturbed their political position and economic activities; the end of the slave trade that came with the French conquest in 1895 led to their disappearance as an economically distinct group.

ANTAMBAHOAKA. The Antambahoaka live on the east coast of Madagascar, in the lower valley of the Mananjara River. They claim to be descended from the Zafiraminia (q.v.) and are one of the groups in Madagascar to show Islamic influences.

ANTANAIMORO. Antanaimoro is a military camp situated on the outskirts of Antananarivo (q.v.). At the time of the crisis that led to the fall of the Ramanantsoa regime (q.v.), it was occupied by the Groupe Mobile de Police, the renamed version of the Forces Républicaines de Sécurité (q.v.), the main military support of the First Republic (q.v.), which had been displaced by the regime of General Ramanantsoa. In December 1974 Colonel Bréchard Rajaonarison (q.v.) and supporters of his aborted coup against the regime fled there after the discovery of the plot. Although the camp was the site of open revolt against his regime, Ramanantsoa did not have the political strength to attack it, and the men who assassinated his successor, Richard Ratsimandrava (q.v.) on February 11, 1975, were members of the GMP from the camp. After the assassination, the camp was attacked both by the army and by an Antananarivo mob, and the assassins as well as Rajoanarison and his supporters were captured.

ANTANANARIVO (18°55′S, 47°31′E). Founded in the mid–seventeenth century under the name Analamanga, Antananarivo was one of the first strongholds of the Merina (q.v.). The early city was situated on a hill, or *rova* (q.v.), overlooking the Ikopa and Betsiboka rivers, at a point where the rivers formed marshes suitable for rice cultivation. At the time of Andrianampoinimerina's (q.v.) conquests, Antananarivo was the most important of the Merina kingdoms; tradition records that it took three attempts before the city was finally conquered about 1793. Andrianampoinimerina made it a second capital, and under subsequent rulers it became the main capital of the country. At the time of the French conquest the city had a population of about 75,000, over half of whom were slaves.

The French made Antananarivo, renamed Tananarive, the capital of the whole territory, concentrated the administrative, economic, and educational apparatus of the colonial regime in the city, and made it the center of the island's transportation system. By the end of the colonial period Tananarive had a population of about 250,000. Although subsequent regimes have largely drawn their top political personnel from regions outside the capital, the primacy of Antananarivo (the name was changed again after the May 1972 Revolution, q.v.) has not been challenged. It now has a population of nearly one million, larger than that of the other five provincial capitals combined. It remains the economic as well as the political center of the island.

ANTANANARIVO ANNUAL. Started by James Sibree in 1875, the *Antananarivo Annual* appeared until 1900. Written largely by missionary authors, it contained observations on different aspects of Malagasy life and on the customs of various Malagasy groups.

ANTANANARIVO PROVINCE. Located at the center of Madagascar, in the Highlands (q.v.), Antananarivo province is the fastest growing of the Malagasy provinces, in part due to natural population growth and in part due to immigration from other parts of the island. The capital, Antananarivo (q.v.), is located here, and most of the island's industry is located either in Antananarivo or in Antsirabe (q.v.) to the south. As the seat of the former Merina Empire (q.v.) and center of mission activities in the nineteenth century, the province also has the densest educational network of the island. Its economy rests on services, some industry, and agriculture, in particular the cultivation of rice. In spite of immigration, its population is still largely Merina (q.v.).

ANTANDROY. The Antandroy, or "People of the Thornbush," inhabit the arid southernmost tip of Madagascar. Like many

Malagasy ethnic groups, they have incorporated over time people from other groups, particularly Sakalava (q.v.), Bara (q.v.), and Antanosy (q.v.). Organized into kinship groups, the Antandroy are largely cattle herders, often on a semi-nomadic basis. Given the poverty of their region, which is arid at best and subject to droughts, the Antandroy are also an important source of migrant labor for the rest of the island. Their estimated population in 1974 was 412,000.

ANTANKARANA (*also* Antakarana). The Antankarana live in northern Madagascar, in the region around Antseranana (q.v.). A small group, estimated to be about 46,000, their development reflects an early influence by Arabs (q.v.) and late Sakalava (q.v.) influence. Their region is one of the major cash-crop areas of Madagascar, specializing in the cultivation of cloves and vanilla, and the Antankarana are a major source of labor for the spice plantations.

ANTANOSY. The Antanosy live in a region stretching inland from Taoloñaro (q.v.). Like many other southern groups, their ruling clans claim descent from the Arabicized Zafiraminia (q.v.). Like the ruling clans of the Antaimoro (q.v.), they possess writings in Arabic characters known as *sorabe* (q.v.). Their economy is based on herding and on work in the sisal (q.v.) plantations of their region. Their population is estimated to be about 182,000

ANTOKON'NY KONGRESIN'NY FAHALEOVANTENAN'I MADAGASIKARA. *See* AKFM.

ANTONGIL BAY (15°30′S, 49°50′E). Antongil Bay stretches 100 km inland and provides the best harbor on the east coast between Toamasina (q.v.) and Antseranana (q.v.). At the end of the seventeenth century it provided a haven for pirates (q.v.) and later was the first harbor used for trade in slaves, cattle, and rice with the Mascarenes (q.v.), although it lost its position to Foulpointe (q.v.) in 1756. In 1774 Count Benyowski (q.v.) was sent by the Compagnie des Indes Orientales (q.v.) to establish a permanent settlement there, but the establishment did not match his reports of it. After the company sent a mission of inspection that revealed Benyowski's fabrications, Antongil Bay was definitively abandoned in favor of Toamasina (q.v.).

ANTSERANANA (12°25′S, 49°20′E). Originally Diégo-Suarez (q.v.), Antseranana is the site of Madagascar's best harbor, formerly a French naval base, which was handed over to the Malagasy government in 1973 after the renegotiation of the cooperation agreements (q.v.) between the two countries. The arsenal and dry dock attached to the base were nationalized as SECREN, or the Société d'Études de Constructions et de Réparations Navales, and the arsenal was transformed into a factory for the construction of agricultural machinery. The factory was not successful, and the dry dock fell into disuse. There were plans to repair both as part of an attempt to revive the Malagasy economy.

Antseranana itself is Madagascar's third most important port, serving for the export of the cash crops of the interior of the province of Antseranana (q.v.) and as a point of transshipment to the Seychelles and the Comoro Islands.

ANTSERANANA PROVINCE. The northernmost of the Malagasy provinces, Antseranana is isolated from the rest of the island by the Tsaratanana Massif. It was created in 1956 from the northern parts of Toamasina (q.v.) and Mahajanga (q.v.) provinces. It is the richest province after Antananarivo, growing a variety of cash crops, including coffee (q.v.), perfume plants (q.v.), vanilla (q.v.), pepper, and cloves. It has periodically threatened to separate itself politically from the rest of the island. The main Malagasy ethnic group in the province is the Antankarana (q.v.), followed by the Sakalava (q.v.), Tsimihety (q.v.), and Betsimisaraka (q.v.). The plantations attract migrant labor from the south, and the area has also been subject to immigration from non-Malagasy groups, particularly in the island of Nosy Be (q.v.) and the port of Antseranana (q.v.).

ANTSIRABE (19°55′S, 47°2′E). Located 163 km south of the capital, Antananarivo, Antsirabe was founded in 1869 by Norwegian missionaries attracted by the cool climate and the mineral springs found in the area. During both the Merina Empire (q.v.) and the colonial period it was a favored spa, and a rail line from Antananarivo was extended there in 1923. Since independence it has become one of the major industrial centers of Madagascar. The main military academy is located in Antsirabe.

ANTSIRABE COLLOQUIUM. This meeting was convened at Antsirabe (q.v.) by Philibert Tsiranana (q.v.), president of the republic and of its dominant party, and the Parti Sociale Démocrate (q.v.), in an attempt to expand the PSD's base by absorbing some of the other Malagasy parties. It held its first meeting on October 21, 1961. Most of the thirty-five other parties in existence at the time, including the AKFM (q.v.) and the Union Sociale et Démocratique de Madagascar (q.v.) attended. Meetings at Antananarivo continued through November, and a second colloquium was held at Antsirabe on December 27, but it broke up with no agreement on a common program. In the meantime, however, the PSD had attracted the Rassemblement National Malgache (q.v.) and had been joined on an individual basis by other prominent politicians, such as the nationalist leaders Jacques Rabemananjara (q.v.) and Joseph Ravoahangy (q.v.). It also attracted the support, and later the membership, of factions of the UDSM and of the Rassemblement Chrétien de Madagascar (q.v.). With its majority position consolidated in this way, the PSD had no further need to pursue the attempt at regrouping undertaken at the colloquium, and there were no further meetings.

ARABS. Arabic or Islamic influence in Madagascar has been strong since at least the eleventh century, as the island became incorporated into the western Indian Ocean trading network the Arabs dominated. Early Arab maps show the approximate location of Madagascar, called alternately "Waqwaq" and "Komr." Arab trading centers were established on the coast of Madagascar at such locations as Vohemar (q.v.), and the ruling clans of several Malagasy groups, most notably the Antaimoro (q.v.) and the Sakalava (q.v.), claim to be of Arab descent. Malagasy was first written in Arabic script, in sacred writings called *sorabe* (q.v.). Although the main Arab settlements were eliminated after the arrival of Europeans in the western Indian Ocean, groups of Arab-Swahili traders known as Antalaotra (q.v.) remained on the west coast until the end of the nineteenth century.

AREMA Antokin'ny revolosiona malagasy, *or* ''Vanguard of the Malagasy Revolution''; *in* French, Avant-garde de la Révolution Malgache). AREMA was founded by Didier Ratsiraka (q.v.) in March 1976 to be the central, or regime, party of the Democratic Republic or Madagascar (q.v.), after negotiations with other political groups to form a single party had broken down. It was the first party to apply and be admitted to the Front National pour la Défense de La Révolution (q.v.), which united the legal parties of the republic. The organization of the party parallelled that of the decentralized collectivities (q.v.), with the basic unit being the *fokontany* cell. It was not clear, however, that the intermediate levels between the base and the center undertook many activities outside election time. The national level was also not clearly organized, and the national congress never met. As secretary-general of the party, Didier Ratsiraka named the members of the political bureau.

Like the regime party of the First Republic (q.v.), the Parti Social Démocrate (q.v.), AREMA was established with the active participation of the territorial administration; like the PSD, the party was a loose coalition of divergent interests. In the late 1970s and 1980s these divisions became especially acute, and the party developed a split between a ''left'' or ''presidential'' AREMA that supported the socialist policies of Didier Ratsiraka, and a ''right'' AREMA headed by the then minister of finance, Rakotovao-Razakaboana (q.v.). The split ended when Ratsiraka reasserted his control over the party after winning the 1982 presidential elections, although many of the policies advocated by the dissident group were adopted during the series of negotiations with the International Monetary Fund (q.v.) for relief from Madagascar's debts.

In spite of its divisions, AREMA was able to dominate elections to the Assemblée Nationale Populaire (q.v.) and to the councils and presidencies of the decentralized collectivities. In the legislative elections of May 1989, it gained 66% of the vote and 120 of 137 seats in the assembly. During the crisis that led to the fall of the regime, AREMA joined other parties supporting President Ratsiraka in the Mouvement Militant pour le Socialisme Malagasy (q.v.). After the first elections of the Third Republic (q.v.), AREMA disappeared, and Ratsiraka announced the formation of a new party, the Vanguard for Economic and Social Recovery.

AREMA had several auxiliary organizations, of which the most important was AREMA Women, headed by Ratsiraka's wife, Céline (q.v.), and her sister, Hortense Raveloson-Mahasampo (q.v.). There was also an AREMA-run union federation, SEREMA, and an AREMA-run cooperative organization. *See also* COOPERATIVES; ELECTIONS; UNIONS.

ARIDY, CELESTIN (1919–). The meeting that decided to create the Parti Social Démocrate (q.v.) was held at Aridy's home. A native of Nosy Be, he was a teacher who had attended the Ecole le Myre de Vilers (q.v.) and the teachers' college at Montpellier. Under the First Republic (q.v.) he served as chief of the then province of Diégo-Suarez from 1960 to 1965, when he became secretary of state for social affairs in charge of public health and then secretary of state for agriculture in charge of western development.

ASIAN IMMIGRANTS. *See* CHINESE; INDO-PAKISTANIS.

ASSEMBLEE NATIONALE POPULAIRE (National People's Assembly). The Assemblée Nationale Populaire was the legislature of the Democratic Republic of Madagascar (q.v.). Composed of 137 deputies, it held its inaugural session July 28–30, 1977. It normally met for four months of the year, from October to December, but could be called into session at other times. Its agenda was established by the president of the republic in consultation with the president of the ANP, Lucien Xavier Michel Andrianarahinjaka (q.v.), a major figure of the Second Republic, and its political bureau. The assembly was dominated by the regime party, AREMA (q.v.), and the turnover of deputies was relatively high. Although the assembly lacked real power, it did serve as a forum for the expression of discontent. It delayed the passage of the 1987 investment code for several months, and in 1988 three opposition parties—MFM (q.v.), MONIMA (q.v.), and Vonjy (q.v.)—refused to vote for the budget. The last election to the ANP was held on May 28, 1989, with AREMA winning 120 of the 137 seats. The operations of the assembly were suspended in 1992 during the period of transition to the Third Republic (q.v.), and in the new constitution it was replaced by a bicameral legislature composed of a national assembly and a senate. See also *ELECTIONS.*

ASSOCIATION DES ETUDIANTS D'ORIGINE MALGACHE. The AEOM was founded in France in 1934 by Rakoto Ratsimamanga. At first a cultural and social club, after the Rebellion of 1947 (q.v.) it became one of the major voices of nationalist sentiment and played an important role in the campaign for amnesty (q.v.) for those convicted or complicity in the uprising and for the repeal of the Annexation Law of 1896 (q.v.). Under Richard Andriamanjato (q.v.), who became its president in 1956, it developed links with the International Student Union based in Prague. *See also* UNION DES ETUDIANTS MALGACHES.

AUGAGNEUR, VICTOR (1855–1931). A deputy from the Rhône district of France, Augagneur was the first civilian governor-general of Madagascar, occupying the post from 1905 to 1910. Under his administration extensive work was done on the island's transportation system, including the continuation of the Tananarive–East Coast railroad (q.v.). Augagneur continued the work of his predecessor, General Gallieni (q.v.), in constructing the framework of the colonial system. He revised the *indigénat* (q.v.) and established the conditions by which the Malagasy could acquire French citizenship. A strongly anticlerical republican, Augagneur cut the subsidies traditionally granted to the mission schools and forbade the holding of classes in buildings that were also used for religious services. The result was a drastic decline in the numbers attending school. As an economy measure he closed the regional schools that Gallieni had established in an attempt to reduce the dominance of Antananarivo and its elite in education and recruitment to the administration. After leaving Madagascar, Augagneur returned to the French National Assembly, and later served as governor-general of French Equatorial Africa. *Further information may be found in the Bibliography following this Dictionary.*

AVOTSE. *See* COOPERATIVES.

-B-

BAIBOHO. These are river banks, largely located on west coast rivers, that receive alluvial deposits at the time of annual floods. They provide an area for cultivation, particularly of rice and of cotton.

BANKING SYSTEM. As part of its attempt to gain control of the Malagasy economy, the Ramanantsoa regime (q.v.) established after the May 1972 Revolution (q.v.) undertook a reorganization of the banking system. The reorganization was pursued by the successor Democratic Republic of Madagascar (q.v.). In 1973 Madagascar left the Franc Zone (q.v.), and the Institut d'Emission Malgache, which had been run jointly with the French, was taken under Malagasy control and renamed the Banque Centrale de la République Malgache. In 1975 the existing private banks in Madagascar were nationalized; and three specialized banks were created: the Bankin'ny Indostria, or "Bank for Industry"; the Bankin'ny tantsaha mpamokatra, or "Bank for Peasant Producers"; and the Banky Fampandrosoana ny Varotra, or "Bank for the Encouragement of Commerce." The banking system has had uneven success, and the Bank for Peasant Producers in particular has neither attracted the savings nor undertaken the investments that were expected of it.

The banking system was one of the targets of the liberalization policies begun in the late 1980s, particularly since the banks' ill-regulated lending activities helped fuel inflation. The Bank for Industry was opened to private capital, but both the DRM and the government of the Third Republic (q.v.) have resisted pressures to open the other two banks, even as they have attempted to gain better control over their activities.

BARA. With a population estimated at 228,000 in 1964, the Bara are a seminomadic group living in south central Madagascar, with Ihosy (q.v.) as their main town. They claim to have come to this territory from the east, pushed out by pressure from the Tanala (q.v.). Although the Bara contain many groups that come together and split up, by the end of the nineteenth century there were three major kingdoms, or groups: the Bara Iantsantsa in the eastern part of the territory, the Bara Be in the center, and the Bara Imamo in the western part (''kingdom'' is used loosely here since the basis of the Bara economy at the time—beyond herding—was cattle and slave raiding, and the 6 kings were essentially those who could establish themselves as heads of the raiding parties). In spite of the establishment of a Merina outpost at Ihosy, the Bara were generally able to resist the imposition of rule by the Merina Empire (q.v.). The French arrived in 1897, but it took ten years and the execution of a leader of the Bara Be, Lahitafika (q.v.), before the territory was conquered. The modern economy of Bara territory is still based on cattle herding, but rice cultivation, largely for subsistence purposes, has become increasingly common. See ANDRIAMANELY.

BARGUES, ROBERT. Bargues served as governor-general of Madagascar from February 1950 to October 1954. During his period in office, the political controls imposed after the Rebellion of 1947 (q.v.) began to be eased, and the Malagasy electorate was expanded from 256,930 to 885,000. Political activity at the level of the municipalities was also increased. Bargues refused to allow French political parties to establish themselves in Madagascar and attempted to limit political discourse to economic development issues. He was succeeded by André Soucadaux (q.v.).

BAS-MANGOKY. The delta of the Mangoky River, which drains western central Madagascar, receives extensive alluvial deposits during the flood season and has the potential for high-yield agricultural production. The Bas-Mangoky was the site of a major, and not entirely successful, attempt to develop the production of cotton, first during the colonial period and then during the First Republic (q.v.).

BEDO, JOSEPH. Bedo, one of the major figures of the government of the Democratic Republic of Madagascar (q.v.), was born in Toamasina province. His political career began during the First Republic (q.v.), and he served as director of the Agency for Internal and External Documentation (security) in the Ministry of the Interior from 1970 to 1972. In 1976 he became secretary to the president in charge of the Inspectorate General of Finance, Army, and Gendarmerie, and in 1982 he became minister of transportation, food supplies and tourism. In 1987 he became minister of justice, a post he held until August 1991, when Guy Razanamasy (q.v.) established a government designed to incorporate opposition figures.

BEFELATANANA. A medical school was established by Governor-General Gallieni in 1897 at the Befelatanana Hospital in Tananarive to train Malagasy medical auxiliaries for the colonial health system. The school and its students have played an important role in Malagasy politics. The 1915 secret society Vy Vato Sakelika (q.v.) was centered on the school, and such graduates as Joseph Ravoahangy (q.v.) were important figures in the nationalist movement (q.v.). In 1972 the school served as a detonator for the May 1972 Revolution (q.v.) when its students went on strike to protest the subordination of their degrees to those handed out under French auspices by the Faculty of Medicine of the University of Madagascar. In 1977 the school was closed and its functions divided between the Faculty of Medicine and training programs for midwives and paramedical personnel.

BEMANANJARA, JEAN. A native of Toamasina province, Bemananjara was a longtime minister of foreign affairs of the

Democratic Republic of Madagascar (q.v.). He served as director of the cabinet of the minister of foreign affairs of the last government of the First Republic (q.v.) but was also active in the regimes that succeeded it. He was a member of the Conseil National Populaire du Développement (q.v.) during the Ramanantsoa regime (q.v.) and was minister of transportation in the short-lived government of Richard Ratsimandrava (q.v.). After the coming to power of Didier Ratsiraka (q.v.) in June 1975, he continued as minister of transportation and food supplies, leaving the post to become director of the president's personal cabinet in 1982. He was named minister of foreign affairs in 1983, a post he held until August 1991.

BEMOLANGA. A deposit of oil-bearing shale covering over 400 square kilometers is located at Bemolanga in the Morafenobe region of Mahajanga province. In 1981 during the All-Out Investment Policy (q.v.) period, surveys financed by a loan from the European Investment Bank were carried out in the hope that exploitation of the deposits would make Madagascar self-sufficient in petroleum. Studies suggested, however, that extraction of the oil would be prohibitively expensive, and no investors were found to undertake the task. *See also* PETROLEUM.

BENYOWSKI, MAURICE AUGUSTE DE ALADAR, COUNT (d. 1786). A member of the Hungarian nobility, Benyowski participated in a Polish revolt against the Russians in 1768. He was captured and sent to Siberia, from which he managed to escape and make his way to Canton in 1770. There he proposed his services to the Compagnie des Indes Orientales (q.v.), which sent him to Antongil Bay (q.v.) to found a settlement in 1774. He sent back glowing reports of the founding of cities and the establishment of an alliance network of Malagasy rulers. A commission of inquiry demonstrated that the reports were fabrications, and Benyowski was recalled to France. Instead he went to Britain and the United States, where he was able to raise enough money to equip a ship, the *Intrepid*, and engage some more "volunteers," as he called his associates. Benyowski returned to

Antongil Bay in 1785 and expelled the French garrison, proclaiming himself emperor of Madagascar. The French sent a retaliatory mission, and Benyowski was killed in the battle that followed their arrival.

BETSILEO. The Betsileo inhabit central Fianarantsoa province in the southern Highlands (q.v.) of Madagascar, claiming to be descended from groups that arrived there from the east coast at around the fifteenth century. With a population estimated at 920,600 in 1974, they are the third largest ethnic group on the island. Like the Merina, their society was divided into endogamous castes of nobles, commoners, and slaves, and the Betsileo noble clans were called *hova.* In the late seventeenth and eighteenth centuries several kingdoms developed in what is now Betsileo territory, including Isandra (q.v.) in the west and Lalaingina (q.v.) in the east. Betsileo territory was invaded by the Merina Empire (q.v.) around 1815, and was rapidly conquered, the Merina establishing a southern capital at Fianarantsoa (q.v.) in 1830. The eastern part of Betsileo territory was heavily involved in the Rebellion of 1947 (q.v.), but the rebels were not able to capture Fianarantsoa itself. The modern Betsileo economy is dominated by rice cultivation, largely irrigated, and the Betsileo have a reputation for being the best rice cultivators of the island. Because of population densities they also emigrate to other parts of the island, particularly to the middle west of Mahajanga province (q.v.). Since Fianarantsoa province is second only to Antananarivo province in the density of its educational network, there are many Betsileo to be found in the administration. The Betsileo also had several representatives among the political elite of the Democratic Republic of Madagascar (q.v.), including the president of the Assemblée Nationale Populaire (q.v.), L. X. M. Andrianarahinjaka (q.v.).

BETSIMISARAKA. Madagascar's second largest ethnic group, the Betsimisaraka were estimated to number 1,134,000 in 1974, and inhabit the east coast of the island from Mananjary in the south to Antongil Bay (q.v.) in the north. The Betsimisaraka are a loosely knit group divided into several subgroups. During the eighteenth century, the northern Betsimisaraka were united in the Betsimisaraka Confederation (q.v.) under the leadership of the Zanamalata (q.v.). The most important port in Madagascar, Toamasina (q.v.), is located on their territory, and they were an early target of the expansion of the Merina Empire (q.v.), which occupied the port in 1817. During the colonial period the Betsimisaraka, like the Tanala (q.v.), were subject to seizures of land for plantations and to forced labor for the plantations and for the Antananarivo-Toamasina railroad. Their territory was one of the major centers of the Rebellion of 1947. The Betsimisaraka economy is a mixed agricultural one, with extensive cultivation of rice and of cash crops (particularly coffee) and, in the north, vanilla and cloves. Several leading Malagasy politicians have been Betsimisaraka, including the nationalist leader Jacques Rabemananjara (q.v.) and the president of the Democratic Republic of Madagascar (q.v.), Didier Ratsiraka (q.v.).

BETSIMISARAKA CONFEDERATION. The Betsimisaraka Confederation was started after 1712 by Ratsimilaho (q.v.), the son of a pirate and of a Malagasy chief's daughter. Ratsimilaho assembled the other Zanamalata (q.v.) chiefs of the Fenoarivo (q.v.) region and was able to conquer territory along the coast from Fenoarivo to the port of Toamasina (q.v.) and to move inland, putting pressure on such groups as the Sihanaka. From this position they were able to control the trade with the Mascarenes (q.v.) that was crucial to their economy and that of inland groups. After Ratsimilaho's death in 1750, however, the confederation began to disintegrate. Ratsimilaho's successors, Zanahary (who died in 1767), Iavy (who died in 1791), and Zakavola (who died in 1803), were never able to exercise the authority that he had. By the end of the eighteenth century, the confederation had lost its control over Toamasina to Creole traders under the leadership of Jean René (q.v.). The confederation was unable to resist the attacks of the Merina Empire (q.v.), which occupied Toamasina in 1817. The Zanamalata staged a rebellion against Merina rule in 1826, but it was put down. *See also* BETSIMISARAKA-SAKALAVA RAIDS.

BETSIMISARAKA-SAKALAVA RAIDS. Although pirates were eliminated from the western Indian Ocean by the first quarter of the eighteenth century, the area was not always well patrolled by the navies of the great powers of the time. From about 1785 to 1820 the Betsimisaraka descendants of the pirates and the Sakalava, with whom they had been linked by a dynastic marriage earlier in the century, assembled fleets of pirogues and attacked the Comoro Islands, the shipping around the islands, and the east coast of Africa. The islanders sent requests for help to the sultan of Zanzibar and to the British at the Cape and Mauritius, but without success. The attacks stopped only with the Merina conquest of the Betsimisaraka and much of Sakalava territory. *See also* ZANAMALATA.

BEZAKA, ALEXIS. Bezaka was a mayor of Toamasina (q.v.) from 1957 to 1964 and a member of the first Loi-Cadre (q.v.) government council, having been elected at the head of a list entitled Defense of Provincial Interests that he later turned into the Union National Malgache (q.v.). As mayor of Toamasina (Tamatave) he convened the 1958 Tamatave Congress (q.v.) of parties which demanded immediate independence for Madagascar, an action that led to his expulsion from the government council. In 1958 he founded the Rassemblement National Malgache (q.v.) and followed the rest of the party when it merged with the regime party of the First Republic (q.v.), the Parti Social Démocrate (q.v.). He was expelled from the PSD and defeated as mayor of Toamasina for persistent public criticism of the regime. In 1968 he founded the Parti Démocrate Chrétien de Madagascar, but without electoral success. After the May 1972 Revolution (q.v.), he supported a ''yes'' vote in the referendum that led to the establishment of the Ramanantsoa regime (q.v.) but was critical of that regime's policy of *fokonolona* reform (q.v.). He went into exile in France at the time of the founding of the Democratic Republic of Madagascar (q.v.), and maintained his criticism of regime. In 1987 he announced the formation of the Union des Opposants Malgaches de l'Extérieur, or ''Union of External Malagasy Opponents.''

BEZANOZANO. One of several groups practicing *tavy,* or slash-and-burn agriculture, the Bezanozano live along the boundary of the forest zone, between the Merina (q.v.) and the Betsimisaraka (q.v.). They were one of the first groups conquered by the Merina Empire (q.v.) at the beginning of the nineteenth century, and were used as porters between the Highlands and the coast. They increasingly adopted Merina customs, including irrigated rice culture. Their population is estimated to be about 60,500.

BEZARA, JUSTIN. Elected to the French senate in 1947 as a member and leader of the Mouvement Démocratique de la Rénovation Malgache (q.v.), Bezara had his parliamentary immunity lifted and was tried for complicity in the Rebellion of 1947 (q.v.). He was sentenced to forced labor on the prison island of Nosy Lava (q.v.) and was released in 1954. He returned to political activity in his home city of Diégo-Suarez and joined the Union des Peuples Malgaches (q.v.). In 1956 he became mayor of Diégo-Suarez and was a member from Diégo-Suarez in the Loi-Cadre (q.v.) representative assembly. He was a minister in the Loi-Cadre government council, but his political orientation was very different from that of the Parti Social Démocrate (q.v.), which was establishing itself as the dominant party, and he did not have a post in the government after independence in 1960.

BINAO (1867–1923). A granddaughter of Andriantsoly (q.v.), Binao became ruler of the Bemihisatra group of the Sakalava (q.v.) in 1881, nominally controlling a territory that included the island of Nosy Be (q.v.) and the mainland opposite. Her kingdom had already been under pressure from the advance of the Merina Empire, and she assisted the French during the Franco-Malagasy War of 1883–1885 (q.v.). The protectorate (q.v.) established at the end of the war disappointed her since it recognized Merina control over the island as a step to extending the protectorate beyond the territory directly controlled by the empire. She supported the French again during the Franco-Malagasy War of 1895 (q.v.), however, and refused to joined the Sambirano Revolt of 1898 (q.v.). Under the French *politique des races* (q.v.), she was confirmed as ruler of an internal protectorate established in her territory.

BLANQUET DE LA HAYE, JACOB (d. 1677). When the Compagnie des Indes Orientales (q.v.) obtained royal permission to abandon the settlement at Fort-Dauphin (q.v.) in 1669, they sent Blanquet de la Haye to remove the settlers and to explore the possibility of establishing trading posts in India. He arrived at Fort-Dauphin in 1670, where he alienated both settlers and local rulers. He proceeded to the Ile de Bourbon (q.v.), but returned to Fort-Dauphin in June 1671, when he removed most of the settlers, leaving behind the Comte de Champmargou and a garrison of forty soldiers. After unsuccessful attempts to set up French settlements in India, Blanquet de la Haye returned to Fort-Dauphin in December 1674, to find that most of the garrison, including Champmargou, had been massacred, and that the others had either fled to the interior or been picked up by passing boats.

BLEVEC, BERTRAND-HERCULE (1792–1866). A French military officer, Blevec succeeded Sylvain Roux as commander of the French settlement on the Ile Sainte-Marie in 1823. He aided the Betsimisaraka (q.v.) in their resistance against Merina (q.v.) attempts at conquest. Unrest in the area, however, and the final Merina conquest, resulting in the decisive redirection of trade to Toamasina (q.v.), led to the abandonment of the settlement in 1830.

BOINA. Boina was a northern Sakalava (q.v.) kingdom established at the beginning of the eighteenth century by groups from the Menabe kingdom to the south under the leadership of Andriamadisoarivo, who had lost a dispute over the succession to a brother. The kingdom absorbed the groups already living on its territory, including the Antalaotra (q.v.) traders along the seacoast. The port of Mahajanga (q.v.) was established and in 1745 became the capital of the kingdom. Boina dominated the trade between the coast and the interior for the rest of the century. At the beginning of the nineteenth century, the Merina Empire began to seize lands in Boina, and occupied Mahajanga in 1824. The ruler of Boina,

Andriantsoly (q.v.), fled to the Comoro Islands (q.v.), and his sisters fled to Nosy Be and later to the mainland, where they founded the kingdom of Bemihisatra.

BOTOKEKY, LAURENT. Botokeky was minister of education and then of culture, including education, from the time of the founding of the First Republic (q.v.) until 1972. A teacher from Morondava, he participated in the creation of the dominant party of the First Republic, the Parti Social Démocrate (q.v.), serving as treasurer of the party's steering committee. Prior to the creation of the First Republic, he had been a member of the French senate. As minister of education he was critical of the demands for Malgachization (q.v.) of the educational system and for improved access to it. He was one of the main targets of the May 1972 Revolution (q.v.) and resigned during the early stages of the revolution. His attempts to win elective office in the subsequent Ramanantsoa regime (q.v.) were unsuccessful.

BOUDRY, ROBERT. Boudry was the secretary-general of the French colonial administration in Madagascar in 1946 and was generally sympathetic to Malagasy aspirations for increased political autonomy. His transfer in 1946 was part of the hardening of the administration that preceded the Rebellion of 1947 (q.v.). Boudry continued to take an interest in Malagasy affairs and was one of the critics of the Tananarive trial (q.v.) and an early advocate of amnesty for those convicted at the trial. *Further information may be found in the Bibliography following this Dictionary. See also* GOVERNOR-GENERAL.

BOURBON, ILE DE. See REUNION.

BRADY (d. 1835). A mulatto from Jamaica, and a sergeant in the British army, Brady was one of the military assistants sent by Sir Robert Farquhar (q.v.) to train the armies of Radama I (q.v.) after the treaty of 1816. He assisted in the transformation of the army of the Merina monarchy (q.v.) into a standing force capable of undertaking the wars of conquest planned by Radama. He married a Malagasy, rose to the rank of general, and died a wealthy man in 1835.

BRAZZAVILLE CONFERENCE. This conference on the future of France's colonial possessions, held from January 30 to February 8, 1944, came to an ambiguous set of conclusions. Although it recommended increased representation of the colonial populations in French political institutions, the decentralization of imperial administration, and the development of the "political personality" of each colony, it rejected the possibility of self-government for the colonies. Malagasy nationalists tended to give the conference recommendations an optimistic interpretation, seeing the conference as a stage in the loosening of the French colonial system.

BRITISH INVASION. After the Japanese victories in the Far East, including the capture of Singapore on February 15, 1942, the British feared that they might try to establish a base in the western Indian Ocean, thereby threatening South Africa and the supply lines to India. Madagascar, under a Vichy-appointed governor, was considered a possible target. The British, therefore, invaded Madagascar on May 5, 1942, beginning with an attack on the naval base at Diégo-Suarez. The British captured the main coastal cities, and on October 5 Tananarive was declared an open city. Control over Madagascar was handed to the Free French forces on January 7, 1943. The episode increased French suspicion of British intentions toward Madagascar, especially since the Free French had not been included in the invasion itself. Nationalist groups had been in contact with the occupying forces, and after the war they were often accused of being the agents of the "Anglo-Saxons."

BRUNET, AUGUSTE. Brunet was secretary-general of the colonial administration in Madagascar and served as acting governor-general from March 1923 to February 1924. He resigned from the colonial service to enter politics and served as deputy from Réunion.

-C-

CAMERON, JAMES (1800–1875). Born in Scotland, Cameron trained as a carpenter and joined the London Missionary

Society (q.v.) as an artisan missionary. He served in Madagascar from 1826 to 1835 and from 1862 until his death in 1875. As well as his missionary activities, Cameron undertook a large number of economic and building projects for the government of the Merina monarchy (q.v.). He set up the first printing shop and developed factories for the making of soap, bricks, and sulfur. When the missionaries were expelled by Queen Ranavalona I (q.v.) in 1835, Cameron was invited to remain, on the condition that he give up his missionary work. He refused, and moved to Cape Town. After the death of the queen and the succession of Radama II (q.v.), Cameron returned to Antananarivo, where he continued his building activities, including several of the capital's churches and a stone shell for the royal palace. When he died in 1875, he was given a state funeral.

CAPE PEAS. Cape peas were introduced to Madagascar from South Africa as early as the seventeenth century. They have been a major export crop in the southwest of the island, where they are grown in alluvial deposits along riverbanks known as *baiboho* (q.v.). Production and exports have declined since 1980, however, from about 20,000 metric tons a year to about 400 metric tons.

CARTEL DES REPUBLICAINS. The Cartel des Républicains was formed in October 1958 by Philibert Tsiranana (q.v.), leader of the Parti Social Démocrate. It linked his party with the Union Démocratique et Sociale de Madagascar (q.v.) of Norbert Zafimahova (q.v.) to oppose the parties that had advocated a "no" vote in the referendum on the establishment of the Fifth French Republic (q.v.) in future elections. The PSD and the UDSM were the two largest parties in the legislature and were able to form a majority. The cartel disintegrated as the PSD attracted some of the members of the UDSM and of other parties and was able to form a majority by itself.

CATHOLIC CHURCH. About 25% of the Malagasy population is affiliated with the Catholic church. The first church missions on the mainland of Madagascar were begun in 1861 by Marc Finaz (q.v.). Preceded by the London Missionary Society (q.v.), the Catholic church established itself to the south of Antananarivo (q.v.), in Fianarantsoa (q.v.), and on the coasts, although it also competed with Protestant churches in Imerina. With the coming of the colonial period, the church had an ambiguous relationship with the colonial administration. It was preferred to the Protestant denominations because it was staffed by French, but most colonial governors were anticlericals who were suspicious of church activities. In 1953 the bishops published a letter recognizing the legitimacy of Malagasy aspirations to independence that was criticized both by the French settlers and by the governor-general of the day, Bargues (q.v.). In 1956 Madagascar officially ceased to be mission territory, although missionary activity continues. The first Malagasy bishop was consecrated in 1948.

After independence in 1960, the Catholic church continued to be a political presence in the island. Its educational network—two presidents, Tsiranana (q.v.) of the First Republic (q.v.) and Ratsiraka (q.v.) of the Democratic Republic of Madagascar (q.v.), attended the Collège Saint Michel in Antananarivo—its press and its foreign ties have combined to give it a position independent of government that allows it to be critical of regime policies. Under the Democratic Republic of Madagascar (q.v.) the church was one of the main voices of opposition. In 1984 a ''Bishops' Letter'' described the characteristics of a dictatorship in terms that clearly indicated the regime; then, in 1987, a message from Pope John Paul II deplored the deterioration of the moral climate of the regime, and in the same year another ''Bishops' Letter'' attacked the growth of the wealth of the elite in the face of the misery of the poor. The Catholic churches, like the Protestant churches, had links with the Kung Fu movements (q.v.) that threatened the regime in 1984.

After 1987 the church press continued to attack the government of the Democratic Republic. In the crisis of 1991 the Catholic churches, linked with the Protestant churches in the FFKM, or Federation of Malagasy Christian Churches (q.v.), at first attempted to mediate between Ratsiraka and his opponents. After the massacre of Iavoloha (q.v.) the FFKM joined the opposition and contributed to the demise of the regime.

CAYLA, LEON (1881–1965). A career colonial administrator, Cayla had already been stationed in Madagascar before serving as governor-general there from 1930 to 1939. He arrived with orders to control the developing nationalist movement, which had just staged the May 19, 1929, demonstration (q.v.), and his name is associated with the Décret Cayla (q.v.), which gave the colonial administration increased powers to arrest and detain those it considered guilty of activities likely to increase hatred of the colonial regime. His administration was marked by arrests of Malagasy nationalists and their French sympathizers, suspensions of newspapers, and a tight control on the labor market that eased only with the coming to power of the Popular Front (q.v.) in France in 1936. In response to the economic crisis of the 1930s Cayla reduced the size of the administration and pursued a program of public works that included completion of the Fianarantsoa–Côte Est railroad (q.v.), improvements to the port of Toamasina, and the development of an air travel network. Much of this work was undertaken through a compulsory labor organization known as the Service de la Main-d'Oeuvre pour les Travaux d'Intérêt Général (q.v.). Cayla returned to Madagascar from July 1940 to April 1941 as the Vichy (q.v.) regime's replacement for Marcel De Coppet, who had contemplated siding with the Free French (q.v.) in 1940.

CENSORSHIP. Madagascar has both one of the oldest presses in Africa and one of the oldest censorship laws, passed under the Merina Empire (q.v.). Censorship was strengthened under the colonial regime, which first forbade newspapers in the Malagasy language and later, when this ban was relaxed, required a newspaper to have a French citizen as the managing editor. In 1959 the Tsiranana government, to become the First Republic (q.v.) in 1960, passed a law making it a crime to publish articles that would cause outrage to national and community institutions (the community referred to is the French Community, (q.v.). Censorship was briefly lifted after the May 1972 Revolution (q.v.), but returned with the entrenchment of the Ramanantsoa regime (q.v.) and the establishment of the Democratic Republic of Madagascar (q.v.). In 1973 an Order of Journalists under the control of the Ministry of Information was created, and journalists were required to be licensed. In August 1975 the new DRM passed a law allowing the regime to suspend any journal harmful to public order, national unity, or morality. Newspapers were checked by the Ministry of Information and Ideological Guidance, by a unit in the president's office, and by the regime political party, AREMA (q.v.). Film distribution was nationalized in 1975, and both radio and television were government run.

The abolition of censorship was one of the demands of the opposition groups that mobilized to end the Second Republic. In March 1989 President Ratsiraka (q.v.) announced the end of press censorship. Control over broadcasting was also relaxed. Like the other reforms produced by Ratsiraka in his attempt to retain power, these were not enough to satisfy the opposition.

CHARTER OF THE MALAGASY REVOLUTION. Also known as the *Boky Mena,* or "Red Book," the charter is based on a series of broadcasts President Didier Ratsiraka (q.v.) made in August 1975 as part of the campaign for the referendum on the establishment of the Democratic Republic of Madagascar (q.v.). The charter was the formal ideological basis of the Malagasy political system, and adherence to its principles was the precondition for legal political participation. It begins by exalting the Malagasy nation and identifying the Democratic Republic with the nationalist tradition of the Menalamba (q.v.), Vy Vato Sakelika (q.v.), and the martyrs of the Rebellion of 1947 (q.v.). Although the regime declared itself to be Marxist, the charter minimizes the importance of class conflict within the nation and argues that the main conflict is that between the Malagasy nation and neocolonialism. The revolution is declared to be compatible with religion, small-scale private property, and rule by social elites if they share the goals enunciated in the charter. Five "pillars of the revolution" were identified: oppressed workers and peasants, progressives, young intellectuals, women "as such," and the military. The charter promises the decentralization of economic benefits and political power, increased access to education, and a nationalist and "progressive" foreign policy. Although political discourse in the Democratic Republic of Madagascar was much more pluralistic than the limits of the charter suggest, it was never disavowed as the basis of the regime.

CHEVIGNE, PIERRE DE. De Chévigné served as governor-general of Madagascar from February 1948 to February 1950. Although he had no previous colonial experience, he had served with the Free French (q.v.) forces during the Second World War, and was given the task of restoring the colonial system after the Rebellion of 1947 (q.v.). He ordered the execution of the person identified as "general" of the uprising, Samuel Rakotondrabe (q.v.) and strictly enforced the state of siege, preventing any reconstitution of the Mouvement Démocratique de la Rénovation Malgache (q.v.) and keeping up administrative pressure on former members.

CHINESE. Madagascar has a Chinese population listed in the 1966 census as about 9,000, largely concentrated on the east coast and central Highlands. The Chinese first came to Madagascar to work on the Antananarivo-Côte Est railroad, but most came in later waves of immigration, largely from the area around Canton between the two world wars. The Second World War and the Communist takeover of mainland China put an effective end to immigration. They established themselves as small merchants at first and, like the Indo-Pakistanis (q.v.) on the west coast, gradually came to dominate the retail and wholesale markets on the island, and the collection of cash crops and rice. Like the Indo-Pakistanis their businesses were the targets of nationalizations under the Ramanantsoa regime (q.v.) of 1972–1975 and the subsequent Democratic Republic of Madagascar (q.v.). The liberalization of government economic policy after 1983 permitted the Chinese to return to their commercial activities.

CHURCHES. Nearly half the population of Madagascar is affiliated with a Christian church, with an estimated 25% of the population being Catholic and 21% Protestant. The establishment of Christian churches in Madagascar began with the arrival of missionaries from the London Missionary Society (q.v.) in 1817, at the invitation of Radama I (q.v.), king of the Merina Empire (q.v.), and the churches established were at first closely connected with royal power. The LMS missionaries were expelled in 1835 by Ranavalona I (q.v.) but returned after her death in 1861, and were followed by other missions (q.v.). The position of the church was buttressed in 1869 by the conversion of Ranavalona II (q.v.) and her prime minister, Rainilaiarivony (q.v.). Because of the official position of Protestant Christianity in the Merina Empire, its churches, especially those derived from the LMS, tended to recruit among the upper classes of Antananarivo province, while the Catholic church (q.v.) recruited more to the south, on the coasts, and among the lower classes of Imerina. At the village level, rivalry between the two denominations was often acute.

After the French conquest, the church networks, particularly those of the Protestants, provided rare opportunities for education and employment not controlled by the colonial regime, and were often a basis for nationalist activities. After independence, the control of the churches over educational networks, publications, and money permitted them to maintain a stance independent of successive governments. Under the Democratic Republic of Madagascar (q.v.), the most articulate critic of the regime, until the formation of the Alliance Démocratic Malgache (q.v.) in 1988, came from the churches and particularly from the bishops of the Catholic church. In 1970 the FJKM (Fiangonan'i Jesosy Kristy eto Madagasikara, q.v.) was founded to link the Protestant churches of the Highlands, the French Evangelical churches, and the Quaker churches.

In 1980 the FFKM, or Federation of Malagasy Christian Churches (q.v.), linked the Protestant and Catholic denominations of Madagascar. The FFKM played a major role in the transition to the Third Republic (q.v.). It at first attempted to mediate between President Ratsiraka (q.v.) and the opposition groups working under the title of Comité des Forces Vives (q.v.), but after the massacre at Iavoloha (q.v.) the FFKM declared its solidarity with the opposition and joined forces with them to overthrow the regime.

CLOVES. *See* SPICES.

CLUB DES 48. Supposedly an organization of the Merina (q.v.) economic elite based in the capital, the club was frequently referred to during the Ramanantsoa regime (q.v.) of 1972–1975 as a conservative force pushing the regime in the direction of state capitalism rather than popular or scientific socialism. It is probable that the notion of a 'club'' exaggerates the degree of formal organization, although the elite of the capital form a tightly knit group with many interconnections.

CODE OF 305 ARTICLES. This legal code, published in 1881, represented an attempt to rationalize the legal system of the Merina Empire (q.v.) and was part of the strategy of Prime Minister Rainilaiarivony (q.v.) to protect his rule from outside pressure by adopting the legal characteristics of the European countries responsible for the pressure. The code was intended to be applied only in Imerina (q.v.), while the Betsileo (q.v.) had their own code, and other areas of the empire were ruled in large part indirectly. The code included provisions barring foreign ownership of Malagasy territory, a provision that was to lead to disputes with the French.

COFFEE. Although there are some indigenous species of coffee in Madagascar, commercial cultivation first started in the mid–nineteenth century with arabica species introduced from Réunion. Under local growing conditions, however, the species proved vulnerable to *Hemileia vastrix,* which also arrived from Réunion about 1880. Arabica was replaced by hardier varieties, of which the most common today is robusta. Coffee was one of the main crops grown by French settlers (q.v.), particularly on the east coast, but in the period between the two world wars, they were gradually displaced by Malagasy cultivators. The Rebellion of 1947 (q.v.) led to a further abandonment of European plantations, and by independence 90% of commercialized coffee was grown by the Malagasy. Coffee is now cultivated on the east coast and in some areas of the north.

Coffee was once Madagascar's most important export, but it has been surpassed by vanilla as a revenue generator. Exports of coffee have declined in volume in recent years, from 63,500 metric tons in 1989 to 43,500 in 1991. *See* EXPORTS.

COLLEGE SYSTEM. Under the colonial regime, the electorate of Madagascar was organized into two "colleges", one for French citizens and the other for the majority of Malagasy having "indigenous status." Elected bodies were also divided into colleges that met separately. At first the college of French citizens had a majority of seats, but this majority was gradually reduced. In 1956, after the passage of the Loi-Cadre (q.v.), the college system was abolished. *See also* INDIGENAT.

COLLOQUE D'ANTSIRABE. *See* ANTSIRABE COLLOQUIUM.

COMITE DE REDRESSEMENT ECONOMIQUE ET SOCIAL (Committee for Economic and Social Recovery). The CRES was established by the power-sharing agreement (q.v.) of October 31, 1991, as one of the institutions of the transition to the Third Republic (q.v.). It was a consultative body of about 130 members, presided over by two of the leaders of the opposition to the Democratic Republic of Madagascar (q.v.): Manandafy Rakotonirina (q.v.) and Richard Andriamanjato (q.v.). Although its functions were never clearly defined, it did manage to produce a plan for the economic recovery of the island in April 1993.

COMITE DES FORCE VIVES (Committee of Active Forces). Also known by the Malagasy *Hery Velona,* the Comité des Forces Vives was formed in March 1990 to unite groups working for the overthrow of President Didier Ratsiraka (q.v.) and the Democratic Republic of Madagascar (q.v.).

Groups joining included the AKFM-Renouveau (q.v.), led by Richard Andriamanjato (q.v.); the MFM (q.v.), led by Manandafy Rakotonirina (q.v.); and the Union Nationale pour le Développement et la Démocratie (q.v.), led by Albert Zafy (q.v.), as well as representatives from unions and church groups.

The CFV pressed for the removal of Ratsiraka from office and an end to the DRM. In the summer of 1991 it began a series of demonstrations and general strikes, and in August it named a "transitional government," with retired general Jean Rakotoharison (q.v.) as president and Zafy as prime minister. The MFM withdrew from the Comité over this "insurrectional" act, but continued to cooperate with it. During the months of August and September, the CFV "government" occupied ministries and continued to stage general strikes. Efforts by Prime Minister Guy Razanamasy (q.v.) to expand his government to include members of the CFV were at first rejected, but after pressure from the armed forces, government and opposition signed the power-sharing agreement (q.v.) of October 31, 1991, stripping Ratsiraka of most of his powers and setting up the institutions to manage the transition to the Third Republic.

The transition period was dominated by the CFV, and its candidate, Albert Zafy, won the runoff election for president of the Third Republic with 66% of the vote. *See also* ELECTIONS; FFKM; IAVOLOHA.

COMITE DE SOLIDARITE DE MADAGASCAR. Also known as COSOMA, this committee was founded in 1948 under the aegis of the French Communist party to aid those prosecuted for their part in the Rebellion of 1947 (q.v.). Active in both France and Madagascar, it first concentrated on supplying the political prisoners of 1947 and their families with food, clothing, and legal assistance. Later it undertook campaigns for the amelioration of the conditions of imprisonment and for amnesty (q.v.). Its efforts were in part responsible for the transfer of the MDRM deputies (q.v.) from prison in Corsica to restricted residence in France. The COSOMA also served as an organizational base for nationalists who were prevented from overtly political activity. Among the Malagasy active in the committee were Richard Andriamanjato (q.v.) and Gisèle Rabesahala (q.v.).

COMITE DU SALUT PUBLIC. This "Committee of Public Safety" was founded during the Second World War by the nationalist figure Ravelojaona (q.v.) to try to defend the farmers of the Highlands (q.v.) against the exactions of the Office du Riz. In 1945 its activities took a more directly political turn when it sent a letter to the French government demanding independence for Madagascar. Although Ravelojaona did not join the Mouvement Démocratique de la Rénovation Malgache (q.v.) after the war, other members of the committee did, and the networks established by the Comité du Salut Public were used as a basis for the party's expansion.

COMITE NATIONAL POUR L'OBSERVATION DES ELECTIONS (National Election Observation Committee.) The CNOE was formed in 1989 by lawyers and church groups to monitor the series of elections announced for that year by President Didier Ratsiraka (q.v.) of the Democratic Republic of Madagascar (q.v.). It challenged the results of the presidential elections of March, claiming that Ratsiraka had received only 47% of the vote rather than the 62% he claimed. After the elections the CNOE joined with other groups, including the Comité des Forces Vives (q.v.), to work for the removal of Ratsiraka and the end of the DRM.

COMMERCIAL COMPANIES. With the imposition of French colonial rule, French trading and commercial companies took over the Malagasy economy. The three most important were the Marseillaise, the Lyonnaise, and the Société de l'Emyrne, a subsidiary of the Rochfortaise. These companies handled the wholesale end of Madagascar's import-export business. Through their preferred access to credit and ability to extend credit to smaller businesses down the chain of distribution, they were able to dominate trade on the island. Another company, the Havraise, had a monopoly of shipping to and from the island and dominated the island's two major banks. The activities of the first three companies earned them the title "the three crocodiles of the island." The First

Republic (q.v.) did little to diminish the power of the commercial companies, and they were among the targets of the nationalization measures of the Ramanantsoa and Ratsiraka regimes. The Marseillaise was the last to be nationalized, in 1976.

COMMISSION MIXTE FRANCO-MALGACHE.This was an advisory commission created in December 1943 at the instigation of the Free French commissioner for colonies, René Pleven, in response to demands of both Malagasy and settlers for a restoration of some degree of representation. The commission was to be composed of an equal number of Europeans and Malagasy named by the governor-general. Before it could begin operation, however, it was superseded by the Conseil Représentatif (q.v.).

COMMISSION MIXTE FRANCO-MALGACHE (2).This commission was established at the time of the renegotiation of the Cooperation Agreements (q.v.) between France and Madagascar in 1973. Relations between the two countries were so difficult at the time, however, that the commission did not meet until 1977. It now meets on an annual basis to discuss the amount and distribution of French aid to Madagascar, particularly in the area of technical assistance. Other issues, including French assistance in the relief of Madagascar's debts, are handled through other channels. *See also* DEBT CRISIS; FRANCE.

COMMUNE DE MOYEN EXERCICE. Under the colonial system a commune de moyen exercice was an urban area with an elected municipal council and an administrator-mayor appointed by the governor-general. By the 1950s there were twenty communes de moyen exercice in Madagascar, including the capital, Tananarive. In 1955 a French law on municipal organization in Africa and Madagascar created the communes de plein exercice (q.v.) with mayors chosen by the councils.

COMMUNE DE PLEIN EXERCICE. Created by French law in 1955, the commune de plein exercice had an elected council and a mayor elected by the council. The first communes de plein exercice in Madagascar were the provincial capitals: Tananarive, Fianarantsoa, Tamatave, Majunga, and Tulear. Diego-Saurez became a commune de plein exercice when the province of Diégo-Suarez was created in November 1956. The law also merged the French and Malagasy colleges of the councils, and the municipal councils elected in 1956 served as a political base for many of the early figures of the First Republic (q.v.). After internal independence in 1958, the remaining municipalities became communes de plein exercice. In 1960 Tananarive, which had consistently elected mayors from opposition parties, was given a special status with the elected mayor subordinate to an appointed prefect. *See also* COLLEGE SYSTEM.

COMMUNES RURALES. Rural communes, grouping several villages, with an elected council and mayor were established by the First Republic (q.v.) in 1959 in an attempt to coordinate rural development efforts. In general this system of rural organization was not considered a success. Villagers complained of a lack of resources for development and of the authoritarian attitude of the administration, while administrators complained of corrupt and inefficient rural councils and mayors. *See also* SYNDICATS DES COMMUNES.

COMMUNES RURALES AUTONOMES MODERNISEES. After the failure of the Communes Autochtones Rurales, the CRAM were created in another attempt to increase rural agricultural productivity. Under this scheme a small number of the more promising CAR were to be provided with extra development funds and encouraged to experiment with new crops and techniques. By 1953 seventeen CRAM were in operation. Their effectiveness was limited, however, by administrative insistence on crops that provided a quick monetary return and on mechanization in circumstances where it was not always suitable. The fact that the CRAM were run by the territorial administration and largely boycotted by the agricultural services also made their operation difficult.

COMORIANS. Many Comorians came to Madagascar after the Second World War in response to overcrowding on their home islands. By 1970 it was estimated that there were approximately 60,000 Comorians in Madagascar and that they formed close to a majority of the population in the port city of Mahajanga (q.v.). In that city, and in Antseranana (q.v.) where they were also numerous, they constituted a large proportion of the urban proletariat and often had difficult relations with the Malagasy because of competition for jobs and because the Comorians had been extensively employed in the colonial police force. At the time of independence in 1968, many Comorians chose to return to French citizenship. When the 1973 renegotiation of the Cooperation Agreements (q.v.) between Madagascar and France ended the special status French citizens had enjoyed in Madagascar, an exodus of Comorians began. In 1976, anti-Comorian riots broke out in Mahajanga, leaving over 1,000 dead. Most of the remaining Comorians were repatriated by a joint effort of the Comoro and Malagasy governments. About 15,000 to 20,000 remain, most living in the capital, Antananarivo (q.v.). In recent years there has been some revival of Comorian immigration. *See also* COMORO ISLANDS.

COMORO ISLANDS. The Comoro Islands, of which the largest are Njazidja (Grande-Comore), Nzwani (Anjouan), Mwali (Mohéli), and Mahore (Mayotte), are located in the Indian Ocean north of Madagascar. The closest, Mayotte, is 320 km away. It is possible that the earliest settlers of Madagascar came via the Comoro Islands, and the Comoros and Madagascar were part of the western Indian Ocean trading network that predated the arrival of Europeans in the area. At the turn of the eighteenth century, the Sakalava (q.v.) and Betsimisaraka (q.v.) sent raiding expeditions against the islands, and in 1831 the king of the Boina Sakalava, Andriantsoly (q.v.) fled to Mahore after the capture of his kingdom by the Merina Empire (q.v.) and became a sultan there. Both Madagascar and the Comoros were incorporated in the French Empire, and from 1912 to 1946 the islands were administered from

Madagascar. The Democratic Republic of Madagascar (q.v.) supported the creation of the new state of the Comoro Islands in 1976, and protested the separation of the island of Mayotte, which remained under French control. Relations with the government of Ali Soilih were damaged, however, by the attacks on Comorians (q.v.) in Mahajanga (q.v.) and other cities in December 1976. When Soilih's government was overthrown by a group of mercenaries in 1978, the government of Madagascar condemned the new regime and protested the ties it developed with South Africa. Relations did not return to normal until 1985.

COMPAGNIE DES INDES ORIENTALES. The company was created by Cardinal Richelieu in 1642 under royal patent to develop a French presence in the Indian Ocean (q.v.) and in India itself. The establishment of a settlement in Madagascar was among its charges, and an attempt was made at Fort-Dauphin (q.v.) beginning in 1642. The company's charter was reconfirmed in 1654, but its history was troubled by the involvement of its founders in political difficulties in France and by competition with the British and Dutch in the Indian Ocean and in India. The attempt to settle in Madagascar was abandoned after the massacre of the garrison in 1674, and its other enterprises were not significantly more successful. It was taken over by the Crown, renamed the Compagnie Française des Indes Orientales, and in 1717 given a formal monopoly over the slave trade (q.v.) from Madagascar. The monopoly was never effective, and was ended in 1767.

CONCESSIONS. The French colonial regime gave large land grants to companies and settlers as part of its agricultural development policy. In all about 900,000 hectares were granted as concessions, 500,000 to five companies: Suberbie, la Compagnie de la Grand Ile, la Compagnie Franco-Malgache de la Culture, Sambrana, and Delhorbe. The remaining land went to smaller companies and to about 2,000 individuals. It was expected that the concessions would play a major role in the production of cash crops for export, but much of the land remained unworked, though unavailable for cultivation by the Malagasy. The concessions, particularly along the east coast, were one of the main targets of the Rebellion of 1947 (q.v.). After the creation of the Democratic Republic of Madagascar (q.v.) in 1975, the concessions were nationalized as part of the land reform (q.v.) policy. Although the land was claimed both by the descendants of the original owners and by the Malagasy who had been employed on the concessions, most of the land turned into state farms. *See also* AGRICULTURAL POLICY.

CONFEDERATION GENERALE DU TRAVAIL (CGT). In 1948 the French union movement split into two sections: the CGT keeping the prewar name and affiliating with the French Communist party, and Force Ouvrière (q.v.) having a looser association with the French Socialist party.

CONGREGATIONS. The congregations were introduced in 1896 to organize the Indian and Chinese populations of Madagascar. Under this system, which the French had previously developed in Indochina, where the Chinese or Indian male adult population numbered more than nine, they were required to form a congregation and choose a leader who would be their intermediary with the administration. Individual direct contact with the administration and islandwide organization were discouraged.

CONGRES NATIONAL POPULAIRE. After the May 1972 Revolution (q.v.) the leader of the new government, General Ramanantsoa (q.v.), agreed to the demands of the leaders of the groups involved in the demonstrations that had precipitated the revolution for a national congress to discuss the political future of Madagascar. Many of these leaders wanted the change of regime to lead to a fundamental restructuring of Malagasy politics and society and saw the gathering as a constituent congress that would draw up plans for a political system based on their ideas. By the time the congress convened on September 4, 1972, however, Ramanantsoa had consolidated his position so that he was no longer dependent on the more radical groups involved in the May events and had established a government that was much more conservative than they had wished. On the eve of the congress he declared a state of siege, effectively preventing further demonstrations, and announced that he was preparing a new constitution to be submitted to a nationwide referendum on October 8. These two actions undercut the purpose of the congress, as did quarrels among the delegates from various groups and various parts of the island, and it ended without having been able to draft a plan for the type of radical direct democracy hoped for by some participants. See also KIM; RAMANANTSOA REGIME.

CONGRESS OF PROVINCIAL ASSEMBLIES. After the success of the "yes" vote in the Referendum on the Constitution of the Fifth French Republic (q.v.) Philibert Tsiranana (q.v.) convoked the assemblies of Madagascar's provinces to Antananarivo to vote on the future status of the island. The congress voted for the status of autonomy within the French Community, and on October 15, 1958, Governor-General Soucadaux (q.v.) proclaimed the achievement of autonomy and the "caducity" of the Annexation Law of 1896 (q.v.). The Loi-Cadre Government Council (q.v.) became a provisional government, and the existing legislature was dissolved, to be replaced by a new national assembly with constituent powers.

CONSEIL DE LA REPUBLIQUE. This was the second house of the French legislature under the Fourth Republic (q.v.), replacing the senate of the Third Republic (q.v.). Madagascar was to have five senators, two elected by French citizens and three elected by Malagasy having "indigenous" status. Following the successes of the Mouvement Démocratique de la Rénovation Malgache (q.v.) in elections to the Assemblée Nationale, however, the administration decided to have the senators jointly elected by the two colleges of the provincial assemblies. Under these circumstances, one MDRM senator, Justin Bezara (q.v.), was elected, on March 30, just after the outbreak of the Rebellion of 1947 (q.v.). His parliamentary immunity was lifted in August so that he could be tried for complicity in the uprising. *See also* COLLEGE SYSTEM; INDIGENAT.

CONSEIL MILITAIRE POUR LE DEVELOPPEMENT. The Military Council for Development, established by the 1975 constitution of the Democratic Republic of Madagascar (q.v.), was the official parliament of the Malagasy armed forces. Composed of fifty members chosen by the president of the republic from lists submitted by different branches of the military, it met twice a year in closed sessions. Reports of its deliberations suggest that it did not provide a major arena for military politics in Madagascar or a major channel for communication between the armed forces and the regime. Rather, discussion, so far as reported, tended to concentrate on technical aspects of development projects and law-and-order issues, such as the repression of banditry. The post of president of the council was often used as a semiretirement position to remove senior officers from direct political activity. *See also* MILITARY.

CONSEIL NATIONAL POPULAIRE DU DEVELOPPEMENT (National People's Development Council). This 162–member assembly was established as a consultative body during the military-led regime of General Gabriel Ramanantsoa (q.v.). Elected in 1973, it included some former members from the regime party of the First Republic (q.v.), the Parti Social Démocrate (q.v.), but most members listed themselves as "nonpartisan, favorable to the regime." The CNPD itself rarely met, but its permanent commission, led by the Protestant minister Michel Fety (q.v.), played a more important role in the politics of the Ramanantsoa regime (q.v.). The council itself met once after the establishment of the Democratic Republic of Madagascar (q.v.) on November 5, 1975. It was formally dissolved on March 31, 1976, to be replaced by the Assemblée Nationale Populaire (q.v.).

CONSEIL REPRESENTATIF. This council was established on March 23, 1945. It was to be composed of sixty members, half of them Malagasy. One-third of the Malagasy members were to be named by the governor-general and the others were to be elected by local notables (q.v.). It was replaced by the more directly elected Assemblée Representative established after the creation of the Fourth French Republic (q.v.).

CONSEIL SUPERIEUR DES COLONIES. The Conseil Supérieur des Colonies was a largely phantom body designed to represent France's colonies under the Third Republic. In its early period of existence members were usually French citizens and usually named by the colonial administration. In 1939 the first election in Madagascar to the council was held, and the nationalist leader Ravelojoana (q.v.) was elected.

CONSEIL SUPERIEUR DES INSTITUTIONS (Superior Council of Institutions). The CSI was formally the highest institutional authority of the First Republic (q.v.). It consisted of five members, two named by the president of the republic, two named by the president of the assembly, and one by the president of the senate. The council played a role in legitimizing the transfer of power from Philibert Tsiranana (q.v.) to General Ramanantsoa (q.v.) in 1972, from Ramanantsoa to Colonel Richard Ratsimandrava (q.v.) in 1975, to the Directoire Militaire (q.v.) after Ratsimandrava's assassination, and to Didier Ratsiraka (q.v.) and the Democratic Republic of Madagascar (q.v.) in June 1975. Under the Democratic Republic of Madagascar, it was replaced by the Haute Cour Constitutionnelle.

CONSEIL SUPREME DE LA REVOLUTION. The Supreme Council of the Revolution was the formal political executive body of the Democratic Republic of Madagascar (q.v.). Established by the 1975 constitution, it was charged with the task of assisting the president of the republic in the "conception, orientation, and oversight of national policy and the preservation of internal and external national sovereignty." Immediately after Didier Ratsiraka (q.v.) took power in June 1975, the council consisted of the officers of the Military Directorate (q.v.) that had been formed after the February assassination of President Richard Ratsimandrava (q.v.). In 1976 it was enlarged to include civilians, and eventually became a largely civilian body of approximately twenty-two members named by the president, two-thirds directly and one-third from a list supplied by the Assemblée Nationale Populaire (q.v.). The CSR was presided over by the president of the republic, and its doyen (oldest member) replaced the president as head of state in his absence. Although the council included representatives of all parties who are members of the Front National pour la Défense de la Révolution (q.v.), it was dominated by the regime party, AREMA (q.v.)

The council also had seven commissions: the plenary commission, which dealt with foreign affairs and the national plan; the defense commission, composed only of military councillors, which dealt with military questions; and commissions for finance and agriculture; food supplies, agriculture, and tourism; industry and commerce; culture and society; and justice and administration. The commissions dealt with questions as assigned by the president. Although appointment to the CSR often served as a form of semiretirement, it also served as a power base for some commissioners and was the scene of some political struggles. In December 1982 Monja Joana (q.v.) attempted to use his position as doyen of the council to commandeer radio time to protest his defeat by Ratsiraka in the recent presidential election, an action which led to his removal from the council (though he later returned). In April 1989 another party leader and rival candidate in the March presidential elections, Manandafy Rakotonirina (q.v.), was ejected from the council for his persistent opposition to President Ratsiraka. *See also* ELECTIONS.

In the last days of the Second Republic, Ratsiraka used the CSR as part of his efforts to stay in power. Members whose support was doubtful were ejected, and Monja Jaona, and the leader of Vonjy (q.v.), Gilbert Sambson (q.v.), returned to the council. The council was abolished in February 1992 by the power-sharing agreement (q.v.) that opened the transition to the Third Republic (q.v.).

CONSEILS DE DISTRICT. These councils, to be elected by the notables (q.v.) of rural areas, were established in 1944. Their role was purely consultative, and in many districts they rarely met.

CONSEILS DES NOTABLES. Conseils des notables elected by village chiefs were established by Gallieni (q.v.) in 1903, in an attempt to create a reliable political organization in the countryside. They became operational in the 1920s, but dissatisfaction with their usefulness led to reorganization in 1926 and 1930.

CONSTITUENT ASSEMBLIES. Two constituent assemblies were held before the establishment of the Fourth French Republic (q.v.). The first was elected in October 1945, and the second in June 1946, after the French electorate had rejected the consitution drafted by the first Constituent Assembly. The second college of the Malagasy electorate sent two delegates to the constituent assemblies: the nationalist leaders Joseph Raseta (q.v.) and Joseph Ravoahangy (q.v.). Elections to the assemblies constituted the first legal nationwide political activity, and the two delegates were chosen by a restricted electorate largely on the basis of personal followings and their reputations as nationalist figures. It was during their stay in Paris that the two leaders founded the Mouvement Démocratique de la Rénovation Malgache (q.v.). In Paris they attempted to secure autonomy if not independence for Madagascar. In February 1946 they sent a memorandum to the minister for the colonies calling for the abrogation of the Annexation Law of 1896 (q.v.) and in March submitted a motion to the assembly calling for autonomy for Madagascar.

Reaction to this motion was so hostile that they withdrew it and submitted another calling for negotiations over Madagascar's status. This also met with a hostile response, and a third motion calling for a referendum in Madagascar was pending when the constituent Assembly ended its work. In the second Constituent Assembly the Malagasy delegates continued to urge the holding of a referendum on Madagascar's status, but without success. They were also disappointed with the second constitution's provisions for the colonies, which allowed very little autonomy and treated the overseas territories as integral parts of France with no prospect for future independence. *See also* COLLEGE SYSTEM; REBELLION OF 1947.

CONSTITUTION, THIRD REPUBLIC. The constitution of the Third Republic (q.v.) was passed by the National Forum (q.v.) on March 31, 1992, in spite of violent objections from the supporters of the Democratic Republic of Madagascar (q.v.). The constitution establishes a dual executive, with a largely ceremonial president elected for a five-year term that can be renewed once and a prime minister elected by and responsible to the lower house of the legislature. The legislature is composed of two houses, a national assembly that is directly elected by proportional representation and a senate that is indirectly elected. Two-thirds of the senators are elected by a college of representatives of local government bodies and one-third are chosen by the president from lists submitted by registered economic and social organizations. The constitution was submitted to a referendum (q.v.) on August 19, 1992, and passed with 66% of the vote.

CONSTITUTIONAL REFERENDUM, AUGUST 19, 1992. This referendum, to approve the constitution (q.v.) of the Third Republic (q.v.), asked voters, "Do you accept this draft Constitution, reaffirming national unity and advocating democracy, to usher in the Third Republic?" Defenders of the Democratic Republic of Madagascar (q.v.) staged violent protests during the referendum campaign and prevented the holding of the referendum in Antseranana and Toamasina, but the constitution was approved by 66% of those voting.

COOPERATION AGREEMENTS. The cooperation agreements between France (q.v.) and the First Republic (q.v.) were negotiated in 1960, as Madagascar moved toward independence. They provided for Franco-Malagasy cooperation in several areas. In military affairs they provided for training in France for Malagasy officers and for the maintenance of French officers in the Malagasy military (q.v.) until Malgachization (q.v.) of the officer corps was completed. The agreements also maintained French bases at Ivato (an airport outside the capital, Antananarivo) and at Diégo-Suarez (q.v.). In education the agreements maintained the equivalence of Malagasy degrees with French degrees and put the University of Madagascar under a rector nominated by the French Ministry of Education. In financial affairs the agreements kept Madagascar in the Franc Zone (q.v.). Other agreements provided for a supply of French technical assistants (q.v.) in the educational system and in the administration. The maintenance of ties with France that the accords created was resented by the opposition to the First Republic, and a demand for their renegotiation was one of the slogans of the May 1972 Revolution (q.v.). They were renegotiated in 1973, and most of the arrangements were ended. *See also* EDUCATION; RAMANANTSOA REGIME.

COOPERATIVES. Both the postwar nationalist movement and the First Republic (q.v.) experimented with the establishment of peasant cooperatives. The post–1975 Democratic Republic of Madagascar (q.v.) attempted to use cooperatives as part of a major reorganization of rural production. The first plan for the formation of cooperatives, published in 1977, was closely modeled on the system in operation in North Korea, and envisaged a situation in which land was owned by the cooperative, or at least was worked jointly. This plan met with little success and was subjected to two revisions. The final version simply established cooperation in agricultural work and in the acquisition of tools and material. In addition to the state cooperative system, there was a rival system operated by the regime party, AREMA (q.v.), that included a network of stores called PROCOOP, and that was used to channel resources more directly to regime supporters. Other parties, most notably the MFM (q.v.) and MONIMA (q.v.), attempted both to take control of state cooperatives and to establish their own. The MONIMA cooperative network, AVOTSE, was at one time quite extensive, but eventually ran into financial difficulties from which the regime refused to rescue it.

COPPET, MARCEL DE (1881–1968). De Coppet served as governor-general of Madagascar twice, from 1939 to 1940 and from 1946 to 1948. A member of the French Socialist party, he had previously served in Madagascar from 1905 to 1910 and as governor-general of French West Africa. In 1939 De Coppet mobilized the island for the French war effort, and at the time of the fall of France in June 1940, declared first for the Free French (q.v.) and then, after the British attack on the French fleet at Mers el-Kébir, for the Vichy regime (q.v.). He was recalled to France and replaced by Armand Annet (q.v.), whom the Vichy government considered to be more reliable. His return to Madagascar after the war aroused some hopes in nationalist circles, since one of his acts in 1939 had been the enlargement of Malagasy representation on the Délégations Economiques et Financiéres (q.v.); however, he had received instructions to block the rise of the nationalist party, the Mouvement Démocratique de la Rénovation Malgache (q.v.). His vacillating policies, which alternately raised and disappointed nationalist hopes, may have contributed to the Rebellion of 1947 (q.v.), and he left blamed by both the settlers and the nationalists.

CORN. *See* AMERICAN CROPS.

COROLLER, ARISTIDE. Born in Mauritius (q.v.) about 1797 or 1802, Coroller was the secretary (and possibly the nephew, as he claimed) of Jean René (q.v.), whom he succeeded as governor of Toamasina (q.v.) under the Merina Empire (q.v.) in 1826. As governor of the port, he played a crucial role in dealing with the traders established there and with the representatives of the British and French governments.

COTIER. This term is used to refer to the non-Merina populations of Madagascar, not all of whom live near the coast. It is a political term, designed to draw a contrast between the status of the Merina (q.v.) and that of the other groups. Although contested, the Merina-Côtier division has been the basis for political organization, as in the formation of the Parti des Deshérités de Madagascar (q.v.) and the Parti Sociale Démocratique (q.v.), the dominant party of the First Republic.

The division was revived by President Ratsiraka (q.v.) in the transition to the Third Republic (q.v.), which replaced the regime that he had headed. Ratisraka accused his opponents of trying to reestablish Merina dominance, and his followers in several coastal provinces attempted to set them up as components of a federation. The attempt was not successful.

COURRIER DE MADAGASCAR.The *Courrier de Madagascar* was Madagascar's largest newspaper during the First Republic (q.v.). French-owned, it took a pro-French and pro-regime stand. Its offices and plant were burned at the time of the May 1972 Revolution (q.v.), and it was succeeded by *Madagascar Matin* (q.v.), which was in turn succeeded by *Madagascar Tribune.*

CUNHA, TRISTAN DA. A Portuguese explorer, Da Cunha was sent to investigate Madagascar after its existence had been reported by Diégo Diaz (q.v.). He explored the coast of the island, attacking some Islamic settlements, but finding no evidence of gold or spices he abandoned any plans for further activity there.

-D-

DEBT CRISIS. Madagascar's debt crisis was precipitated by a combination of internal and external factors. The All-Out Investment Policy (q.v.), initiated in 1978, involved large-scale borrowing from both public and private quarters. At the same time, attempts to gain control of the collection and distribution of rice were leading to shortages that made the importation of an increasing quantity of rice necessary, while the instability of industrial policy perpetuated a decline in industrial production that had begun under the Ramanantsoa regime (q.v.). Madagascar's 1973 departure from the Franc Zone meant that an increasing share of imports had to be paid for in American dollars. Externally, a decline in the prices of Madagascar's most important exports, particularly coffee, and rises both in the price of oil and in interest rates also contributed to the crisis. By early 1980 the Malagasy government had to approach the International Monetary Fund (q.v.) for assistance, and in June of the year a first agreement involving 64.5 million in special drawing rights was signed.

Since then, Madagascar's economic policy (q.v.) has largely been dominated by the debt crisis and its consequences. Attempts to resolve the crisis have involved a large number of international actors. The country's major public bilateral creditor is France (q.v.), and its largest multilateral creditor is the World Bank (q.v.). Money is also owed to private banks, particularly in France and the United States, and to the states of the former Soviet Union (q.v.), which was a major supplier of petroleum (q.v.). Conditions for the continuance of IMF aid have included several devaluations of the Malagasy franc, the abandonment of state trading monopolies, and the drafting of a new and more liberal investment code.

The crisis has followed several stages. The 1980 agreement was suspended when the IMF decided that the Malagasy government had not fulfilled the conditions for the aid, but was resumed and followed by a new agreement for 109 million in special drawing rights in April 1981. In 1984, and again in 1986 and 1987, a rescheduling of debts involving the IMF, the London Club (q.v.) of private banks, and the Paris club of public creditors occurred. (The Soviet Union rescheduled the Malagasy debt in 1984.) The rescheduling was accompanied by more loans from, in particular, France, the United States, and the IMF. This rescheduling was not enough to resolve the crisis, which had its basis not only in the debt itself, but also in declining productivity and financial mismanagement. By the end of 1987 it was estimated that Madagascar's external debt was over $3.2 billion and that debt-servicing was taking over 50% of export earnings. In October 1988 Madagascar became the second country after Mali to receive exceptional rescheduling of its debts as provided for by the Toronto Plan (q.v.). Madagascar has also had some of its debt annulled. In spite of these measures, total debt was estimated at about $3.9 billion in 1990.

Activity on the debt reduction front was suspended by the political crisis of 1991. Production declined, civil servant strikes prevented the collection of government revenues, payment on all debts except for those owing to international institutions stopped, and the IMF suspended interaction with the Malagasy government. Negotiations have resumed with the installation of the Third Republic (q.v.). *See also* ECONOMY.

DECENTRALIZED COLLECTIVITIES. Established by the 1976 Charter of the Decentralized Collectivities, the territorial organization of the Democratic Republic of Madagascar (q.v.) was an attempt to blend the direct democracy proposed by earlier champions of *fokonolona* reform (q.v.) and the centralization that was both traditional to Malagasy administration and required by the type of socialism espoused by the founders of the Democratic Republic. At the base of the system was the *fokontany,* a term preferred by the designers of the system to the term *fokonolona,* corresponding to the village or urban neighborhood. There are 11,373 *fokontany.* These are grouped into 1,250 districts, or *firaisampokontany* which are in turn grouped into 110 regions, or *fivondronampokontany.* At the summit of the system are the six *faritany,* which correspond exactly to the six provinces of earlier regimes. At the *fokontany* level the population elects a council which then chooses an executive whose president is also directly elected. Elections to the other levels are indirect, with the people's council at each level sending delegates to the next higher level. *Faritany* councils also included the province's deputies to the Assemblée Nationale Populaire (q.v.). The *fokontany* also have *vatoeka,* or economic committees, charged with local economic planning and liaison with the economic activities of the central ministries, but there is some debate about how effective these have been. Administrative committees at the higher levels are charged with coordinating the work of territorial and functional ministries. Each level is supervised by the level above, and provinces and urban areas come directly under the supervision of the Ministry of the Interior. The decentralized communities are also under the tutelage of the Ministry of Information and Ideological Guidance, and the president's office.

In the transition to the Third Republic (q.v.) the elected officials of the decentralized collectivities, in majority members of the DRM regime party, AREMA (q.v.), were dismissed and replaced by appointed delegations.

DECRET CAYLA. This law, decreed by Governor-General Cayla (q.v.) in December 1929, attempted to restrain the growing Malagasy nationalist movement (q.v.) and particularly the activities of the Ralaimongo group (q.v.). Among other provisions, it required each newspaper to have a French citizen as managing editor, and empowered the administration to seize publications carrying articles likely to incite hatred of the colonial administration.

DELEGATIONS ECONOMIQUES ET FINANCIERES. The Economic and Financial Delegations were established in 1924 by Governor-General Olivier (q.v.) in response to demands for a greater voice in decisions on the colony's taxes and budgets. The Delegations had separate European and Malagasy sections, with the Malagasy delegates being elected by the Conseils des Notables (q.v.). The Malagasy section met rarely, in closed session, and had only a consultative role.

DEMOCRATIC REPUBLIC OF MADAGASCAR. The Democratic Republic of Madagascar was established on June 15, 1975, when the Directoire Militaire (q.v.) that had taken power after the assassination of President Richard Ratsimandrava (q.v.) chose naval captain Didier Ratsiraka (q.v.) as the new president. He announced the choice of Marxist socialism as the ideological orientation of the DRM. The creation of the new republic was ratified in a referendum (q.v.) in December 1975. Among the institutions of the DRM were the Front National pour la Défense de la Révolution (q.v.), which grouped the political parties of the regime, and the Conseil Suprême de la Révolution (q.v.), which was an executive organ grouping representatives of those parties. As well as the president, there was also a government headed by a prime minister. The unicameral legislature was called the Assemblée Nationale Populaire (q.v.), and there was a legislature of the military (q.v.) called the Comité Militaire pour le Développement (q.v.).

Didier Ratsiraka was the first and only president of the Democratic Republic of Madagascar. Weakened by internal political and economic failures, the debt crisis (q.v.), and by the international collapse of Marxist regimes, the republic was finally successfully challenged by an opposition movement called the Comité des Forces Vives (q.v.). After a period of instability that began in 1989, it was replaced by the Third Republic (q.v.) in 1992. *See the Introduction and Chronology above for key dates in the history of the DRM.*

DIAZ, DIEGO (*also* Diogo). Diaz was commander of one of twelve ships of a Portuguese fleet commanded by Pedralvares Cabral sailing for India. His ship was blown off course and touched on the coast of Madagascar in 1500. It was after this that Madagascar was reliably situated on European maps of the western Indian Ocean.

DIEGO-SUAREZ. Now Antseranana (q.v.), Diégo-Suarez was named after two Portuguese admirals, Diégo Diaz (q.v.) who first sighted Madagascar in 1500, and Fernando Suarez, who sighted the bay itself in 1506. The bay at Diégo-Suarez is one of the best natural harbors in the western Indian Ocean, and has attracted many users. It served as a base for pirates (q.v.) in the early eighteenth century, being the site of the International Republic of Libertalia. In the nineteenth century the French were attracted to the bay, and the protectorate (q.v.) of 1885 gave them the right to construct installations there. The fortifications of the modern base were begun in 1900 by Colonel Joseph Joffre, later known for his role in the Battle of the Marne in the First World War. An arsenal and dry dock were added later. During the Second World War, it was in part British fear that the port would be used as a base for attacks on South Africa that led to the British invasion (q.v.) of Madagascar in 1942. After the war, Diégo-Suarez served as the headquarters for the French Indian Ocean fleet until 1973, when it was handed over to the Malagasy government after the renegotiation of the Cooperation Agreements (q.v.) between France and Madagascar.

DIRECTOIRE MILITAIRE. The Military Directorate was established by the Malagasy armed forces on February 12, 1975, immediately after the assassination of Colonel Richard Ratsimandrava (q.v.). The directorate had eighteen members, drawn from both the army and the gendarmerie, and from all regions of the country. It was led by the ranking general of the army, Gilles Andriamahazo (q.v.). Among its members were the future president, Didier Ratsiraka (q.v.), and two of his brothers-in-law. One of Ratsimandrava's rivals for power, Roland Rabetafika, attempted to find a place on the directorate, but was rejected and later accused of complicity in the assassination. It was the task of the directorate to maintain order in the country and in the armed forces while it settled the question of succession to the presidency.

Over a period of four months Ratsiraka was able to put together a coalition that included, after some hesitation on their part, the bulk of Ratsimandrava's supporters. On June 15, 1975, the directorate declared Ratsiraka the new president of the republic and dissolved itself. *See also* MILITARY; TRIAL OF THE CENTURY.

DRURY, ROBERT (1687–1733). Drury was born in London and went to sea at the age of twelve. He was shipwrecked off the coast of Madagascar about 1701 and became a slave of the local ruler. He traveled extensively through western Madagascar until he escaped and returned to London in 1717. The authorship of his book of reminiscences is disputed, since many attribute it to the author of *Robinson Crusoe,* Daniel Defoe, and claim that it is a pastiche of Drury's memories and other sailors' tales. The descriptions of groups and territories in the book are corroborated by other sources, however, as is his vocabulary of the Malagasy of that time and place.

DUPRE, JULES-MARIE (1813-1881). A career naval officer, Dupré became commander of the French Indian Ocean fleet in 1861. After the death of Queen Ranavalona I (q.v.), he was sent to negotiate a treaty with her son, Radama II (q.v.). He achieved the opening of Madagascar to French activities that Ranavalona had refused. There were two treaties: a public treaty that arranged for an opening of trade and recognized the validity of the terms of the Lambert Charter (q.v.), and a secret treaty that recognized French sovereignty over the territory ceded to France by other Malagasy, notably Sakalava (q.v.) rulers. The secret treaty was not recognized by the French government, but the public treaty was ratified. Dupré also joined with Lambert (q.v.) in creating the Compagnie de Madagascar to take advantage of the new opportunities. In 1863, however, Radama II was killed in a coup d'état, and the treaties were denounced by the new queen, Rasoherina (q.v.), and her government. Dupré urged the French government to invade Madagascar to punish the

Merina government, but without success. He later became governor of Réunion (q.v.).

DUSSAC, PAUL (1896–1938). A French citizen born in Russia where his father had fled after the fall of the Paris Commune, Dussac settled at Diégo-Suarez in 1922. He was a supporter of the Malagasy nationalist movement, and in particular of the Ralaimongo group (q.v.). At the time, Malagasy newspapers were required to have French managing editors, and he collaborated on several journals, helping to found new versions as the colonial administration closed down the previous ones. The journals included *L'Aurore Malgache, La Nation Malgache,* and *La Prolétariat Malgache.* Dussac was imprisoned for his involvement in the May 19, 1929, demonstration (q.v.) and freed only after the liberalization of political life that followed the coming to power of the Popular Front (q.v.). He attempted to found a Malagasy communist party, but was disavowed by the French Communist party. In 1937 he returned to France, where he died.

DUVEAU, Roger. Duveau was elected by the college of French citizens of Madagascar to the Constituent Assemblies (q.v.) that established the French Fourth Republic, and later became a deputy in the National Assembly (q.v.). In 1954 he served briefly as secretary for overseas France. As a planter himself and delegate of the first college, he at first represented settler interests and opposed the end of the college system (q.v.) of elections. He became more sympathetic, however, to the extension of political participation and to the granting of an amnesty (q.v.) to those convicted of complicity in the Rebellion of 1947 (q.v.). In 1956 he was elected to the National Assembly by the second college.

-E-

ECOLE LE MYRE DE VILERS. This school, named after the first administrator of the 1885 French protectorate (q.v.), was established by General Gallieni (q.v.) in 1897. It was the highest level of state education available in Madagascar and served as a training school for Malagasy civil servants and teachers. The president of the First Republic (q.v.), Philibert Tsiranana (q.v.), was a graduate of the school, as were many members of his cabinet.

ECONOMY. The Malagasy economy is dominated by agriculture, which occupies about 81% of the active population and accounts for almost all exports. *See Table 2.* The production of rice for local consumption and the raising of cattle are the most important agricultural activities, while the export crops consist largely of coffee and tropical spices. The nonagricultural sector of the economy is dominated by services, and industrial production employs about 50,000 people.

The economy has historically suffered from a lack of connection between sectors and regions, in part resulting from problems of transportation and communication, as well as from natural disasters, especially cyclones. Asserting national control over the economy has also been a problem. During the French colonial period the economy was dominated by French commercial companies (q.v.) and Asian intermediaries, a situation that continued after independence under the First Republic (q.v.). The Ramanantsoa regime (q.v.), which controlled the island from 1972 until early 1975, attempted to gain control of the economy by leaving the Franc Zone, nationalizing some major industries, setting up state trading companies, and establishing an investment code that required firms to establish local headquarters and encourage Malagasy participation in management and ownership.

Further nationalizations and an attempt to increase state control of the economy (via devices such as state farms) followed from the Marxist orientation of the Democratic Republic of Madagascar (q.v.), established under President Didier Ratsiraka (q.v.) in 1975. In October 1979 Ratsiraka announced the adoption of an "All-Out Investment Policy" (q.v.) to be financed by "Omni-Directional Borrowing." The failure of this investment policy, the increase in debt that it entailed, and such external factors as the second oil crisis and the fall of prices for Madagascar's exports led to the collapse of the Malagasy economy, a collapse from which the country has yet to recover. Both agricultural and indus-

TABLE 2 Economic Overview

Population	11,673,000
% Urban	25
GDP per capita	U$230
GDP by sector (%)	
Agriculture	33
Industry	13
Services	54
Economically active population, by sector	
Agriculture	87
Industry	4
Services	9

Sources: World Bank, *World Tables, 1990;* and *Africa Research Bulletin,* August 16–September 15, 1992.

trial production have declined or remained stable over the 1980s, with a slight increase at the end of the decade reversed by the 1991 political upheaval that led to the fall of the DRM and the creation of the Third Republic (q.v.).

In 1980 the Malagasy government appealed to the International Monetary Fund for assistance in its debt crisis (q.v.) and signed a first agreement that year. Subsequent agreements have followed, as has the rescheduling and annulment of much of the Malagasy debt by other creditors. The conditions for this assistance have led to the reversal of earlier economic policies. Regulation of the price of agricultural goods has been replaced by floor and ceiling prices, and the monopolies of the two state trading companies have been ended, although the government retained control of the collection and marketing of cloves and coffee, which together provide a major share of Madagascar's export earnings. In January 1988 the minister of finance announced the closure of all state companies except JIRAMA, which handles water and electricity, and SOLIMA, the oil refinery. In 1990 the government negotiated the creation of an industrial free zone on the east coast south of Toamasina with the Hong Kong–based Far East Group.

The suffering brought about by the economic decline, the

debt crisis, and the structural adjustment programs was one of the factors that enabled the opposition to the DRM to mobilize the crowds to overthrow the regime. The successor Third Republic (q.v.) has attempted to restore government accounts by improving the collection of revenue, particularly customs duties, and by restraining increases in the size of the civil service. It has promised further privatization of state-owned firms and liberalization of state control of trade, although it has not yet agreed to reduce its presence in the banking sector. The country remains heavily dependent on foreign aid, however, of which France provides about 40%, both for investment and for balance-of-payments support.

EDUCATION. Education in the Western sense began in Madagascar with the establishment in 1821 of schools run by the London Missionary Society (q.v.) at the request of Radama I (q.v.), ruler of the Merina Empire (q.v.). The school system at first recruited its pupils from the upper classes of the capital, Antananarivo, but was later extended to the villages of Imerina. Malagasy was the main language of instruction at the primary level, and Malagasy and English were used at the secondary level. The schools served as the main training and recruiting ground for the Merina administration, and since recruitment took place as a form of conscription, the schools were not always welcome. When the Catholic missions came to Madagascar in 1861, they extended the educational network south to Fianarantsoa (q.v.) in Betsileo (q.v.) territory. In 1886 primary education was made compulsory in Imerina, and it is estimated that at the time of the colonial conquest there were 137,000 students in the Protestant-run system and 27,000 in the Catholic system.

Early French governors were suspicious both of the perpetuation of British influence through the Protestant system and of church-run education in general. In 1906 Governor-General Augagneur (q.v.) forbade the use of languages other than French and the holding of classes in religious buildings, and school attendance fell accordingly. The colonial power also expanded the system, however; after the failure of an attempt by Gallieni (q.v.) to set up regional colleges, the state system of education was centered on Antananarivo, with the most important postsecondary institutions—the medical school at Befelatanana (q.v.) and the Ecole Le Myre de Vilers (q.v.)—located there. An Institute of University Studies was created in 1955, but did not develop into a university until after independence. French was the language of instruction at the secondary level, while policy on the language to be used at the primary level varied. At the time of independence, Madagascar had the highest school-participation rate of France's African colonies. About one-third of the eligible population was in school, one-half in the mission network.

By the time of independence in 1960, education had become a valued commodity, and the First Republic (q.v.) was under considerable pressure to expand the system. Expansion did take place, but largely at the primary level. At the higher levels the system was sharply pyramidal, with a series of cutoff points of which the most important were the examination for entry into secondary school, the examination between the first and second levels of secondary education, and the baccalaureate, which entitled the holder to pass on to the new University of Madagascar (q.v.) created in 1960. Unemployment among school dropouts became an increasingly serious problem. The system was also criticized for its emphasis on French culture, particularly at the university level, where the equivalence of Malagasy and French diplomas arranged for in the Cooperation Agreements (q.v.) between France and the First Republic meant that the curriculum of the University of Madagascar had to follow that of French universities. Demands for Malgachization (q.v.) of the curriculum and staff of the secondary schools and the university mobilized a growing student opposition in the late 1960s. The fall of the First Republic in the May 1972 Revolution (q.v.) was precipitated by strikes and demonstrations staged by students and school dropouts.

Under the Ramanantsoa regime (q.v.) and the Democratic Republic of Madagascar (q.v.) which followed the Revolution of 1972, the educational system was expanded until it absorbed 25% of the national budget. Standards, especially for the baccalaureate, were relaxed, and the number and value of university scholarships were increased. Attempts were made to introduce Malagasy as a language of instruction and to revise the curriculum to give a larger role to the study of Malagasy culture and history. At the university, most of the French professors left, to be replaced by Malagasy, and, under the Democratic Republic, instructors from the Soviet Union began to teach there in growing numbers. As part of the All-Out Investment Policy (q.v.) of the Democratic Republic, university centers were created in the provincial capitals, including one at Antananarivo that was seen as an attempt to create a regime counterweight to the University of Madagascar. Although the regime promised to end private education, both the church and, to a lesser degree, the nonreligious private system survived.

In spite of the increases in expenditure, the relationship between the regime and students remained difficult. The expansion of state activity under the Democratic Republic did not solve the problems of employment for school dropouts and graduates, and the system itself suffered during the austerity of the 1980s. Both the university and the secondary school system were the scenes of frequent strikes and demonstrations, and students provided support for parties critical of the regime, like MONIMA (q.v.) and the MFM (q.v.), as well as for such antiregime groups as the Kung Fu (q.v.). In November 1986 President Ratsiraka sponsored an attempt to reform the system by limiting the right to repeat academic years and by centralizing instruction in the third and fourth years at two of the seven university centers. Reaction to the proposed reform led to demonstrations and riots that resulted in some deaths, and the proposal was eventually withdrawn.

Students and teachers were prominent participants in the strikes and demonstrations that led to the collapse of the DRM, and the current president of the Third Republic (q.v.), Albert Zafy (q.v.), is a professor at the University of Madagascar. *See the Chronology above for key dates of university and secondary school strikes since 1975. See also* FEDERATION DES ASSOCIATIONS D'ETUDIANTS DE MADAGASCAR; SYNDICAT DES ENSEIGNANTS ET CHERCHEURS DE L'ENSEIGNEMENT SUPERIEUR.

ELECTIONS, DEMOCRATIC REPUBLIC OF MADAGASCAR. The adult population of the Democratic Republic of Madagascar (q.v.) directly elected the president of the republic, the members of the Assemblée Nationale Populaire (q.v.), and the council and president of the executive of the lowest level of the decentralized collectivities (q.v.). Although for reasons of party infrastructure and administrative interference the electoral results were dominated by the regime party, AREMA (q.v.), other parties did contest elections and win votes. All parties wishing to run candidates in elections were, however, required to belong to the Front National pour la Défense de la Révolution (q.v.).

There were three series of elections during the existence of the DRM. In December 1975 a referendum approved the constitution of the republic and the nomination of Didier Ratsiraka (q.v.) as president by a majority of 94.5% of the votes cast. In March 1977 elections to the newly created *fokontany* councils were held. AREMA gained 88.2% of the seats, with its strongest results in the provinces of Toamasina and Mahajanga. The AKFM (q.v.) was second, with 8.3% of the seats, gaining its best results in Antananarivo province. MONIMA (q.v.) gained 1.8% of the seats, mainly in Toliara province, while Vonjy (q.v.) gained 1.4% scattered in Antananarivo and the southeast of Fianarantsoa province. In June, elections to the Assemblée Nationale Populaire were held, although the distribution of seats had been agreed to in advance. AREMA had 112 of the 137 seats; the AKFM, 16; Vonjy, 7; and UDECMA (q.v.), which had received almost no votes in the earlier election, had 2 seats. The MFM (q.v.) boycotted both elections, and MONIMA boycotted the election for the ANP.

Elections were held again in 1982 and 1983. Ratsiraka postponed the legislative and local elections until after the presidential election, in which his only opponent was Monja Jaona (q.v.). Ratsiraka won with 80% of the vote, although he had only 50% in the capital. In elections to the decentralized collectivities and the ANP, AREMA won 65% and 64% of the vote, respectively. At the local level, the AKFM, with 12% of the vote, was the closest party, while in the elections to the ANP, it was the MFM, with 11%, that was the second party.

Presidential elections were held again on March 12, 1989 (advanced from November in response to growing unrest). There were four candidates: Ratsiraka, Monja Jaona, Manandafy Rakotonirina (q.v.), and Marojama Razanabahiny (q.v.). Ratsiraka won with 62% of the vote, down from his 1982 total. Rakotonirina gained 20% of the vote, Razanabahiny 15%, and Monja Jaona only 3%

The last elections held under the DRM were the elections to the ANP and to the councils of the decentralized collectivities, held in May and September 1989, respectively. In the legislative elections, AREMA won 120 seats; the MFM, 7; Vonjy, 3; AKFM-Renouveau (q.v.), 3; the AKFM, 2; and MONIMA, 1 seat. In the elections to the local councils, AREMA also reaffirmed its dominance, but the high abstention rates, particularly in urban centers, were a truer indication of the weakness of the regime, which was to disappear, replaced by the Third Republic (q.v.), in 1992.

ELECTIONS, THIRD REPUBLIC. The first election to be held under the Third Republic (q.v.), successor to the Democratic Republic of Madagascar (q.v.), was the referendum to approve the constitution of the new republic. In spite of disruptions caused by supporters of the former DRM, the constitutional referendum of August 19, 1992, resulted in the approval of the new constitution by 66% of those voting. The subsequent elections for president and deputies to the National Assembly were delayed several times by political instability. The presidential election involved two stages, a first round and a runoff election between the two leading candidates in the first round. In the first stage of the presidential election, held on November 25, 1992, there were eight candidates, including Didier Ratsiraka (q.v.), president of the DRM, and Albert Zafy (q.v.), candidate of the Comité des Forces Vives (q.v.), which had been responsible for the overthrow of Ratsiraka. Other candidates included Manandafy Rakotonirina (q.v.), leader of the MFM; Jacques Rabemananjara (q.v.), a figure from the First Republic (q.v.); and Ruffine Tsiranana, daughter of the president of the First Republic, Philibert Tsiranana (q.v.). Ratsiraka and Zafy emerged as the two leading candidates, with 28.3% and 48%

of the vote respectively. In the runoff election held on February 10, 1993, Zafy received 66.6% of the vote and Ratsiraka 33.4%. Elections to the National Assembly were held on June 16, 1993.

ELECTRICITE ET EAU DE MADAGASCAR. Madagascar's largest utilities company, the EEM was financed by a French investment group based in Lyons. In 1908 the company received a license to produce and distribute electric current and water in Madagascar. It was criticized both for the slow rate at which it extended its services and for the high prices it charged. The firm was nationalized in 1976, and the state company JIRAMA (*Jiro sy Rano Malagasy,* or ''Malagasy Electricity and Water'') was created. A disagreement over recompense for the expropriation continued until 1984.

ELLIS, WILLIAM (1794–1872). William Ellis was a missionary attached to the London Missionary Society (q.v.). His first posting was the Society Islands and Tahiti, but on his return to London in 1824 he began work for the foreign-contact section of the society. In 1835 he was sent to Madagascar to attempt to negotiate the return of the Protestant missionaries who had been expelled by Queen Ranavalona I (q.v.). He landed at Toamasina (q.v.) but was not allowed to proceed to the capital. He tried again in 1854, and was finally invited to Antananarivo in 1858, although his efforts to arrange a return of the missionaries were not successful. After the queen's death, Ellis and the LMS returned to Madagascar at the invitation of her son, Radama II (q.v.), with whom Ellis had had contacts during his visit. Ellis reestablished the mission and acted as advisor to the king, returning to London in 1865. *Further information may be found in the Bibliography following this Dictionary.*

ETHNIC GROUPS. Madagascar is generally considered to have eighteen ''ethnic groups,'' although some authors argue for the existence of twenty-one. This disagreement is indicative of the fluid nature of ethnicity in Malagasy society. Most groups have subdivisions that are as important as the groups themselves, and the dispute over the number of groups arises from disagreements over when the differences become important enough that the group constitutes a separate subgroup. Most groups, even those that developed centralized political institutions, never had a single political system covering the whole group. The Merina monarchy (q.v.) is the exception to this rule. The Sakalava (q.v.) monarchies date from the seventeenth, and possibly even the sixteenth century, but the Betsimisaraka (q.v.) Confederation and the Betsileo (q.v.) kingdoms date from the eighteenth century. A group name like the Tanala (q.v.), or "People of the Forest," is essentially a geographical description. Many customs are either local or shared by many groups; the Malagasy language, although spoken in a variety of dialects, is shared by all. Through interaction in the nineteenth century, however, and the extensive administrative and political use of the concept in the colonial period, ethnic identity does have importance, and the ethnic balance of political and administrative institutions—including the military—is paid attention to, whether the goal is ethnic balance or ethnic imbalance.

EVOLUES. Under the colonial system, évolués were Malagasy who qualified for French citizenship. Access to this status required a certain level of education and an attestation of good character from the local colonial administrator. French citizenship freed its holder from the requirements of the indigénat (q.v.), including forced labor. It was not easy to acquire this status, and in 1939 there were barely 8,000 Malagasy holding French citizenship.

EXPORTS. Madagascar's main exports are agricultural products and some minerals. *See Table 3.* Except for vanilla, cloves, and Cape peas, the amount of each commodity that Madagascar exports is only a fraction of world production, and it has little control over prices. In general, prices for Madagascar's exports have been declining over the last decade, and uncertainties of supply as well as corruption in the collection and marketing of exports have also reduced export income. Before the colonial period Madagascar's exports went mainly to the Mascarene (q.v.) Islands and to a variety of countries, including the United States and Great Britain.

TABLE 3 Export Commodities, 1991
(in thousands of metric tons)

Coffee	43.5
Cloves	13.0
Pepper	1.8
Vanilla	0.6

Source: Africa Research Bulletin, April 16–March 15, 1993.

During the colonial period trade was monopolized by France, and after independence, the First Republic (q.v.) enjoyed privileged access to the French market. With the change of regime in 1972 and the creation of the Democratic Republic of Madagascar (q.v.) in 1975, an attempt was made to diversify trading partners. The share of France as a market decreased, but the domination of Western countries did not. Tropical agricultural products continue to be the most important components of Madagascar's exports. Depending on world prices, either coffee or vanilla is the most important, followed by the other, while cloves and pepper are usually next in importance. *See also* SPICES.

FAHAVALO. The *fahavalo* were groups of bandits who gathered in areas outside the effective control of the Merina Empire (q.v.), beginning with the northwest, as it began to collapse after the Franco-Malagasy War of 1883 (q.v.). They drew their numbers from deserters from the war itself, and refugees from the increase in forced labor that occurred after 1885 as the Merina government attempted to repay the indemnity to France exacted by the treaty that ended the war. By 1888 they had come close enough to the capital to attack Ambohimanga (q.v.), and in 1890 they attacked Antananarivo (q.v.) itself. After the French conquest of 1895, they began to attack French targets as well as officials of the Merina monarchy, Malagasy Christians, and missionaries. Some of their activities merged into the Revolt of the Menalamba (q.v.).

FAMADIHANA. Referred to in English as "the turning of the dead," the *famadihana* is a ceremony that consists of removing the bones of dead ancestors from the family tomb and giving them new shrouds. Cattle are sacrificed and long ceremonial speeches called *kabary* are made. The ceremony is found throughout Madagascar, although it is especially common in the Highlands. Some writers argue that it is not a traditional ceremony but took its present form in the nineteenth century in response to changes introduced by the extension of the Merina monarchy.

FANJAKANA. *Fanjakana* is the Malagasy word for "government" or "administration" and is often used to indicate something that is alien to local society.

FARQUHAR, SIR ROBERT. Farquhar was the governor of Mauritius (q.v.) after the British took the island from the French in 1814. Eager to preserve British influence in the Indian Ocean, he entered into contact with Radama I (q.v.), ruler of the expanding Merina monarchy (q.v.), in 1815, sending a mission to the Merina capital. In 1817 he sent sergeants Hastie (q.v.) and Brady (q.v.) to the Merina capital, Antananarivo, to demonstrate the advantages of British-style military training. On October 23, 1817, a treaty was signed in which Radama agreed to abolish the slave trade (q.v.) in return for an indemnity and British recognition as the king of all Madagascar. Farquhar also agreed to provide assistance for the training of the Merina armies. When Farquhar went on leave to England, his replacement refused to pay the indemnity. Farquhar returned to Mauritius in 1820 and renegotiated the treaty.

FEDERATION DES ASSOCIATIONS DES ETUDIANTS MALGACHES. The FAEM was the main student organization at the University of Madagascar during the First Republic (q.v.). It alternated between demands limited to the improvement of student amenities and those which were more political in nature, until the slogan of "Malgachization" (q.v.) brought the two sets of interests together. Although the FAEM participated in the May 1972 Revolution (q.v.), it was by no means the most radical of the groups involved in that event.

FENERIVE. *See* FENOARIVO.

FENOARIVO (18°26′S, 46°34′E). A port lying south of the Ile Sainte-Marie (q.v.) on the east coast, Fenoarivo was an early center for the slave trade with the Mascarenes. It was also the center from which the Zanamalata (q.v.) launched the formation of the Betsimisaraka Confederation (q.v.).

FETY, MICHEL (1921–). A Protestant minister from Toamasina province, Fety was active in the First Republic (q.v.) and the Ramanantsoa regime (q.v.). He was one of the first members of an official body to criticize the government's behavior in the suppression of the peasant uprising of April 1971, and became president of the permanent commission of the Conseil National Populaire du Développement (q.v.) during the Ramanantsoa period. In this capacity he supported the *fokonolona* reform (q.v.) of Colonel Richard Ratsimandrava (q.v.). At the last meeting of the CNPD after the establishment of the Democratic Republic of Madagascar (q.v.) in 1975, he attempted to defend the assassinated colonel's view of the reform, but was criticized for romanticism by the defenders of the new regime.

After the installation of the DRM, Fety more or less disappeared from official political life. On July 29, 1992, however, a small group of armed civilians seized the Antananarivo radio station, claiming to act in Fety's name. The attempted coup quickly collapsed.

FFKM (Fikombonan'ny Fiangonana Kristiana eto Madagascar, *or* "Council of Christian Churches of Madagascar"). The FFKM was founded in 1980 to bring together the Catholic church and the major Protestant churches of Madagascar. It played an important role in the transition from the Democratic Republic of Madagascar (q.v.) to the Third Republic (q.v.). In August and December 1990, it convened assemblies of political groups to discuss the reform of the political system. When groups supporting the regime refused to attend, the assemblies turned into gatherings of opposition forces. In the political crisis of the summer of 1991, the FFKM at first attempted to mediate between President

Ratsiraka (q.v.) and the opposition Comité des Forces Vives (q.v.), but after the massacre of demonstrators at the presidential palace of Iavoloha (q.v.), it sided definitively with the opposition and participated in the negotiations that led to the power-sharing agreement (q.v.) of October 31, 1991.

FIAKARA. A native of Toliara province, Fiakara was commander of the army garrison of Antananarivo at the time of the 1975 assassination of President Richard Ratsimandrava (q.v.). He also served as a judge in the "Trial of the Century" (q.v.) of those accused of plotting the assassination. An early member of the regime party, AREMA (q.v.), he ws named to the Conseil Suprême de la Révolution (q.v.) in 1977.

FIANARANTSOA (21°26′S, 47°0′E). Fianarantsoa was established as the southern capital of the Merina Empire (q.v.) in 1830 on the site of a Betsileo (q.v.) village. It was a major site of mission activity, particularly after the arrival of the Catholic missions in 1861. After the French conquest in 1895, it served as a base for the extension of colonial rule to the south, and a French military camp was established there.

FIANARANTSOA–COTE EST RAILROAD. This railroad was built between 1926 and 1937 to connect the provincial capital of Fianarantsoa with the East Coast port of Manakara and to allow an outlet for the coffee-growing regions between the two cities. It is 163 km long, and the steep slope of Madagascar's eastern escarpment and the persistent rains and occasional cyclones create major problems of maintenance.

FIANARANTSOA PROVINCE. Fianarantsoa province is located in the southern part of the Highlands (q.v.). Its capital, Fianarantsoa (q.v.), was an administrative center for the Merina Empire (q.v.) and the site of intensive mission activity. It was also used as an administative center by the French. As a result, Fianarantsoa province has an infrastructure second only to that of Antananarivo province (q.v.). Its economy is dominated by agriculture: rice in the north, cattle in the south, and cash crops, especially coffee, on the coast.

The dominant ethnic group is the Betsileo (q.v.), with Bara (q.v.) to the south and Tanala (q.v.) and Antaifasy (q.v.) to the east.

FIANGONAN'I JESOSY KRISTY ETO MADAGASIKARA. The FJKM, or Church of Jesus Christ in Madagascar, was founded in 1970 to link the Protestant (q.v.) denominations derived from the London Missionary Society (q.v.), the French Evangelical Churches (q.v.), and the Quakers. In 1980 the churches composing the FJKM joined with the Catholic church to form the Council of Malagasy Churches, or FFKM (q.v.), which played a major role in the transition to the Third Republic (q.v.). *See also* MISSIONS.

FIFTH FRENCH REPUBLIC. The Fifth French Republic was established in 1958, after the passage of its constitution in the Setember 28 referendum of that year. The constitutional provisions for the overseas territories, including Madagascar, established a French Community, in which the overseas members would enjoy internal autonomy, while France handled questions of defense, foreign relations, and monetary affairs. All of France's African colonies, with the exception of Guinée, accepted the constitution and the status of autonomy within the French Community. Internal and international pressures to full independence were too great, however, and in January 1959 the Federation of Mali, grouping Senegal and the current state of Mali, asked for full independence, and in December 1959 Madagascar asked for its independence. *See also* FIRST REPUBLIC.

FINAZ, MARC (1815–1880). A French Jesuit, Finaz began missionary work in Réunion (q.v.) in 1846. In 1855 he went to the capital of the Merina Empire (q.v.), Antananarivo, disguising his identity as a priest because of the ban on mission activity decreed by Queen Ranavalona I (q.v.). Finaz became a friend and counselor of the future Radama II (q.v.) and was implicated in the 1857 plot to unseat Ranavalona and replace her with her son. He left the capital after the plot was discovered, but returned in 1862, after the queen's death, to direct the establishment and expansion of Catholic missions in Madagascar. He died in Antananarivo in 1880. *See also* CATHOLIC CHURCH; MISSIONS.

FIRST REPUBLIC. The First Malagasy Republic began its existence as an autonomous state in the French Community, established by the constitution of the Fifth French Republic (q.v.) in September 1958. The constitution of the First Malagasy Republic was passed on April 20, 1959. It provided for a quasi-presidential system along the lines of the Fifth French Republic, with the exception that there was no prime minister, the president being both head of state and head of government. The constitution provided for a bicameral legislature with a National Assembly (q.v.) and a Senate (q.v.). There was also a constitutional court, or Conseil Supérieur des Institutions (q.v.).

In December 1959 the government of Madagascar requested the granting of full independence, and on June 26, 1960, this independence, and the ''caducity'' of the Annexation Law of 1896 that had made Madagascar a French colony, were proclaimed in Antananarivo. Independence had been accompanied by the signing of a series of cooperation agreements (q.v.) between Madagascar and France that maintained a French economic, military, and political presence on the island. Opponents of the First Republic referred to these agreements as the ''original sin'' that damned the republic from birth.

Although the First Republic was dominated by a single political party, the Parti Sociale Démocrate (q.v.) under the president of the republic, Philibert Tsiranana (q.v.), it was technically a multiparty system, with two continuing parties of opposition, the AKFM (q.v.) and MONIMA (q.v.), and many other ephemeral parties. The PSD clearly dominated the administration and political system, however, and after 1965 controlled all but three seats in the National Assembly and all the seats in the Senate.

The First Republic had a conservative foreign policy, firmly aligning itself with France on the Western side of the Cold War. Under Tsiranana, it avoided groups like the Organization of African Unity (q.v.), which it considered too radical, and maintained relations with states not generally in favor at Third World gatherings, such as South Korea, South Vietnam, and at the end of the 1960s South Africa (q.v.). In spite of the ''social democratic'' character of the PSD, internal policy was also conservative. The colonial administrative framework was maintained, as were colonial policies like the head and cattle taxes, while Malgachization (q.v.) of the upper reaches of the administration and the military (q.v.) proceeded slowly. The educational system remained tied to the French system by means of the equivalency of higher Malagasy diplomas with the corresponding French diplomas.

The end of the First Republic began with Tsiranana's illness in 1970. A Peasant Rebellion (q.v.) in 1971 added further instability, and finally the May 1972 Revolution (q.v.) brought about the fall of the republic and its replacement by the civil-military Ramanantsoa regime (q.v.). *See the Introduction above for a further history of the First Republic.*

FISHING. Madagascar's fishing industry is not well developed, and problems of transportation mean that ocean fish are not widely consumed in the inland portions of the island. Various attempts have been made to establish a fishing industry and processing plants, but without success. Japanese tuna-fishing boats that had been operating in Malagasy waters withdrew in 1976, and the most important remaining activity is shrimp fishing along the west coast, often in conjunction with Japanese capital. Agreements have been signed with the European Community to develop tuna fishing, and the basic agreement was extended for a further three years in May 1992. Freshwater fish are caught mainly by individuals to supplement family diets.

FLACOURT, ETIENNE DE (d. 1660). De Flacourt was the agent sent by the Compagnie des Indes Orientales (q.v.) to restore its settlement at Fort-Dauphin (q.v.) after the first attempt of 1642 had disintegrated in quarrels among the settlers. He arrived in 1648 and proceeded to refortify the settlement and send out exploring parties over much of southern Madagascar to establish trading networks. In 1653 he returned to France to raise interest in the colony and wrote a history and a dictionary of Malagasy. In 1660 he set out on a return journey to Madagascar, but his ship was attacked by the Dutch and blown up.

FOKONOLONA REFORM. Reform of the territorial administration and a change in the nature of government-populace relations had been one of the goals of the radical elements of the May 1972 Revolution (q.v.) that led to the fall of the First Republic (q.v.) and the installation of the Ramanantsoa regime (q.v.). After 1972 the idea was taken up by Ramanantsoa's minister of the interior, gendarmerie colonel Richard Ratsimandrava (q.v.). Using the slogan ''popular control of development,'' Ratsimandrava proposed to resolve the perennial problem of popular suspicion of government by returning as much decision-making power as possible to the level of the village community, or *fokonolona.* Popularly elected councils were to take over many of the functions of local control that had been the role of the territorial administration, and economic councils were to establish local development plans. Regional and national plans were to follow from the local plans rather than the other way around. The territorial administration was to enter the villages only at their invitation.

The implementation of the reform ran into several problems, including the reluctance of the territorial administration to administer a policy aimed at ''dynamiting'' the state structures on which their power rested. At the time of his assassination in 1975, Ratsimandrava was pursuing the reform and encouraging peasant expression of grievances against the administration. Although this radically populist vision of *fokonolona* reform died with him, it had aroused enough enthusiasm that the subsequent Democratic Republic of Madagascar (q.v.) was obliged to carry out a version of it, revised in the direction of increased centralization, and to adopt much of its terminology and many of its slogans. *See also* DECENTRALIZED COLLECTIVITIES.

FONDATION CHARLES DE GAULLE (*also* Fondation de L'Enseignement Superieur). This foundation was created in 1960 to group the Institute of University Studies (about to become the University of Madagascar), (q.v.), assorted research institutes, and the Ecole Nationale d'Administration. The president of the republic was the president ex officio of the foundation.

FONDS D'INVESTISSEMENT POUR LE DEVELOPPEMENT ECONOMIQUE ET SOCIAL. More commonly known by its initials, FIDES, this fund was established in 1946 to provide long-term loans for infrastructure and other economic development projects in France's overseas territories. In Madagascar it helped to finance the Communes Rurales Autonomes Modernisées (q.v.) and projects for the development of coffee and sugar cultivation.

FORCE OUVRIERE. In 1948 the French union movement split over the issue of affiliation with the French Communist party. One section, the Confédération Générale du Travail (q.v.), affiliated with the party, while Force Ouvrière maintained looser links with the French Socialist party.

FORCED LABOR. Most precolonial political units in Madagascar had a system of obligatory labor owed to the collectivity or to the ruler. Under the Merina Empire (q.v.) the *fanampoana,* as this system was usually called, was extended to public works, to porterage, to the maintenance of a standing army, and to recruitment for the administration. Migration to escape the demands of the monarchy was not uncommon. In 1896 the French governor-general, Gallieni (q.v.), instituted a decree requiring all healthy males between the ages of sixteen and sixty to furnish a maximum of fifty days labor for public works and supply convoys. Later, Malagasy permanently employed by Europeans were exempted, but this system was often abused through the sale of work certificates. In 1926 the system was tightened and made more onerous by the introduction of SMOTIG, or service de la Main-d'Oeuvre des Travaux d'Intérêt Général (q.v.). Forced labor was abolished throughout the French African empire in 1946, but subsequent regimes have often required labor for various "development" projects, particularly the building and repair of roads and bridges.

FORCES REPUBLICAINES DE SECURITE. The FRS was a paramilitary force, about 2,000 men strong in 1972, that was created in 1966 by the minister of the interior, André Resampa (q.v.), and attached to the Ministry of the Interior. As long as Resampa was minister of the interior he took a personal interest in recruitment to the force, usually drawing its men from his home base of Morondava, and the FRS was considered to be his personal army. It did not react to his downfall, however, and by the time of the May 1972 Revolution (q.v.) was the only force willing to defend the First Republic (q.v.). It was the FRS raid on students assembled at the University of Madagascar on the night of May 12 that set off the demonstrations that turned into the May Revolution, and it was its act of firing on the crowd assembled at the Antananarivo Hôtel de Ville that turned the opinion of the capital decisively against the regime.

After the First Republic was replaced by the Ramanantsoa regime (q.v.), the FRS was renamed the Groupe Mobile de Police, but not otherwise reformed, and in fact was generally ignored by the regime. Colonel Bréchard Rajaonarison (q.v.), whose attempted coup at the end of December 1974 led to the fall of the Ramanantsoa regime, took refuge at the GMP camp at Antanaimoro (q.v.) and held out there until the assassination of Richard Ratsimandrava (q.v.) in February 1975. Ratsimandrava's assassins were members of the GMP from the Antanaimoro camp. After the reorganization of the military (q.v.) under the Democratic Republic of Madagascar (q.v.) the GMP/FRS was disbanded.

FORESTS. Much of Madagascar was originally covered with forests, but now all that remains are some reforested areas in the Highlands (q.v.) and the remnants of the rain forest of the east coast. Deforestation began at an early period, particularly in the Highlands, and nineteenth century visitors to the Merina (q.v.) capital, Antananarivo (q.v.), remarked on the bare appearance of the surrounding countryside. Deforestation has occurred as land is cleared for agriculture, as wood is harvested for fuel, and because of the practice of *tavy,* or slash-and-burn agriculture. Attempts to ban this style of agriculture under successive regimes, and to make reforestation a "national duty," have not been conspicuously successful. The deforestation has resulted in serious erosion and in the silting up of river mouths, particularly along the west coast.

FORT-DAUPHIN. Now Taolañaro (q.v.), Fort-Dauphin received its name at the time of an attempted French settlement under the Compagnie des Indes Orientales (q.v.) in 1642. The settlers at first attempted to establish themselves at Saint Lucy's Bay to the north, but moved to the more secure ground of the peninsula that forms one side of the Fort-Dauphin harbor. Etienne de Flacourt (q.v.) was sent there in 1646 and managed to keep the settlement in operation, but after his death it stagnated and was closed in 1674 after the massacre of most of its garrison. Fort-Dauphin continued to be used as a port to provide supplies, largely cattle, for the Mascarenes (q.v.) after the settlement was abandoned, and in 1768 the company made another attempt to establish a settlement there, under the Comte de Maudave. He abandoned the effort in 1771, leaving only a small post that was conquered by the troops of the Merina Empire in 1825.

FOULPOINTE (*also* Mahavelona) (17°41′S, 49°31′E). A harbor lying between Toamasina (q.v.) and Antongil Bay (q.v.) on the east coast, Foulpointe was one of the early stations for the slave trade between Madagascar and the Mascarenes. In 1756 the Compagnie des Indes Orientales (q.v.) established a post there, and in 1758 Foulpointe replaced Antongil Bay (q.v.) as the official center of company activities on the east coast, a position it lost to Toamasina in 1800. It was subsequently occupied by the forces of the Merina Empire (q.v.). In 1826 the Betsimisaraka (q.v.) attacked the post the Merina had established, but were defeated, and their Zanamalata (q.v.) leaders were taken to Antananarivo (q.v.) where they were later executed.

FOURTH FRENCH REPUBLIC. The Fourth French Republic was established in October 1946, when the French electorate approved the second constitution submitted to it by the

Constitutional Assemblies (q.v.). Under the constitution of the Fourth Republic, what were called the Territoires d'Outre-Mer, or Overseas Territories, were grouped in the French Union and elected members of the National Assembly and the Senate according to the college system (q.v.) whereby French citizens and a restricted electorate of those under the regime of the *indigénat* (q.v.) voted separately. The constitution of the Fourth Republic considered the Overseas Territories to be an integral part of France, a conception that led to the wars in Indochina and Algeria and contributed to the collapse of the republic in 1958. Disappointment at this conception was one of the contributing factors to the Rebellion of 1947 (q.v.) in Madagascar. It was not until the passage of the Loi-Cadre (q.v.) in 1956 that a greater measure of autonomy was granted to the African colonies, including Madagascar. The movement from autonomy to independence was completed under the Fifth French Republic (q.v.).

FRANC ZONE. The Franc Zone is a monetary association of France and its former colonies. Its agreements provide for free convertibility of the former colonies' currencies into French francs in return for the holding of their reserves in French francs and use of the Paris Exchange for their transactions in other currencies. The First Republic (q.v.) joined the Franc Zone by the Financial Cooperation Agreement of June 1960. As part of the renegotiation of the Cooperation Agreements (q.v.) undertaken by the Ramanantsoa regime (q.v.) in 1973, Madagascar left the Franc Zone. With the arrival of the debt crisis of the 1980s there have been periodic rumors that Madagascar would apply for readmission, but it has not yet done so.

FRANCE. France established a protectorate (q.v.) over Madagascar in 1885, after the Franco-Malagasy War of 1883–1885 (q.v.). After the invasion of 1895, it established a second protectorate but annexed the island outright after the Revolt of the Menalamba (q.v.). It ruled Madagascar as a colony until 1958, when the constitution of the Fifth French Republic (q.v.) established the French Community, and Madagascar gained internal autonomy within the community. In 1960

Madagascar became fully independent, but the First Republic (q.v.) maintained close ties with France, arranged in a series of Cooperation Agreements (q.v.). After the May 1972 Revolution (q.v.), the Ramanantsoa regime (q.v.) renegotiated the agreements, ending the close links. Relations between Madagascar and France became more distant with the creation of the avowedly Marxist Democratic Republic of Madagascar (q.v.) in 1975. Nationalizations (q.v.) of French firms, Malagasy criticism of French policy in the Comoro Islands (q.v.), and territorial disputes over the ''scattered islands'' of the Indian Ocean all provided friction in the relationship. There was some improvement in the relations in 1977, when the Franco-Malagasy Commission established in 1973 met for the first time and agreed to a resumption of French assistance in the educational system. The rapprochement between France and Madagascar was furthered by the deepening of Madagascar's debt crisis (q.v.). In 1984 Madagascar agreed to pay an indemnity to the French firm Electricité et Eau de Madagascar (q.v.) in return for French help in its dealings with the International Monetary Fund (q.v.). In 1989 France agreed to a substantial reduction of Madagascar's debt. Throughout, France remained Madagascar's first customer and most important supplier of imports (q.v.).

By the time of the collapse of the Democratic Republic of Madagascar, France had regained much of its former position of influence, a position that was strengthened after 1989 by the ending of Soviet assistance to the regime. French teachers returned to the island, and French soldiers moved in as trainers to the presidential guard. During the crisis of 1991, French authorities tried at first to bring about a compromise between President Ratsiraka (q.v.) and his opponents in the Comité des Forces Vives (q.v.), but after the massacre of demonstrators at the presidential palace of Iavoloha on August 10, 1991, the French began putting pressure on Ratsiraka to resign, offering him asylum in France. The French government firmly supported the government of the Third Republic (q.v.).

FRANCO-BRITISH CONVENTION. In August 1890 the French and British governments signed a convention that settled their rivalry in the western Indian Ocean. In the convention, the French government recognized the newly established British protectorate in Zanzibar in return for recognition of the French version of its protectorate (q.v.) over the Merina Empire (q.v.). This effectively signaled that Great Britain would not intervene in future French efforts to secure their position in the island.

FRANCO-MALAGASY WAR, 1883–1885. In February 1883 Admiral Pierre, commander of the French Indian Ocean fleet, was ordered by the minister of the navy, François De Mahy (q.v.) to attack the port of Mahajanga (q.v.) and to present the government of the Merina Empire (q.v.) with an ultimatum demanding recognition of the French claim to territory in the protectorate treaty it had signed with Sakalava (q.v.) rulers in the northwest of the island, permission for foreigners to own land in Madagascar, and the opening of trade. Pierre bombarded Mahajanga, and went to the port of Toamasina (q.v.) to receive the answer to the ultimatum. When there was no reply, he bombarded and occupied the port. A change of government intervened in France, however, and the new government was less enthusiastic about the pursuit of the war. Pierre died while on his way to France to justify his actions, and his successor, Admiral Galiber, had instructions to try a more cautious approach. The Merina government was not prepared to fight and win any decisive engagements, and the war ended without a clear victory on either side, although the subsequent treaty went part way to establishing French claims to the island by giving France a limited protectorate (q.v.) over the Merina Empire and a base at Diégo-Suarez (q.v.).

FRANCO-MALAGASY WAR, 1895. The Franco-Malagasy War of 1895 began after a series of disagreements over the implementation of the Protectorate of 1885 (q.v.). On November 16, 1894, the French National Assembly voted the credits necessary to pursue a war against the Merina Empire (q.v.) with the objective of establishing French rule in Madagascar. Although Toamasina (q.v.) was captured in December 1894, the actual conquest began from Mahajanga on the west coast, where the French landed with a force of 14,733 commanded by General Duchesne, planning to follow the Betsiboka and Ikopa rivers to the Merina capital, Antananarivo (q.v.). The expedition proved to be more difficult than expected, although largely because of natural obstacles. The campaign started at the beginning of January, in the rainy season, and it was necessary to accompany the progress of the army with the construction of a road. After six months of advancing at a rate of 3 km a day, with high mortality rates, largely from fever, Duchesne formed a flying column that reached Antananarivo on September 23, 1895. The capital was bombarded, and Queen Ranavalona III (q.v.) and her government surrendered on October 1. A treaty establishing a new French protectorate was signed the same day. The French conquest of Madagascar was not complete with the collapse of the Merina state, however. In Imerina itself, the Revolt of the Menalamba (q.v.) against the imposition of French rule lasted until 1898, and other ethnic groups of the island also staged rebellions against the French.

FREE FRENCH. After the German invasion and the fall of France, General Charles De Gaulle (q.v.) and other members of the French army and some French politicians fled to London and attempted to continue the fight against the Germans. Other members of the French government had fled to unoccupied territory in France where they established the Vichy regime (q.v.) and made peace with the Germans. Madagascar was originally under the control of the Vichy regime. With the British invasion of 1942 (q.v.), however, the Vichy administration was removed from Madagascar and in January 1943 control over the island was handed back to the Free French. Many Malagasy nationalists had hoped that they, rather than the French, would take power, and relationships between the Free French administration and the Malagasy were further embittered by the extraction of labor and material, including food, from the island in support of the French war effort. *See also* OFFICE DU RIZ.

FRENCH COMMUNITY. *See* FIFTH FRENCH REPUBLIC.

FRENCH EVANGELICAL CHURCH. The French Evangelical church was invited to Madagascar in 1896 by Governor-General Gallieni (q.v.) to counteract the influence of British Protestants, such as the London Missionary Society (q.v.). It was instrumental in moving Protestant activity to the coastal regions of Madagascar. Churches derived from the French Evangelical church are the second largest of the Protestant (q.v.) denominations in Madagascar, and have been active in working for Protestant unity.

FRENCH UNION. *See* FOURTH FRENCH REPUBLIC.

FRONT DEMOCRATIQUE MALGACHE. *See* PARTI DEMOCRATIQUE MALGACHE.

FRONT NATIONAL MALGACHE. The FNM was an electoral committee formed to support the candidacies of Roger Duveau (q.v.) and Philibert Tsiranana (q.v.) to the French National Assembly in 1956. After the election it tried to organize as a political party, but its turn to a more nationalist direction, advocating immediate independence, led Tsiranana to distance himself from the party. He founded the Parti Social Démocrate (q.v.) later in 1956. After the 1958 Tamatave Congress (q.v.), the FNM was one of the parties that founded the opposition AKFM (q.v.).

FRONT NATIONAL POUR LA DEFENSE DE LA REVOLUTION. The constitution of the Democratic Republic of Madagascar (q.v.) provided for the creation of a National Front for the Defense of the Revolution to "motivate and guide the spirit of the Revolution" and to "embody the unity of the nation's masses." In order to have a legal existence, political parties had to join the FNDR and accept, at least formally, its principles. The FNDR was composed of the president of the DRM, the prime minister, the president of the Assemblée Nationale Populaire (q.v.), and of three representatives from each of the member parties. In practice, the FNDR was not able to fulfill its task of containing opposition to the regime, and when it was convoked in

August 1989, to discuss changes to the constitution of the DRM, it had not met since 1982. In March 1990 the constitution of the DRM was amended to allow the formation of parties outside the FNDR, and the institution ceased to exist.

-G-

GALLIENI, JOSEPH SIMON (1849–1916). Gallieni was the first governor-general of Madagascar, from 1896 to 1905, having previous experience of military campaigns and administration in West Africa and Indochina. He was appointed, with civil and military powers, after the outbreak of the Revolt of the Menalamba (q.v.). On his arrival, he presided over the end of the Merina monarchy (q.v.) and the establishment of the colonial system of rule. He executed the uncle and an advisor of Queen Ranavalona III (q.v.), exiled the queen, and moved into the palace of Ambohitsara. The Menalamba Revolt and the Sambirano Rebellion (q.v.) in the west were put down, although it was not until 1904 that the south was subdued by Gallieni's second-in-command, Hubert Lyautey (q.v.).

Gallieni presided over the creation of tariff barriers that reserved the Malagasy market to the French, the arrival of settlers (q.v.), and the granting of concessions (q.v.) to French commercial companies (q.v.). He instituted the *indigénat* (q.v.) to rule the Malagasy and experimented with various systems of administration. At first, he tried the *politique des races* (q.v.), or system of internal protectorates, which attempted to diminish reliance on the agents of the Merina Empire (q.v.) by ruling non-Merina groups through their indigenous systems. The variety of systems, however, and their lack of responsiveness to the directives of the colonial administration led to the gradual abandonment of the system, and its replacement by a system of more direct rule.

Gallieni also created a system of state schools to counterbalance the schools created by the missions (q.v.), many of which were run by the London Missionary Society (q.v.) and gave education in English. He also made an attempt, later abandoned by his successors, to establish training schools for Malagasy administrators outside the Merina-dominated Highlands. In Antananarivo, he established a medical school at Befeletanana (q.v.) and the Ecole Le Myre de Vilers (q.v.). Gallieni also gave some attention to the infrastructure, staring a road system and the Antananarivo to Toamasina railroad, instituting forced labor for the purpose.

Although he initially saw Madagascar as a colony of settlement, and encouraged settlers both from his own troops and from Réunion (q.v.), Gallieni later concluded that large-scale settlement was not appropriate for the island. When he left Madagascar he continued his military career and at the outbreak of the First World War in August 1914 he was military governor of Paris, and organized the defenses of the first Battle of the Marne. He became minister of war in 1915, and died in 1916.

GARBIT, HUBERT (1869–1933). Garbit was acting governor-general of Madagascar from 1914 to 1917 and governor-general from 1920 to 1923. He had already served as chief military officer of the island from 1905 to 1910. He was charged with mobilizing Madagascar's contribution to the French defenses in the First World War, and recruited over 45,000 Malagasy to serve in France, raised 5 million francs, and sent large quantities of raw materials. In 1917 he went to France to command the Malagasy troops there. Garbit was popular with the settlers (q.v.) for his dismantling of the Vy Vato Sakelika (q.v.) organization of nationalists, but was criticized by the nationalists and their sympathizers for the methods he had used in his mobilization effort. In his second term as governor-general, Garbit made further attempts to control the nationalist movement, including strengthened press censorship, restrictions on meetings, and laws on "vagabondage." He also attempted to grant some representation to the Malagasy by creating a Malagasy section of the Délégations Economiques et Financières (q.v.). He gave considerable attention to the development of the infrastructure, particularly the railroads (q.v.).

GAULLE, CHARLES DE (1890–1970). De Gaulle was the leader of the Free French (q.v.) during the Second World War, and president of the French Fifth Republic (q.v.) from 1958 to 1969. He visited Madagascar in August 1958 as part of his campaign in favor of the Referendum on the Constitution of the Fifth Republic (q.v.). His failure to promise amnesty (q.v.) for the prisoners of the Rebellion of 1947 (q.v.) or an abrogation of the Annexation Law of 1896 (q.v.) disappointed the strongly nationalist groups, who campaigned for a "no" vote in the referendum. The groups campaigning for a "yes" vote cited his promise that under the Fifth Republic Madagascar would have its own government, as in the days of the Merina Empire (q.v.).

GOATS. Goats are raised in the southwest of Madagascar, where they are indigenous, possibly after an early introduction by the Arabs (q.v.). Since 1914 they have been crossbred with Angora goats. They are raised mainly by the Mahafaly (q.v.) for their wool, but also are used for meat in times of famine.

GOVERNOR-GENERAL. Under the French colonial system, Madagascar was ruled by a governor-general appointed by the president of the Republic, in principle for a five-year term. He was responsible to the Ministry of Colonies, and all correspondence with the Ministry went through his office. He headed both the civil and military administration, named or nominated other administrative officers, and had the authority to promulgate laws and decrees. His second-in-command was called the secretary-general. After the 1956 Loi-Cadre (q.v.), the title of governor changed to high commissioner, and his powers were modified.

GRANDIDIER, ALFRED (1836–1921); GRANDIDIER, GUILLAUME (1873–1957). Father and son, the Grandidiers were the foremost French scholars of Madagascar of their period. Both wrote extensively on all aspects of Madagascar, and they compiled the *Collection des Ouvrages Anciens Concernant Madagascar,* a collection of earlier writings on the island. *Further information may be found in the Bibliography following this Dictionary.*

GROUPE D'ETUDES COMMUNISTES. A Groupe d'Etudes Communistes was started in Antananarivo in 1946 by Pierre Boiteau (q.v.), but attracted few members, although the future president of the First Republic (q.v.), Philibert Tsiranana (q.v.), was briefly a member. The group had faded away by 1955.

GROUPE MOBILE DE POLICE. *See* FORCES REPUBLICAINES DE SECURITE.

-H-

HASTIE, JAMES. A former sergeant in the Indian army, James Hastie was sent by Sir Robert Farquhar (q.v.) to Antananarivo in 1817 to help train the armies of the Merina monarchy (q.v.). In 1820 he was appointed British resident agent in Antananarivo.

HAUTE AUTORITE D'ETAT (High State Authority). The HAE was established by the power-sharing agreement (q.v.) of October 31, 1991, to manage the transition from the Democratic Republic of Madagascar (q.v.) to the Third Republic (q.v.). It was to be presided over by Albert Zafy (q.v.), a leader of the opposition to the DRM. The establishment of the HAE was delayed when Zafy objected to what he considered to be excessive representation of the supporters of DRM President Didier Ratsiraka (q.v.). The composition of the HAE was revised to include six supporters of Ratsiraka, seven from the opposition MFM (q.v.), and eighteen from Zafy's Comité des Forces Vives (q.v.). It began operation in January 1992.

HELLVILLE (13°25′S, 48°16′E). Also known as Andoany, Hellville is the most important city on the island of Nosy Be (q.v.). It was named after Admiral de Hell, governor of Réunion, who signed a treaty of protection in 1841 with rulers of the Boina (q.v.) Sakalava (q.v.), who had taken refuge there after the capture of their kingdom by the Merina Empire (q.v.). Hellville is the island's fourth most important port, handling both local and long-distance traffic.

HIGHLANDS. Sometimes erroneously called the Plateaux, the Highlands are the central part of Madagascar, including the territory of the Merina (q.v.) and Betsileo (q.v.). The term can also have political significance, since the Highlands have a more developed infrastructure than the other parts of the island and are considered to be a privileged region.

HOVA. A noble caste for the Betsileo (q.v.), and a commoner caste for the Merina (q.v.). The evolution of the Merina monarchy in the nineteenth century saw power pass to an oligarchy dominated by hova clans led by the Andafiavaratra (q.v.). The Merina state of the time was often erroneously called the Hova state.

-I-

IAVOLOHA. The palace of the president of the Democratic Republic of Madagascar (q.v.), located eight miles south of the capital, Antananarivo (q.v.), Iavoloha was built for Didier Ratsiraka (q.v.) by North Korean technicians. The main part of the palace was built as a replica of the royal palace of Antananarivo, but the installations also included extensive fortifications and bunkers as well as a military camp. On August 10, 1991, a crowd of over 400,000 antiregime demonstrators marched on the palace. The presidential guard fired on the crowd, killing over a hundred people, including two bodyguards of opposition leader Albert Zafy (q.v.), and wounding Zafy himself. Ratsiraka's efforts to blame the regular armed forces were unsuccessful, and the massacre caused external donors and internal groups like the FFKM (q.v.), which had been attempting to achieve a compromise between Ratsiraka and his opponents, to align themselves definitively with the opposition.

IHARANA. *See* VOHEMAR.

IHOSY (22°24′S, 46°8′E). Ihosy is located where the road from Fianarantsoa (q.v.) and Antananarivo (q.v.) divides, with one branch going to Toliara (q.v.) and the other to Taoloñaro (q.v.). It was established as the southernmost outpost of the Merina Empire (q.v.) in Bara (q.v.) territory, on a spot overlooking the current city. In January 1897 it was occupied by the French and used as a base for the conquest of the south.

IKONGO. Located in the southern part of Tanala territory, Ikongo has been the site of several kingdoms, usually headed by a royal caste, the Zafirambo, which claims descent from the Islamicized Zafiramina (q.v.) and which is considered to have arrived in the area during the seventeenth century. Authority was usually exercised in conjunction with representatives of common clans. In 1836 a rebellion against the Merina Empire (q.v.), which had conquered large parts of Tanala territory and imposed the payment of tribute (including slaves), broke out, centered in Ikongo and led by a member of the royal family, Tsiandrofa. After a series of engagements, formal recognition of the separation of the region was granted in 1862 by Radama II (q.v.). Ikongo was also the center of Tanala resistance to French colonial rule and of the Insurrection of 1904–1905 (q.v.).

ILE SAINTE-MARIE (*also* Nosy Ibrahim *or* Nosy Boraha) (16°50′S, 49°55′E). Situated between Antongil Bay (q.v.) and Foulepointe (q.v.), the Ile Sainte-Marie served as a haven for pirates (q.v.) at the end of the seventeenth and the beginning of the eighteenth centuries. The Compagnie des Indes Orientales (q.v.) established a trading post there. In 1750 Queen Betia signed the island over to the French, who attempted to occupy it, but abandoned their post after the garrison was massacred in 1754. In 1821 the agent of the Compagnie des Indes Orientales, Sylvain Roux, made another attempt to establish a trading post there. The French, under Roux's successor, Blevec (q.v.), built another fort. The island is now a center of clove production.

IMERINA. The home territory of the Merina (q.v.).

IMPORTS. Madagascar's imports are dominated by petroleum (q.v.), food, particularly rice (q.v.), and raw materials for processing. Reliable statistics are difficult to establish, and the estimations of the Malagasy government differ significantly from those of the World Bank (q.v). Madagascar's main suppliers are France, the United States, and Japan. Under the Democratic Republic of Madagascar (q.v.), the Soviet Union supplied significant amounts of petroleum and military equipment that did not appear in the trade statistics. As a result of the debt crisis (q.v.) that began in 1981, the economic programs that have been adopted to deal with the crisis, and the economic difficulties created by the political crisis of 1991, there have been recurrent severe shortages of imported goods in Madagascar, causing hardship particularly in urban regions, but also contributing to the deterioration of the country's infrastructure, transportation, and industrial plant.

INDIAN OCEAN. The Democratic Republic of Madagascar (q.v.) was an active proponent of projects to have the Indian Ocean declared a demilitarized zone. French bases at Ivato, an airport near Antananarivo (q.v.), and at Diégo-Suarez had already been eliminated under the previous Ramanantsoa regime (q.v.), in which the president of the DRM, Didier Ratsiraka (q.v.), had been foreign minister. Although the DRM developed ties with the Soviet Union after its establishment in 1975, and for a time permitted the presence of Soviet aircraft-spotting stations on its territory, it did not allow its harbors to be used as bases. Madagascar also supported United Nations resolutions declaring the Indian Ocean a "peace zone."

INDIGENAT. The *indigénat* was the legal system under which the large majority of Malagasy not qualifying for French citizenship were governed. It added to the infractions contained in the criminal code another series of offenses—including delays in tax payments, the failure to grow certain crops, and failure to provide compulsory labor—that those possessing the status of French citizenship were not subject to being charged with. Offenses under the *indigénat* were usually tried not by the regular justice system but by the district officers assisted by two notables or Malagasy administrators. Decisions were validated by the governor-general. The actual content of the rules and punishment of the *indigénat* varied, but in Madagascar the system gave more attention to labor control and to censorship than was usual in the other African colonies.

INDONESIA. Indonesia was historically the major customer for Madagascar's exports of cloves, which it uses largely in the manufacture of cigarettes. It stopped buying Malagasy cloves in 1983, however, in part because of increases in its own production, but also because of Malagasy attacks on its position in East Timor and because of the excessive demands of the Malagasy negotiator for a special commission. *See also* SPICES.

INDO-PAKISTANIS. Indian merchants, mainly from the part of the subcontinent that is now Pakistan, began arriving in Madagascar during the nineteenth century, often via East Africa. They usually settled on the west coast of Madagascar, and were known as Karany, or Karana. With time they also established themselves in the Highlands. Today there are an estimated 15,000 people of Indo-Pakistani descent in Madagascar; most are Muslim. Like the Chinese (q.v.), they are engaged primarily in wholesale and retail trade, the collection of crops, and, more recently, in industrial activities and the ownership of plantations. Their activities were the target of the nationalizations of commercial networks carried out by the Ramanantsoa regime (q.v.). Under the Democratic Republic of Madagascar (q.v.) they and their shops were also the target of mob violence. *See also* CONGREGATIONS.

INDRIANJAFY, GEORGES THOMAS. Minister of justice of the Democratic Republic of Madagascar (q.v.) from 1976 to 1982, Indrianjafy had served as director of the Ecole Nationale d'Administration under the First Republic (q.v.) from 1968 to 1972. A native of Mahajanga province, he served in the Ministry of Information during the Ramanantsoa regime (q.v.). He was a founding member of the political bureau of the DRM regime party, AREMA (q.v.). In the early 1980s he was identified with the "right AREMA" faction critical of the socialist policies of the regime and was one of the ministers removed when the faction was purged in 1982. He was retired to a post on the Conseil Suprême de la Révolution (q.v.).

INDUSTRY. Industry accounts for about 15% of Madagascar's GDP and occupies about 4% of the active population. The main centers of industrial production are Antananarivo (q.v.), Antsirabe (q.v.), and Toamasina (q.v.). The main industries process agricultural products and textiles, as well as cement, soap, cigarettes, and beer. Under the Democratic Republic of Madagascar (q.v.), the state nationalized many industries and undertook new industrial activities itself as part of its All-Out Investment Policy (q.v.). Among the sectors affected were oil refining and the textile industry. The industrial sector has suffered from a lack of spare parts and raw materials since the debt crisis (q.v.) of the 1980s, and produces at less than capacity. Plans to repair and revitalize the industrial plant are part of the foreign aid packages that have been put together in recent years. Withdrawal of the state from industrial activity and the increased attraction of foreign private investment are also part of the economic plans. More liberal investment codes were passed in 1987 and in 1990, and in 1990 the government negotiated the creation of an industrial free zone with the Hong Kong firm, Far East Group. *See also* ECONOMY; WORLD BANK.

INSURRECTION OF 1904–1905. One of the last rebellions against the imposition of French colonial rule, this insurrection began in the southeast of Madagascar and quickly spread throughout the south, involving mainly the Tanala (q.v.) and the Bara (q.v.). The insurrectionists attacked both French military posts and Malagasy administrators. The nature of the southern terrain made suppression of the rebellion difficult.

INTERNAL PROTECTORATES. *See* POLITIQUE DES RACES.

INTERNATIONAL MONETARY FUND. The IMF was established in 1945 to stabilize fluctuations in rates of exchange.

Countries belonging to the IMF maintain deposits with it that they can borrow against in times of shortage of foreign exchange. There are also special drawing rights that allow countries to borrow amounts in excess of their reserves with the fund. Since the emergence of the debt crisis (q.v.) in developing countries, the IMF has played a major role in providing funds to Third World countries and in determining responses of developed countries to the crisis. IMF aid is contingent upon restructuring programs that usually include reductions of government expenditure, the liberalization of foreign trade, and the reduction of government intervention in the economy. Madagascar first approached the IMF for aid in 1980, and has made several agreements with the fund since then. *See the Chronology above for additional information. See also* TORONTO PLAN; WORLD BANK.

INVESTMENT CODES. Since independence, Madagascar has had four codes covering foreign investment. The first, passed in 1961 under the First Republic (q.v.), empowered the government to grant a range of advantages and concessions to new investors, including exemption from import and export taxes and protection in the local market. The second, passed in 1973 under the Ramanantsoa regime (q.v.), was more restrictive, and required new investors to include local capital and to move Malagasy into management positions. The third, passed in 1987 by the Democratic Republic of Madagascar (q.v.) under pressure from the International Monetary Fund (q.v.), removed the restrictions of the second, and attempted to attract investment by offering a relaxation of government regulation. The 1987 code aroused some controversy, and was criticized in the Assemblée Nationale Populaire (q.v.) as being too liberal. In spite of this criticism, the continuing debt crisis and pressure from Western donors led to a further liberalization of controls and increase in incentives in the code of 1990.

ISANDRA. Isandra was a kingdom established in the southeastern section of Betsileo (q.v.) territory at the beginning of the eighteenth century, with a capital at Mahazoarivo. It was the most prestigious of the Betsileo kingdoms, and Andriamanalimbetany, who ruled from about 1750 to 1790, dominated the other Betsileo kings. The authority of the ruler within the kingdom was weak, however, and Andriamanalimbetany's successor declared himself a vassal of the approaching Merina Empire (q.v.) in return for Merina support in reinforcing his powers.

ISOTRY. Isotry is one of the poor neighborhoods of the Malagasy capital, Antananarivo (q.v.). Youth of the neighborhood, often organized as ZOAM (q.v.), have played an important role in political events in the capital, particularly the May 1972 Revolution (q.v.).

ISTASSE, COMMANDANT. Istasse was the commanding officer of the Forces Républicaines de Sécurité (q.v.) and chief aide of André Resampa (q.v.), minister of the interior of the First Republic (q.v.), until the May 1972 Revolution (q.v.). He was a participant in the attempted coup plotted by Colonel Bréchard Rajaonarison (q.v.), which precipitated the fall of the Ramanantsoa regime (q.v.) that succeeded the First Republic. Like Rajaonarison, he fled to the Antanaimoro (q.v.) camp after the failure of the coup. He was tried for complicity in the assassination of Colonel Richard Ratsimandrava (q.v.) but, as with the other defendants in the "Trial of the Century" (q.v.), the charges against him were dismissed.

-J-

JAOTOMBO, FERDINAND. A native of Antseranana province, Joatombo was a captain in the army in 1975, and was a member of the Directoire Militaire (q.v.) that took power after the assassination of President Richard Ratsimandrava (q.v.), with the additional post of deputy to the president of the Directoire, Gilles Andriamahazo (q.v.). He supported the claim to office of Didier Ratsiraka (q.v.), and when Ratsiraka took power in June 1975, he became a member of the Conseil Suprême de la Révolution (q.v.). In 1977 he was a founding member of the political bureau of the regime party, AREMA (q.v.).

JARISON, JEAN FRANCOIS (1914–). Jarison was born in Toamasina province and, like many politicians of the First Republic (q.v.), attended the Ecole Le Myre de Vilers (q.v.) and started his career in the colonial administration. He was an early member of the Parti des Deshérités de Madagascar (q.v.). He was president of the provincial assembly of Toamasina province in 1958 and a member from that province of the Assemblée Représentative in Antananarivo. In 1960 he was elected to the National Assembly (q.v.) on Jacques Rabemananjara's (q.v.) Miara-Mirindra (q.v.) list, which later merged with the Parti Social Démocrate (q.v.). Under the First Republic he was minister of labor and social legislation and after 1967 minister of public health and population. He was the father of the wife of Etienne Ratsiraka (q.v.), brother of Didier Ratsiraka, president of the Democratic Republic of Madagascar (q.v.).

JINA (*also* JINY). JINA, or Jeunesse Nationale, was a secret society founded on the east coast of Madagascar in 1943 by a group of nationalists including Monja Jaona (q.v.). Like the other secret society founded at the time, PANAMA (q.v.), JINA advocated the end of the colonial system, if necessary by an armed uprising. It is probable that it was these two secret societies that provided much of the planning and leadership for the Rebellion of 1947 (q.v.).

JOHASY, BARTHELEMY (1927–). Born in the Vangaindrano region of Southern Madagascar, Johasy started as an employee of the colonial administration and, under the First Republic (q.v.), alternated between the territorial administration and economic posts. In 1968 he became minister in charge of the budget, and when the powers of the regime's strongman and minister of the interior, André Resampa (q.v.), were reduced, Johasy, known for his quarrels with Resampa, was named minister attached to the presidency in charge of internal affairs. He was in this post at the time of the outbreak of the May 1972 Revolution (q.v.), and in the absence of President Tsiranana (q.v.) it was Johasy who gave the order for the arrests of student leaders that precipitated the revolution. When the First Republic was overthrown, Johasy retired from politics.

-K-

KABARY. A long, elaborate speech laced with copious proverbs and references to the wisdom of the ancestors, the *kabary* is a standard part of any Malagasy ceremony. *Kabary* given by rulers were a common feature of public life in precolonial Madagascar, and the *kabary* of the founder of the nineteenth century Merina monarchy (q.v.), Andrianampoinimerina (q.v.), are preserved in the *Tantaran'ny Andriana eto Madagasikara* (q.v.). As the Merina monarchy centralized, the royal *kabary* changed in nature from a dialogue between ruler and people to a speech punctuated at intervals by the rhetorical question, "Is it not so, my people?"

KAMISY, COLONEL. Colonel Kamisy was the head of President Ratsiraka's (q.v.) bodyguard, and had testified for the prosecution in the 1983 Officer's Trial (q.v.) of three army and gendarmerie officers accused of plotting to overthrow the president. He was found dead near the gendarmerie headquarters at Antsirabe in May 1984. Gendarmerie involvement in the killing was suspected but never proven, and the incident was symptomatic of the difficult relations between Ratsiraka and the armed forces at the time. *See also* MILITARY.

KARANY. Karany, or Indian, traders were active on the coasts of Madagascar, particularly on the southwest coast, from the beginning of the nineteenth century. They dominated the slave trade that continued on the coast until the French conquest and had by then amassed enough capital to move into other branches of trade. At present, the term "Karany" is used to designate anyone of Indo-Pakistani (q.v.) descent.

KOMITY IRAISAN'NY MPITOLONA (Comité Commun de Lutte, *or* "United Action Committee," *most commonly known by the initials* KIM). During and after the May 1972 Revolution (q.v.), the groups most directly involved in the revolt formed a coordinating committee. With about sixty members, the KIM included delegates from student groups, teachers' organizations, workers, and the *lumpenproletariat* of Antananarivo as represented by the ZOAM (q.v.). The committee claimed that its action in leading the May Revolution gave it a mandate to direct the future development of Malagasy politics and contested the claim of the Ramanantsoa regime (q.v.) to a legitimacy other than that conferred by the revolution. After the coming to power of Ramanantsoa the KIM held weekly study sessions and staged several demonstrations against aspects of his policy, but was unable to prevent the consolidation of a regime that excluded it. In an attempt to expand their support, the members of the committee attempted to establish KIM in provincial cities in preparation for the Congrès National Populaire (q.v.) that was to be held in Antananarivo in September 1972. The significance of the congress was diminished by Ramanantsoa's announcement of a constitutional referendum to be held that October, and the congress itself disintegrated into quarrels between members of the Antananarivo KIM and the more conservative provincial delegates. The committees disintegrated after the congress, but many of their members were later active in the MFM (q.v.).

KOTO, ROBERT. An economist from Toliara, Koto was an early supporter of Didier Ratsiraka (q.v.) and served as a presidential advisor at the beginning of the Democratic Republic of Madagascar (q.v.). In 1977 Ratsiraka named him to the political bureau of the newly established regime party, AREMA (q.v.) and to the Conseil Suprême de la Révolution (q.v.). In 1982 Koto attempted to run against Ratsiraka for president, attracting the support of conservative elements who blamed the socialist orientation of the regime for the country's economic crisis. Koto's candidacy was ruled illegal on the grounds that he was not presented by any of the parties belonging to the Front National pour la Défense de la Révolution (q.v.), and he was removed from his official posts.

KUNG FU. Like the ZOAM (q.v.), the Kung Fu is an organization of youths in Antananarivo. Inspired by the martial arts films of Bruce Lee, these ''self-defense'' societies began to appear in the capital in the late 1970s and gained adherents during the economic crisis of the early 1980s. They were created in part in opposition to the ZOAM and the regime-sponsored groups of ZOAM known as the Tanora Tonga Saina, or TTS (q.v.), but differed from them in having a wider social base of recruitment, in having some adult leaders, and in having branches in provincial cities. They had links with the churches, which at the time were critical of the regime, and with non-AREMA (q.v.) political parties. In the 1982 presidential election campaign they provided the bodyguard for the opposition candidate, Monja Jaona (q.v.).

By 1984 the Kung Fu clubs claimed over 10,000 members, and were said to have secret sections in the armed forces. The regime responded by banning the practice of the martial arts in September 1984, setting off a riot that culminated in the burning of the offices of the Ministry of Youth. In December 1984 groups of Kung Fu attacked the neighborhood bases of the TTS, aided by the population of the neighborhoods who resented the thuglike behavior of that group. It is estimated that between 100 and 250 TTS were killed. The failure of the army and gendarmerie to intervene brought their relations with the regime to a crisis, and it was not until President Ratsiraka (q.v.) had consolidated his hold on the military by moving stronger supporters into key posts and had mended his fences with groups like the churches that he was able to move against the Kung Fu. On July 31, 1985, the army and gendarmerie attacked Kung Fu strongholds in Antananarivo and provincial cities, killing several hundred, including their leader, Pierre Mizael Rakotoarijaona.

Two hundred forty-five members were arrested and were brought to trial in March 1989. Twenty-eight were given sentences ranging from two years in prison (considered to have already been served during their thirty-month imprisonment) to two years suspended. The others were acquitted. Although the groups themselves are still illegal, there are still active Kung Fu sections, particularly in the capital.

-L-

LABORDE, JEAN (1805–1878). Laborde was a Gascon sailor, shipwrecked on the east coast of Madagascar in 1831. He made his way to the court of the Merina monarchy (q.v.) at Antananarivo, where he was presented to Queen Ranavalona I (q.v.). Laborde established himself in Madagascar, marrying Emilie Roux, the daughter of Sylvain Roux, a former agent of the Compagnie des Indes Orientales (q.v.) in Madagascar. He was soon given the task of developing the Merina economy, in spite of Ranavalona's suspicion of the type of Westernization represented by the missionaries. Using conscript labor, he established a factory complex at Mantasoa, where textiles, paper, sugar, weapons, and other commodities were produced. He also experimented with new plants and with livestock breeding. Laborde built a new royal palace, and was given responsibility for the education of the heir to the throne, Prince Rakoto, later Radama II (q.v.). In 1857 he was implicated in a plot to remove the queen from the throne to hasten the prince's succession, and expelled. After his departure the laborers at the Mantasoa complex rose up and destroyed the establishment, and it was abandoned. Laborde spent the years from 1857 to 1861 in exile in Réunion (q.v.) but returned after Ranavalona's death. He continued his economic activities and served as French consul from 1862 to 1878. After his death, the disposition of his property in Madagascar, which he left to two nephews, was an important source of discard between the French and Merina governments. *See also* LABORDE LEGACY.

LABORDE LEGACY. When Jean Laborde (q.v.) died in 1878, he left his estates in Madagascar to two nephews, who laid claim to the property according to the terms of the Franco-Merina Treaty of 1868, which the French interpreted as allowing them to acquire property in Madagascar. The government of the

Merina Empire (q.v.) under Prime Minister Rainilaiarivony (q.v.) maintained that foreigners could not own land in Madagascar, but could only have a lifetime interest in it. The French government took up the cause of the Laborde heirs, in order to establish the principle of the possibility of acquiring property in Madagascar. The issue was further treated in the Code of 305 Articles (q.v.), promulgated by the Merina government in 1881, which explicitly banned the sale of land to foreigners. The French protested, and the issues raised by the Laborde legacy were one of the causes of the Franco-Malagasy War of 1883–1885 (q.v.).

LAHIFOTY. *See* ANDRIANDAHIFOTY.

LAHITAFIKA. Lahitafika was the son of Ramieba, king of the Bara-Be (q.v.). When Ihosy (q.v.), the most important town in Bara territory, was occupied by the French in January 1897, relations between the newcomers and the two Bara leaders were at first uneventful. In March, however, the French captured Ramieba, and began building roads, establishing other settlements, and trying to collect taxes. A series of uprisings followed. Lahitafika was charged with organizing them and was executed, but Ramieba was able to escape from detention.

LAKATONIANJA. Lakatonianja is a rock shelter in northern Madagascar near Antseranana (q.v.). It contains several archaeological sites, the earliest of which has been radiocarbon dated to about A.D. 707. Later sites, dating from about the twelfth century, contain ceramics from the Middle East, suggesting that Lakatonianja was part of the Islamic trading network that operated along the coast of Madagascar. *See also* ARABS; VOHEMAR.

LALAINGINA. Lalaingina was an important Betsileo (q.v.) kingdom that developed at the end of the seventeenth century, with a capital at Mitonga. The economy of the kingdom rested on agriculture and on trading slaves for firearms with the Sakalava (q.v.) to the west. In 1805 the ruler of the kingdom, Raindritsara, was killed in battle, and the kingdom was divided among his sons. This division weakened the kingdom, and it was incorporated into the Merina Empire (q.v.) in 1815.

LAMBERT, JOSEPH. Joseph Lambert was a French trader operating in Antananarivo in the last years of the reign of Ranavalona I (q.v.). With his countryman Jean Laborde (q.v.) he formed part of the circle of the heir to the throne, later Radama II (q.v.). In 1855 Radama granted Lambert a charter for the development of the island, later called the Lambert Charter (q.v.), to come into effect when Radama succeeded to the throne. In 1857 Lambert participated in a plot to overthrow Ranavalona and replace her with Radama, and was exiled when it was discovered. Lambert returned to the island on Ranavalona's death, and served as Radama's ambassador to Paris and London. When his charter was revoked by the succeeding government of Rasoherina (q.v.), Lambert demanded compensation and was backed by the French government. He received an indemnity of 1 million francs for himself and his company in 1865.

LAMBERT CHARTER. The Lambert Charter was signed in 1855 between Joseph Lambert (q.v.) and the then Prince Rakoto, later Radama II (q.v.). The charter, which was to take effect after the prince succeeded to the throne on the death of his mother, Queen Ranavalona I (q.v.), gave Lambert and his associates concessions of land and mineral rights in Madagascar, the right to undertake public works, and the right to mint the currency of the Merina Empire (q.v.), in return for 10% of the profits from the undertakings. Alienation of land to foreigners was against the practice of the Merina state, and this and other provisions of the charter offended both the patriotism and economic interest of the ruling oligarchy. The charter contributed to the sense of grievance against Radama II that led to his assassination in 1863. The Lambert Charter was denounced by the new government of Queen Rasoherina (q.v.), and on payment of an indemnity to the French government, the Merina government received the original copies of the charter, which were burned in a public ceremony in 1865.

LAND REFORM. Although there is some inequality of land holdings in Madagascar, and sharecropping (q.v.) is common in several areas, the land reform policy undertaken by the Democratic Republic of Madagascar (q.v.) after 1975 set as one of its goals the reduction of the number of small holdings. As a result, the reform concentrated on the expropriation of large holdings owned by foreign planters and companies, often unexploited, rather than on redistribution of land among Malagasy. The first expropriations occurred in 1974 under the Ramanantsoa regime (q.v.) and concerned about 28,000 hectares of holdings over 100 hectares in size in the Mananjary district of Fianarantsoa province. These same plantations had been targets of the Rebellion of 1947 (q.v.). Subsequent expropriations, particularly in the region around Lake Alaotra (q.v.) and the Sakay (q.v.) totaled nearly 100,000 hectares. In general the land has been handed over to cooperatives (q.v.) or exploited as state farms rather than redistributed to individual cultivators.

LAROCHE, HIPPOLYTE (1848–1914). Laroche was the first French resident-general assigned to Madagascar after the 1895 French conquest of the island. A career administrator with experience in Algeria, he arrived in January 1896 with the task of administering the 1895 protectorate in a manner that would leave the internal administration of the Merina Empire (q.v.) intact. The March Revolt of the Menalamba (q.v.), however, precipitated a crisis in French control that was exacerbated by quarrels between Laroche and the general in charge of French forces in Madagascar, Voyron. In July the French minister of colonies, André Lebon, arranged the passage of a law ending the protectorate and replacing it with colonial status. He also removed Laroche and replaced him with General Joseph Gallieni (q.v.), to whom he gave both civil and military authority. Laroche's last act as resident was the abolition of slavery. He returned to France and entered politics. *See also* ANNEXATION LAW.

LASTELLE, NAPOLEON DE (1802–1856). De Lastelle was a French trader established in the Mascarenes (q.v.). Beginning in 1829 he handled most of Madagascar's trade with the outside world and undertook some activities on the island itself, including the development of coffee and cocoa plantations. He collaborated with Jean Laborde (q.v.), whom he had presented to Queen Ranavalona I (q.v.). His activities ceased when Malagasy ports were closed to trade after the 1845 Anglo-French bombardment of Toamasina, but he continued to live in Toamasina where he was connected with the Fiche family who controlled the city. *See also* RENE, JEAN.

LECHAT, EUGENE. A French citizen and administrator, Lechat was one of the founders of the Parti Social Démocrate (q.v.) of the First Republic (q.v.). He was director of regional schools from 1951 to 1957 (many early members of the PSD were recruited from the state teaching staff) and member of the Assemblée Representative from Fianarantsoa province after 1957. Under the First Republic he adopted Malagasy citizenship and was successively minister of public works and posts and telecommunications and minister of equipment and communications.

LEGENTILHOMME, PAUL. Legentilhomme was a general with the Free French (q.v.) forces. He became governor of Madagascar after the British handed control of the island back to the French in January 1943. He left the island in May. *See also* BRITISH INVASION.

LE MYRE DE VILERS, CHARLES-MARIE. Le Myre de Vilers was the first French resident in Antananarivo under the terms of the 1885 treaty establishing the French protectorate (q.v.) over the Merina Empire (q.v.). He had served in the French navy, as a prefect in France, and in the administration in Algeria and Cochin China. As resident, he quarreled with the Merina prime minister, Rainilaiarivony (q.v.), over the terms of the protectorate, and in particular over whether giving France control over the empire's "external relations" meant that foreign consuls within Madagascar were also accredited to the resident rather than to the Merina court. He left Madagascar in 1896 to become a deputy from Cochin China in the French National Assembly, where he joined the Third Republic's (q.v.) colonial lobby. In 1894 he returned to

Antananarivo to present the French demands for an extension of their powers under the protectorate. He presented Rainilaiarivony with an ultimatum on October 25, which the latter refused. Le Myre de Vilers left Antananarivo on October 27 and sent word of the refusal to Paris where, on November 16, the National Assembly voted the funds necessary for the invasion of Madagascar. In 1896 Le Myre de Vilers was the rapporteur of the commission of the National Assembly that recommended passage of the Annexation Law of 1896 (q.v.).

LE VACHER DE LA CASE (d. 1671). Le Vacher de la Case joined the French settlement at Fort-Dauphin (q.v.) in 1656. After quarrels with the commander of the Fort-Dauphin garrison, the Comte de Champmargou, he fled inland, and married the daughter of a Malagasy ruler, who inherited her father's position on his death. De la Case traveled widely in the southern part of the island and made alliances with many local groups. In spite of his quarrels with the settlement at Fort-Dauphin, he continued to supply it with food and to defend it when necessary. His death in 1671 was a contributing factor to the ultimate destruction of the settlement.

LIBYA. Closer relations with Libya were part of the post-1972 radicalization of Malagasy foreign policy. Libya has furnished some aid to Madagascar, including support for the extension of Islamic studies at the University of Madagascar and a personal gift of more than one million dollars to President Ratsiraka (q.v.). Madagascar supported the Libyans in the debates in the Organization of African Unity (q.v.) over the location of the 1982 summit. Libyan aid has not, however, been a major factor in Madagascar's attempts to resolve its debt crisis.

LIGUE DE DEFENSE DES INTERETS FRANCO-MALGACHES. The League for the Defense of Franco-Malagasy Interests was formed by Madagascar's settler (q.v.) community in 1946 in response to the rise in nationalist organizations, like the Mouvement Démocratique de la Rénovation Malgache (q.v.), and in reaction against what the settlers saw as the weakness displayed by the colonial administration in dealing with the movements. It was one of several settler pressure groups. *See also* PRESENCE FRANCAISE.

LIGUE FRANCAISE POUR L'ACCESSION DES INDIGENES DE MADAGASCAR AUX DROITS DES CITOYENS FRANCAIS. This organization was founded in Paris in 1920 by the nationalist leader Jean Ralaimongo (q.v.) with the patronage of Anatole France and André Gide. It attempted to lighten the restrictions imposed by the regime of the *indigénat* (q.v.).

LOI-CADRE. The Loi-Cadre was passed by the French legislature in June 1956, and its provisions were carried out in 1957. It was designed to liberalize the political structures of France's African colonies, including Madagascar, and introduced universal adult suffrage, abolished the two-college system (q.v.), and created a government council with seven elected members and four to five appointed members that was to have some of the executive powers of a cabinet. Special provisions applied to Madagascar included the strengthening of the powers of the provincial level of government in response to the fears of the colonial administration and some Malagasy political figures that increasing the autonomy of the central political system would lead to Merina (q.v.) dominance of the system. A sixth province, Diégo-Suarez (now Antseranana, q.v.), was also created. The division was still less than that applied to French East and West Africa, however. After the Loi-Cadre, at the provincial level a French chef de province worked with a council and an assembly. The central government consisted of the French high commissioner (formerly governor-general), the government council, with a vice president who had some of the powers of a prime minister, and an assembly, whose members were chosen by the provincial assemblies. The Loi-Cadre disappointed nationalist groups because it did not abrogate the law of annexation and because there was no provision for amnesty for the prisoners of the 1947 rebellion. The first (and only) Loi-Cadre elections were held in March 1957, and in them Philibert Tsiranana (q.v.), future president of the First Republic (q.v.), became vice president of the government council.

LOI-CADRE GOVERNMENT COUNCIL. This council was established by the Loi-Cadre (q.v.) of 1956. Composed of seven members elected from the assembly, and four to five appointed by the French high commissioner, it was intended to assume some of the executive powers formerly held by the French governor-general, who became a high commissioner under the law. The high commissioner served as president of the council. There was only one Loi-Cadre Government Council, chosen in 1957. Its elected members included Philibert Tsiranana (q.v.) as vice president, and Gervais Randrianasolo, Paul Longuet, Alfred Ramangasoavina (q.v.), Justin Bezara (q.v.), Philippe Raondry, and Alexis Bezaka (q.v.). The work of the council was overtaken by events, as Madagascar gained autonomy in the French Community (q.v.) in 1958, and the then independence in 1960.

LOMBARDO, RAYMOND (1914–). A French citizen born in Madgascar, Lombardo was active in the nationalist movement before and after the Second World War. He edited a bilingual newspaper, *Fraternité-Fihavanana,* that was critical of the administration and, with Pierre Boiteau (q.v.), attempted to found a Group d'Etudes Communistes (q.v.) in Antananarivo in 1946. He served as a Communist party member of the Consultative Assembly of the French Union in 1947. He was accused of complicity in the Rebellion of 1947 (q.v.), and the assembly lifted his parliamentary immunity on the condition that he be tried in France.

LONDON CLUB. The ''London Club'' is comprised of the private banks making loans to Third World countries. In the case of Madagascar, the club includes seventy-eight creditor banks, dominated by French and American banks, and has a managing committee cochaired by the Chase Manhattan Bank and the Banque Nationale de Paris. In August 1987 the London Club agreed to reduce the amount of Malagasy loans due between 1987 and 1992 from $136.6 million to $77.2 million, with the remainder due between 1992 and 1996. It also examined the possibility of converting some of the debt into local investments. *See also* DEBT CRISIS; TORONTO PLAN.

LONDON MISSIONARY SOCIETY. The LMS was founded in London in 1795 as the Missionary Society, and changed its name to the London Missionary Society in 1818. It was composed mainly of Congregationalists, with some members from the evangelical wing of the Church of England. The first LMS missionaries went to Tahiti, Guyana, Cape Province, and India. In 1815 it was encouraged by the governor of Mauritius (q.v.), Sir Robert Farquhar (q.v.), to send missionaries to the Merina monarchy (q.v.) with whose king, Radama I (q.v.), Farquhar was negotiating a treaty of friendship. The first missionaries, David Jones and Thomas Bevan, arrived with their families at Toamasina in 1818. All fell ill with malaria, and only Jones survived. He returned to Mauritius, but returned with James Hastie, whom Farquhar had engaged to train the Merina army, in 1820, and proceeded to the Merina capital, Antananarivo. Other missionaries, notably James Cameron (q.v.) and William Ellis (q.v.), followed. In the following years LMS missionaries were instrumental in transcribing the Malagasy language into Latin characters, beginning an education system, and undertaking economic activities which included a building program in Antananarivo. The missionaries were forbidden to proselytize, but managed to attract adherents.

In 1835 Queen Ranavalona I (q.v.) expelled the missionaries as part of her strategy of returning to Malagasy traditions, but Malagasy Christians maintained a clandestine church organization. Missionaries began coming back with the relaxation of Ranavalona's rule in the late 1850s and returned in force after her death in 1861. Other denominations, including the Catholic church (q.v.), arrived, but the LMS kept the advantage of its earlier establishment and close connections with the Merina monarchy (q.v.). At times these connections were a source of tension, since it was the strategy of the Merina state under Prime Minister Rainilaiarivony (q.v.) after the conversion of the queen and prime minister in 1869 to use the church as a state religion and its schools as a means of compulsory recruitment to the administration. The different times of arrival and different strategies of operation of the Christian missions meant that the

LMS strength was concentrated in the Highlands (q.v.) of Madagascar, and often in the upper ranks of society.

After the French conquest of 1895, the LMS and its adherents were suspected of pro-British and nationalist sentiment, and their churches and educational network came under attack. The French Evangelical church (q.v.) arrived to take up some of the work that had been done by the LMS; however, denominations derived from the London Missionary Society churches remain the largest of the Malagasy Protestant (q.v.) denominations.

LUMIERE. Published in Fianarantsoa (q.v.) by the Catholic church (q.v.) from 1935 to 1975. *Lumière* was for many years Madagascar's most important journal of political comment. During the First Republic (q.v.) it took a stance increasingly critical of the regime and was one of the first newspapers to attack the regime for the repression of the Peasant Rebellion of 1971 (q.v.). In subsequent regimes it was more difficult to maintain this posture, and the imposition of a more rigorous system of censorship (q.v.) under the Democratic Republic of Madagascar (q.v.) led to the closure of the newspaper. Its tradition of critical comment has been carried on by *Lakroan'i Madagasikara* under Rémi Ralaibera (q.v.).

LYAUTEY, LOUIS-HUBERT (1854–1934). A career army officer, Lyautey served as the second-in-command to General Gallieni (q.v.) in the assertion of French control in Madagascar, with special responsibility for southern Madagascar. From his base in Fianarantsoa (q.v.) he used what he called the *tache d'huile,* or "oil-spot," policy, developed earlier in his service in Indochina. It consisted of establishing a series of outposts from which French control would then spread to the surrounding countryside. Among the outposts used for this purpose were Ambalavao (q.v.) and Ihosy (q.v.).

-M-

MADAGASCAR. The origin of the name of Madagascar, like the origin of the Malagasy, is mysterious. In his *Travels,* Marco

Polo refers to "Madeigascar" or "Mogelasio." Early geographers located the "island of Madagascar" north of Zanzibar, and it is now considered probable that Marco Polo was in fact referring to Mogadiscio (Magadishu) on the African coast. After the Portuguese discovery of the island in 1500, however, it was called Madagascar, as well as by the Portuguese-given name of Saint Lawrence's Island (q.v.).

MADAGASCAR MATIN. *Madagascar Matin* is Madagascar's largest circulation newspaper, and the successor to the *Courrier de Madagascar* (q.v.), whose plant was burned at the time of the May 1972 Revolution (q.v.). Although it is French-owned like its predecessor, it publishes articles in both French and Malagasy. It is generally favorable to the regime but has still been subject to censorship (q.v.) from time to time.

MADAGASIKARA OTRONIN'Y MALAGASY. *See* MONIMA.

MAHAJANGA (17°0′S, 47°0′E). The most important port on the west coast of Madagascar, Mahajanga was officially founded in 1745, when the capital of the Boina (q.v.) kingdom was moved there. It had, in fact, served as a port for years before. Throughout the eighteenth century, it was the major port for the slave trade (q.v.) with the Arabs (q.v.). It was captured by the troops of the expanding Merina Empire (q.v.) in 1824, and by invading French forces in 1895. It is still Madagascar's second most important port, after Toamasina (q.v.) and has the most diverse population of Madagascar's provincial capitals, with large numbers of Indo-Pakistanis (q.v.) and, until the attacks of 1976, many Comorians (q.v.). The development of the harbor has been hampered by silting and the lack of deep-water facilities.

MAHAJANGA PROVINCE. Mahajanga province covers the northwest of Madagascar. Its main ethnic groups are the Sakalava (q.v.) and the Tsimihety (q.v.), but there is also considerable immigration from other parts of Madagascar. The economy rests on agriculture and stock raising, with large-scale cotton production on the lower Mangoky river. *See also* BAS-MONGOKY.

MAHY, FRANCOIS DE. A deputy from Réunion (q.v.) in the National Assembly of the French Third Republic, De Mahy was one of a group of overseas deputies (q.v.) who were an important part of the colonial lobby of the republic. De Mahy himself had credentials as a staunch republican and held office both in the National Assembly itself and in successive governments of the Third Republic. In 1883 he was minister of the navy and colonies in the monthlong Fallières cabinet, and profited from the occasion to assert a French protectorate over the northwest of Madagascar. His action was only partly supported by the following government. The Franco-Malagasy War of 1883 (q.v.) led to the imposition of the protectorate (q.v.) of 1885, which De Mahy criticized as not giving France sufficient powers in Madagascar. De Mahy supported the 1895 invasion of the island, and was president of the commission of the National Assembly that recommended passage of the Annexation Law of 1896 (q.v.), which made Madagascar a French colony.

MAINTY. A slave caste. *See also* SLAVERY.

MAJUNGA. *See* MAHAJANGA.

MALGACHIZATION. After independence in 1960, the meaning of Malgachization was limited to the (slow) movement of Malagasy into the posts in the military and administration still held by the French. By the time of the May 1972 Revolution (q.v.) the term had acquired a broader meaning, including the establishment of national control over the economy, and the reform of the educational system, particularly at the secondary and postsecondary level, to provide an education in Malagasy that reflected the national culture.

Under the Ramanantsoa regime (q.v.) policies pursued in the name of Malgachization included the establishment of state trading companies, the drafting of an investment code requiring foreign-owned companies to move Malagasy into management and shareholding positions, and the renegotiation of the Cooperation Agreements (q.v.) with France. In education, Malgachization was more controversial. Although Malagasy is spoken throughout the island, there are many dialects, and written Malagasy uses the Merina (q.v.) dialect. When the government proposed to substitute Malagasy for French as the language of secondary education in 1973, anti-Merina riots broke out in several coastal cities, leading to some deaths and to an exodus of Merina from the provinces. Although the regime denounced the riots as the work of the recently ousted Parti Social Démocrate (q.v.), it also established a commission to try to establish a common Malagasy language based on all the dialects.

The introduction of Malagasy at the secondary level also created problems of transition at the university level, where some education continued to be conducted in French. As part of the post-1980 rapprochement with France, the teaching of French at the secondary level has been increased, and the number of professors from France has also increased.

Malgachization also implied a modification of curriculum and research. *The results in the area of history can be seen in the Bibliography of this volume.* Since 1972 there has been a great increase to the amount of writing about Madagascar done by Malagasy and an attempt to do justice to the history of regions outside the Highlands.

MAMPILA, JAONA (d. 1979). A native of Toliara and a lieutenant colonel in the gendarmerie, Mampila served as chief of the province of Mahajanga during the Ramanantsoa regime (q.v.). He was named commander in chief of the gendarmerie by Richard Ratsimandrava (q.v.) in February 1975, and held the post until Didier Ratsiraka (q.v.) took power in June of that year. He served as minister of the interior in the first Ratsiraka government and later as minister of defense. A close associate of the president, he was named to the Conseil Suprême de la Revolution (q.v.) in 1976.

MANGOKY. *See* BAS-MANGOKY.

MANIOC. *See* AMERICAN CROPS.

MANJAKAMIADANA. Manjakamiadana is the royal palace of the Merina (q.v.) monarchy. It consists of a wooden building, constructed for Queen Ranavalona I (q.v.) under the supervision of Jean Laborde (q.v.), and an outer stone shell, built by James Cameron (q.v.) for Ranavalona II (q.v.). It is now a museum.

MANJAKAVAHOAKA. *See* UNION DES SOCIAUX DEMOCRATES DE MADAGASCAR.

MANTASOA. Sixty kilometers east of Antananarivo, Mantasoa was the site of a major industrial complex constructed by Jean Laborde (q.v.) during the Merina Empire (q.v.), taking advantage of the presence of iron deposits and the availability of water and wood. After Laborde was exiled to Réunion following an attempted coup against Ranavalona I (q.v.), the conscript laborers who had built and run the installation destroyed it. Much of the complex is now covered by an artificial lake.

MARIANO, LUIS. Mariano was a Portuguese Jesuit based in Mozambique charged with exploring the possibility of missionary activity on the west coast of Madagascar. He made trips to the coast, and especially to Boina Bay in 1614, 1616, and 1619, and visited the northwest in 1630. Although he made no converts, his accounts of his visits provide extensive information about Malagasy societies and political units of the area. Exploring what is now Sakalava (q.v.) territory, he reported a society of villages based on agriculture and the raising of goats and cattle.

MARO, RAYMOND (d. 1979). Maro, from the province of Antseranana, was a close associate of President Didier Ratsiraka (q.v.) during the early years of the Democratic Republic of Madagascar (q.v.). He was named to the Conseil Suprême de la Révolution (q.v.) when it was expanded to include civilians in 1976, and was a founding member of the political bureau of the regime party, AREMA (q.v.). He served as an AREMA representative on the Front National pour la Defense de la Révolution. Formerly active in the

André Resampa (q.v.) wing of the Parti Social Démocrate (q.v.), he was one of the links between the Ratsiraka regime and influential figures from the First Republic (q.v.).

MAROSERANA (*also* Maroseranana). The Maroserana dynasty is the founding dynasty of the Sakalava (q.v.) kingdoms. Members founded the first important kingdom, that of Menabe (q.v.), in the sixteenth century, and spread northward, usually as losers in dynastic quarrels led their followers to found a new kingdom. The status of ruler still exists in many contemporary Sakalava societies, and ceremonies centered around *dady* (the remains of former kings) are still celebrated.

MARSON, MAX VALERIEN. A captain in the gendarmerie in 1975, Marson was a representative from Fianarantsoa province in the Directoire Militaire (q.v.) that took power in 1975 after the assassination of Richard Ratsimandrava (q.v.). After the DM had chosen Didier Ratsiraka (q.v.) as president, Marson became a founding member of the new regime's central party, AREMA (q.v.), and a member of the Conseil Suprême de la Révolution (q.v.).

MASCARENES. The Mascarene Islands include Réunion (q.v.) and Mauritius (q.v.). By the eighteenth century, as their plantation economy developed and required slaves and food, they became important trading partners of Madagascar. The islands were originally under French control, but after the Napoleonic Wars, the British took over Mauritius and the Seychelles, leaving the French with Réunion. Throughout the nineteenth century, contacts continued to be important. It was the British governor of Mauritius, Sir Robert Farquhar (q.v.), who opened official contacts with the Merina (q.v.) monarchy in 1815, while Réunionese traders and some settlers were active on the east coast around Toamasina (q.v.) even earlier. At the end of the nineteenth century, deputies from Réunion were an important part of the pro-colonial lobby in France, and it was a Réunionese deputy serving as minister of the navy, De Mahy (q.v.), who gave the orders that started the Franco-Malagasy War of 1883–1885 (q.v.).

On May 16 the regime gave in to the demand for the return of the prisoners, but by then the demonstrators, whose number grew each day, were demanding the ouster of President Tsiranana and the establishment of a military regime. Tsiranana appealed for help to the French, who had 4,000 paratroopers stationed at Ivato airport, but on May 17 the French embassy announced that its troops would be used only to defend French lives and property. On the same day the commander of the gendarmerie, Richard Ratsimandrava (q.v.), informed Tsiranana that the Malagasy armed forces were no longer willing to defend the regime. On May 18 the commanding general of the armed forces, Gabriel Ramanantsoa, announced that Tsiranana had handed power over to him.

The May Revolution was regarded as a triumph of Malagasy nationalism, a ''Second Independence'' that, more than the formal independence of 1960, constituted a fulfillment of the hopes of the Rebellion of 1947 (q.v.). The hopes of the more radical participants in the revolution for a more complete change in Malagasy politics and society were not fulfilled, however. *See also* KOMITY IRAISN'NY MPITOLONA.

MAYEUR, NICHOLAS (1747–1809). Born in France, Mayeur moved with his family to the Ile de France (Mauritius, q.v.) in 1750, and by 1763 was living on the east coast of Madagascar and working as an interpreter for the Compagnie des Indes Orientales (q.v.). Mayeur traveled extensively throughout Madagascar, visiting Fort-Dauphin (q.v.), the coast, and the region around Diégo-Suarez (q.v.). He was also involved in Count Benyowski's (q.v.) attempt to establish an ''empire'' on the east coast. Mayeur was the first European to see the Merina (q.v.) capital, Antananarivo (q.v.), which he visited in 1776. In 1788 Mayeur returned to the Ile de France, where he remained except for one last visit to Madagascar, 1796–1797.

MENABE. The Menabe is the northern region of Tanala (q.v.) territory. In the nineteenth century one of the area clans, the Zafiakotry, cooperated with the expanding Merina Empire (q.v.) to establish themselves as rulers over the others with a capital at Ambohimanga du Sud. They were not, however, able to maintain this position.

MENALAMBA. The revolt of the Menalamba, or ''Red Shawls,'' is considered to have begun with the killings of the Johnson family of Quaker missionaries on November 2, 1895. The revolt itself was a complicated affair involving many different groups, and was directed simultaneously against the French invaders, who had captured Antananarivo at the beginning of October of that year, against the corruption and abandonment of traditional customs of the Merina empire (q.v.), held by the rebels to be responsible for the loss of Antananarivo, and against those considered responsible for the Merina empire's decline, including officials of the Merina government, Malagasy Christians, and European missionaries. The rebels included deserters from the Merina army and *fahavalo* (q.v.) as well as local dignitaries and members of the Merina administration.

Groups called Menalamba existed in many areas of Imerina, usually on its borders, and were not always well coordinated either in terms of action or of goals. They revived many traditional practices, including use of the royal talismans, or *sampy* (q.v.), and claimed to be acting in the name of and on orders from Queen Ranavalona III (q.v.). On the other hand, they also attacked the practices and personnel of the queen's government, and some of the groups established rival monarchs. The uprising lasted until 1898, and it is estimated that it may have involved as many as 300,000 people out of a population of one million, and that between 50,000 and 100,000 died either from the uprising or from famine and disease resulting from the disruption it caused.

The most immediate result of the uprising was the end of the Merina (q.v.) monarchy. An Annexation Law transforming Madagascar from a protectorate to a colony was passed on August 6, 1896, and General Joseph Gallieni (q.v.) was sent to Antananarivo to put down the uprising. On his arrival he arrested two councillors of the queen, a commoner and minister of the interior from the powerful Tsimiamboholahy (q.v.) clan, Rainiandriamampandry, and an uncle of the queen, Prince Ratsimamanga, and had them put to death for complicity in the uprising, a complicity that was never proven and that is most improbable. In February 1897 the monarchy itself was abolished, and the queen and several members of her family and entourage were sent into exile.

The Menalamba rising itself came to an end at the end of 1898, but it was not the last of the uprisings against the imposition of colonial rule. Later, its example was cited by the organizers of the Rebellion of 1947 (q.v.). *See also* RABEZAVANA; RABOZAKA.

MERINA. Madagascar's largest ethnic group, with an estimated population of 1,933,000 in 1974, the Merina inhabit the central Highlands (q.v.) of Madagascar and are centered on the capital, Antananarivo (q.v.). The time of their arrival in Madagascar and the time and means by which they arrived and established themselves in the center of the island are not known, although Merina traditions state that upon their arrival in the Highlands they conquered and absorbed a group of previous inhabitants called the Vazimba (q.v.). By the sixteenth and seventeenth centuries, kingdoms had begun to appear and the subsequent history of the Merina is one of coalescing and splitting units of social organization until the final unification of the kingdoms under Andrianampoinimerina (q.v.) in the late eighteenth century. Under Andrianampoinimerina's successors the Merina monarchy extended its power to other parts of Madagascar, establishing the Merina Empire (q.v.). Through the activities of the London Missionary Society (q.v.), an educational system was established, and by the time of the French conquest in 1895, through conquest, education, and trade, the Merina were the dominant group in the island. They were, and to some degree still are, to be found throughout the island as administrators, traders and shopkeepers, teachers, and pastors.

The French made some attempts to reduce this domination, but because they relied extensively on Merina personnel at the lower levels of the colonial administration, and because they concentrated educational facilities in the Antananarivo, which became the colonial capital, the domination continued to be important. After the Second World War, the French tried to create an elite drawn from non-Merina groups, commonly referred to as Côtiers (q.v.), as a counterweight to the more nationalistic Merina. It was this elite, under Philibert Tsiranana (q.v.), that formed the nucleus of the ruling group of the First Republic (q.v.). Although developments since independence have greatly reduced the disparities between the Merina and the other groups, the province of Antananarivo still has the advantage in educational, economic, and communications infrastructure, and mutual feelings of distrust between the Merina and other groups remain an element of Malagasy politics.

MERINA EMPIRE. The extension of the area controlled by the Merina (q.v.) monarchy beyond the boundaries of the home territory of Imerina began after the 1810 with the expeditions of the successor of Andrianampoinimerina (q.v.), Radama I (q.v.). Radama extended the territory controlled by the Merina east to the port of Toamasina, south into Betsileo (q.v.) territory, and west into the territory of the Sakalava (q.v.). His conquests were continued by his successors, and by the late nineteenth century the Merina Empire occupied about two-thirds of Madagascar, including the territory to the south of Imerina as far as Ambalavao (q.v.), most of the central and southern east coast, the port of Mahajanga (q.v.), and a corridor of land through Sakalava territory to the port. It also had outposts at Toliara (q.v.) and Fort-Dauphin (q.v.) that were usually reached by water.

The empire was governed by a variety of systems. Imerina was directly ruled by the administration under the monarch and prime minister, and Betsileo territory was also directly controlled by the administration, although with a different set of laws. The other parts of the empire were governed through local rulers, under the supervision of Merina civil-military governors. Several of the groups incorporated in the empire had violently resisted conquest by the Merina armies, and when internal difficulties and external pressures, which became acute after the Franco-Malagasy War of 1883–1885 (q.v.), loosened the grip of the imperial forces, many areas moved out of imperial control and into active revolt. The empire was also plagued in its later years by the development of *efitra,* territories on its outside fringes that were occupied by escaped slaves, fugitives from conscription and forced labor, and escaped convicts. The administration of the empire was not able to reassert control over these areas, another sign of its weakening prior to the French conquest of 1895.

The existence of the Merina Empire has influenced modern politics in Madagascar. Fears of a reassertion of Merina dominance over what are called the Côtiers (q.v.) split the nationalist movement, colored the composition of the First Republic (q.v.), and can still reappear.

MERLIN, MARTIAL (1860–1935). Merlin was a career colonial official who served as governor-general of French Equatorial Africa in 1908, and succeeded Garbit (q.v.) as governor-general of Madagascar in September 1917. During his stay in Madagascar he continued mobilization for the war effort, but restricted the ''voluntary'' recruitment of the previous administration and made some effort to improve local rice supplies. In response to settler pressure for more representation in the decisions of the colonial administration, he set up the practice of regular meetings of the presidents of the island's chambers of commerce. In January 1918 Merlin left Madagascar to become governor-general of French West Africa.

MFM (Mpitolona ho amin'ny Fanjakan'ny Madinika, *or* ''Party for Proletarian Power''). The MFM was founded in 1972 by Manandafy Rakotonirina (q.v.) and other radical participants in the May 1972 Revolution (q.v.). Inspired equally by the experience of its organizers as opposition to the First Republic (q.v.) and by the radical ideas of the day, the party had an organization that was partly overt and partly clandestine. Its doctrine at first argued that a violent revolution was a necessary prelude to the establishment of an egalitarian socialist state, a position that it formally abandoned in 1980. The party led a precarious existence under the Ramanantsoa regime (q.v.), which it saw as having prevented the full development of the May revolution. In 1973 it attempted to hold a demonstration commemorating that revolution, but the demonstration was banned and several of the party's leaders were arrested. The MFM also had reservations about the practicality and sincerity of the *fokonolona* reform (q.v.) of Colonel Richard Ratsimandrava (q.v.). Although it formed part of the Left Front that supported Didier Ratsiraka (q.v.) after the assassination of Ratsimandrava, the party's leadership was not fully convinced of the revolutionary potential of the regime, and it spent some time in opposition, even being banned for a period in 1976, before joining the Front National pour la Défense de la Révolution (q.v.) in 1977.

The party's relationship with the Ratsiraka regime continued to be ambiguous. The MFM supported Ratsiraka against more conservative groups but maintained its semiclandestine structure and was involved in several acts of opposition to the regime, including attacks on regime officials in Nosy Be and other parts of the north in 1981. It was rumored to have contacts with the Kung Fu (q.v.) groups that threatened the regime at the end of 1984. Although the party supported Ratsiraka's candidacy in the presidential election of 1982, in the spring of 1987 it formed an opposition alliance with two other parties and in the presidential election of March 1989 its leader, Rakotonirina, ran against Ratsiraka.

The party also changed ideological direction in the late 1980s, espousing the adoption of liberal market policies as the solution to Madagascar's economic problems. In October 1990, it changed its name to Militant Party for the Development of Madagascar. The MFM played an active role in the events that led to the downfall of the Ratsiraka regime, as one of the groups founding the Comité des Forces Vives (q.v.). The MFM separated itself from this opposition alliance in July 1991, when its members created a "transitional government" and began occupying government offices, but it continued in opposition to the regime and participated in the power-sharing agreement that arranged the transition to the Third Republic (q.v.). The party was disappointed, however, when Rakotonirina's showing in the presidential election of 1992 was much less than expected. *See also* ALLIANCE DEMOCRATIQUE DE MADAGASCAR; ELECTIONS.

MIARA-MIRINDRA. This list of candidates to the legislative elections of 1960 in Toamasina province was put together by

Jaques Rabemananjara (q.v.) and Alexis Bezaka (q.v.). It ran against an official list of candidates from the Parti Social Démocrate (q.v.) but itself contained many PSD figures. It won 192,000 votes against 85,000 for the PSD, and 25,000 for the AKFM (q.v.). After the election, Rabemananjara was granted a post in the PSD government, and Miara-Mirindra merged with the PSD.

MIGRATIONS. Malagasy oral traditions record extensive individual and collective migrations in premodern times, usually in a westerly and northerly direction from the east coast inland. At present, two types of migration exist. The first involves permanent migration from areas of high population concentration and is composed largely of Merina (q.v.), Betsileo (q.v.), and Tsimihety (q.v.) moving into western Madagascar. The second involves temporary migration (annual or for a limited number of years) by people, usually from the south of the island, in search of work in industry and on plantations. Displacement as far north as Antseranana (q.v.) is not uncommon.

MILITARY. The armed forces of the First Republic (q.v.) had their origin in the transfer of Malagasy personnel serving in the French army. They developed in time into several military and paramilitary organizations. In addition to an army of about 4,000 and a navy and air force of about 500 each, there was a gendarmerie force of about 4,500. These forces were covered by military cooperation agreements with the French government, and at the time of the May 1972 Revolution (q.v.) still had nearly as many French as Malagasy officers. There were two other forces not covered by the cooperation agreements: the Service Civique (q.v.), to which most conscripts were sent, and which was used mainly for rural public works; and the Forces Républicaines de Sécurité (q.v.), attached to the Ministry of the Interior and used as a political police. The army was commanded by General Gabriel Ramanantsoa (q.v.), who had served with distinction in the Second World War and in Indochina, and had two Malagasy colonels, Roland Rabetafika (q.v.) and Bréchard Rajaonarison (q.v.). The gendarmerie, which was directly attached to the president's office, had been commanded since 1969 by a Malagasy, Colonel Richard Ratsimadrava (q.v.).

The composition and role of the armed forces was a source of some tension during the First Republic. The slow rate of Malgachization (q.v.) of the officer corps was a cause of resentment, and the Malagasy government asked for, and received, an increase in the number of French paratroopers stationed at Ivato airport—from 2,000 to 4,000—after the wave of coups in African countries in 1966. The regular army was considered by the regime to be ''too Merina'' (q.v.) and the gendarmerie, recruited from other regions of the island and the lower strata of Merina society, was well enough armed to serve as a counterweight. The Service Civique was resented by the population as a new form of forced labor, and the FRS was resented for its role in breaking up demonstrations. The military played a crucial role in the downfall of the First Republic. The action of the FRS in firing on a student demonstration in Antananarivo turned the demonstration into the May 1972 Revolution, while the refusal of the army and the gendarmerie to defend the regime forced Tsiranana (q.v.) to resign. As the ranking officer, Ramanantsoa became the new head of state.

Divisions among the military were also a major cause of instability during the Ramanantsoa regime (q.v.), and it was an attempted coup by Bréchard Rajaonarison that led to Ramanantsoa's resignation in January 1975. The direct blame for the assassination of his successor, Ratsimandrava, was attributed to men from the FRS. After Ratsimandrava's assassination, a Military Directorate (q.v.) ruled until June 1975, and picked his successor, naval captain Didier Ratsiraka (q.v.). After he took power, Ratsiraka reorganized the armed forces in an attempt to reduce the divisions and maintain his own control over them.

Considered one of the ''five pillars of the revolution,'' the national People's Army of the Democratic Republic of Madagascar (q.v.) grew to over 30,000 and consumed about one-third of the national budget. The largest section was the Development Army, composed of the old Service Civique, the infantry, and the engineering corps. The army, with a special antiriot unit, shared policing duties with the gendarmerie, but also had an extensive economic role. It conducted several agricultural projects, maintained roads, and helped with transportation during the rice harvest. It also ran the national military service, which enrolls over 5,000 female and male conscripts, most of whom are sent as teachers to rural areas. The air force and navy were merged, and the gendarmerie left largely untouched. The most politically significant change was the creation of elite military units with a level of armament above that of the other forces. These included the Intervention Force of former paratroopers and naval marines directly under the authority of the president, and the president's security guard and security regiment, recruited from among regime supporters and trained by North Korean officers.

Relations between the Ratsiraka regime and the armed forces were often strained. *See Chronology above for dates of coup attempts.* The Counseil Militaire pour le Développement (q.v.), a military "legislature," did not act as a real channel of communication between the regime and the military. The longtime minister of defense, Guy Sibon (q.v.), a strong supporter of Ratsiraka, died in 1986, and was replaced by Ratsiraka's brother-in-law, Christophe Raveloson-Mahasampo (q.v.). Raveloson-Mahasampo was a controversial figure, and was removed to placate the opposition to the regime in February 1991.

During the crisis of 1991, the military played its role largely behind the scenes. It distanced itself from the massacre at Iavoloha (q.v.), which had been the act of the Presidential Guard, and made it clear that it would not undertake similar actions to defend the regime. The "president" of the transitional government proposed by the Comité des Forces Vives (q.v.) in the summer of 1991 was retired general and commander in chief Jean Rakotoharison (q.v.). The armed forces put pressure on the opposition movements and the regime to reach a power-sharing agreement and a transitional regime. Military representatives also participated in the institutions that set up the Third Republic (q.v.). *See also* OFFICE MILITAIRE NATIONALE POUR LES INDUSTRIES STRATEGIQUES; OFFICE MILITAIRE

POUR LA PRODUCTION AGRICOLE; OFFICERS' TRIAL.

MINERALS. Madagascar has a variety of mineral resources, but few large deposits. Iron was the first mineral to be exploited, and there is evidence of iron mining in the central Highlands (q.v.) as early as the sixteenth century. Gold was also discovered at an early period and was a source of income for the Merina Empire (q.v.). During the colonial period, concessions (many of which were never taken up) were granted for the mining of gold, graphite, rock crystal, and mica. The largest deposit of gold was discovered in the Andavokoera region south of what was then Diégo-Guarez (q.v.) in 1907, and production reached 3.7 tons in 1909, only to fall off sharply afterward. Graphite and mica were developed during the First World war for military use, and continued to be important until after the Korean War, when their place was taken by synthetics. There are also deposits of coal, the most important located in the southwest near the Sakoa River, a tributary of the Onilahy. The quality of the coal is not high, however, and the problems of transporting it have so far proven prohibitive. There are deposits of oil-bearing shale at Bemolanga (q.v.), but a cheap technology for extracting the oil does not exist. The Malagasy government, in conjunction with foreign oil companies, searched for offshore petroleum (q.v.) for most of the 1980s, but without discovering significant deposits. Of Madagascar's minerals, graphite and chromite are the most important sources of export income.

MISSIONS. Although there were some exploratory attempts to establish missions in Madagascar—such as the seventeenth century efforts of Luis Mariano (q.v.)—the first missionary establishment of any size in Madagascar came in 1817 when the London Missionary Society (q.v.) sent missionaries to Antananarivo at the invitation of the king of the Merina Empire (q.v.), Radama I (q.v.). The missionaries were expelled in 1835 by Radama's successor, Ranavalona I (q.v.), as part of her attempt to minimize Western influences. They returned at her death in 1861, however, accompanied by other denominations. The Catholic church (q.v.) had already established missions on the French-held Ile Sainte-Marie (q.v.) and Nosy Be (q.v.) and came to Antananarivo in 1861, extending their influence south to Fianarantsoa (q.v.) and to the coasts. The British Society for the Propagation of the Gospel came in 1864, Norwegian and American Lutherans in 1866, and the Society of Friends (Quakers) in 1867. The French Evangelical Society came in 1897. The churches (q.v.), hospitals, and school networks established by the missionaries covered much of the Highlands (q.v.) and to a lesser degree the coasts at the time of the French conquest. Under the French, the hospitals and the LMS medical school at Befelatanana (q.v.) were taken over by the state, but the educational networks remained in church hands. The missions handed control of the churches over to the Malagasy at varying rates, with the Lutherans being the slowest.

MONIMA (Mouvement National pour l'Indépendance de Madagascar; *in 1967 renamed* Madagasikara Otronin'ny Malagasy, *or* "Madagascar supported by the Malagasy"). MONIMA was founded in 1958 by Monja Jaona (q.v.), who had been active in the postwar nationalist movement as a leader of the secret society JINA (q.v.). At the time of its founding MONIMA advocated immediate independence and a "no" vote in the Referendum on the Constitution of the Fifth French Republic (q.v.). The party briefly supported the Parti Social Démocrate in the late 1950s when the party moved Madagascar to independence, but it spent most of the First Republic in opposition. Administrative harassment during this period reduced the party to its local bases around Toliara (q.v.) and the party was ordered dissolved for its involvement in the Peasant Rebellion (q.v.) of April 1971. Its intransigent stand won it the support of educated youth no longer satisfied with the official opposition provided by the AKFM (q.v.) in the late 1960s, but by the time of the May 1972 Revolution (q.v.) it had lost much of this support to the groups that were later to form the MFM (q.v.).

MONIMA criticized the Ramanantsoa regime (q.v.) that followed the May Revolution for what it saw as conservativism and pro-Merina (q.v.) bias, and saw the *fokonolona* reform (q.v.) of President Richard Ratsimandrava (q.v.) as an attack on its rural bases. Relations with the Democratic Republic of Madagascar (q.v.) of Didier Ratsiraka (q.v.) were tempestuous. MONIMA participated in the institutions of the republic, but in 1977 Monja Jaona took the party out of the Front National pour la Défense de la Révolution. This split the party into two groups, Vondrona Socialista MONIMA, which attacked Monja Jaona's "dictatorial tendencies" and returned to the Front, and MONIMA Ka Miviombio, which remained true to him. Monja Jaona brought his branch of the party back into the Front in 1981, but still ran against Ratsiraka in the 1982 presidential election. In 1987 MONIMA joined other parties in the Alliance Démocratique de Madagascar (q.v.), in opposition to the regime party, AREMA (q.v.).

Under the Democratic Republic, MONIMA lost much of its support in Toliara province to AREMA, and reemerged as a party of urban opposition with sections in the University of Madagascar and in 1984 links with the Kung Fu groups (q.v.). In 1983 Monja Jaona was elected to the Assemblée Nationale Populaire (q.v.) as a deputy from the capital. The party remains very much dominated by the leader, however, and has had difficulty in creating any organizational network.

Monja Jaona ran against Ratsiraka in the 1989 presidential election, but gained only 3% of the vote. In August 1989 he returned to the Conseil Suprême de la Révolution, and MONIMA returned to a position supporting the regime. In March 1990, when multiparty politics resumed, MONIMA joined the regime party, AREMA, and other parties backing Ratsiraka against the opposition to form the Mouvement Militant pour le Socialisme Malagasy (q.v.). MONIMA continued to support Ratsiraka during the transition to the Third Republic (q.v.), backing his demand for a federal constitution. This support has continued into the Third Republic.

MONIMA KA MIVIOMBIO. *See* MONIMA.

MONJA JAONA (1910–). Born in southern Madagascar of Antandroy (q.v.) stock, Monja Jaona was active as an evangelist in Toliara province before the Second World War. He began his career denouncing the abuses of the existing colonial system, and was frequently the target of administrative retaliation. During the Second World War, he was placed under house arrest at Manakara, on the east coast, where he founded the secret society JINA (q.v.). After the war he became a member of the Mouvement Démocratique de la Rénovation Malgache (q.v.), but his activities resulted in imprisonment in September 1946. He was still in prison at the outbreak of the Rebellion of 1947 (q.v.), in which many MDRM leaders were killed or imprisoned. He continued to be active in politics and was elected to the provincial council of Toliara province (q.v.). In 1958 he founded MONIMA (q.v.), in opposition to what was to become the regime party of the First Republic (q.v.), the Parti Social Démocrate (q.v.). He refused to join that party after independence, and was ousted from his position as mayor of Toliara (q.v.), which he had held since 1959, in 1961. Monja Jaona continued to oppose the policies of the First Republic, and when the Peasant Rebellion of 1971 (q.v.) broke out, he accepted responsibility for it. He was arrested, and sent to the prison island of Nosy Lava (q.v.). He was released by the May 1972 Revolution (q.v.), but did not completely support the subsequent Ramanantsoa regime (q.v.), being suspicious of its attempts at *fokonolona* reform (q.v.).

Under the Democratic Republic of Madagascar (q.v.), Monja Jaona was a supporter, but more often an opponent of the regime. He first joined the Front National pour la Défense de la Révolution (q.v.) and accepted a seat on the Conseil Suprême de la Révolution (q.v.). He took MONIMA out of the FNDR in 1977, however, leading to a split in the party. He returned to the FNDR in 1981, but ran against President Didier Ratsiraka (q.v.) in the presidential elections of 1982, gaining 19.8% of the vote. Declaring the results a fraud, he called for a general strike and the overthrow of the regime, and was once more placed under house arrest. He was released to run in the legislative elections of 1983, where he won a seat in Antananarivo.

Monja Jaona ran against Ratsiraka in the 1989 presidential election, but this time there were two other candidates,

Manandafy Rakotonirina (q.v.) and Marojamo Razanabahiny (q.v.), and Monja Jaona gained only 3% of the vote. In August 1989 Monja Jaona resumed his seat on the Conseil Suprême de la Révolution, and in the ensuring crisis he supported Ratsiraka against his opposition. In 1990 he led MONIMA into the Mouvement Militant pour le Socialisme Malagasy (q.v.), an alliance of parties supporting Ratsiraka against the opposition Comité des Forces Vives (q.v.), and in the transition to the Third Republic (q.v.) he joined the forces demanding a federal constitution. On March 31, 1992, Monja Jaona led a crowd of Ratsiraka supporters in a march on the National Forum (q.v.), which was drafting the constitution for the Third Republic, and was wounded when troops defending the meeting place fired on the crowd. He has continued to support Ratsiraka since.

MORA, ETIENNE. An economist from Toamasina province, Mora was one of the early supporters of President Didier Ratsiraka (q.v.). He was one of the first civilians named to the Conseil Suprême de la Révolution (q.v.) in 1976. His connections with important figures from the First Republic (q.v.) formed a useful link between the two regimes. Mora retired from the CSR in 1985.

MOUVEMENT DEMOCRATIQUE DE LA RENOVATION MALGACHE. The MDRM, Madagascar's most important nationalist party, was created in Paris in February 1946, through the action of the two Malagasy delegates to the Constituent Assemblies (q.v.) of the French Fourth Republic (q.v.), Joseph Raseta (q.v.) and Joseph Ravoahangy (q.v.). They recruited a Malagasy intellectual living in Paris, Jacques Rabemananjara (q.v.), to run as a third candidate in the upcoming legislative elections, and in Madagascar branches of the party were first set up as electoral committees. The party grew rapidly, particularly in the Highlands (q.v.), recruiting from established nationalist figures and returning veterans of the Second World War. It also attracted the participation of the secret societies JINA (q.v.) and PANAMA (q.v.) that had been established during the war. In spite of administrative resistance, and the creation of an opposing party, the Parti des Deshérités de Madagascar (q.v.), the MDRM was successful electorally, winning 71% of the vote in the Malagasy college in the November 1946 elections to the French National Assembly and returning its three candidates as deputies. In the January 1947 elections to Madagascar's five provincial assemblies, the MDRM won all the seats in Tananarive and Tamatave provinces, and majorities in Fianarantsoa and Tulear, losing only in Majunga province.

The MDRM was considered by the colonial authorities to be the chief organizer of the Rebellion of 1947 (q.v.). The deputies were arrested, the party itself was banned, and many members were arrested and sent to prison or executed. It seems clear now that the party as an organization was not directly responsible for the uprising. During its existence, however, it was divided between advocates of a parliamentary route to autonomy and those, including the members of the secret societies, who advocated a rebellion against colonial rule. It was this section, in conjunction with others not directly affiliated to the party, that organized the rebellion. *See also* TANANARIVE TRIAL.

MOUVEMENT MILITANT POUR LE SOCIALISME MALGACHE (Militant Movement for Malagasy Socialism). The MMSM was formed in March 1990 by supporters of the president of the Democratic Republic of Madagascar (q.v.), Didier Ratsiraka (q.v.), and included his party, AREMA (q.v.), MONIMA (q.v.), and some members of the AKFM (q.v.) and Vonjy (q.v.). The MMSM organized resistance to the opposition Comité des Forces Vives (q.v.) and to the establishment of the Third Republic (q.v.).

MOUVEMENT NATIONAL POUR L'INDEPENDANCE DE MADAGASCAR. *See* MONIMA.

MOUVEMENT SOCIAL MALGACHE. This movement was launched by the Catholic mission in Madagascar to provide a counterweight to the Mouvement Démocratique de la Rénovation Malgache, considered by the mission to be too nationalistic and Protestant-dominated. It dissolved after the

Rebellion of 1947 (q.v.) and the disappearance of the MDRM.

MPITOLONA HO AMIN'NY FANJAKANA'NY MADINIKA. *See* MFM.

-N-

NATAI, JEAN-JACQUES (1920–). Born in Moramanga, in Mahajanga province, Nataï was one of the founders of the dominant party of the First Republic, the Parti Social Démocrate (q.v.). He was trained as a dentist, and at first worked in the colonial health services. He was president of the Government Council of Mahajanga province in 1958, and in 1960 he held the post of chief of the province. In 1965 he became secretary of state for agriculture in charge of western development, and in 1967 minister of agriculture.

NATIONAL ASSEMBLY. The legislature of the First Republic (q.v.) had as its lower house a National Assembly of 125 members. Deputies to the National Assembly were elected by the list system or by proportional representation. The Malagasy version of this system differed from others in that a list gaining 55% of the vote in its district won all the seats. The exception was the district of the city of Antananarivo, where a strict system of proportional election was followed.

NATIONAL FORUM. This forum was held in Antananarivo (q.v.) from March 22 to March 31, 1992, to discuss the future constitution of the Third Republic (q.v.). The draft constitution had already been discussed in the transitional institutions established by the power-sharing agreement (q.v.) of October 31, 1991, and in regional forums, whose delegates composed the National Forum. The greatest conflict took place, not in the forum itself, but between the forum and the supporters of the Democratic Republic of Madagascar (q.v.), who wanted the forum to consider a federal form of state. Violent demonstrations, and an attempt on the life of the leader of the transition, Albert Zafy (q.v.), forced the forum to move from its meeting place in Antananarivo to a military camp outside the city, where it completed its deliberations.

NATIONALIST MOVEMENT. The Malagasy nationalist movement started with both advantages and disadvantages. The existence of a previously independent state, the Merina Empire (q.v.), served as an early rallying point, but an ambiguous one, since restoration of the empire was not appealing to the non-Merina (q.v.) peoples of the island. A single language and a high degree of education were advantages, but were counteracted by a high degree of control by the government authorities that made any kind of open political activity impossible. The first organization that had a membership beyond the capital was the Vy Vato Sakelika (q.v.) based at Befelatanana (q.v.) medical school and suppressed by the colonial authorities in 1915. After the war, Jean Ralaimongo (q.v.) in company with French sympathizers animated a loosely knit group often known as the Ralaimongo group (q.v.) that extended its geographic coverage beyond the Highlands (q.v.) and its social coverage beyond the elite. The nationalist movement first aimed at the limited goal of securing the rights of French citizens for the Malagasy, and freeing them from the restrictions of the *indigénat* (q.v.), but after the May 19, 1929, demonstration (q.v.) in Antananarivo (q.v.) began to work for independence. Political activity was repressed during the Second World War, but after the war a restricted Malagasy electorate was given the right to send delegates to the two Constitutional Assemblies (q.v.) that decided on the constitution of the Fourth French Republic (q.v.) and to the National Assembly. A party grouping many established nationalist leaders, the Mouvement Démocratique de la Rénovation Malgache (q.v.), was formed and was able to elect its candidates to the two constitutional assemblies and the three deputies' seats. The party was divided, however, into a wing that advocated independence through peaceful means, and a wing, based on the secret societies PANAMA (q.v.) and JINA (q.v.), that advocated a rebellion. In March 1947 the Rebellion of 1947 (q.v.) broke out, and the MDRM was accused of organizing it. The party was dissolved, and its leaders were either killed or imprisoned. The trauma of the rebellion and the severity of control that followed it dampened signs of nationalist activity for most of the next decade. People with nationalist leanings gravitated to unions (q.v.) and to ostensibly nonpolitical organizations, like the Comité de Solidarité de Madagascar (q.v.). Nationalist forces reappeared after the liberalization of political life that followed the passage of the Loi-Cadre (q.v.), and parties were formed advocating immediate independence. In 1958 they assembled in the Tamatave Congress (q.v.) to demand independence and urge the rejection of the French Community proposed in the Referendum on the Constitution of the Fifth French Republic (q.v.). Their audience was sufficiently large that Madagascar had the second highest number of negative votes of France's African colonies.

NATIONALIZATIONS. The first nationalizations undertaken after the May 1972 Revolution (q.v.) occurred during the Ramanantsoa regime (q.v.) when the arsenal at Diégo-Suarez (now Antseranana, q.v.) and Electricité et Eaux de Madagascar (q.v.) were taken over. When Didier Ratsiraka (q.v.) took power in June 1975, he announced a series of nationalizations as part of the transition to an economy based on Marxist socialism. Enterprises nationalized included the French-owned banks, the Compagnie Marseillaise de Madagascar (q.v.), insurance companies, and the film distribution network. Later the Malagasy government acquired majority participation in the Société Malgache des Transports Maritimes and the oil refinery at Toamasina. By 1978 it was estimated that the state controlled about 61% of firms operating in Madagascar. After the economic collapse of the early 1980s, however, the state withdrew from many sectors of economic activity, including the market, and plans were announced to dispose of most state firms. Activities targeted for privatization include the insurance sector, meat processing, textiles, and the distribution of petroleum products. Under the Democratic Republic of Madagascar (q.v.), there were accusations that most of the privatized firms had been acquired by families with connections to President Ratsiraka (q.v.). The pace of privatization is expected to increase under the Third Republic (q.v.). *See also* ECONOMY.

NONALIGNED MOVEMENT. A grouping of states not aligned with either of the Cold War superpowers was first suggested at the Bandung Conference of Afro-Asian states in 1955. The movement was founded at the Belgrade Conference in 1961. The First Republic had adopted a policy of alignment and declared anticommunism, and it neither asked nor was invited to join the movement. After the May 1972 Revolution (q.v.) Foreign Minister Didier Ratsiraka (q.v.) took Madagascar into the movement as part of his radicalization of the country's foreign policy. As president of the Democratic Republic of Madgascar (q.v.) he attempted to make a place for Madagascar in the radical wing of the movement, supporting attempts to demilitarize the Indian Ocean (q.v.) and accepting the thesis that the states of the socialist bloc were the natural allies of the Third World. After the arrival of the debt crisis (q.v.), however, Ratsiraka was critical of the failure of socialist states to provide assistance, accusing them of behaving like the imperialist powers, and he criticized the movement itself for its failure to achieve a united front on the crisis.

NORTH KOREA. After the Soviet Union (q.v.), North Korea was the socialist country with which the Democratic Republic of Madagascar (q.v.) had the closest relations. President Ratsiraka (q.v.) expressed admiration for North Korean leader Kim Il Sung, for North Korea's passage from an agricultural to an industrial economy, and for Kim's philosophy of *Juche,* or self-reliance. North Korea provided training, officers, and weapons for the president's security guards, supplied weapons for the armed forces and assistance in their economic projects, and provided the first (unrealized) model for the Malagasy system of cooperatives (q.v.). North Koreans also built the presidential palace and military camp at Iavoloha (q.v.). By the time of the fall of the Democratic Republic of Madagascar, however, Korean influence had been much reduced by the rapprochement with the West occasioned by Madagascar's debt crisis (q.v.).

NOSY BE. An island off the coast of Antseranana province (q.v.), Nosy Be was originally occupied by Arab settlements and by the Antankarana (q.v.). In the 1830s groups of Boina Sakalava (q.v.) came to the island as refugees from the Merina Empire (q.v.). In 1841 Admiral de Hell, governor of Réunion, signed a treaty of protection with the Sakalava rulers. Settlers from France and Réunion followed, establishing plantations for growing perfume plants (q.v.), and spices (q.v.). Nosy Be is now one of the main areas of Madagascar in which these crops are grown. In 1981 and 1982 it was the site of antigovernment demonstrations protesting corruption in the handling of the commercialization of vanilla.

NOSY LAVA. Nosy Lava is located on the west coast of Madagascar, opposite Analalava. Originally a burial ground for Sakalava (q.v.) royalty, it was used during the colonial period as a prison camp for long-term convicts. Political prisoners, such as the suspected members of Vy Vato Sakelika (q.v.), were also sent there. Subsequent regimes have continued to use the island for this purpose.

-O-

OFFICE DU RIZ (Rice Bureau). The Office du Riz was established in 1944 as part of the mobilization of Madagascar's resources for the French war effort. It was greatly resented for its practice of forcing farmers to sell their entire crops at low prices and then selling restricted quantities back to them at considerably higher prices. As a result of its activities, corruption and a black market in rice developed. Defense against the Office du Riz was a rallying point for nationalist activities, and resentment against the Office was one of the factors contributing to the Rebellion of 1947 (q.v.). *See also COMITE DU SALUT PUBLIC.*

OFFICE MILITAIRE NATIONALE POUR LES INDUSTRIES STRATEGIQUES (National Military Office for Strategic Industries). Created in 1977, OMNIS is composed of military officers and directly attached to the president's office. It is responsible for mineral exploration and research, and has played a role in recent oil exploration on the island. It controls the island's chromite-mining activities, and is responsible for running the arsenal at Antseranana (q.v.).

OFFICE MILITAIRE POUR LA PRODUCTION AGRICOLE (Military Office for Agricultural Production). Established in 1979 and composed of army units, OMPIRA took over several of the foreign-owned plantations expropriated after 1975. The Office had responsibility for many of the army's agricultural projects, including the ''100,000 hectares of rice'' scheme, and undertook production of some export crops, including coffee and vanilla.

OFFICERS' TRIAL. In 1977 three officers of the Malagasy armed forces—Major Andriamaholison (q.v.) of the gendarmerie, Captain Rakotonirina (q.v.) of the army, and Captain Rakoto (q.v.) of the gendarmerie—were arrested and charged with conspiracy against the state. They were not tried until October 1983, at a time of crisis for the regime of President Ratsiraka (q.v.), and commentators speculated that the three officers, with a variety of military and political ties, were being tried to set an example to others. The trial had been preceded by the trial of army colonel Auguste Rasolofo (q.v.) and others arrested and accused of having plotted to assassinate Ratsiraka in 1982, and the relatively light sentences handed down in that trial had led to protests from the regime. The sentences in the officers' trial were severe: house arrest for life for Andriamaholison and Rakotonirina, and ten years at forced labor for Rakoto. All appealed their sentences, although Rakoto later withdrew his appeal. The appeals of the others were dismissed.

OLIVIER, MARCEL (1879–1945). A career colonial administrator, Olivier was governor-general of Madagascar from 1924 to 1930. He established the Délégations Economiques et Financières (q.v.), advisory councils designed to meet settler demands for more representation, set up a bank to issue currency (the Banque de Madagascar et des Comores), conducted a survey of land and revised landholding laws, and completed the Fianarantsoa–Côte Est railroad (q.v.). He also organized the Service de Main-d'Oeuvre des Travaux d'Intérêt Général (q.v.) (SMOTIG) to channel forced labor to government projects. Olivier's period in Madagascar was a time of increasing nationalist activity, in part inspired by policies like the land surveys and SMOTIG, that culminated in the riots of May 19, 1929. *Further information may be found in the Bibliography following this Dictionary.*

OMBIASY. The *ombiasy* are priests of the Antemoro (q.v.) and Antanosy (q.v.) groups. In precolonial times they were renowned for their skills based on interpretation of the *sorabe* (q.v.) writings, their practice of divination (called *sikidy*) that consists of reading patterns of grains, and their powers to create individual talismans known as *ody* and official talismans known as *sampy* (q.v.). They served as advisors to the rulers of many kingdoms, including those of Betsileo (q.v.) territory and the Merina (q.v.) monarchy.

ORGANISATION COMMUNE AFRICAINE ET MALGACHE. This organization, the continuation of the Union Africaine et Malagache (q.v.), groups France and its former African colonies. The First Republic (q.v.) under Philibert Tsiranana (q.v.) preferred OCAM to the Organization of African Unity (q.v.). The Democratic Republic of Madagascar (q.v.) under Didier Ratsiraka (q.v.) considered OCAM to be a form of neocolonialism and did not participate in the meetings.

ORGANIZATION OF AFRICAN UNITY. The Organization of African Unity was founded in 1963. Madagascar was one of the original members, although the founders of the organization rejected the suggestion of President Tsiranana (q.v.) that the body be named the Organization of African and Malagasy Unity. The First Republic (q.v.) maintained its distance from the OAU, preferring the exclusively Francophone Organisation Commune Africaine et Malgache (q.v.). With the radicalization of Malagasy foreign policy under the Ramanantsoa regime (q.v.), Madagascar came to play a more active role in the organization. Under President Ratsiraka (q.v.) of the Democratic Republic of Madagascar (q.v.) the country at first attempted to carve out a role in the organization. Madagascar was one of the first countries to recognize the Saharan Democratic Arab Republic and to support its membership in the organization. The OAU also supported Madagascar's claim to the ''scattered islands'' surrounding it. In later years, however, President Ratsiraka criticized the OAU for an excess of talk and a lack of unity.

ORSTOM PLOT. ORSTOM was originally called the Office du Recherche Scientifique pour les Territoires d'Outre-Mer; it is now the Office du Recherche Scientifique et Téchnique d'Outre-Mer. During the First Republic (q.v.), sociologists working for the organization had contacts with Malagasy intellectuals critical of the regime. In October 1971 a group of Malagasy and French sociologists from ORSTOM were arrested and accused of preparing a Maoist plot against the regime. No plot was ever proved, and the members of the group still in detention were released after the May 1972 Revolution.

OVERSEAS DEPUTIES. Under the Third French Republic (q.v.), French citizens of the overseas territories—which included Algeria, Réunion, Cochin China, French India, and the Antilles—elected deputies to the French National Assembly. The overseas deputies were an important part of the colonial lobby of the Third Republic, and since they were usually long-term deputies they often rose to influential positions. Among the deputies who were interested in the French position in Madagascar were François De Mahy (q.v.) of Réunion, and Charles-Marie Le Myre de Vilers (q.v.) of Cochin China.

-P-

PANAMA. The Parti Nationaliste Malgache, or PANAMA, as it was known, was a secret society founded during the Second World War and connected at first with the Comité du Salut Public (q.v.). Using networks of Protestant pastors and teachers, it spread first in the area around the capital and then to Toliara, Toamasina, Diégo-Suarez, and Mahajanga. It advocated immediate independence for Madagascar, if necessary by a violent revolution. After the war it cooperated with the Mouvement Démocratique de la Rénovation Malgache (q.v.). Along with another secret society, JINA (q.v.), PANAMA probably supplied much of the planning and leadership for the Rebellion of 1947 (q.v.). The society was dissolved by the colonial administration in May 1947.

PANGALANES CANAL. The Pangalanes Canal is a channel of partially navigable lagoons that stretches for 652 km along the east coast south of Toamasina (q.v.). The lagoons, called *pangalanes,* are separated by outcropping. Attempts to connect the lagoons in order to provide a sheltered waterway down the east coast have been undertaken by various regimes, beginning with the Merina Empire (q.v.). The expense of the project and the opposition of the secondary ports of the east coast to the channeling of traffic to Toamasina have prevented completion of the full route.

PARTI DEMOCRATIQUE MALGACHE. The PDM was founded in 1945 by the longtime nationalist leader, Ravelojaona (q.v.). It advocated independence based on the principles of the United Nations Charter (q.v.) but rejected the more radical line of the Mouvement Démocratique de la Rénovation Malgache (q.v.). Its main support came from the Protestant elite of the capital, and after the Rebellion of 1947 (q.v.) it led a shadowy existence without real influence, under the name Front Démocratique Malgache. In 1955 it renamed itself the Parti Libéral Chrétien (q.v.), but dissolved shortly thereafter.

PARTI DES DESHERITES DE MADAGASCAR. PADESM was founded in Toliara in 1946 in response to the earlier creation of the Mouvement Démocratique Malgache (q.v.). Among its early leaders were Pascal Velonjara (q.v.), Felix Totolehibe (q.v.), Philibert Tsiranana (q.v.), and Raveloson-Mahasampo (q.v.). The party rejected immediate independence and expressed its gratitude to the colonial power for freeing the "disinherited" of Madagascar from the domination of the Merina (q.v.) elite. It recruited outside Merina areas and among the nonelite of the Highlands. In spite of administrative favor, it was never able to win elections at the national level. PADESM did better at the provincial level, winning 13 of 18 seats in Mahajanga, 8 of 18 in Fianarantsoa, and 7 of 18 in Toliara in the 1947 elections to the Malagasy college of the provincial assemblies. After the Rebellion of 1947 (q.v.) PADESM denounced the MDRM as the instigator of the revolt, but it too lost much of its cohesion with the disappearance of its rival. Party leaders tended to run in subsequent elections supported by personal election committees. In 1956 it suffered a final split between leaders like Tsiranana, who supported the Loi-Cadre (q.v.), and leaders like Raveloson-Mahasampo, who opposed even this grant of autonomy as premature. The supporters of Tsiranana went on to found the Parti Social Démocrate (q.v.), while the others usually withdrew from politics.

PARTI LIBERAL CHRETIEN. The PLC was founded in 1955 by a group, including Gabriel Razafintsalama (q.v.) and Prosper Rajaobelina (q.v.), who had previously been connected with the Parti Démocratique Malgache (q.v.). It advocated autonomy within the French Union (q.v.) but was unable to attract an audience and disappeared shortly after its founding.

PARTI NOUVEAU DEMOCRATE DE L'OCEAN INDIEN. One of Madagascar's few openly Marxist parties, the Parti Nouveau Démocrate de l'Océan Indien was founded in Tamatave in 1956 by the journalist Jacques Titus. It received no encouragement from the French Communist party, which was hostile to any attempt to create an overtly communist party in Madagascar, and was unable to spread outside Tamatave. Titus abandoned this effort, but later made other attempts to found a communist organization in Madagascar.

PARTI SOCIALE DEMOCRATE. Originally the Parti Social Démocrate de Madagascar et des Comores, the PSD was founded in Mahajanga in 1956 by Philibert Tsiranana and a group of associates that included Calvin Tsiebo (q.v.), Laurent Botokeky (q.v.), and André Resampa (q.v.). The Party's founders, many former members of the Parti des

Deshérités de Madagascar (q.v.), were mainly civil servants from modest coastal families. In 1956 the PSD supported the Loi-Cadre (q.v.) and advocated the abrogation of the Annexation Law of 1896 (q.v.). It was opposed to immediate independence, however, and favored the maintenance of a close relationship with France after independence. The party received the active support of the French high commissioner, André Soucadaux (q.v.), who was, like Tsiranana, a member of the French Socialist party. Although there were too many parties for the PSD to dominate the Loi-Cadre representative assembly, it was able to gather enough support among the members to have Philibert Tsiranana elected vice president of the assembly and leader of the government council.

Between 1957 and the coming of internal autonomy in 1958 the PSD absorbed several of the parties that had appeared at the time of the Loi-Cadre. After 1958 the party was able to use its control of the administration under André Resampa, who was both secretary-general of the party and minister of the interior, to destroy the power bases of most of the surviving opposition leaders, and in the elections of 1965 only the AKFM managed to win any seats in the legislature, gaining 3 out of 108. Although the party remained in power until the May 1972 Revolution, it was always plagued by factional disputes, which increased as Tsiranana's health declined, and by 1970 the party was divided among groups loyal to Tsiranana, those supporting his minister of foreign affairs, Jacques Rabemananjara (q.v.), and those supporting Resampa. In 1971 Tsiranana attempted to regain control of the party by ousting Resampa as secretary-general and minister of the interior.

After the May 1972 Revolution, the PSD continued a legal existence until the anti-Merina riots of 1972–1973, which the Ramanantsoa regime (q.v.) attributed to agitation by local PSD leaders. The party was then declared illegal and disbanded. In 1974 Tsiranana and Resampa reconciled and formed the Parti Socialiste Malgache (q.v.), which was banned in 1975 after the assassination of the then president of Madagascar, Richard Ratsimandrava (q.v.). Under the Democratic Republic of Madagascar (q.v.), former PSD officials still active in politics found their way into Vonjy (q.v.) and the regime party, AREMA (q.v.). When the DRM permitted the formation of new parties in March 1990, André Resampa revived the Parti Social Démocrate.

PARTI SOCIALISTE MALGACHE. The Parti Socialiste Malgache was born of the reconciliation between André Resampa (q.v.) and Philibert Tsiranana (q.v.) after the May 1972 Revolution (q.v.). Immediately after the revolution, Tsiranana had maintained the Parti Social Démocrate (q.v.) in existence, while Resampa had created the Union Socialiste Malgache (q.v.). Neither formula met with success, and in March 1974 the two men created the PSM to regroup the forces opposed to the Ramanantsoa regime (q.v.). The new party took over the headquarters of the PSD. After the assassination of Colonel Richard Ratsimandrava (q.v.) in February 1975, the party headquarters, in which Resampa had taken refuge, was destroyed by an Antananarivo mob and the PSM itself was banned.

PATUREAU, FERDINAND. A native of Toamasina province, and married to the sister of Didier Ratsiraka's (q.v.) wife, Patureau was a member of the Directoire Militaire that took power after the assassination of Colonel Richard Ratsimandrava (q.v.), when he was a commandant in the army and one of Ratsiraka's supporters in the Directoire. After Ratsiraka was named president in June 1975, Patureau moved to the Conseil Suprême de la Révolution (q.v.). In February 1976 he was named director of the Office Militaire Nationale pour les Industries Stratégiques (q.v.), a post that he resigned in September of that year to enter the private sector.

PEASANT REBELLION, APRIL 1971. The peasant rebellion that began in the south of Madagascar on April 1, 1971, was a response to government efforts to maintain taxation levels in the region after an epidemic of anthrax had destroyed the herds that the population depended on for income. Much of the leadership of the revolt was provided by the region's party of opposition to the First Republic (q.v.), MONIMA (q.v.). Its leader, Monja Jaona (q.v.), went into hiding, and when captured took responsibility for the uprising. He was deported to

Nosy Lava (q.v.), as were over five hundred others. The severity of the government suppression of the rebellion gradually became known in the rest of Madagascar and reaction to it was part of the alienation of opinion—both in the general public and in the military (q.v.), where the gendarmerie had participated in the suppression—that contributed to the collapse of the regime in the May 1972 Revolution (q.v.).

PERFUME PLANTS. Madagascar grows a wide variety of plants used in the manufacture of perfume, mainly in the northwest around Nosy Be. Among the most important are ylang-ylang, vetiver, and lemongrass. Ylang-ylang is the only one of these plants to constitute an important export in recent times.

PETROLEUM. Madagascar produces no petroleum, and guaranteeing and paying for adequate supplies has been a continuing problem for successive governments of the island. Under the Democratic Republic of Madagascar (q.v.), the Soviet Union was a major supplier of oil until 1988, when it suspended deliveries because Madagascar could no longer meet the payments. It has since been replaced by Iran and Libya, and potentially by South Africa.

Madagascar has tried to develop its own supplies by exploring the possibility of extracting petroleum from the oil-bearing shale at Bemolanga (q.v.) and by looking for off-shore deposits. Exploration agreements were signed in 1981 and 1982 with Mobil, Occidental, and Petrocanada to look for oil off the west coast of the island. The search was resumed in 1988, and contracts were signed with Shell, Amoco, and BHP, with exploration still concentrated on the west coast. Some deposits have been found, but they have not yet come into operation.

PHILIPPE, JEAN (d. 1984). Philippe was commander in chief of the gendarmerie from 1977 to 1984. His death in November of that year left the gendarmerie without a direct commander at the time of the December Kung Fu (q.v.) incidents.

PIERRE, SIMON. Simon Pierre was an early advisor to President Didier Ratsiraka (q.v.). In the early days of the Democratic

Republic of Madagascar (q.v.), he served as a commissioner attached to the Conseil Suprême de la Révolution (q.v.) and was a founding member of the political bureau of the regime party, AREMA (q.v.). An agricultural engineer from Fianarantsoa province, he was named minister of rural development and agrarian reform in 1976. In 1982, at the time of the "right AREMA" crisis, he was removed from his post and "promoted" to the Conseil Suprême de la Révolution (q.v.) amid veiled presidential accusations of disloyalty. He returned to favor in 1985, however, and was named minister of information and ideological guidance. He lost the post when the ministry was abolished in September 1989.

PIQUE, ALBERT (1853–1917). Albert Piqué, governor-general of Madagascar from 1910 to 1914, was a career colonial servant with experience in Indochina and West Africa. His period in office saw the conquest of the last resistance groups in the west of the island, and the consolidation of direct French control with the abandonment of the system of internal protectorates established by General Gallieni (q.v.). Piqué made several attempts to develop the colonial economy and started the construction of the Antananarivo-Antsirabe railroad. *See also* POLITIQUE DES RACES.

PIRATES. Because of the attractive trade routes that cross the western Indian Ocean, there has always been some pirate activity around Madagascar. Large-scale European piracy began after 1684, when advancing colonization and increased naval patrols drove the pirates from their bases in the Caribbean. Madagascar was attractive because of the lack of any powerful naval presence in the area and because it was near three important routes: trade to and from the Indies, trade up and down the East African coast, and pilgrim traffic to Mecca. Several pirates, including William Kidd, moved their bases to Madagascar, settling along the northeast and northwest coasts, especially in Antongil Bay (q.v.), the Ile Sainte-Marie (q.v.), and Diégo-Suarez Bay (q.v.), where the pirate Misson founded the "International Republic of Libertalia."

By the 1730s the growing presence of the French and

British navies and the development of the convoy system of shipping led to the elimination of the pirates from their Malagasy bases. On the east coast, however, their descendants, the Zanamalata, founded and provided a ruling dynasty for the Betsimisaraka Confederation (q.v.) and, in conjunction with the neighboring Sakalava, conducted raids on the Comoro Islands (q.v.) at the end of the eighteenth century. *See also* BETSIMISARAKA-SAKALAVA RAIDS.

PLANQUE, EDOUARD (1893–1945). Planque was a member of the French Communist party and active in support of the Malagasy nationalist movement after the First World War. He was arrested and imprisoned after the May 19, 1929, demonstration (q.v.). At the outbreak of the Second World War, he returned to France, where he was arrested in 1941. He died at Dachau in 1945.

POLITIQUE DES RACES. When he took over as governor-general at the beginning of French colonial rule, General Gallieni (q.v.) wanted to administer the island without excessive reliance on the existing administration of the Merina Empire (q.v.), which the French had supplanted. Drawing on his experience in Indochina, he introduced the *politique des races,* a policy of governing the different groups of the islands through their traditional institutions and rulers. Also known as the system of internal protectorates, the *politique des races* proved unsatisfactory. Local political institutions had their own purposes and were hard to adapt to the requirements of colonial rule, while local rulers often either worked against the French or lost authority for working with them. The policy was abandoned by Governor-General Albert Piqué (q.v.) in favor of direct administration with Malagasy ''auxiliaries'' at the lower levels.

POPULAR FRONT. The Popular Front government was a coalition of French parties of the left, of which the most important were the Socialist and the Communist parties. It was in office from June 1936 to June 1937. Although most of its attention was taken up by French domestic policies, it did undertake some liberalization of the colonial system. In Madagascar this included the release of people imprisoned for nationalist activities, the legalization of Malagasy unions (q.v.), and the relaxation of press censorship (q.v.).

PORTOS, AUGUSTIN AMPY. Portos was born in Antseranana province. He began his career in the First Republic (q.v.), serving as chief of the personal cabinet of the then minister of the interior, André Resampa (q.v.). During the Ramanantsoa regime (q.v.), he was a senior civil servant in the Ministry of Foreign Affairs, whose minister was Didier Ratsiraka (q.v.). When Ratsiraka took power in 1975, Portos became minister of justice, and in 1976 minister of the interior. Also a member of the political bureau of the regime party, AREMA, Portos was considered to be one of the ''strongmen'' of the DRM. He lost his post as interior minister in August 1991, when Guy Razanamasy (q.v.) was called on to form a government of reconciliation including opposition figures. Portos was succeeded by Colonel Charles Rakotoharison.

PORTS. Madagascar has eighteen official ports, fourteen of which can handle international traffic, and four that handle only cabotage, or internal traffic. The dominant port is Toamasina (q.v.) on the east coast, followed by Mahajanga (q.v.) on the west coast, Anteseranana (q.v.), Hellville (q.v.), and Toliara (q.v.). The ports on the east coast are subject to destructive cyclones, while those on the west coast must deal with silting.

POWER-SHARING AGREEMENT. This agreement, first proclaimed on October 31, 1991, was an accord between President Ratsiraka (q.v.) of the Democratic Republic of Madagascar (q.v.) and his opposition, the Comité des Forces Vives (q.v.), on the institutions and processes for the transition to the Third Republic (q.v.). The original agreement removed most of Ratsiraka's powers, but left him the post of commander in chief of the armed forces. It set up four transitional institutions: the presidency, the government of Prime Minister Guy Razanamasy (q.v.), a Haute Autorité d'Etat (q.v.) to be presided over by opposition leader Albert

Zafy (q.v.), and a Comité de Rédressement Economique et Social (q.v.) to be chaired by two other opposition leaders, Manandafy Rakotonirina (q.v.) and Richard Andriamanjato (q.v.). The agreement was repudiated on November 7 by Zafy, who had been out of the country when it was reached, on the grounds that it left Ratsiraka in control of the armed forces and gave his supporters excessive representation on the transitional institutions. After considerable negotiation, the agreement was amended to meet Zafy's objections, and was proclaimed on January 9, 1992.

PRESENCE FRANCAISE. Présence Française was an organization of conservative settlers (q.v.) supported by the commercial companies (q.v.) and the large coastal planters. In the period after the Second World War it dominated the French-citizen college of Madagascar's territorial and provincial assemblies and elected leaders such as Roger Clément (q.v.) to posts in the French legislature. It also supported conservative candidates in the Malagasy college. The movement declined, however, as the island moved to autonomy, and its candidates began losing to the liberal settler organization, the Entente Franco-Malgache. In 1957 Roger Clément announced his support for the Loi-Cadre (q.v.) and the movement toward autonomy that it implied.

PROCOOP. PROCOOP was the network of cooperatives set up by the regime party of the Democratic Republic of Madagascar (q.v.), AREMA (q.v.), in part with the proceeds of a personal loan from Libya to President Ratsiraka (q.v.) in 1979. The director of PROCOOP was Ratsiraka's sister-in-law, Hortense Raveloson-Mahasampo (q.v.). Undertakings of the cooperative network included an automobile factory in Fianarantsoa and agricultural projects.

PROTECTORATE, 1885. The first French protectorate over the Merina Empire (q.v.) was established by the treaty, signed on December 17, 1885, that ended the Franco-Malagasy War of 1883–1885 (q.v.). The treaty provided that the Merina government would pay France an indemnity of 10 million francs and gave the French the right to establish a base at

Diégo-Suarez (q.v.). In addition, the French would exercise control over the external affairs of Madagascar and would send a resident to Antananarivo with a military escort to administer the terms of the protectorate. Quarrels over the interpretation of the treaty began even as it was signed, and the first French resident, Le Myre de Vilers (q.v.), saw his role as that of asserting further French control over the island, while the Malagasy prime minister, Rainlaiarivony (q.v.), saw his role as that of minimizing even the degree of control provided for in the treaty. By 1894 the French were determined to establish their claim to the island, and they sent Le Myre de Vilers, by then a deputy to the National Assembly, to Antananarivo to demand a revision of the protectorate establishing the right to control the conduct of foreign affairs, to grant land concessions to foreigners, to station troops, and to undertake public works. It was the refusal of the Merina government to agree to these terms that led to the Franco-Malagasy War of 1895.

PROTECTORATE, 1895. After their conquest of Madagascar in 1895, the French established a protectorate, with a treaty signed by Queen Ranavalona III on October 1. Under the protectorate, the occupying power took over control of both the internal and external affairs of the island, but left the monarchy and most of the administration of the Merina Empire (q.v.) intact. This arrangement was unstable, and the Revolt of the Menalamba (q.v.), which broke out in November 1895, was blamed by the French on the machinations of the monarchy and its supporters. In 1896 the monarchy was abolished, and on August 6, 1896, a law was passed declaring Madagascar a French possession.

PROTESTANTS. Approximately 21% of the Malagasy population is affiliated with a Protestant church. The largest denomination—Congregationalist—was established by the London Missionary Society (q.v.), which began mission (q.v.) activity in Madagascar in 1817. It is followed in size by churches founded by the French Evangelical Society, which began work in 1897. Other denominations are the Anglicans, Quakers, and Lutherans. The churches agreed to a division of territory at the end of the nineteenth century whereby the Quakers and Lutherans concentrated more on the southern parts of Madagascar. There are also breakaway syncretistic churches, but they do not have the importance in Madagascar that they do in other African countries. After the French conquest, the English-based Protestant churches were suspected of furnishing networks for the nationalist movement (a suspicion that was not totally unfounded), and Protestant church leaders suffered heavily in the repression of the Rebellion of 1947 (q.v.). The main Protestant churches became organizationally independent of their mother churches in 1958, although missionary activity continues. In 1970 the FJKM (Fiangonan'i Jesosy Kristy Eto Madagascar) linked the churches derived from the London Missionary Society, the French Evangelicals, and the Quakers, and a later, less active, federation added the southern, mission-oriented churches. In 1980 the FFKM, or Federation of Malagasy Christian Churches, including the Catholic church, was established.

PROVINCES. ''Province'' has been applied to a variety of administrative units in Madagascar since the French conquest. The first five of today's provinces—Fianarantsoa, Tananarive (now Antananarivo), Majunga (now Mahajanga), Tamatave (now Toamasina), and Tulear (now Toliara—were created in November 1946, in part as an attempt to break the cohesion of the island's nationalist movement. The province of Diégo-Suarez (now Antseranana) was created from portions of Tamatave and Majunga provinces in 1956. The provinces had a two-college assembly which also served as an electoral college for the territorial assembly in Tananarive. The 1956 Loi-Cadre (q.v.) increased the power of the provinces, but the coming of internal autonomy in 1958 with the subsequent elimination of provincial-based opposition plus the centralization of the ruling PSD greatly weakened their position. A part of this weakening was the substitution of an appointed for an elected chief in 1963. The provinces were retained under the *fokonolona* reform of the Democratic Republic (q.v.) and rebaptized *faritany*.

PROVINCIAL COUNCIL. Under the First Republic (q.v.), the provincial councils were composed of the provinces' deputies and senators and a group of general councillors whose number varied from province to province. The councils' powers were limited, extending mainly to primary education, cultural affairs, and sports. The provincial councils were suspended by the Ramanantsoa regime (q.v.) in 1973 and their functions transferred to the province chiefs.

-R-

RABEARIMANANA, GABRIEL. A geography professor at the University of Madagascar and a member of MONIMA (q.v.), Rabearimanana served as an advisor to President Didier Ratsiraka (q.v.) in the early days of the Democratic Republic of Madagascar (q.v.). In 1977, when MONIMA party leader Monja Jaona (q.v.) took the party out of the Front National pour la Défense de la Révolution (q.v.) and began opposing the regime, Rabearimanana joined with other members in protesting this "arbitrary action." They left the party and founded Vondrona Socialista MONIMA and successfully applied for readmission to the FNDR.

RABEMANANJARA, JACQUES (1913–). An important Malagasy political figure from 1945 to 1972, Jacques Rabemananjara received his higher education in France and was living in Paris as a writer and poet connected with the Présence Africaine group at the end of the Second World War. He joined the two Malagasy delegates to the French Constituent Assemblies (q.v.), Joseph Raseta (q.v.) and Joseph Ravoahangy (q.v.), to found the Mouvement Démocratique de la Rénovation Malgache (q.v.) and ran as the MDRM candidate in the November 1946 elections to the French National Assembly. As a Betsimisaraka (q.v.) Catholic, he added ethnic and religious balance to the MDRM group of leaders. With the other two MDRM deputies (q.v.), Rabemananjara was accused of complicity in the Rebellion of 1947 (q.v.). On October 4, 1948, he was sentenced to life imprisonment at forced labor, a sentence that was later commuted to imprisonment in Corsica and in 1955 to assigned residence in Paris, where he took up his literary activities again.

In 1957 Rabemananjara was released from the restrictions of assigned residence, but not permitted to return to Madagascar. By 1960 he had made his peace with the new regime of Philibert Tsiranana (q.v.) and returned to Madagascar in July 1960. In the September 1960 elections to the Malagasy National Assembly, he ran in Toamasina province at the head of the Miara-Mirindra (q.v.) list, which gained sixteen seats in the assembly. Although the list ran against an "orthodox" list of candidates from Tsiranana's Parti Social Démocrate (q.v.), it included some PSD supporters, and Rabemananjara himself was made minister of agriculture in the new government. He joined the PSD officially in 1961, becoming successively minister for the economy and, in 1967, minister of foreign affairs.

Rabemananjara was widely considered to be a possible successor to Tsiranana. By the early 1970s, however, his prestige had declined, in part because of the agreements he had negotiated with South Africa as foreign minister and in part because of accusations of corruption. After the fall of the First Republic (q.v.) in 1972, Rabemananjara returned to exile in Paris.

He returned to Madagascar after the fall of the Democratic Republic of Madagascar (q.v.), and ran in the presidential elections of 1992, offering himself as a "transitional pope" and gaining the support of some of the more conservative elements of the Comité des Forces Vives (q.v.), including General Jean Rakotoharison (q.v.). *Further information may be found in the Bibliography following this Dictionary.*

RABEMANANJARA, RAYMOND. Although not related to Jacques Rabemananjara, Raymond Rabemananjara was also active in nationalist politics after the Second World War and was one of the founders of the Mouvement Démocratique de la Rénovation Malgache. In the period before independence, he was active in trying to form a popular Christian party. In 1956 he formed the Union Travailliste et Paysanne (q.v.), and in the 1956 municipal elections he ran unsuccessfully in

Antananarivo on a list called "Union et Action Communale." *Further information may be found in the Bibliography following this Dictionary.*

RABEONY, JOSEPH. General Joseph Rabeony was head of the Service Civique branch of the Malagasy military (q.v.) in the last years of the First Republic (q.v.). In 1976 he replaced General Gilles Andriamahazo as president of the Comité Militaire pour le Développement, serving in this capacity until 1984.

RABESAHALA, GISELE (1930–). Born into a politically active family, she began her own political activities in the early 1950s in organizations grouping Malagasy nationalists and French sympathizers like Pierre Boiteau. In the pre-independence period she served as secretary-general to the Comité de Solidarité Malgache (q.v.) and worked on the executive of FISEMA, the Malagasy union affiliated to the French Confédération Générale de Travail (q.v.). She was also a member of the editorial board of the nationalist newspaper *Imongo Vaovao.* Rabesahala was one of the founders of the AKFM (q.v.), and became secretary-general in 1959. Under the Democratic Republic of Madagascar (q.v.) she was an AKFM representative to the Front National pour la Défense de la Révolution (q.v.) and a member of the Assemblée Nationale Populaire (q.v.) for Antananarivo. Rabesahala was considered to be one of the Marxist hardliners of the AKFM and the DRM, and became minister for revolutionary art and culture in 1977. In September 1989 the name of the post was changed to the minister of culture, and in the August 1991 government of Guy Razanamasy the ministry was abolished and she was removed from government office.

RABETAFIKA, ROLAND. A member of a noble Merina (q.v.) family, and a graduate of Saint-Cyr, Rabetafika was one of three colonels in the Malagasy armed forces at the time of the May 1972 Revolution (q.v.). When General Gabriel Ramanantsoa (q.v.) took power after the revolution, he appointed Rabetafika to head his personal cabinet and gave him responsibility for the management of the army (including promotions), for the intelligence activities of the Deuxiéme Bureau, and for the direction of the economy. In the factional disputes that characterized the Ramanantsoa regime (q.v.), Rabetafika's personal ambition and his preference for a state-run capitalist economy clashed with the ambitions and more socialist options of Colonel Richard Ratsimandrava (q.v.) and naval captain Didier Ratsiraka (q.v.).

As director of the economy, Rabetafika was responsible for the creation of the state marketing companies and eventually became identified with the mismanagement and corruption that characterized their activities. In December 1974 the Deuxième Bureau discovered the existence of a coup plot, led by Colonel Bréchard Rajaonarison (q.v.), who accused the regime and Rabetafika in particular of corruption and a pro-Merina bias in military promotions. The discovery of the plot, and its consequences, led to the fall of the Ramanantsoa regime, and Ratsimandrava and Ratsiraka were able to block Rabetafika's attempts to succeed Ramanantsoa. When Ratsimandrava was assassinated after one week in power, on February 11, 1975, Rabetafika was one of the main suspects, both because of thwarted ambition and because Ratsimandrava had been using the intelligence services of his Ministry of the Interior to investigate reports of corruption. Rabetafika was denied a seat on the Directoire Militaire (q.v.) that succeeded Ratsimandrava, and was arrested and added to the number of the accused in the "Trial of the Century" (q.v.) in April 1975. The case against him was dismissed in June 1975. He was later promoted to the rank of general of division and given the largely honorary post of inspector-general of the armed forces that Rajaonarison had held before him.

RABEZAVANA. Rabezavana was an official in the administration of the Merina Empire (q.v.) and one of the leaders of the resistance of the Menalamba (q.v.) against the imposition of colonial rule. The group that he led was able to capture the royal city of Ambohimanga (q.v.). He surrendered to the French in June 1897, but escaped and was recaptured twice, and finally exiled to Réunion. He was returned to Madagascar in 1899, where he died in 1900 under mysterious circumstances.

RABOTOSON, FRANCOIS DE PAUL. Rabotoson was minister of education of the Democratic Republic of Madagascar (q.v.) from 1976 to 1977. Removed from his post because of the continuing turmoil in the sector, and in particular because of a strike in the schools of technical education that involved several violent outbreaks, he was named secretary-general to the Conseil Suprême de la Révolution (q.v.).

RABOZAKA. Rabozaka was a Protestant minister and official of the Merina Empire (q.v.) who was one of the leaders of the revolt of the Menalamba against the imposition of French rule. His group rose in March 1896, the traditional period of the *fandroana,* and threatened the capital, Antananarivo. He surrendered in February 1898, and was exiled to Réunion.

RADAMA I. King of Imerina from 1810 to 1828, Radama continued the work of his father, Andrianampoinimerina (q.v.), of extending the boundaries of the Merina (q.v.) monarchy. He conquered the territory east of Imerina, taking the port of Toamasina (q.v.) in 1817, and engaged in less successful warfare with the kingdoms of the Sakalava (q.v.) to the west. He also moved south, into the territory of the Betsileo (q.v.). He began diplomatic contacts with outside powers, signing a treaty with the British governor of Mauritius, Sir Robert Farquhar in 1817, in which he agreed to abandon the slave trade in return for recognition of his claim to be king of Madagascar, payment of an indemnity, and British sponsorship of his efforts to modernize his kingdom. Under this sponsorship missionaries from the London Missionary Society (q.v.) came to the island to transliterate the Malagasy language into the Latin alphabet, set up an educational system, and establish small industries. Under James Hastie (q.v.), British soldiers participated in the training of the Malagasy army, which Radama made a standing force for the first time. Radama, who was a skeptic in religious matters (although he did consult *ombiasy* [q.v.], as had his father), limited the proselytizing activities of the missionaries, but he also minimized the ritual aspects of the monarchy. When he died in 1828 he was succeeded by his first wife and cousin, who ruled as Ranavalona I (q.v.).

RADAMA II (1829–1863). Known in his youth as Prime Rakoto or Rakotond-Radama, Radama II was the son of Ranavalona I (q.v.) and was accepted as the son of Radama I (q.v.), who had died eighteen months before his birth. Although her reign was marked by a closure against Western influences, Ranavalona saw that her son had some education and did little to limit his contacts with such Europeans as Jean Laborde (q.v.). By the end of Ranavalona's reign Prince Rakoto had become the focus of hopes for a lessening of authoritarian rule and for a reopening of the country to outside contacts, and he had gathered around him a counter-court of like-minded Malagasy. An attempt to anticipate the succession and stage a coup in 1857 led to the expulsion of Laborde, but left the prince in line to succeed.

When Ranavalona died in 1861, Radama proceeded to put into operation the opening that had been promised. The death penalty and ordeal by poison were abolished, as were rituals like circumcision and the *fandroana.* In addition Radama abolished import and export duties and began to implement the Lambert Charter (q.v.), which granted the French-based Compagnie de Madagascar extensive land and mineral rights on the island in return for 10% of the company's profits.

Radama's changes aroused considerable opposition. The ruling elite of his mother's reign were disturbed by the attack on their control of the Merina economy, and by Radama's reliance on a group of advisors drawn from outside their ranks, called the Menamaso, or "Red Eyes." (The reasons given for the name vary: the Menamaso had a reputation for being dissolute, and "red eyes" might refer to this. Others claim that "red eyes" could refer to courage, or that they resulted from late nights spent poring over state papers.) Most of the Menamaso came from aristocratic families from the south of Imerina, rather than from the Andafiavaratra (q.v.) families of the north who had helped establish the Kingdom.

The abandonment of central royal rituals also disturbed

the population, and an epidemic of spirit possession, called *Ramaneniana,* broke out in the countryside and spread to Antananarivo. Those affected claimed to be possessed by the spirits of the royal ancestors come to reproach their unworthy descendant. In March 1863 the *fandroana* was not held. At the same time, the Andafiavaratra were criticizing Radama II for the terms of the Lambert Charter and demanding that he stop his association with the Menamaso. Radama refused, and at the beginning of May the Andafiavaratra, led by Raharo (q.v.), son of the prime minister of Ranavalona I, staged a coup. The Menamaso were killed, and in the night of May 11–12 Radama himself was strangled. He was succeeded by his first wife and cousin, who ruled as Rasoherina (q.v.). Raharo became prime minister and husband of the queen.

RADIO, CELESTIN. A doctor from Fianarantsoa province, Radio was a member of the Front National pour la Défense de la Révolution (q.v.) of the Democratic Republic of Madagascar (q.v.) as vice president of one of its member parties, Vonjy (q.v.). He was minister of social affairs in the weeklong government of Colonel Richard Ratsimandrava (q.v.) in 1975, and was minister of public works in the second government of President Didier Ratsiraka (q.v.) in 1976. He also served as minister of public administration, a post he left in 1982 to join the Conseil Suprême de la Révolution (q.v.).

RAHARIJAONA, HENRI. A former ambassador to France, Raharijaona was along with Nirina Andriamanerisoa (q.v.), one of the authors of the new Malagasy investment code.

RAHARO (*also known as* Rainivoninahitriniony). One of the leaders of the conservative faction in the Merina court of the early nineteenth century, Raharo was the son of Rainiharo (q.v.), husband and prime minister of Ranavalona I (q.v.), and the brother of Rainilaiarivony (q.v.), who was to rule as prime minister for most of the second half of the century. When his father died in 1852, Raharo became commander in chief of the Merina armies. He at first supported Ranavalona's successor, Radama II (q.v.), and became his prime minister, his brother taking over as commander in chief. Disturbed by Radama's growing moves to Westernization, however, and by the growing influence of a group of advisors called the Menamaso, Raharo led the coup d'état that overthrew and assassinated the king in May 1863. He became the prime minister and husband of the new queen. Rasoherina (q.v.). Raharo soon become unpopular with the ruling group because of his excessive conservatism and his irrascible character, and in 1864 he was removed from his post and sent into exile on his estates. He was succeeded by his brother, Rainilaiarivony.

RAHATOKA, SALOMON. An administrator from southeast Fianarantsoa province, Rahatoka was director-general of the Ministry of the Interior from 1969 to 1972. After the May 1972 Revolution (q.v.) he became an advisor to the new head of state. General Gabriel Ramanantsoa (q.v.). He was minister of public works in the first government of Didier Ratsiraka (q.v.) and in 1976 was named to the Conseil Suprême de la Révolution (q.v.). In 1977 he became ambassador to the Federal Republic of Germany.

RAILROADS. Madagascar's railroads were all constructed before the Second World War. The oldest, the Antananarivo–Côte Est, which runs for 360 km from Antananarivo (q.v.) to Toamasina (q.v.), was started under Gallieni (q.v.) and finished in 1913. A spur line from Moramanga to the rice-growing area of Lake Alaotra (q.v.), a distance of 168 km, was finished in 1922, and another line from Antananarivo to Antsirabe (q.v.), a distance of 158 km, was finished in 1923. A separate line, the Fianarantsoa–Côte Est railroad, from Fianarantsoa (q.v.) to the port of Manakara, a distance of 163 km, was finished in 1938. The lines running to the coast are difficult to maintain, both because of the steep grade and because of the frequent cyclones and heavy rains that characterize the east-coast climate.

RAINILAIARIVONY (1828–1896). Prime minister of the Merina Empire (q.v.) from 1864 to 1895. Rainilaiarivony was a member of the Tsimiamboholahy clan (q.v.), which had helped the founder of the kingdom, Andrianampoinimerina (q.v.), seize power from his uncle. His father, Rainiharo (q.v.), had served as prime minister from 1828 to 1851, and his brother, Raharo (q.v.), from 1861 to 1864. In his youth, Rainilaiarivony received some mission education, participated in his family's commercial and military activities, and served as private secretary to Queen Ranavalona I (q.v.). He was one of the leaders of the coup that overthrew her successor, Radama II (q.v.).

Rainilaiarivony joined in the plot that removed his brother from the office of prime minister in 1864, and became prime minister and husband of Queen Rasoherina (q.v.). He continued as prime minister for the remaining years of the Merina state, placing on the throne and marrying the two succeeding sovereigns, Ranavalona II (q.v.) and Ranavalona III (q.v.).

It was Rainilaiarivony's goal as prime minister to preserve Madagascar from domination by foreign powers and to preserve the economic and political position of the ruling oligarchy of which his clan was an important part. This involved a certain degree of Westernization, symbolized by the conversion of Rainilaiarivony and Ranavalona II to Christianity in 1869. This conversion entitled the Merina kingdom to consideration as a "civilized" country, and secured his leadership of the growing Protestant faction in the kingdom. He also presided over the creation of two written legal codes, in 1868 and 1881. Rainilaiarivony continued his royal predecessors' attempts to modernize the army and create a territorial administration. In 1881 he created a cabinet with eight ministries: Interior, Foreign Affairs, Justice, Defense, Commerce, Industry, Finances, and Education.

In practice Rainilaiarivony continued to handle most important matters, and this excessive personalization and centralization of power contributed to the difficulties the Merina state had in dealing with the crisis presented by French pressure at the end of its existence. In 1883 the first Franco-Malagasy War (q.v.) demonstrated the weakness of the army and state apparatus, and led to the imposition of an indemnity and a protectorate (q.v.) for external matters. Rainilaiarivony's remaining years as prime minister were marked by increasing popular discontent and by court intrigues inspired by his age and by the prospect of a struggle for his succession. In 1894 the French delivered an ultimatum demanding a strengthening of their protectorate. Rainilaiarivony refused, and the second Franco-Malagasy War began. After the French victory in October 1895, Rainilaiarivony was exiled to Algiers, where he died in 1896. His body was returned to Madagascar to be buried with his family.

RAJAOBELINA, PROSPER (1913–1975). An author as well as a political activist, Rajaobelina was linked with Gabriel Razafintsalama (q.v.) in several post–Second World War moderate nationalist groups. Under the First Republic, he was director of the Ecole nationale d'Administration from 1960 to 1967. He also carried out several diplomatic missions.

RAJAONAH, PIERRE. A native of Antananarivo province with attachments to MONIMA (q.v.), Rajaonah was minister of rural development and agrarian reform in the first (1975) government of the Democratic Republic of Madagascar (q.v.). He was killed in August 1976, in the same helicopter crash that took the life of Prime Minister Joel Rakotomalala (q.v.).

RAJAONARISON, BRECHARD. Rajaonarison was one of three colonels in the Malagasy armed forces at the time of the May 1972 Revolution (q.v.) and the installation of the military-civilian regime led by General Gabriel Ramanantsoa. Unlike the other colonels—Roland Rabetafika (q.v.), who became Ramanantsoa's personal second-in-command, and Richard Ratsimandrava (q.v.), who became minister of the interior—Rajaonarison was given the largely honorific post of inspector-general of the army. He attributed this slight to his Côtier (q.v.) origins and to his lack of status as a former noncommissioned officer promoted to the officer corps at the time of independence. At the end of 1974, he began plans for a coup to overthrow the by then discredited Ramanantsoa regime (q.v.). His plot was discovered by Rabetafika's intelligence services, and he fled to the Antanaimoro military camp (q.v.)

outside Antananarivo. The camp was controlled by the largely côtier Groupe Mobile de Police (q.v.). From the camp Rajaonarison issued communiqués accusing the Ramanantsoa regime of corruption, of disgracing the armed forces, and of preferring Merina officers to others in promotions.

As the crisis proceeded, it was evident that Rajaonarison had some support for his point of view. Not only was he visited by figures from the regime displaced by the May 1972 Revolution, such as former president Philibert Tsiranana (q.v.) and André Resampa (q.v.), but regime supporters, including the brother of Didier Ratsiraka also came to the camp. In the face of this support, the regime did not dare attempt to dislodge him from Antanaimoro. The crisis led to the fall of General Ramanantsoa and to the naming of Richard Ratsimandrava as president on February 5, 1975. After the assassination of Ratsimandrava on February 11, the army did attack the camp, and Rajaonarison was arrested. Along with 305 others he was tried for complicity in the assassination in the ''Trial of the Century'' (q.v.), which began on March 21, 1975. The charges against Rajaonarison and the other defendants were dismissed, however, and he was retired from the army.

RAKOTO, ABEL. Gendarmerie captain Abel Rakoto was one of three officers arrested in 1977 and charged with conspiracy against the state. In 1983 he was sentenced to ten years at forced labor, while the others were given sentences of deportation for life. Although all three appealed their sentences, Rakoto later withdrew his appeal. *See also* OFFICER'S TRIAL.

RAKOTO, PRINCE. *See* RADAMA II.

RAKOTOARIJAONA, DESIRE. Rakotoarijaona was a commandant in the gendarmerie at the time of the 1975 assassination of Richard Ratsimandrava (q.v.) in whose weeklong government he had served as minister of finance. Rakotoarijaona became one of the members from Antananarivo province in the Directoire Militaire (q.v.), which took control of the country and elected Didier Ratsiraka (q.v.) as Ratsimandrava's successor in June 1975. With the other members of the Directoire, he became a member of the Conseil Suprême de la Révolution (q.v.) in 1975. In 1977 he succeeded Justin Rakotoniaina (q.v.) as prime minister, and in 1983 he was named to the political bureau of the regime party, AREMA (q.v.). In February 1988 he resigned his post as prime minister, in part for health reasons and in part because of growing political disagreements with President Ratsiraka.

RAKOTOHARISON, JEAN. Rakotoharison became commander in chief of the Malagasy armed forces in August 1976, and was commander at the time of the 1984 Kung Fu (q.v.) attack on the Tanora Tonga Saina (q.v.) bases in Antananarivo. The army was criticized for its failure to intervene rapidly in the incident, and Rakotoharison was already suspect for his independent attitude and links with the MFM (q.v.). Three days after the assault he was removed as commander in chief and "promoted" to the post of head of the Comité Militaire pour le Développement. He later retired from the military. In 1991 Rakotoharison joined the opposition to the Democratic Republic of Madagascar (q.v.). In July 1991 he agreed to serve as president of the countergovernment set up by the Comité des Forces Vives (q.v.). In the 1992 election for the presidency of the Third Republic (q.v.), he supported the candidacy of Jacques Rabemananjara (q.v.).

RAKOTOINDRAINY, LUCIEN (1931–1987). A native of Antananarivo province, Rakotoindrainy served as military chief of the province of Fianarantsoa during the Ramanantsoa regime (q.v.), holding the rank of lieutenant colonel in the army. Considered to be a loyal supporter of President Didier Ratsiraka (q.v.), he was named commander in chief of the Malagasy armed forces after the Kung Fu (q.v.) incidents of December 1984, although he had not previously held a command post. He died in June 1987.

RAKOTOMALALA, JOEL (1929–1976). The first prime minister of the Democratic Republic of Madagascar (q.v.), Rakotomalala came from Fianarantsoa province and began officer training in France in 1957. He joined the Malagasy army at the time of independence, and after the May 1972 Revolution (q.v.) became minister of information in the Ramanantsoa regime (q.v.). He was promoted to lieutenant colonel in 1973. Rakotomalala held the position of minister of posts and telecommunications in the weeklong government of Richard Ratsimandrava (q.v.) and became a member of the Directoire Militaire (q.v.) that took power after Ratsimandrava's assassination. Rakotomalala was one of the main organizers of the referendum that ratified the DM's choice of Didier Ratsiraka (q.v.) as president, and in January 1976 he became prime minister. He was killed in a helicopter accident on July 30, 1976.

RAKOTOMALALA, LOUIS. A bank employee in Antananarivo, Rakotomalala was active in nationalist politics during and after the Second World War. Although he had been a member of the Comité du Salut Public (q.v.) during the war, after the war he helped found the Mouvement Social Malgache (q.v.) rather than adhering to the Mouvement Démocratique de la Rénovation Malgache (q.v.) as had many other activists in the CSP. In the 1957 provincial elections he ran on the Liste de Défense des Droits du Peuple with Alfred Ramangosoavina and Gabriel Razafintsalama (q.v.), but he did not follow Ramangosoavina into alliance with the dominant Parti Social Démocrate (q.v.).

RAKOTOMANGA, MIJORO. A lieutenant colonel in the gendarmerie in 1975, Rakotomanga was an assistant to Richard Ratsimandrava (q.v.), minister of the interior in the Ramanantsoa regime (q.v.), and successor to General Ramanantsoa. Although he was not a member of the Directoire Militaire (q.v.) that ruled after Ratsimandrava's assassination, he was named head of the gendarmerie when Didier Ratsiraka (q.v.) took power in June 1975. He was replaced in this role in August 1977 by his second-in-command, Jean Filippe (q.v.).

RAKOTOMAVO, PASCAL. Rakotomavo was a longtime advisor to President Didier Ratsiraka (q.v.) on financial matters.

He was head of the state insurance company, ARO (Assurance Reassurances Omnibranches), and in 1982 was named minister of finance, succeeding Rakotovao-Razakboana (q.v.), leader of the antipresidential "right AREMA." He later became minister in the president's office with responsibility for finance and economy. In 1989 he became special counselor to the Conseil Suprême de la Révolution (q.v.), a post that disappeared when the CSR was abolished in 1992.

RAKOTONDRABE, SAMUEL (d. 1948). Rakotondrabe was a merchant in Antananarivo whom the colonial administration identified as the "general" of the Rebellion of 1947 (q.v.). He was captured, and then executed on July 19, 1948, three days before the beginning of the Tananarive Trial (q.v.).

RAKOTOND-RADAMA, PRINCE. *See* RADAMA II.

RAKOTONDRAVO-RADAODY, LAURENT. Rakotondravo-Radaody was a founding member of the AREMA political bureau. He was also the assistant director of the personal staff of Didier Ratsiraka (q.v.).

RAKOTONIRINA, MANANDAFY (1938–). A sociologist at the University of Madagascar and ORSTOM, Rakotonirina led the radical opposition to the First Republic (q.v.) in the late 1960s and early 1970s. He worked at first in conjunction with MONIMA (q.v.), but after a quarrel with the party's leader, Monja Jaona (q.v.), he assembled his own group based at the university. The journal of the group, *Ny Andry* (q.v.), criticized the regime for its continued ties with France and for the continuation of a colonial-style authoritarian relationship with the population. It also criticized French domination of the University of Madagascar and the failure of studies at the university to deal with what it saw as the problems of Malagasy society. Rakoktonirina's activities were instrumental in politicizing groups of unemployed youth in the capital, called ZOAM (q.v.), and in creating the alliances between those groups and student groups that culminated in the May 1972 Revolution (q.v.).

After the May revolution, Rakotonirina founded the MFM

(q.v.), or Party for Proletarian Power, and criticized the Ramanantsoa regime (q.v.) for failing to pursue the goals of the revolution. Several riots were blamed on the MFM, and Rakotonirina himself spent some time in jail. When the Democratic Republic of Madagascar (q.v.) was created in 1975, Rakotonirina at first maintained a distant attitude, and the MFM boycotted the institutions of the regime and the first set of elections. Rakotonirina took the MFM into the Front National pour la Défense de la Révolution (q.v.) in July 1977; he himself joined the Conseil Suprême de la Révolution (q.v.), becoming head of its economic commission. During the economic crisis of the 1980s, Rakotonirina became increasingly critical of the regime and increasingly prone to argue for the virtues of the market as a cure for those difficulties. In March 1987 he joined the leaders of other parties in creating the Alliance Démocratique Malgache (q.v.) with the purpose of opposing the regime's economic policies, and in the presidential elections of March 1989 he ran against President Didier Ratsiraka (q.v.), coming in second, with 19.3% of the vote.

Rakotonirina was one of the founders of the Comité des Forces Vives (q.v.), formed to work for the overthrow of Ratsiraka and the DRM. He took the MFM out of the alliance in July 1991, when the CFV named a countergovernment and began occupying government offices, declaring that this step was too "insurrectional" for his tastes. He continued to work with the opposition, and joined the power-sharing agreement (q.v.) that set up the transition to the third Republic (q.v.), sharing the chairmanship of the Committee for Economic Revival with Richard Andriamanjato (q.v.). Rakotonirina ran for president in the 1992 election, but came in a distant third to Ratsiraka and the winner, and other leader of the CFV, Albert Zafy (q.v.).

RAKOTONIRINA, MARSON. A captain in the army and a former aide of General and President Ramanantsoa (q.v.), Rakotonirina was one of three officers arrested in 1977 and charged with conspiracy against the state. Tried in 1983, Rakotonirina was sentenced to deportation—in effect, permanent house arrest. An appeal of the sentence was rejected in 1987. *See also* OFFICERS' TRIAL.

RAKOTONIRINA, STANISLAS. An employee of the Comptoir National d'Escompte in Antananarivo, Rakotonirina was the first elected mayor of the capital. He began his political career as a member of the provincial assembly from the Mouvement Démocratique de la Rénovation Malgache (q.v.). After the Rebellion of 1947 (q.v.) he was arrested but later acquitted of participation in the uprising. He returned to political activity and ran unsuccessfully for the provincial assembly and the French National Assembly, always losing to more "moderate" candidates. He founded the Union des Indépendants de Tananarive (q.v.) to contest the 1956 municipal elections, which he won. After the passage of the Loi-Cadre (q.v.), which promised increased autonomy for Madagascar, Rakotonirina attempted to extend the UIT beyond the capital. Although he was not successful in this, he was elected to the Antananarivo provincial assembly and by the provincial assembly to the Assemblée Représentative. In the campaign for the Referendum on the Constitution of the Fifth French Republic (q.v.) Rakotonirina advocated a "no" vote. He always refused to ally with other parties, however; he did not join the parties that formed the AKFM (q.v.) after the referendum, finding them too much under communist influence and, although a Catholic, did not join in efforts to to found a party based on the mission network. In October 1958 the head of the Loi-Cadre Government Council, Philibert Tsiranan (q.v.),was able to form a new majority on the Antananarivo municipal council with the cooperation of Louis Rakotomalala (q.v.), and Rakotonirina was ousted as mayor, to be replaced by Rakotomalala. Tsiranana also succeeded in having Rakotonirina ousted from his position in the governing council of Antananarivo province. In the election of 1960 he also lost his seat in the National Assembly. Rakotonirina died in Paris in 1976.

RAKOTOVAHINY, ARSENE. A founder of the Parti Social Démocrate (q.v.), Rakotovahiny had been an ally of Philibert Tsiranana (q.v.) from the early 1950s. participating with him in the Front National Malgache (q.v.). In the 1960 election, he led the "orthodox" PSD slate in Toamasina province against the Miara-Mirindra (q.v.) slate of Jacques Rabemananjara (q.v.). The failure of his list greatly reduced his political influence, and it was Rabemananjara who moved into the Tsiranana government as minister.

RAKOTOVAO, JOHANESA (1899–1966). Rakotovao was a Lutheran minister who was a leader of the Committee for Amnesty for the prisoners of the Rebellion of 1947 (q.v.). With Gabriel Razafintsalama (q.v.) he was a founder of the short-lived Parti Libéral Chrétien (q.v.).

RAKOTOVAO-RAZAKABOANA. A native of Antananarivo province, Rakotovao-Razakaboana was minister of finance of the Democratic Republic of Madagascar (q.v.) from 1975 to 1982. He had previously served as director of the Planning Bureau under the Ramanantsoa regime (q.v.) and in 1975 was considered to be close to the AKFM (q.v.). Although he was a founding member of the regime party, AREMA (q.v.), and head of its Antananarivo section, his political position increasingly differed from that of President Ratsiraka, until by 1980 he was considered to be the center of a ''right AREMA'' opposing the socialist options of the ''left,'' or presidential, AREMA. Rakotovao-Razakaboana's position was strengthened by the confidence that officials of the International Monetary Fund (q.v.) placed in him during early negotiations to resolve Madagascar's economic crisis. His performance in the 1982 presidential campaign, however, when he failed to rally a large enough majority of the vote for Ratsiraka's candidacy, led to a final break between the two men. Rakotovao-Razakaboana was relieved of his position as finance minister and ''promoted'' to the Conseil Suprême de la Révolution (q.v.).

RALAIBERA, REMI. A Catholic priest and editor of the church's main political journal, *Lakroan'i Madagasikara,* Ralaibera was a critical commentator on Malagasy politics beginning in the later days of the First Republic (q.v.). He was one of the nonstudents arrested at the time of the May 1972 Revolution (q.v.). He was originally supportive both of the Ramanantsoa regime (q.v.) and of the Democratic Republic of Madagascar (q.v.) but became increasingly critical of the corruption and political and economic failure of the regimes. *See also* CATHOLIC CHURCH; CHURCHES.

RALAIMONGO, JEAN (1884–1942). The most important leader of Madagascar's interwar nationalist movement, Ralaimongo was born to a Betsileo (q.v.) family and attended the Normal School of the French Protestant Mission. He served in France in the First World War, and after the war remained in Paris where he helped found the Ligue Française Pour l'Accession des Indigènes de Madagascar aux Droits des Citoyens Français (q.v.), of which he became the secretary-general. He also participated in journals critical of France's colonial policy such as *L'Action coloniale* and *Le Libéré.*

In 1923 Ralaimongo returned to Madagascar at the same time as Joseph Ravoahangy (q.v.), with whom he frequently collaborated. There he founded a series of newspapers, including *L'Opinion,* which were usually seized and forced out of operation by the colonial authorities. He spent much of his time under house arrest but continued to attempt to organize peasant resistance to the *indigénat* (q.v.). During a period of liberty he helped organize the May 19, 1929, demonstration (q.v.) at the Excelsior Theater in Antananarivo and was arrested and sentenced to house arrest in the Antalha district. He died there in 1942. *See also* RALAIMONGO GROUP.

RALAIMONGO GROUP. This name was given to a group of nationalists centered around Jean Ralaimongo (q.v.) and active after the First World War. The group was the first nationalist group to make a concerted effort to reach beyond the elite of Antananarivo. As well as Ralaimongo, the group included Joseph Ravoahangy (q.v.), Joseph Raseta (q.v.), Abraham Razafy (q.v.), and Jules Ranaivo (q.v.). Among its European sympathizers were Paul Dussac (q.v.), Edouard Planque (q.v.), and Ignace Albertini (q.v.). The Ralaimongo group at first demanded the end of the *indigénat* (q.v.) and the extension of the rights of French citizens to the Malagasy, but after the May 19, 1929, demonstration (q.v.) in Antananarivo began to demand independence. Several members of the group were active in the post–Second World War

Mouvement Démocratique de la Rénovation Malgache (q.v.).

RAMAHATRA, PRINCE (1858–1938). Prince Ramahatra was the cousin and brother-in-law of Queen Ranavalona III (q.v.) and a member of the Catholic group of the Merina court. In 1895 he was minister of war and a member of the Grand Council of the kingdom, where he frequently quarreled with the prime minister, Rainilaiarivony (q.v.). After the French conquest he joined the French "pacification" of the Vakinakaratra region south of Tananarive and served in the French colonial administration until 1913. In 1921 he became the first Malagasy appointed to the Conseil d'Administration of the colony.

RAMAHATRA, VICTOR. Army lieutenant colonel Victor Ramahatra became prime minister of the Democratic Republic of Madagascar (q.v.) in February 1988. A native of Antananarivo province considered to be a "president's man," he had been minister of public works since 1982. He presided over the collapse of the regime and was replaced as prime minister (after having offered his resignation several times) by Guy Razanamasy (q.v.) in August 1991, as part of Ratsiraka's efforts to placate his opposition.

RAMAKAVELO. Ramakavelo was an officer in the Service Civique section of the Malagasy military (q.v.) at the time of the May 1972 Revolution (q.v.). Under the Ramanantsoa regime (q.v.) he served in the internal security organization attached to the president's office, the Deuxième Bureau, under the direction of Roland Rabetafika (q.v.). When Colonel Richard Ratsimandrava (q.v.) became president, he named Ramakavelo head of his military cabinet, with responsibilities that included assuring his own security. Ramakavelo was a representative from Fianarantsoa province in the Directoire Militaire (q.v.) that took office after Ratsimandrava's assassination. He also testified at the "Trial of the Century" (q.v.) of those accused of complicity in the assassination, and presented a theory of a double plot involving former president Tsiranana (q.v.) and Rabetafika.

He subsequently moved back to training responsibilities in the army.

RAMANANTSALAMA, JEAN-BAPTISTE. A former administrator and native of Toamasina province, Ramanantsalama is a founding member of the regime party of the Democratic Republic of Madagascar (q.v.), AREMA (q.v.). He was named to the Conseil Suprême de la Révolution (q.v.) when it was enlarged to include civilian participation in 1976.

RAMANANTSOA, GABRIEL (1906–1979). Ramanantsoa was the second president of Madagascar, and the first general and commander in chief of the Malagasy army, to which he transferred at the time of independence after a distinguished career in the French army. A member of a family related to Merina (q.v.) royalty, he graduated from Saint-Cyr in 1931 and entered a colonial infantry regiment. He served in the defense of France in 1940, and was decorated. From 1943 to 1946 he commanded a company stationed in Madagascar, but was in France attached to the Ministry of Defense at the time of the Rebellion of 1947 (q.v.). He later served in the French army in Indochina and had the rank of colonel at the time of Malagasy independence.

At the time of the May 1972 Revolution (q.v.) the armed forces were seen as a guarantee of stability in the face both of the collapse of the First Republic (q.v.) and of the radical elements leading the May demonstrations. As commander in chief of the army, and a figure considered to be acceptable to the French (who had supported the First Republic until that time, and who had 4,000 paratroopers stationed just outside the capital) Ramanantsoa was a logical successor to President Tsiranana. He first received a grant of "full powers" from the president on May 17, and after the referendum of October 1972 (q.v.) became president in his own right.

Ramanantsoa at first conceived his time in office as a chance to give Madagascar a rest cure from politics.

This respite never occurred, however, and the Ramanantsoa regime (q.v.) was marked by unrest, both on the left and on the right, and by rivalry among its leaders. By late 1974 these quarrels, increasing corruption (rumored to include Ramanantsoa's wife, if not the president himself), and Ramanantsoa's failure to give stronger leadership had brought his regime into discredit. When a disaffected colonel, Bréchard Rajaonarison (q.v.), attempted a coup in December 1974, even former supporters called for Ramanantsoa's resignation, and the two most important members of his government—Richard Ratsimandrava (q.v.) and Didier Ratsiraka (q.v.)—refused to continue to serve under him. After an attempt to remain in office, Ramanantsoa handed power over to Richard Ratsimandrava on February 5, 1975. Ramanantsoa remained in the background during the subsequent assassination of Ratsimandrava and the period of rule by the Directoire Militaire (q.v.) that ended with the coming to power of Didier Ratsiraka. He was retired at the end of 1975 along with other senior generals, and died in Paris in May 1979.

RAMANANTSOA REGIME. This regime, headed by General Gabriel Ramanantsoa (q.v.), succeeded the First Republic (q.v.) after the May 1972 Revolution (q.v.) and lasted until the end of 1974. Although Ramanantsoa himself, and the chief figures of his government—his personal second-in-command, army colonel Roland Rabetafika (q.v.); the minister of the interior, gendarmerie colonel Richard Ratsimandrava (q.v.); and the minister of foreign affairs, naval captain Didier Ratsiraka (q.v.)—were all drawn from the military, the regime also included civilian figures. Its legitimacy was drawn both from the transfer of power effected during the May revolution, when a military-led government seemed to be the only plausible nonrevolutionary alternative to the First Republic, and from the Referendum of October 1972 (q.v.), which established an interim regime to last for five years and charged with the task of preparing more permanent political institutions. The referendum also established an elected consultative legislature, the Conseil National Populaire du Développement (q.v.).

The main policy task of the Ramanantsoa regime was the implementation of the "Malgachization" (q.v.) of the economy, educational system, and foreign policy of the country desired by the participants in the May revolution. The Cooperation Agreements (q.v.) with France were renegotiated, ending the special relationship between France and Madagascar that had characterized the First Republic, some French firms were nationalized, and state companies (q.v.) were established to take control of trade, dominated within the island by non-Malagasy, usually Asian, intermediaries. Malgachization of education was more controversial, and fears that the policy would mean the imposition of the Merina (q.v.) dialect of Malagasy led to riots in other regions as early as December 1972.

Ramanantsoa expected his regime would be a period of apolitical rule, but the country never found the calm he expected. The regime had to contend with resistance both from the displaced politicians of the First Republic and from the radical elements of the May revolution, who saw the regime as the betrayal rather than the culmination of the revolution. The one organized political force that reliably supported the government was the AKFM (q.v.), the major opposition party of the First Republic. The period was also marked by factional disputes among the three leading officers. Personal ambition played a role, but each also had a different vision of Madagascar's future. Rabetafika espoused a state-directed capitalism; Ratsimandrava initiated a form of direct democracy with his *fokonolona* reform (q.v.); and Ratsiraka was attracted by Marxist socialism. In addition, corruption of government officials and directors of the new state companies became increasingly blatant.

When Colonel Bréchard Rajaonarison (q.v.) staged his attempted coup at the end of December 1974, he was able to demonstrate considerable support in the armed forces and among civilian political groups if not for his succession to power, at least for the end of Ramanantsoa's rule. Ramanantsoa dismissed his government in January 1975, and attempted to form a new one. The two figures whose support was essential for any continued credibility, however,—Ratsimandrava and Ratsiraka—refused to serve with him. Each also refused to serve in a government in which the other held any position of power. In the end, Ramanantsoa handed power over to Richard Ratsimandrava on February 5, 1975. *See also* KIM; RESAMPA, ANDRÉ; TSIRANANA, PHILIBERT.

RAMANGOSOAVINA, ALFRED (1917–). Ramangasoavina earned degrees in political science and law in Paris, where he was active in the Association des Etudiants d'Origine Malgache (q.v.). He returned to Madagascar and in 1956 formed the Union des Intellectuels et Universitaires Malgaches (q.v.). He was elected to the Antananarivo provincial council in 1957 on a list for the defense of provincial interests that he formed with Louis Rakotomalala (q.v.). He at first supported rapid movement to independence, and UNIUM was one of the participants at the 1958 Tamatave Congress (q.v.) of nationalistic-minded parties. This led to his dismissal from the Loi-Cadre Governing Council (q.v.) by Philibert Tsiranana (q.v.), the vice president of the council. Ramangasoavina then rejected his earlier stand and made peace with Tsiranana, joining his Parti Social Démocrate (q.v.) in 1960. At independence, he became minister of justice of the First Republic (q.v.) and was considered to be the senior Merina (q.v.) and chief intellectual of the government.

RAMAROHETRA. Ramarohetra was a director of the secret society JINA (q.v.). After the Rebellion of 1947 (q.v.) he was one of the major prosecution witnesses against the MDRM deputies (q.v.), accusing them of direct complicity in the rebellion. At the Tananarive Trial (q.v.), however, he retracted his testimony, claiming that it had been extracted by torture.

RAMAROLAHY, PHILIBERT. A native of Antananarivo province, Ramarolahy served as a noncommissioned officer in the French army,and was promoted to the office corps when he joined the Malagasy army after independence. He served as commander in chief of the army during the Ramanantsoa regime (q.v.). He was the presiding military judge at the ''Trial of the Century'' (q.v.) of those accused of complicity in the assassination of Colonel Richard Ratsimandrava (q.v.), but he stepped down when one of the most important of the accused, Colonel Bréchard Rajaonarison (q.v.), attacked him for complicity in what he called the pro-Merina bias of the armed forces. Ramarolahy retired in September 1975.

RANAIVO, JULES. Born into a Merina (q.v.) family living in Betsileo (q.v.) territory, Ranaivo was a leader of the interwar nationalist movement and, with Paul Dussac (q.v.), founded one of the movement's important journals, *L'Aurore malgache.* At the beginning of the war, he was interned by the colonial administration, and his daughter, who had been active in a Free French (q.v.) group, was executed. After the war he joined the Mouvement Démocratique de la Rénovation Malgache (q.v.) and was elected to the French Conseil de la République (q.v.) on March 30, 1947, just at the moment of the outbreak of the Rebellion of 1947 (q.v.). The announcement of his election was delayed until after his arrest, and his parliamentary immunity was lifted ex post facto. He was condemned to ten years solitary confinement, but was released in 1953. He revived the nationalist journal *Ny Rariny* (''Justice'') and later joined the AKFM (q.v.).

RANAVALONA I (c. 1790–1861). Ruler of the Merina Empire (q.v.) from 1828 to 1861, Ranavalona I was the cousin and first wife of Radama I (q.v.). She succeeded to the throne after his death as the result of coup d'état staged by representatives of the group that had originally helped his father to take power, and led by Rainiharo (q.v.), who became her prime minister and whom she married secretly. Many of the policies of her reign reflected the interests of this group. Ranavalona reversed many of Radama's policies, particularly the opening up to European influences. The teaching activities of the missionaries were stopped, and the missionaries themselves expelled in 1835. Malagasy Christians were suspected of owing loyalty to the foreign powers represented by the missionaries and ordered to give up their beliefs. Many were killed when they refused to do so.

At the same time, Ranavalona encouraged the economic activities of such Europeans as Jean Laborde (q.v.) and James Cameron (q.v.) and attempted to continue Radama's work of conquering the rest of the island and centralizing power in Antananarivo. During her reign the city of Fianarantsoa (q.v.) was founded, a Malagasy dictionary was begun, and a code of laws published. At the end of her reign the queen became increasingly unpopular and in 1857 a coup designed to replace her with her son, Prince Rakoto (later Radama II, q.v.), was attempted. Ranavalona survived the attempt, but after her death in 1861 her policy of closure against European influences was abandoned.

RANAVALONA II (d. 1885). A niece of Ranavalona I (q.v.), and second wife of Radama II (q.v.), Ranavalona II was ruler of the Merina Empire (q.v.) from 1868 to 1885. Her reign marked the beginning of the Christian period of the Merina monarchy, a change foreshadowed at her coronation, where the traditional royal talismans, or *sampy* (q.v.), were replaced by the Bible. The queen and her husband and prime minister, Rainilaiarivony (q.v.), were formally baptized in February 1869. To mark their independence from foreign domination, the ceremony was conducted by Malagasy minister rather than European missionaries. In September 1869 the *sampy* were ordered destroyed (in fact, most were taken into hiding by their quardians, to reappear at the time of the Revolt of the Menalamba [q.v.] in 1896). Ranavalona also presided over the creation of the Palace Church, whose network, very much under the control of Rainilaiarivony, was an important part of the administration of the Merina state in its later years. Her reign was also marked by the publication of the Code of 305 Articles (q.v.) and the Franco-Malagasy War of 1883–1885 (q.v.). She died before the signature of the treaty that established the first French protectorate (q.v.).

RANAVALONA III (1863–1917). Queen of the Merina Empire (q.v.) from 1885 until 1896, Ranavalona was a member of the royal family chosen by Prime Minister Rainilaiarivony (q.v.) to fill what was essentially a figurehead position. She was retained as queen after the French conquest (q.v.) in 1895, but exiled when the French abandoned the protectorate (q.v.) and made Madagascar a colony after the Revolt of the Menalamba (q.v.), a revolt made in her name although probably without her knowledge. Ranavalona died in Algiers in 1917. When her body was returned to Antananarivo in 1939, the occasion set off a major demonstration of nationalist sentiment.

RANDRIAMAROMANANA, ALBERT (1913–1947). Randriamaromanana was a lieutenant in the French army at the time of the outbreak of the Rebellion of 1947. He joined the secret society JINA (q.v.) that year, and was responsible for planning the attack on French installations in Antananarivo. It was called off at the last minute and he was arrested and then executed on April 28, 1947. In 1974 he was given the posthumous position of commander of the Ordre National Malgache.

RANDRIANANJA, CHARLES. A doctor and AKFM (q.v.) deputy from Antananarivo in the Assemblée Nationale Populaire (q.v.), Randriananja succeeded Richard Andriamanjato (q.v.), the party's president and longtime mayor of the capital during the First Republic (q.v.), as president of the Popular Council of the city from 1977 to 1983. He also served as an AKFM representative to the Conseil Suprême de la Révolution (q.v.).

RANDRIANTANANA, JEAN DE DIEU. A captain in the army in 1975, Randriantanana was one of the representatives from Mahajanga province in the Directoire Militaire (q.v.) that ruled the country after the assassination of Colonel Richard Ratsimandrava (q.v.) and that elected Didier Ratsiraka (q.v.) president. A supporter of Ratsiraka, he was named to the Conseil Suprême de la Révolution (q.v.) in 1975. He was one of the founders of the central party of the Ratsiraka regime, AREMA (q.v.).

RAOMBANA (1809–1854). Descendant of an early ruler of Imerina, Raombana was sent to England for his education from 1819 to 1827. When he returned to Antananarivo, he became private secretary to Queen Ranavalona I (q.v.), and was charged with diplomatic missions and the education of the future Radama II (q.v.). He wrote extensively and secretly in English on the history and modern times of the kingdom. *Further information may be found under "Ayache, Simon," in the Bibliography following this Dictionary.*

RARIVOSON, JUSTIN. A former director of Shell-Madagascar, Rarivoson was named minister of economy and commerce in the 1976 government of the Democratic Republic of Madagascar. He was associated with Rakotovao-Razakaboana (q.v.) in the antipresidential "right AREMA" and was removed from office in 1982 along with other members of the group.

RASETA, JOSEPH. Raseta's involvement in nationalist activities began with his membership in Vy Vato Sakelika (q.v.), for which he was arrested in 1915 and sent to the prison island of Nosy Lava (q.v.). He was amnestied in 1921, and continued to be active in nationalist politics in the Ralaimongo group (q.v.), spending much of his time in assigned residence as a result. He was interned in 1940 but after the war returned to Antananarivo and was elected as one of two Malagasy delegates to the Constitutional Assemblies (q.v.) of the Fourth French Republic. In company with the other delegate, Joseph Ravoahangy (q.v.), and with Jacques Rabemananjara (q.v.) he founded the Mouvement Démocratique de la Rénovation Malgache (q.v.) in Paris in 1946. All three were elected as deputies to the French National Assembly in November 1946. After the outbreak of the Rebellion of 1947 (q.v.), Raseta's parliamentary immunity was lifted, and he was tried for complicity in the uprising, although he was in France at the time. The Tananarive trial (q.v.) of 1948 sentenced him to death, a sentence that was commuted to life imprisonment in 1949.

Raseta spent the subsequent years in prison in Corsica and after 1955 in restricted residence in France. He was freed from restricted residence in 1957, but not permitted to return to Madagascar. In July 1959 he made an attempt to return, but was intercepted at Djibouti and returned to France. He finally returned with the other MDRM deputies (q.v.) in July 1960, and stood as a candidate in elections to the Malagasy National Assembly for the AKFM. He did not win a seat, and in 1963 he left the party. Raseta ran unsuccessfully for president against Philibert Tsiranana (q.v.) in 1965. He died in 1979.

RASOHERINA (d. 1868). Rasoherina was queen of the Merina Empire (q.v.) from 1863 to 1868, succeeding her cousin and husband, Radama II (q.v.), who had been killed in a coup d'état provoked by his abandonment of royal traditions and his attacks on the economic and political position of the ruling oligarchy which, led by the Andafiavaratra (q.v.) families, staged the coup. Accordingly, her reign was marked by a return to tradition and by the domination of the oligarchy under the leadership first of Raharo (q.v.) and then of his brother, Rainilaiarivony (q.v.), who were, successively, her prime ministers and husbands. Rasoherina was named queen only after signing a document stating that the wishes of the sovereign became law only upon the agreement of the leaders of the people.

RASSEMBLEMENT CHRETIEN DE MADAGASCAR. The RCM, founded in 1958, was an attempt to form a coalition of Christian parties, and included members from the Parti Démocratique de Madagascar (q.v.) and the Union Sociale Malgache (q.v.). It made a strong showing in the municipal elections of 1959, but split over the issue of participation in the government led by the Parti Social Démocrate (q.v.). Jean François Jarison (q.v.) took his followers first into cooperation with Jacques Rabemananjara (q.v.) and then into the government, while another leader, Michel Randria, opposed participation and was ousted as mayor of Fianarantsoa as a result.

RASSEMBLEMENT DU PEUPLE MALGACHE. The RPM was founded in 1956 by, among others, Michel Randria. It was an attempt to link the Protestants and Catholics of the Highlands (q.v.) on a platform of autonomy within the French Community. The party attempted to expand outside the Highlands, but without success, and Randria later took his followers into the Rassemblement Chrétien de Madagascar (q.v.).

RASSEMBLEMENT NATIONAL MALGACHE (*also* Renouveau National Malgache). After the formation of the AKFM (q.v.), an attempt was made under the aegis of Alexis Bezaka (q.v.) to regroup the other parties that had attended the Tamatave Congress (q.v.). Among the parties that joined were Union Nationale Malgache (q.v.) and the Union des Travailleurs et Paysans (q.v.). Stanislas Rakotonirina (q.v.) was approached to bring his Union des Indépendants de Tananarive (q.v.) into the party, but he refused. The party was strongest in Bezaka's home base of Toamasina province, with some bases in Antananarivo and Fianarantsoa. At the time of the 1960 legislative elections, Bezaka cooperated in forming the Miara-Mirindra (q.v.) list with Jacques Rabemananjara (q.v.), and after the elections the bulk of the party's elected members joined the governing Parti Social Démocrate (q.v.).

RATSIMANDRAVA, RICHARD (1931–1975). President of Madagascar from February 5 to February 11, 1975, Ratsimandrava was born into a Merina (q.v.) family of slave descent. His father was a teacher in Antananarivo and one of the founders of the capital's section of the Parti des Deshérités de Madagascar (q.v.). Ratsimandrava graduated from Saint-Cyr in 1954, and served with the French army in Morocco and Algeria. In 1962 he became a captain in the Malagasy gendarmerie, and in 1969 became a colonel and first Malagasy commander of the gendarmerie. In that capacity he helped organize the suppression of the April 1971 Peasant Rebellion (q.v.) in southern Madagascar.

At the time of the May 1972 Revolution (q.v.) his refusal to commit the gendarmerie to the defense of the First Republic (q.v.) contributed to the fall of the regime, and it was his announcement of the refusal of the gendarmerie and army to undertake this defense to President Tsiranana (q.v.), whose protégé he had been considered to be, that marked the end of Tsiranana's resistance. In the subsequent Ramanantsoa regime (q.v.), Ratsimandrava became minister of the interior. During the factional struggles that marked the regime, he joined with Didier Ratsiraka (q.v.) to present a ''Left Front'' against Ramanantsoa's second-in-command and presumed successor, Roland Rabetafika (q.v.). He used his powers as minister of the interior to put together a populist alliance of the peasantry, the urban *Lumpenproletariat,* and some radical intellectuals, based on his attacks on corruption and his proposals for ''*fokonolona* reform'', a radical restructuring of the country's administration aimed at destroying state power at the local level and instituting "popular control of development."

After the December 1974 coup attempt of Colonel Bréchard Rajaonarison (q.v.), Ratsimandrava joined Ratsiraka in refusing to serve in any future government headed by then president General Gabriel Ramanantsoa (q.v.). When Ratsiraka made his participation in a future government conditional on Ratsimandrava's abandonment of his posts as minister of the interior, head of the gendarmerie, and leader of the *fokonolona* reform, Ratsimandrava's support in the gendarmerie and parts of the army allowed him to prevail, and he became president on February 5, 1975. He vowed to continue his attacks on the state apparatus and on official corruption. On February 11, on his way home from his office, he was assassinated. The trial of the immediate assassins and over 300 other suspects (including former President Tsiranana and Roland Rabetafika) ended with most charges being dismissed, and the responsibility for the assassination has never been formally attributed to any party. Ratsimandrava was promoted to the rank of general posthumously. *See also* DIRECTOIRE MILITAIRE; TRIAL OF THE CENTURY.

RATSIMILAHO (d. 1750). Founder of the Betsimisaraka Confederation (q.v.), Ratsimilaho was the son of an English pirate and a Malagasy mother. He was sent to England for an education, but quickly returned with guns and a plan to extend the authority of the Zanamalata (q.v.) over the east coast of Madagascar. Between 1712 and 1720 he was able to conquer the east coast from Antongil Bay to the port of Toamasina (q.v.) and to threaten other Betsimisaraka groups to the south. He died in 1750. His successors were not able to hold the confederation together; it gradually disintegrated and was absorbed by the Merina Empire (q.v.) after 1815.

RATSIRAKA, CELINE. The wife of the president of the Democratic Republic of Madagascar (q.v.), Didier Ratsiraka (q.v.), Céline Ratsiraka is also the daughter of the founder of the Parti des Deshérités de Madagascar (q.v.) and parliamentarian during the colonial period, Pascal Velonjara (q.v.). In her own right, she was an important political figure in the DRM. With her sister, Hortense Raveloson-Mahasampo (q.v.), she was instrumental in organizing the women's branch of the regime party, AREMA (q.v.), and in running the party's cooperative movement, including the cooperative enterprises PROCOOP (q.v.).

RATSIRAKA, DIDIER (1936–). Born in Toamasina province (q.v.), with a father who had been a colonial administrator and a founder of the Parti des Deshérités de Madagascar (q.v.), Ratsiraka entered the Malagasy navy after studies in France. At the time of the May 1972 Revolution (q.v.) he was serving as naval attaché at the Malagasy embassy in Paris, and was called back to serve as minister of foreign affairs in the Ramanantsoa regime (q.v.). As foreign minister he renegotiated the Cooperation Agreements (q.v.) with France, earning prestige as the one who had brought Madagascar its "Second Independence." In the factional struggles of the regime, he sided with Minister of the Interior Richard Ratsimandrava (q.v.) to form a "Left Front" in opposition to officers like Roland Rabetafika (q.v.). At the time of the attempted coup that brought down the Ramanantsoa regime, Ratsiraka and Ratsimadrava prevented Ramanantsoa's attempts to form a new government by refusing to serve with him. Then Ratsiraka also refused to join a government with Ratsimandrava unless the latter gave up his posts of minister of the interior and head of the gendarmerie. In this struggle Ratsiraka was handicapped by the small size of his primary base of support—the navy—and it was Ratsimandrava who became president on February 5, 1975, forming a government that excluded Ratsiraka.

When Ratsimandrava was assassinated on February 11, Ratsiraka became a member of the Directoire Militaire (q.v.) that took over, and was a candidate for the succession. He was able to put together a coalition that held the balance of power between a conservative group headed by Gilles Andriamahazo (q.v.) and the proponents of a continuation of Ratsimandrava's radical populism, headed by Commandant Soja (q.v.). On June 15 the Directoire chose him as president, and he announced the formation of the Democratic Republic of Madagascar (q.v.) and his determination to chart a course of Marxist socialism.

Ratsiraka was to be the only president of the DRM, serving until his ouster in 1992. In the years between 1975 and 1992 he had faced several crises, including divisions in the regime party, AREMA (q.v.), in the early 1980s; a contested presidential election in 1982 in which his opponent, Monja Jaona (q.v.), called for a general strike and the overthrow of the regime; violent opposition in the form of Kung Fu groups (q.v.) in 1984–1985; and another presidential election in 1989 in which three opposing candidates were able to gain a total of 48.7% of the vote.

There were several reasons for Ratsiraka's difficulties. He was never able to establish firm control of the military (q.v.), his economic policies created considerable opposition, and Madagascar struggled with the consequences of a debt crisis (q.v.) that, in the end, led to a progressive abandonment of internal socialism and a growing rapprochement with Western countries. Growing corruption in governing circles, including his own family, also led to resentment. He was able, however, to manage the divided opposition until 1989, and even later.

In 1991 the opposition united in the Comité des Forces Vives (q.v.) to demand an end to the DRM and the removal of Ratsiraka. Ratsiraka tried to divide the opposition, as he had before, but was not successful. In the power-sharing agreement (q.v.) that ended his rule and prepared the way for the Third Republic (q.v.), he managed to retain his office, but without any real power. He then attempted to mobilize his supporters in political parties and the military to demand the creation of a federal state. When the National Forum (q.v.) rejected this possibility, and the ad hoc committee set up to manage elections rejected his presidential candidacy, Ratsiraka campaigned for the rejection of the proposed constitution of the Third Republic, and then for the de facto creation of a federal state. In several coastal provinces the campaign became violent. In the face of this threat, the ad hoc transitional committee agreed to let Ratsiraka run for president in the 1992 elections. He came second in the first round of the elections, held on November 25, 1992, receiving

28.3% of the vote. In the runoff election, held on February 10, 1993, he again came second to Albert Zafy (q.v.), leader of the Comité des Forces Vives, with 33% of the vote. He has since been accused of complicity in several incidents of violent protest by proponents of a federalist system for Madagascar.

RATSIRAKA, ETIENNE. The brother of President Didier Ratsiraka (q.v.), and married to the daughter of Jarison (q.v.), a cabinet minister during the First Republic (q.v.), Ratsiraka was a civil servant in the Ministry of the Interior at the time of the May 1972 Revolution. He was briefly secretary-general of the ministry, but clashed with the minister, Richard Ratsimandrava (q.v.), over the issue of *fokonolona* reform (q.v.). He moved to become director of the Société Nationale de Commerce (q.v.) a position that he left in 1976 to enter the private sector.

RAVELOJAONA (1879–1956). Born in Antananarivo to a Protestant minister attached to the London Missionary Society (q.v.), Ravelojaona attended the Ecole Le Myre de Vilers (q.v.) and taught in the Protestant mission school system. He founded an organization called the Union Chrétien des Jeunes Gens to unite the educated youth of the capital, but the organization was suppressed by the colonial authorities as a potential center of nationalist activity. In 1913 Ravelojaona wrote a series of articles entitled ''Japan and the Japanese,'' discussing the possibility of modernization while maintaining traditional culture, that is said to have been the inspiration for the formation of Vy Vato Sakelika (q.v.). When that organization was suppressed in 1915 he was arrested and later sentenced to life imprisonment. The charges against him were dismissed on appeal. Although he was never a member of the interwar Ralaimongo group (q.v.), he was elected in 1939 to the Conseil Supérieur des Colonies (q.v.) and during the war organized the Comité du Salut Publique (q.v.). After the war he founded the Parti Démocratique Malgache (q.v.) and ran unsuccessfully against Ravoahangy (q.v.) in the 1945 elections to the French Constituent Assemblies (q.v.). He subsequently formed the

Parti Libéral Chrétien, but was not able to recapture his prewar audience.

RAVELOSON-MAHASAMPO. An administrator in the colonial civil service from Toliara province, Raveloson-Mahasampo was one of the founders of the Parti des Deshérités de Madagascar (q.v.) and ran unsuccessfully against Joseph Raseta (q.v.) in the 1946 elections to the second of the French Constitutional Assemblies. In 1951 he was elected to the French National Assembly from the western district of Madagascar. In 1956, arguing that PADESM had become too centered on Antananarivo, and too interested in autonomy, Raveloson-Mahasampo formed the Union Démocratique Cotière and ran unsuccessfully against Philibert Tsiranana (q.v.) in the same district. In 1957 he was elected to the provincial assembly of Toliara on a list affiliated with the Union Démocratique et Sociale de Madgascar (q.v.), opposing the Parti Social Démocrate (q.v.) list of André Resampa (q.v.). He was also elected to the National Assembly, and became a vice president, but his quarrels with Tsiranana and Resampa prevented him from extending his political influence. His son, Christophe Raveloson-Mahasampo (q.v.), was an important figure in the Democratic Republic of Madagascar (q.v.).

RAVELOSON-MAHASAMPO, CHRISTOPHE BIEN-AIMEE. Son of a founder of the Parti des Deshérités de Madagascar, Raveloson-Mahasampo (q.v.), and married to a daughter of Pascal Velonjara (q.v.) and sister of the wife of Didier Ratsiraka (q.v.), Christophe Raveloson-Mahasampo was a captain in the army at the time of the May 1972 Revolution (q.v.). He was military governor of the province of Toamasina during the Ramanantsoa regime (q.v.) and was named minister of public works in the government of Colonel Richard Ratsimandrava (q.v.). He was a representative of Toliara province in the Directoire Militaire (q.v.) that took power after Ratsimandrava's assassination. After the Directoire elected Ratsiraka president of the Republic in June 1975, Christophe Raveloson-Mahasampo became head of the chief internal security organization, the Direction General d'Investigations et de Documentation (DGID). The service was much criticized both for brutality and for lack of effectiveness, particularly in a series of trials in 1983. Christophe Raveloson-Mahasampo was removed as head of the service in March 1985, as part of Ratsiraka's attempts to placate his opposition. After the death of Guy Sibon (q.v.) in May 1986, however, Christophe Raveloson-Mahasampo, now a general, was named minister of defense in his place. He was dismissed from this post in February 1991 as part of Ratsiraka's effort to meet opposition criticism of his regime.

RAVELOSON-MAHASAMPO, HORTENSE. Wife of Christophe Raveloson-Mahasampo (q.v.), and sister of Céline Ratsiraka (q.v.), Hortense Raveloson-Mahasampo was an active figure in the politics of the Democratic Republic of Madagascar (q.v.). With her sister she was head of the women's branch of the regime party, AREMA (q.v.). She was also involved in the economic activities of the party, including the cooperative PROCOOP (q.v.).

RAVOAHANGY-ANDRIANAVALONA, JOSEPH (1893–1970). Born in Fianarantsoa to a family of the Merina (q.v.) aristocracy, he attended Protestant mission schools, the Ecole Le Myre de Vilers (q.v.), and the medical school at Befelatanana (q.v.). While at Befelatanana he was a founder of Vy Vato Sakelika (q.v.), and when the society was dissolved by the colonial administration he was arrested and sentenced to life imprisonment. He was amnestied in 1921, and took up nationalist activities again, working with the Ralaimongo group (q.v.). He helped found the group's journal, *L'Opinion,* and took over responsibility for it when Jean Ralaimongo (q.v.) was sent to prison. After the May 19, 1929, demonstration (q.v.) in Antananarivo, he was sentenced to assigned residence and not released until 1936. Ravoahangy was also active in the efforts of the Ralaimongo group to establish unions (q.v.) in Madagascar. During the war he was secretary-general of the Syndicat des Agriculteurs et Eleveurs de Madagascar and after the war he was elected to the Constituent Assemblies (q.v.) of the Fourth French Republic and, together with the other delegate,

Joseph Raseta (q.v.), and Jacques Rabemananjara (q.v.), founded the Mouvement Démocratique de la Rénovation Malgache (q.v.). In November 1946 he was elected to the French National Assembly.

After the outbreak of the Rebellion of 1947 (q.v.), his parliamentary immunity was lifted and he was tried as one of the organizers of the revolt and sentenced to death. The sentence was commuted in 1949, and he was sent first to prison in Corsica, and then to assigned residence in France. The sentence was lifted in 1957, but Ravoahangy and the other MDRM deputies were not allowed to return to Madagascar until July 1960. Like Rabemananjara, Ravoahangy made his peace with the new president of Madagascar, Philibert Tsiranana (q.v.) and in the September 1960 elections to the Malagasy National Assembly headed a list of national unity in Antananarivo province. He joined the government Parti Social Démocrate (q.v.) in 1961. Ravoahangy served first as minister of public health and, after 1964, as minister without portfolio in Tsiranana's governments.

RAVOAJANAHARY, CHARLES. A professor at the University of Madagascar, and a native of Antananarivo province, Ravoajanahary was one of the main contributors to the early ideology of the regime party of the Democratic Republic of Madagascar (q.v.), AREMA (q.v.). Under the First Republic, (q.v.) he had been a member first of the AKFM (q.v.) and then of MONIMA (q.v.). After the establishment of the Democratic Republic in 1975, he served as an advisor to President Ratsiraka (q.v.) and was named to the Conseil Suprême de la Révolution (q.v.) when it was enlarged to include civilian members. As the oldest member, he filled the position of doyen and was head of the Political and Ideological Commission. In the early 1980s he supported the antipresidential "right AREMA," led by the minister of finance, Rakotovao-Razakaboana (q.v.), and in 1982 was ousted from his position on the AREMA political bureau and the CSR.

RAVONY, FRANCISQUE. A lawyer and national treasurer of the MFM (q.v.), Ravony led the committee that drafted the MFM's proposed constitution for the end of the Democratic Republic of Madagascar (q.v.). When the opposition to the DRM, the Comité des Forces Vives (q.v.), proposed the creation of a countergovernment in May 1991, he was considered to be a possible prime minister, but when the MFM protested this tactic and withdrew from the CFV, he followed the party. He became deputy prime minister in the government composed of regime supporters and opposition figures named by Guy Razanamasy (q.v.) on November 13, 1991, and held the post through the period of transition to the Third Republic (q.v.).

RAZAFINDRABE, VICTORIEN (c. 1898–1948). A member of a Merina (q.v.) family of slave ancestry, Razafindrabe was a member of the secret society JINA (q.v.) and the head of the section of the Mouvement Démocratique de la Rénovation Malgache (q.v.) in Moramanga, Mahajanga province. He led the Rebellion of 1947 (q.v.) in that sector, and was not captured until September 1948. He died in October of the effects of his period of flight.

RAZAFINDRAKOTO, EMMANUEL. Razafindrakoto was a journalist and member of the Ralaimongo group (q.v.) of nationalists in the interwar period. He collaborated with another nationalist figure, Joseph Ravoahangy (q.v.), in several attempts to create Malagasy unions (q.v.), most of which were declared illegal by the colonial administration. In 1941 he was interned by Governor-General Cayla (q.v.), but after the British invasion of 1942 (q.v.) and the coming of the Free French, he was released in 1943.

RAZAFINTSALAMA, GABRIEL. A journalist in Antananarivo, Razafintsalama was an associate of the nationalist figure Ravelojaona (q.v.) in his later days. He participated in the wartime Comité du Salut Publique (q.v.), and after the war was a founder of the Parti Démocratique de Madagascar (q.v.). In 1955 he also participated in the founding of the Parti Libéral Chrétien (q.v.).

RAZANABAHINY-MAROJAMA, JEROME. A native of Fianarantsoa province, and president of Vonjy (q.v.), Dr.

Razanabahiny began his political career in the First Republic (q.v.) as a member of the 1959 Constituent Assembly. He was a director of the youth branch of the Parti Social Démocrate (q.v.) and a senator. After the May 1972 Revolution (q.v.), he split with the other leaders of the party to support the Ramanantsoa regime (q.v.). He founded Vonjy in 1973, and was elected to the Conseil National Populaire pour le Développement (q.v.). In 1976 he took his party into the Front National pour la Défense de la Révolution (q.v.) and became a member of the FNDR and the Conseil Suprême de la Révolution (q.v.). With the economic crisis of the 1980s, however, Razanabahiny was increasingly critical of regime policy. In March 1987 he joined the leaders of MONIMA (q.v.) and the MFM (q.v.) to create the Alliance Démocratique de Madagascar (q.v.) to oppose government policy, and in March 1989 he ran against Didier Ratsiraka (q.v.) for president of the republic. He came in third, after Ratsiraka and Manandafy Rakotonirina (q.v.), with 14.8% of the vote.

RAZANAMASY, GUY WILLY. In August 1991 Guy Razanamasy, at the time mayor of Antananarivo, was asked by President Didier Ratsiraka (q.v.) to form a government that would include members of the opposition to the Democratic Republic of Madagascar (q.v.). His first government included some opposition figures, but the attempt was rejected by the main opposition groups, including the Comité des Forces Vives (q.v.) and the churches, who demanded the removal of Ratsiraka before they would participate. Razanamasy made several further efforts to form a government of national reconciliation and to end the demonstrations and general strikes staged by the opposition, but without success. It was not until the ratification of the power-sharing agreement (q.v.) of October 31, 1991, in December, that Razanamasy was able to form a government acceptable to the opposition, but with only one member who could be considered to be a supporter of Ratsiraka. Razanamasy continued as prime minister during the period of transition to the Third Republic (q.v.).

REBELLION OF 1947. One of the most serious uprising in postwar Africa, this revolt broke out in the night of March 29–30, 1947, with attacks on French installations and settlers along the eastern region of Madagascar. At its height it reached as far inland as Fianarantsoa (q.v.) and reduced communications between Fianarantsoa and Antananarivo to daytime convoys. The center of gravity of the revolt was the cash-crop region of the east coast, where peasants had been displaced by the creation of plantations and subject to demands for forced labor. It also spread rapidly along the rail lines. The failure of attacks on the French military camp at Fianaratsoa itself, as well as on installations at Diégo-Suarez and Antananarivo, and the quiescence of the western region of Madagascar, prevented the islandwide uprising that the rebels had hoped for. It was late 1947, however, before the French were able to place the Malagasy forces on the defensive, and December 1948 before the revolt could be considered over. Some parts of the island remained under a state of siege until 1956.

Estimates of the death toll of the insurrection vary widely. Immediately after its suppression the French high command put the number of dead at 89,000, of which 550 were non-Malagasy, while a French investigation held from 1950 to 1952 estimated that 11,200 had died, 1,900 during the insurrection itself, 3,000 during its suppression, and 6,300 from disease and malnutrition. Other observers put the toll as high as 100,000.

The colonial administration attributed the responsibility for the uprising to the nationalist party, the Mouvement Démocratique de la Rénovation Malgache (q.v.) and arrested party activists, including the three MDRM deputies.

The party itself was dissolved in May 1947. It is probable that the actual planning of the revolt was carried out by the secret societies PANAMA (q.v.) and JINA (q.v.), recruiting from the party and from groups like unionists and returned soldiers, as well as from peasants who had been displaced by cash-crop agriculture. As the death toll indicates, the revolt was in many ways a civil war, and the Malagasy victims included both rebels and those Malagasy whom the rebels considered collaborators with the colonial system.

The revolt itself wove together longstanding grievances against the very existence of the colonial system and its specific characteristics, and complaints created by the privations of the recent war and by the mobilization of the island's resources for the war effort, as symbolized by the Office du Riz (q.v.). It looked both forward and backward. The goal of the revolt was the establishment of an independent Malagasy state. The Brazzaville Conference (q.v.) and the United Nations Charter (q.v.) had raised hopes that the colonial system was coming to an end, as had the early electoral successes of the MDRM. The revolt also looked back to the previous independent Malagasy state—the Merina monarchy (q.v.)—and was timed to coincide with the traditional period of the precolonial purification ritual, the *fandroana.*

The fact that the revolt was in part a civil war meant that for years the Malagasy had an ambivalent attitude toward it. Many of the members of the governing party of the First Republic (q.v.), the Parti Social Démocrate (q.v.), had been members of the party opposed to the MDRM, PADESM, or the Parti des Deshérités de Madagascar (q.v.), and had both suffered in the revolt and participated in its suppression. It was not until 1967 that the date of the outbreak of the revolt was declared a national holiday, and even then the anniversary issue of the journal *Lumière* (q.v.) was seized. The Democratic Republic of Madagascar (q.v.) considered itself to be the culmination of the hopes of ''the matyrs of 1947,'' and the Charter of the Malagasy Revolution (q.v.) made specific reference to them.

REFERENDUM, OCTOBER 8, 1972. This referendum ratified the position of General Ramanantsoa (q.v.) as head of state after the May 1972 Revolution (q.v.) and the military takeover that followed it. The question was: ''Do you accept the law that will enable General Ramanantsoa and his government of national unity to undertake over a period of five years the structural transformations necessary for reform and to create in political life a climate acceptable to the wishes of the population?'' The law in question eliminated the position of president of the republic, thereby effectively denying Philibert Tsiranana (q.v.), who had nominally kept the office after May 1972, any claim to authority.

REFERENDUM, DECEMBER 1–21, 1975. This referendum marked the official beginning of the Democratic Republic of Madagascar (q.v.) and ratified the coming of Didier Ratsiraka (q.v.) to power. The question posed by the referendum was: "In order to create a new society and to bring about the reign of justice and social equality, do you accept the Charter of the Socialist Revolution and the constitution applying it and do you accept Captain Didier Ratsiraka as president of the Republic?" This question did not invite a negative answer. Of those eligible to vote 92.6% did so, and 94.7% of those voting voted in favor of the referendum.

REFERENDUM ON THE CONSTITUTION OF THE FIFTH FRENCH REPUBLIC. On September 28, 1958, citizens of France's overseas territories as well as the French voted on the constitution of the French Fifth Republic. For the overseas territories, including Madagascar, approving the constitution meant the acquisition of autonomy within the proposed French Community, while rejection of the constitution would lead to immediate independence. In Madagascar the referendum polarized the party landscape. The Parti Social Démocrate (q.v.) and the Union Démocratique et Sociale de Madagascar (q.v.) formed the Cartel des Républicains (q.v.) to campaign for a "yes" vote, while the parties that had attended the Tamatave Congress (q.v.) urged rejection of the constitution. De Gaulle's visit to Antananarivo inspired little enthusiasm, but a later promise that countries choosing autonomy within the French Community could still opt for eventual independence did make it easier for some groups to support a "yes" vote. In spite of this, Madagascar had the highest proportion of votes against the constitution after French Guinea, which rejected it outright. In Madagascar, negative votes were 22% of the total for the whole island, and 50.5% in the province of Antananarivo.

RENE, JEAN (d. 1826). René was a Creole trader who established a trading post at Toamasina around 1798. In 1811 he declared himself "king" of the port, successfully challenging the Zanamalata (q.v.) leaders of the Betsimisaraka Confederacy (q.v.) for control of the area. René and his half brother Fiche served as intermediaries in the trade between Europeans at Toamasina and the developing Merina monarchy (q.v.). In 1817 he signed a treaty with the Merina ruler, Radama I (q.v.), acknowledging Radama's overlordship in return for a reinforcement of his own position.

RESAMPA, ANDRE (1924–). A founder and dominant member of the Parti Sociale Démocrate (q.v.), Resampa was born in Toliara province, and first worked in the colonial administration. In 1952 he was elected to the provincial assembly of Toliara on a list called Union Cotière. In 1956 he participated in the formation of the PSD and in 1957 was elected to the provincial assembly and to the Assemblée Représentative. In 1958 he became minister of education and health, and in 1959 minister of the interior. He was head of the Malagasy delegation that negotiated the Cooperation Agreements (q.v.) with France at the time of Malagasy independence in 1960.

In his early period in power, Resampa was able to use his government offices to reinforce the status of the PSD and his position within it and to use his power in the party to reinforce his weight in the government. His position as minister of education gave him access to the network of state teachers, many of whom were recruited to the party, while accession to the post of minister of the interior put the territorial administration at his disposal. As minister of the interior, he created the Forces Republicaines de Sécurité (q.v.), a paramilitary force under his control. Within the PSD he was considered a member of the more "radical" wing, favorable to extending Madagascar's international contacts beyond the tie with France, and interested in more "socialist" policies than those favored by the president of Madagascar and president of the party, Philibert Tsiranana (q.v.).

Resampa's strong position in the party created jealousies, but throughout the 1960s it appeared unassailable. His downfall began with Tsiranana's illness in 1970. Resampa, who considered himself Tsiranana's logical successor, began a reorganization of the party that moved his successors into posts formerly held by Tsiranana supporters, known as the "Tsimihety clan" because many of them belonged to the same ethnic group as the president. When Tsiranana returned to Madagascar, it was easy to convince him that Resampa was plotting to succeed him. In December 1970 Resampa was removed from his post as vice president and lost most of the powers of the Ministry of the Interior, including control over the territorial administration and the police. These were given to a minister attached to the presidency for internal affairs, Barthélemy Johasy (q.v.) whose previous quarrels with Resampa were well known.

When the Peasant Rebellion of April 1971 (q.v.) broke out, Tsiranana took the point of view that if Resampa had not actually been involved in the revolt, it demonstrated incompetence on his part, occurring as it did largely in his ''fief.'' In June 1971 Tsiranana accused Resampa of plotting with a foreign embassy (understood to be the U.S. embassy) to bring about his downfall. Resampa was arrested and imprisoned on the Ile Sainte-Marie (q.v.), where he remained until the May 1972 Revolution (q.v.) brought down Tsiranana and his government.

After Resampa was released from detention, he at first supported the Ramanantsoa regime (q.v.), lining up the new party he had created, the Union Socialiste Malgache (q.v.), behind the campaign for a ''yes'' vote in the Referendum of October 8, 1972 (q.v.) on the establishment of the regime. He increasingly opposed the regime's policies of loosening ties with France and of *fokonolona* reform (q.v.), however, and accused it of pro-Merina (q.v.) and anti-Côtier (q.v.) bias. He reconciled with Tsiranana, and together they formed the Parti Socialiste Malgache (q.v.) in 1974. When Colonel Bréchard Rajaonarison (q.v.) attempted to overthrow the Ramanantsoa regime in December 1974 and fled with the other plotters to Antanaimoro camp (q.v.), Resampa, along with Tsiranana, made declarations of support for him. When the camp was attacked after the assassination of Colonel Richard Ratsimandrava (q.v.) on February 11, 1975, Resampa was sought, and found to have taken refuge in the old PSD headquarters. He was arrested and charged with complicity in the assassination. The charges against him and the other defendants in the ''Trial of the Century'' (q.v.) were eventually dismissed. Resampa returned to his home town of Morondava. In 1983 he was elected to the local council on the list of Vonjy (q.v.), but the party did not support his attempt to be elected to the higher levels of councils.

When the formation of new parties was authorized in 1990, Resampa left Vonjy to form a revived PSD. He participated in the August 31, 1991, government of Guy Razanamasy, but was not included in the transitional government that was created by the power-sharing agreement (q.v.) that prepared the way for the Third Republic (q.v.).

REUNION. Like the other Mascarenes (q.v.), Réunion was a French possession until the Napoleonic Wars and, after a brief British occupation during the wars, was returned to France. Réunion had long depended on trade with Madagascar for slaves, cattle, and rice to feed its plantation economy, and by the late nineteenth century deputies from Réunion, led by François de Mahy (q.v.), were urging the colonization of Madagascar to provide an outlet for excess population. After the French conquest, about half the settlers (q.v.) who came to Madagascar were Réunionese, and settlement plans continued into the 1950s with the launching of the Sakay (q.v.) project. When the headquarters of the French Indian Ocean Fleet was moved from Diégo-Suarez (q.v.) in 1973, it was transferred to Réunion.

RICHARD, CHRISTIAN REMY. Under the Ramanantsoa regime (q.v.), Richard was elected to the Conseil National Populaire pour le Développement (q.v.) from Toliara province. He was named minister of education in the weeklong government of Richard Ratsimandrava (q.v.). In 1976 he was named minister of youth. Richard was a founding member of the political bureau of the regime party, AREMA (q.v.), and was minister of foreign affairs from 1977 to 1983.

RUPHIN, GEORGES. Under the First Republic (q.v.), Ruphin was director of the study and training center of the Parti Social Démocrate (q.v.), the Fondation Philibert Tsiranana. By the coming of the Democratic Republic of Madagascar (q.v.) in 1975, he was a close advisor of President Didier Ratsiraka (q.v.) and a founding member of the political bureau of the regime party, AREMA (q.v.). In 1977 he was named minister of information, and in 1982 became minister of public administration in order to reassert party control over a ministry that had been led by a minister from another party, Célestin Radio (q.v.). In Guy Razanamasy's (q.v.) August 1991 government, the ministry was abolished and Ruphin was left without a government position.

-S-

SAINT AUGUSTINE BAY. A bay located 37 km south of Toliara (q.v.) on the west coast, Saint Augustine Bay was used by British ships as a stopover on the trip to India starting about 1611. An attempt to found a settlement was made in 1645, but without success. At the end of the seventeenth century, Saint Augustine Bay was used by pirates (q.v.). In the nineteenth century it served as a port for the slave trade, and an international trading community was established on Nosy Be, an island just off the bay.

SAINT LAWRENCE'S ISLAND. In 1500 the Portuguese explorer Diego Diaz (q.v.) named Madagascar (q.v.) Saint Lawrence's Island because he had sighted it on Saint Lawrence's feast day, August 10.

SAINT-MART, PIERRE DE. Saint-Mart was a career officer in the French colonial service who succeeded Paul Legentilhomme (q.v.) as the Free French (q.v.) governor of Madagascar in May 1943. His continued mobilization of the island's resources for the French war effort, including the establishment of the Office du Riz (q.v.), exacerbated bad relations between the colonial authorities and the Malagasy, as did the failure of the authorities to purge the administration of officials associated with the period of Vichy (q.v.) rule. When Saint-Mart was succeeded by Marcel De Coppet (q.v.) in May 1946, nationalist activities were well established, and the leaders who were to form the MDRM, or Mouvement Démocratique de la Rénovation Malgache (q.v.), had already won their first electoral victories. *See also* REBELLION OF 1947.

SAKALAVA. The Sakalava, whose population was estimated at 470,150 in 1972, inhabit the west coast and interior of Madagascar from Toliara (q.v.) in the south to Nosy Be (q.v.) in the north. They are considered to have expanded from their southern base beginning in the late fifteenth century under the leadership of the Maroserana (q.v.) dynasty, absorbing local populations as they went. This movement gave rise to a large number of kingdoms, since disputes over succession were often resolved by the loser's moving away with a group of supporters to found a new kingdom. Among the more important kingdoms were Menabe (q.v.) to the south and Boina (q.v.) to the north. Others were Ambongo, which formed a buffer zone between the two larger kingdoms, and Bemihisatra, founded in the 1830s by refugees from Boina after the capture of Mahajanga (q.v.) by the Merina Empire (q.v.). The original basis of the Sakalava economy was herding, hunting and gathering, and some agriculture. They also came to dominate the trade between the west coast and the interior, first with the Arab (q.v.) and Swahili traders, and then with the Europeans. The economy then came to depend on the exchange of slaves for weapons and other commodities, and the Sakalava in the eighteenth century conducted slave raids themselves and exacted tribute, often in the form of slaves, from neighboring groups, including the Merina.

At the end of the eighteenth century the development of the Merina state permitted the Merina to reverse the pressure, and they occupied large sections of Sakalava territory, including Toliara and Mahajanga, although they were never able to subdue the Sakalava as a whole. Several Sakalava rulers signed treaties of protection with the French to provide a counterbalance to the Merina, although the creation of the French protectorate (q.v.) of 1885, which recognized Merina sovereignty over the island, disappointed many of these rulers. Reaction to the French conquest was varied, with some rulers becoming part of the colonial administration, and others joining in the Sambirano (q.v.) rebellion. The

Sakalava area was largely untouched by the Rebellion of 1947 (q.v.).

The modern Sakalava economy remains oriented around cattle raising, with some agriculture. Their area has been subject to intensive in-migration, both by the Tsimihety (q.v.) to the north and by the Betsileo (q.v.) to the east. The Betsileo, in particular, have brought in agriculture, including rice farming. *See also* BAIBOHO.

SAKAY. The Sakay is a region 100 km to the west of the Malagasy capital, Antananarivo (q.v.). In the early 1950s it was the site of a project designed to establish a modern agricultural system by bringing in settlers from Réunion (q.v.). The scheme was criticized for channeling money to settlement rather than Malagasy agriculture and for displacing the Malagasy herders who had occupied the land. After independence the Malagasy government took over the project, creating SOMASAK (Société Malgache de la Sakay) to settle Malagasy on the land. In 1977 the lands and society became a state farm, and the remaining Réunionese settlers were expelled.

SAMBIRANO REBELLION. The Sambirano rebellion against the imposition of French colonial rule took place in the Sakalava (q.v.) territory of western Madagascar in 1897. The rulers of the different Sakalava kingdoms had originally supported the French in their wars with the Merina Empire (q.v.), expecting that this would remove the Merina occupation of their territory. When it became clear that the French intended to replace the Merina as rulers, the rebellion occurred, but it could not gather the full support of all the rulers, and monarchs like Binao (q.v.) continued to be loyal to the French.

SAMBSON, GILBERT. A native of Fianarantsoa province, Sambson was a member of the political bureau of Vonjy (q.v.) and a Vonjy delegate to the Front National pour la Défense de la Révolution (q.v.) and the Conseil Suprême de la Révolution (q.v.). He was a member of the Conseil Suprême des Institutions (q.v.) and served as a judge and director of national security during the Ramanantsoa regime (q.v.). He was named minister of the interior in the government of Richard Ratsimandrava (q.v.). From 1982 to 1987 he was minister of justice in the Democratic Republic of Madagascar (q.v.). He was removed from the CSR when Vonjy linked itself with the opposition to the Ratsiraka regime, but after the presidential election of 1989 he returned, bringing his faction in the party back to supporting the regime.

SAMPY. The *sampy* were the royal talismans of the Merina (q.v.) monarchy. Originally the amulets of particular clans or regions, they were appropriated at various times by the monarchy as part of its strategy of incorporation of the different groups comprising the kingdom. The *sampy* were responsible for the welfare of the ruler and kingdom and for success in battle. Among the more important were Rabehaza, associated with the monarchy since the seventeenth century; Manjakatsiroa, particularly associated with the founder of the modern monarchy, Andrianampoinimerina (q.v.); and perhaps the most important, Kelimalaza. A nineteenth-century observer described Kelimalaza as "a piece of wood two or three inches long, and as large as the middle finger of a man's hand, wrapped in two thicknesses of scarlet silk about three feet long and three inches wide, the wood pointed at the end, and movable in the silk, with two silver chains, about three inches in length, at either end of the silk." Each *sampy* had a group of guardians. After her baptism in 1869, Ranavalona II (q.v.) ordered the *sampy* burned and removed the privileges of their guardians; however, several of the *sampy* were reconstructed in their regions of origin almost immediately. They reappeared at the time of the French conquest, which many in Imerina attributed to the abandonment of traditional ways by the government, and Kelimalaza in particular played an important role in the revolt of the Menalamba (q.v.).

SECOND COLLEGE. *See* COLLEGE SYSTEM.

SENATE. The Malagasy First Republic (q.v.) had a bicameral legislature with a fifty-four-member senate. The senate consisted of thirty-six "provincial" members, or six per province chosen by the provincial legislatures, and eighteen chosen by the president of the Republic, twelve from lists presented by "representative groups" of the population. The senate's powers were steadily reduced during the First Republic, and the Democratic Republic of Madagascar (q.v.) had a unicameral legislature. The constitution of the Third Republic provided for a senate in which two-thirds of the members are chosen by an electoral college composed of representatives of local governments and interest groups, and one-third chosen from lists put forth by economic, social, and cultural organizations. The term of office for senators is four years. The government is not responsible to the senate, but only to the National Assembly.

SERVICE CIVIQUE. During the First Republic (q.v.), the Service Civique was the branch of the military to which most conscripts were sent. It was used for rural development projects and to staff some rural schools. In 1972 it had approximately 1,500 members. After the establishment of the Democratic Republic of Madagascar (q.v.) in 1975 the Service Civique was merged with the infantry and the engineering corps to create the Development Army. *See also* MILITARY.

SERVICE DE LA MAIN-D'-OEUVRE DES TRAVAUX D'INTERET GENERAL. The SMOTIG was set up in 1926 by Governor-General Olivier (q.v.) to furnish labor for the construction of the Fianarantsoa–Côte Est railroad (q.v.) and other public works. It recruited Malagasy of an age to be subject to military service, and those enrolled lived in camps under military discipline. Although the SMOTIG recruits were supposed to be used on works "of general interest," many were in fact diverted to labor on settler plantations. The French Confédération Générale de Travail (q.v.) attacked the SMOTIG as a form of slavery at meetings of the International Labor Organization, and in 1930 the French government agreed to end the operation. It was not until the installation of the Popular Front (q.v.) government in 1936, however, that the SMOTIG was formally abolished. *See also* FORCED LABOR.

SETTLEMENT. Although there were Creole settlers from the Mascarenes (q.v.) established on the east coast of Madagascar at the time of the French conquest in 1896, large-scale settlement began only after the conquest when the governor-general of the period, Gallieni (q.v.), provided land grants and equipment for his demobilized soldiers and immigrants from Réunion. He was disappointed by the response and on his departure declared that in his opinion Madagascar was not suited to be a colony of settlement. Subsequent governments proceeded with settlement projects, however. In 1926 the French state was declared the owner of all land not enclosed, and in 1929 land surveys were undertaken and credit facilities set up for the encouragement of settlement. By 1939 the settler population was approximately 45,000, concentrated on the east coast, the Highlands, and the cash-crop areas of the north and northwest. Alienation of land for settlement and for large plantations known as concessions (q.v.) caused considerable resentment among the Malagasy, and areas of settlement were among the hardest hit during the March uprising of 1947. The last large-scale settlement scheme was the Sakay (q.v.) project of the 1950s.

SETTLERS. During the colonial period settlers came to Madagascar both from France and from the Mascarenes, particularly Réunion. Often undercapitalized to a degree that could not be remedied by government assistance, and faced with competition from the large concessions (q.v.) and increasingly from Malagasy producers, the settlers sometimes accumulated large debts, and many went bankrupt during the not infrequent depressions in agricultural prices. Their relationship with the colonial administration was also difficult since they objected to the level of taxation and to what they saw as the failure of the administration to provide them with adequate supplies of Malagasy labor. Settler demands for representation and the government desire to mobilize production for the war effort led to the creation in 1915 of a mixed advisory commission of settler representatives and colonial officials. Further demands led to the creation in 1924 of the Délégations Economiques et Financières (q.v.) and to the establishment of a legislature after the Second World War. Settler organizations included the Ligue des Intérêts Economiques de Madagascar, founded in 1925, and the Ligue de Défense des Intérêts Franco-Malgaches (q.v.), founded in 1946. The settler community generally resisted attempts to grant political powers to the Malagasy after the Second World War and particularly after the Rebellion of 1947 (q.v.). By the mid-1950s, however, the community had become divided over the issue, with such settler leaders as Roger Duveau (q.v.) coming to support the 1956 Loi-Cadre (q.v.)

At the time of independence in 1960, there were approximately 70,000 French citizens in Madagascar. It is difficult to measure the impact of independence on the settler community itself since in the early years of independence departures of settlers were compensated for by the influx of French technical assistants. Estimates suggest that the numbers of French declined by half, from about 70,000 at independence to about 35,000 in 1970 and that further departures after the 1975 establishment of the Democratic Republic of Madagascar (q.v.) reduced that number by half again. *See also* COLLEGE SYSTEM.

SHIPPING CONFERENCE OF THE INDIAN OCEAN. This organization, formed after the 1896 French conquest of Madagascar, was comprised of the Nouvelle Compagnie Havraise Péninsulaire, the Messageries Maritimes, and the Scandinavian East Africa Line. It effectively had a monopoly of shipping from Europe to Madagascar and was frequently criticized for high prices and poor service.

SIBON, GUY (d. 1986). Sibon was a captain in the Malagasy navy at the time of the May Revolution of 1972. He served as the military governor of the province of Antseranana under the Ramanantsoa regime, during the weeklong government of Richard Ratsimandrava, and under the Directoire Militaire (q.v.) that took power after Ratsimandrava's assassination. He became minister of defense of the Democratic Republic of Madagascar (q.v.) in 1977, and held the post, rising to the rank of admiral, until his death in a plane crash in 1986.

SIHANAKA. With an estimated population of about 184,000, the Sihanaka live in the northern Highlands (q.v.) of Madagascar, around Lake Alaotra (q.v.), a major rice-growing area. The Sihanaka live both by rice farming and by fishing. Their strategic position along trading routes to the coast subjected them to pressure from both the Betsimisaraka (q.v.) and Merina (q.v.) at the end of the eighteenth and beginning of the nineteenth century. They were able to hold off the Betsimisaraka and engage in slave and cattle raids of their own, but were one of the first groups to be conquered by the Merina Empire (q.v.) and the area was subject to heavy in-migration. The current population is probably a mixture of the original Sihanaka and the Merina immigrants.

SISAL. Sisal plantations were established between the wars in the Taolañaro region of Toliara province and in Antseranana province. Production declined with the discovery of substitutes and by 1959 only the plantations in the Taolañaro region remained. The plantations suffered severely in the drought of 1991–1992, and exports of sisal have largely stopped.

SLAVE TRADE. Before the arrival of Europeans in the western Indian Ocean, the slave trade with Madagascar was conducted by Arab and Indian traders, with the slaves being sent to the Persian Gulf and the Red Sea. With the arrival of Europeans in the sixteenth century, the Americas became the dominant destination. In the mid–eighteenth century, with the development of the plantation economy of the Mascarenes (q.v.), they became the most important destination, and the number of slaves shipped increased. Trading occurred on both coasts, with the important harbors being (on the east coast) Antongil Bay (q.v.), the Ile Sainte-Marie (q.v.), Foulpointe (q.v.), and Toasmasina (q.v.). On the west coast, Mahajanga (q.v.) and Toliara (q.v.) were among the important posts. Slaves were obtained by raiding neighboring peoples, and the rise of the Sakalava (q.v.) monarchies, the Betsimisaraka Confederation (q.v.), and the Merina Empire (q.v.) are all connected with the need to organize these raids, to control the trade, and to defend against being raided. Slaves were traded for weapons and other commodities.

Antislaving treaties were signed between the Merina Empire and the British in 1817, 1820, and 1865, but some degree of slave trading persisted until the French conquest of Madagascar in 1895. One of the factors feeding this trade was the fact that it was a two-way trade, since Madagascar not only exported slaves elsewhere, but also imported slaves, largely from Africa.

SLAVES. Most precolonial Malagasy societies had slaves, usually a mixed group composed of war captives, the poor, and people who had been sentenced to slavery. There was also a more powerful category of royal slaves in societies possessing monarchies. Slaves were considered to be outside society and to lack ancestors.

It was in the Merina Empire (q.v.) of the nineteenth century that the use of slaves—both Malagasy and Africans—was greatest. They were used in part to substitute for freeman occupied by the demands of compulsory labor, the army, and the administration, and in part were used directly for labor. It was estimated that, at the end of the nineteenth century, approximately half the population of Antananarivo province were slaves. The *masombika,* or slaves of African descent, were freed in 1877, and in 1897 the other slaves were freed, but were not given land. In many cases they became sharecroppers on the land of their former masters. The distinction between descendant of slave and descendant of freeborn remains a distinction with some social and political importance.

SOCIETE D'INTERET NATIONAL DE COMMERCIALISATION DES PRODUITS AGRICOLES. This society, known as SINPA, was established by the Ramanantsoa regime (q.v.) in 1972 and became operational in 1973. It was designed to replace the networks of non-Malagasy intermediaries that dominated the collection and distribution of rice. These intermediaries had often been closely connected with supporters of the previous regime, and since rice is the staple food of Madagascar, the possibilities of disruption made their replacement a political necessity. SINPA absorbed the personnel and equipment of other organizations, including the Syndicats des Communes. Almost from the beginning there were problems with corruption, and after the creation of the Democratic Republic of Madagascar (q.v.) in 1975 the organization was placed under the control of a specially created Ministry of Transportation and Food Supply. Problems of inefficiency and corruption continued, and after the economic crisis of the 1980s they were compounded by the collapse of the road infrastructure and a lack of equipment. Many of SINPA's functions are now handled by the army, while others (since the beginning of the IMF-inspired liberalization program in 1983) have been returned to private traders. *See also* ECONOMIC POLICY; SOCIETE NATIONAL DE COMMERCE EXTERIEURE.

SOCIETE NATIONAL DE COMMERCE EXTERIEURE. SONACO was established in 1972 by the Ramanatsoa regime (q.v.) and given the responsibility for the collection of cash crops and the importation and distribution of a range of items, including cooking oil, tires, cement, and batteries. Like the Société National pour la Commercialisation des Produits Agricoles (q.v.), which handled rice, SONACO was designed to replace networks of non-Malagasy intermediaries, but many of these people, usually Indian or Chinese, continued working for it under contract. Again like SINPA, SONACO ran into problems from the beginning, and its first director was jailed for economic crimes. When the French commercial companies (q.v.) that handled the exportation of cash crops were nationalized in 1976, most of SONACO's collection functions were handed over to other agencies. Its import activities were hard hit by the financial crisis of the 1980s, and some of these functions were returned to private traders. Later plans for the reorganization of the Malagasy economy project still further liberalizations of the import sector. *See also* ECONOMIC POLICY.

SOJA. Soja was a captain in the gendarmerie at the time of the May 1972 Revolution (q.v.). Under the Ramanantsoa regime (q.v.) he served as military governor of the province of

Toliara, and in the factional politics of the regime he supported the *fokonolona* reform (q.v.) projects of gendarmerie Colonel Richard Ratsimandrava (q.v.). He was named minister of rural development in the government that Ratsimandrava formed on February 5, 1975. Soja was a representative from the province of Toliara in the Directoire Militaire (q.v.) that took power after Ratsimandrava's assassination, and was both the major exponent of a continuation of Ratsimandrava's policies and one of the contenders for the succession. He was unable to attract a majority to his position, and on June 15 the DM chose Didier Ratsiraka (q.v.) to be president of the Democratic Republic of Madagascar (q.v.). Soja took up the (noncommand) post of inspector of the gendarmerie.

SOLOFOSON, GEORGES. Solofoson was, like President Didier Ratsiraka (q.v.), born in Toamasina province, and served as an advisor to Ratsiraka when the latter was minister of foreign affairs under the Ramanantsoa regime (q.v.). At the time of the establishment of the Democratic Republic of Madagascar (q.v.) in 1975, Solofoson was made director of the cabinet of the presidency of the Conseil Suprême de la Révolution (q.v.), held by the president of the republic. In 1976 he was given responsibility for the organization charged with inspection and control of the state apparatus, army, and gendarmerie. In 1982, after the "right AREMA" crisis, he was named minister of commerce. The ministry was abolished, and Solofoson lost his post, when the August 1991 government of Guy Razanamasy (q.v.) was formed.

SORABE. The *sorabe* are sacred manuscripts written in Malagasy using Arabic script. They include histories and genealogies, works on medicine, and astrology and other forms of divination. Most *sorabe* are in the possession of Antaimora (q.v.) and Antambohoaka (q.v.) scribes, but have been used for divination for other groups. The Bibliothèque Nationale in Paris also has a collection of *sorabe*.

SOUCADAUX, ANDRE. A member of the French Socialist party, Soucadaux became governor-general in 1954 and presided over the transition to independence. It was part of his task to promote the formation of a successor elite, since Malagasy political life had been paralyzed since the Rebellion of 1947 (q.v.). He assisted Philibert Tsiranana (q.v.) in the creation of the Parti Sociale Démocrate (q.v.) and in his rise to the position of vice president of the Loi-Cadre government council (q.v.). After the passage of the Loi-Cadre, the title of governor-general changed to high commissioner.

SPICES. Madagascar produces several tropical spices, of which the most important are cloves, vanilla, and pepper. Vanilla is currently Madagascar's most important export, responsible for 30% of export earnings. In the past, Madagascar dominated world vanilla production, contributing over 50% of the total. Other countries, such as Indonesia, however, have entered the market, cutting into Malagasy sales of vanilla. New, more productive, and more easily grown strains of vanilla are expected to challenge further the Malagasy position. Exports of cloves have also suffered from falling production in Madagascar and falling world prices, due in part to the spread of clove cultivation to such countries as Indonesia and Brazil. Production of pepper has been increasing, but its role in Malagasy export earnings is much less than that of cloves and vanilla.

STIBBE, PIERRE (1912–1966). A French lawyer and veteran of the Resistance, Stibbe defended the MDRM deputies accused of treason after the Rebellion of 1947 (q.v.). He persisted in the defense even though he was severely beaten by unknown assailants upon his arrival in Madagascar. After the trial he continued to defend other African nationalist figures in trouble with French law. *Further information may be found in the Bibliography following this Dictionary.*

SUEZ CANAL. The opening of the Suez Canal in 1869 tilted the strategic balance in the western Indian Ocean to the disadvantage of the strategy of the Merina Empire. British interest shifted to protecting the African areas around the canal, which provided the crucial link to India, and Great Britain was less interested in the Indian Ocean islands—like Madagascar—that overlooked the old route around the southern tip of Africa. This shift of interest culminated in the Franco-British Convention (q.v.) of 1890 in which Great Britain exchanged recognition of France's claims in Madagascar for recognition of Great Britain's protectorate in Zanzibar. In the twentieth century, the closing of the Suez Canal in 1967 created an economic crisis for the First Republic (q.v.) that contributed to its fall in 1972.

SUGAR. Sugar was probably introduced to Madagascar from the Mascarenes (q.v.) around 1800, and grows easily at the lower altitudes along the coast. It was at first grown mainly for subsistence consumption, but after the Second World War industrial processing (by the Société Sucrière de Madagascar, or SOSUMAV) began. Sugar mills are now located in the provinces of Antseranana and Mahajanga, and the largest company is the state-owned Siramamy Malagasy. SIRAMA had difficulties after taking out a loan for expansion in the early 1980s.

SYLLA, ALBERT. A native of Toamasina province, Sylla was one of the founders of the Union Démocratique et Sociale de Madagascar (q.v.). In 1959, as independence was approaching, he led his faction of the party into the governing Parti Social Démocrate (q.v.) and was named minister for foreign affairs. Sylla was killed in a plane accident in 1967 and was succeeded by Jacques Rabemananjara (q.v.).

SYNDICAT D'ENSEIGNANTS ET CHERCHEURS DE L'ENSEIGNEMENT SUPERIEUR. This union of teachers and researchers at the University of Madagascar has been active politically since the last days of the First Republic (q.v.), when its series of seminars on democratization and Malgachization (q.v.) of the educational system helped politicize the student demonstrators who would later stage the May 1972 Revolution (q.v.). Unrest in education (q.v.) has continued to be a problem for succeeding regimes, and SECESS has frequently been involved in strikes at the university. *The dates of university strikes may be found in the Chronology preceding this Dictionary.*

-T-

TAMATAVE. *See* TOAMASINA.

TAMATAVE CONGRESS. This congress, held in Tamatave in May 1958, at the initiative of the aspiring nationalist leader and mayor of the city, Alexis Bezaka (q.v.), was the first gathering of parties interested in moving beyond the framework established by the Loi-Cadre (q.v.) to immediate independence. The congress was attended by a variety of political movements, including the Union du Peuple Malgache, the Front National Malgache (q.v.), the Association des Amis des Paysans, the Comité d'Action Politique pour l'Indépendance de Madagascar, the Union Nationale Malgache (q.v.), the Union Travailliste et Paysan, the GDSM, the Parti Nouveau Démocrate de l'Océan Indien (q.v.), the Parti Populaire Malgache, and the Mouvement Travailliste Chrétien, as well as delegates from the Association des Etudiants d'Origine Malgache (q.v.) and the Union des Intellectuels et Universitaires de Madagascar. One party that might have been expected to attend and did not was the Union des Indépendants de Tananarive (q.v.) of Stanislas Rakotonirina (q.v.).

The congress passed resolutions calling for independence, amnesty (q.v.) for the prisoners of the Rebellion of 1947 (q.v.), and a constitutional assembly elected by universal suffrage. The congress also established a committee that was active in campaigning against the Referendum on the Constitution of the Fifth French Republic (q.v.). Besides Bezaka himself, two other members of the Loi-Cadre Government Council (q.v.)—Justin Bezara (q.v.) and Alfred Ramangosoavina (q.v.)—attended. They were reproached by the vice president of the council, Philibert Tsiranana, (q.v.) and Ramangosoavina and Bezara apologized for their actions. Bezaka did not apologize, leading to the first break between himself and Tsiranana.

After the referendum, an attempt was made to unite the different groups that had attended the congress into a single political party. The parties based on the coast or on Catholic mission networks refused, but the Union du Peuple Malgache, the Front National Malgache, and the Association des Amis des Paysans agreed and formed the AKFM (q.v.), or Independence Congress Party of Madagascar.

TANALA. Literally, ''People of the Forest'', the Tanala live in the rain-forest region of southeastern Madagascar. They practice slash-and-burn agriculture (*tavy*), including the cultivation of some coffee. *See also* MENABE.

TANANARIVE. *See* ANTANANARIVO.

TANANARIVE TRIAL. This trial, of those whom the colonial administration considered the main leaders of the Rebellion of 1947 (q.v.), was held from July 22 to October 4, 1948, in the Palace of Andafiavaratra (q.v.) in Antananarivo (then called Tananarive). Among the accused were the three deputies of the Mouvement Démocratique de la Rénovation Malgache (q.v.)—Jacques Rabemananjara, Joseph Raseta, and Joseph Ravoahangy (q.v.)—as well as members of the party's political bureau and leaders of the two secret societies implicated in the rebellion: PANAMA (q.v.) and JINA (q.v.). The trial shed only limited light on the events of 1947, since most of the actual leaders of the fighting were dead—the man considered by the French to be the ''general'' of the rebels, Samuel Rakotondrabe (q.v.) having been executed three days before the trial began. Some witnesses withdrew their previous testimony on the stand, claiming that it had been extracted by torture.

At the end of the trial, two of the MDRM deputies—Raseta and Ravoahangy—were condemned to death, as were four others. The third deputy—Rabemananjara—was condemned to life at hard labor. The death sentences were upheld by the French appeals court in 1949, but were later commuted to life imprisonment by the French president, Vincent Auriol. A bill granting amnesty (q.v.) to those convicted of complicity in the uprising was passed by the French National Assembly in 1958. *See also* COMITÉ DE SOLIDARITÉ DE MADAGASCAR; STIBBE, PIERRE.

TANORA TONGA SAINA (Revolutionary Youth). The TTS drew its members from the same groups of unemployed youth that had furnished the bases for the bands called ZOAM (q.v.), which had played a central role in the May 1972 Revolution (q.v.) that overthrew the First Republic (q.v.). After the establishment of the Democratic Republic of Madagascar in 1975, some elements of the ZOAM were reorganized by the regime into the "Revolutionary Youth," or *Tanora Tonga Saina,* usually known as the TTS. Nominally under the control of the Ministry of Youth, they were often used to break up, or sometimes to precipitate, strikes and demonstrations. They also continued the ZOAM practice of petty crime and extortion in marketplaces. In December 1984 their strongholds in Antananarivo were attacked by members of the Kung Fu (q.v.) movement with the support of the population. Military units surrounded the neighborhoods, but did not intervene for three days; it is estimated that between 100 and 200 TTS were killed. The TTS and similar groups of unemployed youth have since revived, but with less emphasis on political activities and more on petty crime.

TANTARA'NY ANDRIANA ETO MADAGASIKARA. The *Tantara,* or history of the kings of Madagascar, is a compilation of Merina (q.v.) oral tradition collected by a Jesuit priest, Father Callet, between 1868 and 1881. It deals with the history of Merina kingdoms from the time of their arrival in the Highlands (q.v.) and in particular with the establishment of the modern Merina monarchy under Andrianampoinimerina. The *Tantara* was originally published in Malagasy, but the French edition was published in four volumes from 1936 to 1958, and other editions have since appeared. The *Tantara* represents the traditions of the dominant groups of the nineteenth-century Merina political system, and other bodies of tradition exist giving alternate versions of the same events. *Further information may be found under "Délivré, Alain," in the Bibliography following this Dictionary.*

TAOLAÑARO (25°2′S, 47°0′E). Formerly Fort-Dauphin (q.v.), Taolañaro is now used as a port, handling mainly local traffic and serving as an outlet for the sisal (q.v.) that is produced to the north of the town.

TECHNICAL ASSISTANTS. Under the First Republic (q.v.) French technical assistants staffed posts in the educational system, the administration, and the military. The most important numerically were the technical assistants in the educational system, where they filled 80% of the posts in the university and the state secondary schools. In the administration and the military, they occupied approximately half of the senior posts and dominated the services of President Philibert Tsiranana, where the presidential chief of staff, head of the internal security services of the Deuxième Bureau, and secretary-general of the president's cabinet were all French. The head of the gendarmerie was French until 1969. Demands for the Malgachization (q.v.) of these posts, and the end of the dominant presence of the French technical assistants that this implied, were an important part of the May 1972 Revolution (q.v.) that brought about the fall of the First Republic.

THIRD FRENCH REPUBLIC. The Third French Republic was created following the defeat of Napoleon III's French Empire by the German armies in 1870. The republic itself was not created until 1875, when disputes among monarchists made the creation of a monarchy impossible. Politics in the early period of the Republic was dominated by the need to establish its legitimacy and by quarrels between the revanchists (who argued that revenge against Germany should be the main external goal of France) and the expansionists (who argued that French glory should be recovered by the conquest of an overseas empire). Under the constitution of the Third Republic, French citizens of overseas territories elected deputies to the National Assembly and the less powerful Conseil de la République. In the National Assembly, the overseas deputies (q.v.) were usually both firm republicans and strong supporters of overseas expansion. It was during this period that the Franco-Malagasy Wars of 1883–1885 and 1895 (q.v.) occurred, and that Madagascar was brought under French colonial rule by the Annexation Law (q.v.) of 1896. The Third Republic itself lasted until the German invasion and the fall of France in 1940. *See also* FREE FRENCH; POPULAR FRONT; VICHY.

THIRD REPUBLIC. The Third Malagasy Republic, successor to the Democratic Republic of Madagascar (q.v.), was inaugurated on August 19, 1992, when the Malagasy population passed a referendum on the constitution (q.v.). The main institutions of the Third Republic include a largely ceremonial presidency, a bicameral legislature composed of a National Assembly and a Senate, and a government headed by a prime minister and responsible to the National Assembly.

The Third Republic had its roots in a revolt against the regime of Didier Ratsiraka (q.v.), led by an alliance of the Comité des Forces Vives (q.v.), unions, churches, and parts of the armed forces. The transition period to the republic was characterized by considerable instability, largely the result of actions taken by Ratsiraka and his followers to hang on to power.

TIANDRAZA, REMI. A doctor from Nosy Be in Antseranana province, Tiandraza served as an administrator in the Ministry of Social Affairs under the Ramanantsoa regime (q.v.). In 1975 he became was the first minister of foreign affairs of the Democratic Republic of Madagascar (q.v.). In 1976 he was moved to the Ministry of Scientific Research, and in 1977 became minister of population. In 1982 he was named to the political bureau of the regime party, AREMA (q.v.). As minister of youth, he was responsible for controlling the activities of the Tanora Tonga Saina (q.v.) and other such groups. The rise of the Kung Fu (q.v.) movements and their clashes with the TTS undercut his authority. In 1985 Tiandraza was removed from his ministerial post and "promoted" to the Conseil Suprême de la Révolution (q.v.).

TOAMASINA (18°10′S, 49°25′E). Toamasina is Madagascar's most important port. The harbor, formed by a series of coral reefs, was already in use in the eighteenth century when its greater security and better access to trading routes to the interior brought it dominance over the Ile Sainte-Marie (q.v.) and Antongil Bay (q.v.) as the terminus for trade with the Mascarenes (q.v.). At first controlled by the Betsimisaraka Confederacy (q.v.) and then by Creole traders under Jean

René (q.v.), it was captured by the Merina Empire (q.v.) in 1817. As the chief port of the Merina Empire, Toamasina was subject to periodic attacks by outside powers, including bombardment by the French in 1829 and a Franco-British attack in 1845. It was occupied during the Franco-Malagasy War of 1883–1885 (q.v.). After the French conquest, it was linked by rail to Antananarivo (q.v.) in 1913. Toamasina now handles about 70% of Madagascar's port traffic, although its capacity was severely reduced by a 1986 cyclone. It is also the site of the island's only oil refinery. The refinery stopped operations in 1984 when the debt crisis (q.v.) lowered oil imports as well as the supply of parts needed for repairs, but it has since been put back into operation, and there are plans for its expansion.

TOAMASINA PROVINCE. Toamasina province occupies the central east coast of Madagascar, and contains the island's most important port, the provincial capital of Toamasina (q.v.). It is an important region for the cultivation of cash crops, including coffee, cloves, and some vanilla. It also contains the rice-growing region of Lake Alaotra (q.v.). Like other parts of the east coast, Toamasina was an important center of the Rebellion of 1947 (q.v.). The dominant Malagasy ethnic group in Toamasina province is the Betsimisaraka (q.v.), but there are also important foreign minorities, especially Chinese (q.v.).

TOBACCO. An indigenous form of tobacco exists in Madagascar that is used mainly for chewing. Maryland tobacco was introduced after the First World War, and local production of cigarettes began. In 1964 a government monopoly of production was established. Cigarette production is still one of Madagascar's important industries. *See also* INDUSTRY.

TOLIARA (23°21′S, 43°40′E). Toliara was first developed as a port to handle the slave trade with the Mascarenes in the late eighteenth and nineteenth centuries. It was also the site of a garrison of the Merina Empire (q.v.). After the French conquest it served largely as an administrative center. The port suffers from underdeveloped facilities and the lack of a hinterland.

TOLIARA PROVINCE. Toliara province is the southernmost of Madagascar's provinces, occupied by the Antandroy (q.v.), Antanosy (q.v.), Mahafaly (q.v.), and Sakalava (q.v.) ethnic groups. Although it has two ports—Toliara (q.v.) and Taolañaro (q.v.)—its isolation, the poor quality of the ports themselves, and the lack of a productive hinterland all mean that the ports are underused. Toliara is the most arid of the regions and is subject to periodic droughts that decimate the cattle herds on which its inhabitants depend. It is difficult to grow rice there, and manioc is often used to replace rice when supplies cannot be brought in. Among the cash crops grown in Toliara are sisal (q.v.) and Cape peas (q.v.).

TORONTO PLAN. The Toronto Plan was agreed on at a meeting of developed countries in Toronto in June 1988, and finalized at a meeting of the International Monetary Fund (q.v.) in Berlin that September. It provides debt relief for the poorest countries in the form of reductions of the amount owed and long-term rescheduling of the remaining debt. In October 1988 Madagascar became the second country after Mali to arrange debt relief with its creditors under the plan.

TOTOLEHIBE, FELIX. Totolehibe was a founder of the Parti des Deshérités de Madagascar (q.v.) and was that party's candidate in the western district of Madagascar in the 1946 elections to the French National Assembly. He was the most successful of the PADESM candidates in the election, gaining 19,014 votes to Joseph Raseta's (q.v.) 21,475. In subsequent years he supported the political career of his cousin, Philibert Tsiranana (q.v.).

TRIAL OF THE CENTURY (Antananarivo, 1975). This trial, of those suspected of collusion in the assassination of Colonel Ratsimandrava (q.v.), was held from March 21 to June 12, 1975, before a special military tribunal. Among the 302 accused were three soldiers from the Groupe Mobile de Police (q.v.) who had been found at the site and others suspected of having plotted the assassination, including the leader of the December mutiny, Colonel Bréchard Rajaonarison (q.v.); former president Philibert Tsiranana (q.v.); a former minister of the interior, André Resampa (q.v.); and Ratsimandrava's main rival in the Ramanantsoa government, Roland Rabetafika (q.v.). The trial became an exposé of the quarrels and intrigues of those who had ruled the country since independence. It has been argued that it also served to distract public opinion while the members of the Directoire Militaire (q.v.) that took power after the assassination settled the question of who would succeed Ratsimandrava. On May 16, 270 of the defendants were excused, and on May 17 the military directorate announced the formation of an executive committee headed by Captain Didier Ratsiraka (q.v.). On June 12 the case against the majority of the remaining defendants was dismissed for lack of evidence. Only the three GMP soldiers received sentences of four years each. On June 15 Didier Ratsiraka became head of state. Andafiavaratra Palace was burned during a riot in September 1976, taking the records and archives of the trial with it.

TSIANDROFANA. A ruler of the Tanala (q.v.), Tsiandrofana led a revolt in 1850 that ended with the establishment of de facto independence from the Merina Empire (q.v.). First contacts with the French began in 1890. When the French began to move their armies in after their conquest of 1895, Tsiandrofana urged cooperation, but could not prevent the Tanala from resisting. He died in February 1901, before the conquest was completed.

TSIEBO, CALVIN (1902–). Born in southern Madagascar, Tsiebo was a founder of the Parti Social Démocrate (q.v.) and a vice president of the First Republic (q.v.). He served in the colonial administration and after 1949 was elected to the provincial assembly of Toliara and to the representative assembly. In 1960 he became president of the new National Assembly, leaving the post to become vice president. He was one of the main supporters of President Philibert Tsiranana (q.v.) and was put in charge of the government during Tsiranana's illness in 1970.

TSIHOZONONY, MAHANANGA. A member of MONIMA (q.v.) from Toliara province, Tsihozonony was named to the

Conseil Suprême de la Révolution (q.v.) in 1976. When Monja Jaona (q.v.) took MONIMA out of the regime in 1977, Tsihozonony was one of these who separated from the party to found the Vondrona Socialista MONIMA, which successfully applied for readmission to the Front National pour la Défense de la Révolution (q.v.).

TSIMIHETY. The Tsimihety live in the northwestern part of Madagascar and in 1974 had an estimated population of 558,100. Although traditionally an inland group, they have migrated into Sakalava (q.v.) territory as their herding-based economy expands, and now occupy much of both Mahajanga and Antseranana provinces. They claim to have moved to their current region from areas of the east inland from Maroantsetra and to have absorbed both Sakalava and Sihanaka (q.v.) groups since then. The Tsimihety are notable for their loose social structure and lack of hierarchical political institutions. The president of the First Republic (q.v.), Philibert Tsiranana (q.v.), was Tsimihety, as were many of his associates.

TSIOMEKO. Tsiomeko was a ruler of the Bemihisatra kingdom established by the Boina (q.v.) Sakalava (q.v.) after the capture of their capital, Mahajanga (q.v.), by the Merina (q.v.). In 1839 the advances of the Merina Empire caused her to flee to the island of Nosy Be (q.v.). She applied unsuccessfully for help to the sultan of Zanzibar, and in 1840 signed an agreement for protection with Captain Passot, commander of the French forces in the area. The agreement was formalized in 1841 by the governor of Réunion, Admiral de Hell.

TSIRANANA, PHILIBERT (c. 1910–1978). The only president of the First Republic, Tsiranana was a Tsimihety (q.v.) of peasant ancestry. He attended the Ecole Le Myre de Vilers (q.v.), and at the time of the Rebellion of 1947 (q.v.) was attending the teachers' college of the University of Montpellier. While he was a student in France, he formed the Union des Etudiants Malgaches as a counterweight to the more nationalist and Merina (q.v.)–dominated Association des Etudiants d'Origine Malgache.

When he returned to Madagascar in 1950 he began teaching and became active in politics as a member of the Parti des Deshérités de Madagascar (q.v.). In 1952 he was elected to the provincial council of Mahajanga and was sent as one of its delegates to the representative assembly in Antananarivo. In 1956 he was elected to the French National Assembly from the western electoral district, and while there joined the French Socialist party. On his return to Madagascar, he formed the Parti Social Démocrate (q.v.), with the active encouragement of the French governor-general, Soucadaux (q.v.), who was also a member of the French Socialist party. When the Loi-Cadre Government Council (q.v.) was elected, his PSD was strong enough for him to become its vice president.

Although Tsiranana was more in favor of autonomy than other members of PADESM—a split that had led to his formation of a new party—he was suspicious of further movement toward independence, arguing that internally the Côtier (q.v.) groups were still too weak to avoid domination by the Merina (q.v.) and that externally a small state like Madagascar could fall prey to international communism. He argued for a "yes" vote in the 1958 Referendum on the Constitution of the Fifth French Republic (q.v.), with the rejection of full independence which that implied. In May 1959 he was elected president by the Constituent Assembly of an autonomous Madagascar in the French Union. Pressures for independence were too great, however, and in January 1960 Tsiranana's government began the process of negotiating its full independence. Tsiranana's desire to avoid total separation from France influenced the negotiations, and independence came accompanied by a series of cooperation agreements that maintained a large measure of French influence. On June 26, 1960, independence was proclaimed, and in July Tsiranana brought back the three MDRM deputies whose exile in France had symbolized the divisions of the Malagasy population.

For most of the First Republic Tsiranana, seconded by the secretary-general of the party and minister of the interior, André Resampa (q.v.), was able to maintain his dominance of Malagasy politics. That dominance began to fade when he suffered a stroke at a meeting of the Union Africaine et Malgache (q.v.) at Yaounde in February 1970. He spent the next several months hospitalized in Paris, and when he returned to Madagascar found that the struggle to succeed him had already begun. One of the main participants was André Resampa, whom Tsiranana gradually removed from power, finally accusing him of plotting against the regime and having him arrested in June 1971. In general, Tsiranana had increasing difficulty in controlling political events, coming more and more to rely on a small group of advisors known as the "Tsimihety clan." The Peasant Rebellion of 1971 (q.v.) caused a further loss of prestige. Tsiranana tried to recover his position by staging a presidential election in January 1972, in which he was the only candidate, and in which the members of his government attempted to prove their loyalty by ritual praises. He was elected with 99% of the vote.

By May 1972, however, the crisis in the educational system had turned into the May 1972 Revolution (q.v.), which quickly turned into an attack on Tsiranana and his regime. In spite of his efforts to contain the uprising, Tsiranana was forced to hand power over to General Gabriel Ramanantsoa (q.v.) and was removed as president after the October referendum that ratified the military's seizure of power.

Tsiranana continued to be active in politics during the Ramanantsoa regime (q.v.), reconciling with Resampa to form the Parti Socialiste Malgache (q.v.). He was suspected of complicity in the 1975 assassination of Ramanantsoa's successor, Colonel Richard Ratsimandrava (q.v.), and was one of the defendants at the "Trial of the Century" (q.v.), at which those suspected of involvement in the assassination were tried. Like the other defendants, Tsiranana was released, and the charges against him dismissed. Tsiranana played little part in the subsequent Democratic Republic of Madagascar, and died in 1978.

-U-

UNION AFRICAINE ET MALGACHE. The Union Africaine et Malgache, whose charter was signed in Antananarivo in

September 1961, was formed to link France and its former African colonies when the French Community dissolved as the colonies moved from internal autonomy to full independence between 1959 and 1960. In 1965 the name was changed to Organisation Commune Africaine et Malgache (q.v.). *See also* FIFTH FRENCH REPUBLIC.

UNION DEMOCRATIQUE ET SOCIALE DE MADAGASCAR. The UDSM was founded in 1957 by two brothers from the east coast of Fianarantsoa province, Norbert and Antoine Zafimahova (q.v.). In the 1957 legislative elections, the party gained a majority in both Fianarantsoa and Toliara provinces, and Norbert Zafimahova became president of the Territorial Assembly, in which the UDSM had 36 seats compared with 37 for the Parti Social Démocrate (q.v.) of Philibert Tsiranana (q.v.). The platforms of the two parties resembled each other in their rejection of immediate independence, and they formed the Cartel des Républicains (q.v.) to campaign against the parties that had advocated a "no" vote in the Referendum on the Constitution of the Fifth French Republic (q.v.). After 1958, however, the UDSM began to attempt to expand outside its Fianarantsoa base in competition with the PSD. In response, Tsiranana successfully attracted some UDSM leaders, like Robert Marson (q.v.) and Albert Sylla (q.v.), to the PSD. In the 1958 debates on the constitution that Madagascar would adopt with the coming of internal autonomy, the UDSM lost its battle for the adoption of a parliamentary rather than a presidential form of government, and in the 1959 municipal elections it was unable to maintain control of its bases in Farafangana and Manakara. After these elections, the party split, and a majority of its members in the legislature, led by Albert Sylla, joined the PSD. Norbert Zafimahova reacted by forming the Union des Sociaux Démocrates de Madagascar (q.v.).

UNION DES ETUDIANTS SOCIALISTES MALGACHES. The UESM was formed at the University of Madagascar in 1962. It was the creation of the governing Parti Social Démocrate (q.v.), which considered the existing student group—the

FAEM—too radical. The UESM itself was on the left of the party, however, and pushed for the renegotiation of the cooperation agreements (q.v.) with France and for reform of the educational system.

UNION DES INDEPENDANTS DE TANANARIVE. The UIT was founded by Stanislas Rakotonirina (q.v.) in 1953, and was the main force behind his election as mayor of Antananarivo in 1956. Although it was founded with the assistance of the Catholic mission, it also attracted non-Catholic groups. After the coming of the Loi-Cadre (q.v.) and Rakotonirina's quarrels with the Catholic mission, the UIT entered a period of decline. It did not attend the Tamatave Congress (q.v.) of 1958 or participate in the formation of the AKFM which resulted from the congress. Although the UIT eventually advised a negative vote in the 1958 Referendum on the Constitution of the Fifth French Republic (q.v.), it did not do so until one week before the referendum was to be held. For these reasons the UIT lost its place as the party of Antananarivo nationalism.

UNION DES INTELLECTUELS ET UNIVERSITAIRES MALGACHE. UNIUM was an organization of Antananarivo intellectuals founded in 1956 by, among others, Albert Ramangosoavina (q.v.). It declared that its goal was to "contribute to the elevation of the life of the Malagasy in the political, economic, cultural and social domains." It called for internal autonomy and supported the passage of the Loi-Cadre (q.v.). In 1958 UNIUM attended the Tamatave Congress, which called for immediate independence. Ramangosoavina, however, by now a member of the Loi-Cadre Governing Council, disavowed this action. The union dissolved as its members moved into more overt partisan activity.

UNION DES PEUPLES MALGACHES. This party was a successor to the Parti de l'Union des Peuples Malgaches. It was strongest in Antananarivo, with sections in Toamasina and Diégo-Suarez. In 1956 it supported the candidacy of Stanislas Rakotonirina (q.v.) for mayor of Antananarivo. It attended the Tamatave Congress (q.v.) in 1958,and was one of the parties that united to form the AKFM (q.v.), or Independence Congress Party of Madagascar.

UNION DES SOCIAUX DEMOCRATES DE MADAGASCAR. This party was formed in 1960 by Norbert Zafimahova (q.v.) after his party, the Union Démocratique et Sociale (q.v.), split up over the issue of support for the dominant Parti Social Démocrate (q.v.). Zafimahova's party continued his policy of opposition to the PSD. At the time of the 1965 legislative elections it took the name Manjakavaoaka ("Popular Power"). It was unable to win any seats in the elections.

UNION ET ACTION COMMUNALE. *See* RABEMANANJARA, RAYMOND.

UNION NATIONALE MALGACHE (UNAM). The Union Nationale Malgache was established in Toamasina in 1957. It advocated a degree of independence beyond that granted by the existing Loi-Cadre (q.v.) framework and "moderate" socialism. It attended the Tamatave Congress (q.v.) of 1958, but refused to join the attempt to unify the parties attending the congress in the AKFM (q.v.), or Independence Congress Party of Madagascar.

UNION NATIONAL POUR LE DEVELOPPEMENT ET LA DEMOCRATIE. The UNDD was formed in 1989 by Albert Zafy (q.v.), a professor at the University of Madagascar. Although the UNDD at first claimed an "ecological" ideology, it quickly became one of the leading groups opposing the continuation of the Democratic Republic of Madagascar (q.v.), and in March 1990 joined with other groups to form the Comité des Forces Vives (q.v.), which successfully overthrew the DRM in 1991.

UNION SOCIALISTE MALGACHE. The USM was founded in September 1972 by the former secretary-general of the Parti Social Démocrate (q.v.), André Resampa (q.v.). In the October referendum on the establishment of the Ramanantsoa regime (q.v.), the USM supported a "yes" vote.

Resampa, however, became increasingly critical of the regime's policy of reducing French influence in Madagascar and of what he saw as its pro-Merina (q.v.) bias. This attitude, combined with the USM's lack of success in elections to local councils and the Conseil National Populaire du Développment (q.v.), led to a reconciliation with Philibert Tsiranana (q.v.) and the creation of the Parti Socialiste Malagache (q.v.).

UNIONS. Under the colonial regime, unions for Malagasy were illegal until March 1937, when the right to create unions was extended to Malagasy who could read and write French, a restriction that was removed in August 1938. In spite of this, some Malagasy had belonged to organizations of French civil servants, and in 1909 had formed a mutual aid association that later evolved into a union. In October 1937 the organizers of an attempt to create a Malagasy union were arrested and tried before the court of the *indigénat* (q.v.) for creating an organization that transgressed the restrictions on unionization. It was not until Joseph Ravoahangy (q.v.) began to organize the Syndicat d'Agriculteurs et Eleveurs–CGT that union activity really began. The existing unions were dissolved by the Vichy (q.v.) administrators during the war, however. After the return of the Free French, a Union des Syndicats CGT with both European and Malagasy membership was created in 1943, with Ravoahangy and Boiteau as secretaries-general. It claimed 14,000 members in 1947. After the rebellion of 1947 (q.v.), in which Ravoahangy was condemned to death and later deported, and Boiteau forced to leave Madagascar, the membership of the union collapsed.

Union activity was slow to resume after 1947, and it was not until 1956 that the roots of modern Malagasy unions were laid. In 1956 FISEMA, or *Firaisan'ny Sendika eran'i Madagasikara* ("Federation of Unions of Malagasy Workers"), an offspring of the earlier Confederation Generale du Travail (q.v.), was created. In December of that year Philibert Tsiranana turned the Union des Syndicats Force Ouvière, affiliated with the French Force Ouvrière (q.v.), into the independent Confederation des Travaileurs Malgaches. These joined the one union that had maintained a high level of activity through the period: the Catholic-sponsored union that became independent from the French parent union as the Confederation Chrétienne des Syndicats Malgaches.

The political attachments of the unions continued after independence, with FISEMA affiliating with the opposition AKFM (q.v.) and the regime party, the Parti Social Démocrate (q.v.), creating the FMM, or *Fivondronam'ny Mpiasa Malagasy* ("Union of Malagasy Workers"). The Catholic unions regrouped as SEKRIMA, or *Sendika Kristiana Malagasy* ("Malagasy Christian Unions"). With the coming of the Democratic Republic of Madagascar (q.v.), the union landscape changed again. FISEMA split with the AKFM in 1976 over the issue of its independent participation in the Front National pour la Défense de la Révolution (q.v.). The AKFM founded a new union, FISEMARE, or Federation of Revolutionary Malagasy Workers. The PSD-sponsored union had already declined dramatically in the 1960s for its lack of unity. Finally, the new regime party, AREMA (q.v.), created SENREMA, or *Sendika Revolosionara Malagasy* ("Revolutionary Malagasy Union"). Membership figures for the unions are extremely unreliable. Generally it is agreed that SENREMA is the largest, followed by the Catholic-sponsored SEKRIMA. FISEMA has lost members since its split with the AKFM, and it is not clear that they have been picked up by FISEMARE. Many FISEMA leaders joined SENREMA. The Malagasy union movement has usually been characterized by weakness, in part the result of its political divisions, but also the result of a mobile work force; the seasonal, part-time, or temporary nature of much work; and the existence of a large number of unemployed who can be used as replacements for what are essentially unskilled positions. Among the stronger unions have been those grouping civil servants.

UNITED NATIONS CHARTER. The United Nations Charter, negotiated in San Francisco in 1945, contained a "declaration regarding non-self-governing territories." It declared that in these territories the self-interest of the indigenous inhabitants should be paramount. Nationalists in Madagascar considered that the United Nations Charter gave support to their claims for greater autonomy. Figures like Ravelojaona (q.v.) argued that Madagascar was suited to trusteeship status such as that given to Togo, while some organizers of the Rebellion of 1947 (q.v.) argued that the provisions of the charter meant that the United Nations would come to the assistance of their uprising.

UNITED STATES. The first U.S. consulate, accredited to the Merina Empire (q.v.), was established in Madagascar in 1866. Treaties of friendship were signed in 1867 and 1883. After the French conquest, the consulate continued on a sporadic basis, and at independence was upgraded to an embassy. The First Republic (q.v.) had an ambiguous relationship with the United States. The government was firmly pro-Western and anti-communist, generally supported U.S. foreign policy stands, and permitted the building of a NASA tracking station at Imerintsiatotsika, near Antananarivo (q.v.), in 1963. The Tsiranana (q.v.) regime, however, shared French fears of ''Anglo-Saxon'' designs on Madagascar. In 1971, when the former minister of the interior, André Resampa (q.v.), was accused of plotting with a foreign embassy to overthrow the regime, Tsiranana made it clear that it was the U.S. embassy that he suspected. The U.S. ambassador and much of his staff were recalled, leaving relations at the level of chargé d'affaires.

Relations did not improve when the Democratic Republic of Madagascar (q.v.) announced its Marxist orientation in 1975, and the NASA base was closed. In 1976 two U.S. diplomats were accused of supporting a strike in the technical schools and were expelled, leading to the expulsion of Malagasy diplomats from Washington in retaliation. The United States remained one of Madagascar's chief trading partners, however, and one with whom the balance of trade was favorable to Madagascar. The debt crisis (q.v.) of the early 1980s led Madagascar to seek to improve its relations with Western countries, including the United States. Ambassadors were exchanged again in 1981, and in 1983 the one hundredth anniversary of the 1883 friendship treaty was celebrated.

UNIVERSITY OF MADAGASCAR. The University of Madagascar was established in 1960 by combining several preexisting postsecondary institutions, including the Institut des Hautes Etudes, the Ecole Supérieure des Sciences, and the Ecole Supérieure des Lettres. At the beginning its degrees were given equivalence with French degrees, and its rector was appointed by the French minister of education. It moved to its present location, a place called Ambohitsaina, 2 km outside Antananarivo, in 1967. In 1972 student protests against French domination of their education led to the May 1972 Revolution (q.v.) that overthrew the First Republic (q.v.), and revision of the university system was a priority for the Ramanantsoa regime (q.v.) that followed. Since 1980 university centers have been established in the provincial capitals.

In 1986 the government of the Democratic Republic of Madagascar (q.v.) attempted to reduce expenditure on the system by limiting the numbers of times students could repeat years and restricting upper-level instruction to two of the university centers. The result was a series of strikes and demonstrations that forced the government to withdraw the plan. Projected reforms announced in 1990 were prevented by the instability that followed in 1991 and led to the collapse of the DRM. *See also* EDUCATION.

-V-

VANILLA. Vanilla was introduced to Madagascar from Réunion in the mid–nineteenth century. It is grown along the northwest and northeast coasts, and is Madagascar's most important export, generating about 30% of its export earnings. Production and exportation have been government controlled since 1960, although the operations of the Vanilla Board are currently under review. In recent years Malagasy vanilla has faced increased competition from new producers and artificial vanilla. *See also* SPICES.

VAZIMBA. This name is usually given to the earliest inhabitants of areas in Madagascar, especially those of the Highlands (q.v.), who are considered by local groups to have been established before their own arrival. There are several theories about who the Vazimba actually were. One argues that they were a group distinct from later Malagasy—either African or "Melanesian"—who arrived before the current occupants of the island and were absorbed or driven out by the later arrivals. Other theories argue that the Vazimba represent a premonarchical phase of the later society and may be comprised of groups that lost out in the struggle to establish a more hierarchical form of political system. In many areas, the spirits of the Vazimba are still considered to inhabit their former territory. There is also a present-day group in southwest Madagascar that calls itself Vazimba and claims to have been driven out of earlier territory to the east.

VELONJARA, PASCAL. Velonjara was a founder of the Parti des Deshérités de Madagascar (q.v.) and was the PADESM candidate in the eastern district of Madagascar in the 1946 elections to the French National Assembly, losing to Jacques Rabemananjara by 12,619 votes to 28,227. In 1951 he was successful in winning election to the National Assembly, where he opposed bills to extend amnesty (q.v.) to the prisoners of the Rebellion of 1947 (q.v.). Velonjara's influence extended to the Democratic Republic of Madagascar (q.v.), since three of his daughters married, respectively, Didier Ratsiraka (q.v.), onetime Minister of Defense Christophe Raveloson-Mahasampo (q.v.), and an influential early figure, Ferdinand Patureau (q.v.).

VEZO. The Vezo are a coastal population of seminomadic people who fish for a living on the west coast of Madagascar north of Toliara between the Onilahy and the Mangoky rivers. They are closely related to the Sakalava (q.v.), of whom they are often considered a subgroup.

VICHY. After the German invasion and the fall of France in June 1940, the French parliament met in the southern town of Vichy, in the unoccupied part of France. There it made peace with Germany and established a government under a hero of the First World War, Marshal Philippe Pétain. Most of the administrators of France's African colonies accepted the authority of this government rather than that of the Free French (q.v.) established in London. Marcel De Coppet (q.v.), governor-general of Madagascar, first sided with the Free French and then with the Vichy government. Under the Vichy regime both Malagasy nationalists and the groups of Free French (which included both French and Malagasy) were considered dangers to the regime and prosecuted accordingly. Vichy control over Madagascar ended with the British invasion of 1942 (q.v.), and the surrender of Governor-General Annet (q.v.) in October of that year.

VOHEMAR (*also* Iharana). Vohemar was one of the most important of the Islamic settlements of the northeast coast of Madagascar. Archaeological evidence suggests that the town was established around the fourteenth century and lasted until the seventeenth century. Like other such settlements, it was a trading town, as findings of pottery from China and east Africa suggest. What remains of the town indicates that its culture was a mixture of Islamic and non-Islamic influences.

VONIMBOLA, SAMUEL. A lieutenant in the army in 1975, Vonimbola was a representative from Antseranana province on the Directoire Militaire (q.v.) that took power after the assassination of Richard Ratsimandrava (q.v.). After the establishment of the Democratic Republic of Madagascar (q.v.), Vonimbola was promoted to major and became a rapporteur for the Conseil Militaire pour le Développement (q.v.). In 1982 he was one of several regime figures arrested for illegal vanilla trafficking in his home province.

VONJY IRAY TSY MIVAKY (Popular Force for National Unity). Vonjy was founded in 1973 by Dr. Jerome Razanabahiny-Marojama (q.v.), a former secretary-general of the youth wing of the Parti Social Démocrate (q.v.). The party was formed when Razanabahiny split with the leaders of the PSD, Philibert Tsiranana (q.v.) and André Resampa (q.v.), over the issue of continued support for the Ramanantsoa regime (q.v.). It has provided a home for many former PSD politicians. The party joined the Front National pour la Défense de la Révolution (q.v.) of the Democratic Republic of Madagascar (q.v.) in 1977, but it was always critical of the regime's avowed commitment to Marxist socialism, preferring a brand of social democracy not unlike that practiced by the PSD. Vonjy has consistently done better than predicted in Madagascar's elections, gaining six seats in the Assemblée Nationale Populaire (q.v.) in 1983. The party was split over the issue of supporting Didier Ratsiraka (q.v.) when he ran for a second term as president in 1982. In 1988 it joined the Alliance Démocratique Malgache, and in the 1989 presidential elections, Razanabahiny ran against Ratsiraka, gaining 14.8% of the vote.

Vonjy was weakened when André Resampa, who had been serving as a local official of the party, left in March 1990 to form a renewed PSD. The party split over strategy during the crisis that led to the end of the Ratsiraka regime, with some party members supporting Ratsiraka and others the opposition Comité des Forces Vives (q.v.).

VY VATO SAKELIKA (Iron Stone Network). Usually known by its initials, the VVS was created in 1912 by the students at the medical school at Befeletanana (q.v.) hospital. Members included many such future nationalist leaders as Joseph Raseta (q.v.) and Joseph Ravoahangy (q.v.). Many had been members of an earlier, banned organization, the Union Chrétienne des Jeunes Gens (q.v.). The VVS was important in that, rather than emphasizing the restoration of the Merina (q.v.) monarchy, it discussed the ways in which Western organization and politics could be adapted to local conditions. In this it was inspired by a series of articles by Pascal Ravelojaona (q.v.) on the successful modernization of Japan. The organization also differed from previous nationalist groups in recruiting beyond the capital, having some members from Betsileo (q.v.) territory.

Although this type of organization was forbidden under the *indigénat* (q.v.), the colonial administration generally ignored it until the coming of the First World War in 1914, when it was estimated that the VVS had about 300 members. In December 1915 the colonial administration announced the discovery of a plot, which it said had been formulated by the VVS, to poison the French inhabitants of Antananarivo. Nearly 200 members and suspected members of the VVS were arrested and sent to the prison island of Nosy Lava (q.v.). Eventually 41 of the prisoners were tried, and 34, including Ravoahangy, Raseta, and Ravelojaona, were sentenced to hard labor for from five years to life. Ravelojaona's sentence was overturned on appeal, and the rest were amnestied in 1921.

-W-

WORLD BANK. Officially the International Bank for Reconstruction and Development, the World Bank was founded in 1944 to provide loans for the development of its members. Members of the World Bank must also be members of the International Monetary Fund (q.v.), which was founded at the same time. Although the World Bank was at first occupied with the reconstruction of Europe, it increasingly came to focus on the development of Third World countries. The World Bank has become active in Madagascar since the country's attempts to loosen its reliance on France in the mid-1970s. It was a World Bank report issued in 1978 that provided part of the legitimization for the "All-Out Investment policy" (q.v.) undertaken by the Democratic Republic of Madagascar (q.v.) that year, and the World Bank became Madagascar's largest multilateral creditor. Since the onset of the debt crisis (q.v.) the World Bank has been instrumental in attempting to organize both multilateral and bilateral aid to Madagascar. It established an office in Antananarivo in 1983.

The World Bank has since been involved both in organizing specific aid projects in such sectors as banking and meat processing and in preparing general economic plans for the island. The economic policy slated to run through 1994 calls for further privatizations of government firms and liberalization of the economy, for improvements in the collection of government revenues, and for control over government spending through measures such as the restriction of hiring for the civil service. The plan also points to the social problems created by Madagascar's economic difficulties and to the need for the creation of more social programs.

-X-

No entries

-Y-

No entries

-Z-

ZAFIMAHOVA, ANTOINE. Brother of Norber Zafimahova (q.v.), Antoine collaborated with him in the founding of the Union Démocratique et Sociale de Madagascar (q.v.).

ZAFIMAHOVA, NORBERT. Norbert Zafimahova was born into a powerful family established in Farafangana. At the time of the Rebellion of 1947 (q.v.), in which members of his family were killed, Zafimahova was a member of the representative assembly for the Parti des Deshérités de Madagascar (q.v.). He later served in the Conseil de la République of the Fourth French Republic. In 1956 he participated in the formal break-up of PADESM, founding the Union Démocratique et Socieale de Madagascar in opposition to the Parti Social Démocrate (q.v.) of Philibert Tsiranana. Although he did not accept office on the 1956 Loi-Cadre Governing Council (q.v.), Zafimahova became president of the 1958 assembly, in which his UDSM had 36 out of 90 members to 37 for the PSD. The assembly had the power to draw up a constitution for the status of internal autonomy that Madagascar was to enjoy under the new French constitution. Zafimahova advocated a parliamentary form of government for Madagascar, but the presidential form modeled on the constitution of the Fifth French Republic (q.v.) preferred by Tsiranana was adopted instead.

Throughout the legislature, Zafimahova lost influence as members of his party accepted positions in the government and often joined the PSD. In May 1959 he resigned his presidency, on the point of being censured for absenteeism. In the 1960 presidential election, Zafimahova made an alliance with the Rassemblement Chrétien de Madagascar (q.v.), and ran against Tsiranana, although he lost. After the election some of Zafimahova's former allies, such as Jarison (q.v.), moved into the PSD government. Zafimahova continued to be active in politics, forming the Union des Sociaux Démocrates de Madagascar (q.v.) after the split of the UDSM in 1960, but the control of the PSD over the political system was such that he was never able to be elected.

ZAFIRAMINIA. Literally, ''the Children of Raminia,'' a legendary figure said to have come to the east coast of Madagascar from Mecca and Mangalore in early times. Several dynasties of southern Madagascar, including the Maroserana (q.v.), claim to be descended from the Zafiraminia. Groups calling themselves Zafiraminia were recorded by Portuguese visitors to the region around Fort-Dauphin (q.v.) in 1613, although the visitors commented that the Zafiraminia seemed ignorant of most of the tenets of Islam. The *ombiasy* (q.v.), or ritual specialists who operated throughout Madagascar, also claimed to be Zafiraminia.

ZAFY, ALBERT. The first president of the Third Republic (q.v.) of Madagascar, Zafy was born in Antseranana province. He began his education in France in 1954, graduating with a medical degree, and remaining in France until 1971. He returned to Madagascar and from 1972 to 1975 served as minister of health in the government of General Ramanantsoa (q.v.). When Didier Ratsiraka (q.v.) established the Democratic Republic of Madagascar (q.v.) in 1975, Zafy campaigned against the adoption of the DRM's constitution. He then returned to his post at the University of Madagascar, but emerged in 1989 to found the Union Nationale pour le Développement et la Démocratie (q.v.). In 1990 he joined with other opposition leaders to form the Comité des Forces Vives (q.v.) and began to work to overthrow Ratsiraka and the DRM. When the CFV formed a countergovernment in July 1991, he was named prime minister. When the DRM collapsed, and a power-sharing agreement (q.v.) was set up to manage the transition to the Third Republic (q.v.), Zafy became president of the Haute Autorité d'Etat (q.v.), the central transitional institution. Zafy ran as the candidate of the CFV in the first elections for the presidency of the Third Republic. He gained 48% of the vote in the November 25, 1992, first round, and in the February 10, 1993, runoff election against Didier Ratsiraka, he gained 66.6% of the vote to Ratsiraka's 33.4%.

ZAKARIASY, ALBERT. A Protestant minister and member of the Conseil National Populaire pour le Développement (q.v.) from Toamamsina province, Zakariasy was named minister of foreign affairs in the weeklong government of Richard Ratsimandrava (q.v.), replacing Didier Ratsiraka (q.v.), who had held the post during the Ramanantsoa regime (q.v.). After Ratsimandrava's assassination, Zakariasy supported Ratsiraka and was a founding member of the political bureau of AREMA (q.v.), the regime party of Ratsiraka's Democratic Republic of Madagascar. He continued to sit on the Assemblée Nationale Populaire (q.v.), presiding over the Commission on Infrastructure and Rural Development.

ZANAMALATA. The Zanamalata, or "Children of Mulattoes," were the descendants of pirates (q.v.) and Malagasy living around Antongil Bay (q.v.) on the east coast of Madagascar. After 1712 they were united by Ratsimilaho (q.v.) to form the leadership of the Betsimisaraka Confederation (q.v.), which conquered the area from Antongil Bay to Toamasina (q.v.). At the beginning of the nineteenth century, the confederation was conquered by the Merina Empire (q.v.), which took Toamasina in 1817. The Zanamalata staged a last rebellion against the Merina in 1826, but were defeated. Their leaders were taken to the Merina capital, Antananarivo (q.v.), and executed.

ZOAM. The ZOAM, groups of unemployed youth in Antananarivo (q.v.), began as ZWAM, or Zatovo Western Andevo

Malagasy, which could be loosely translated as "young slave cowboys of Madagascar." They modeled themselves on Clint Eastwood, the hero of the spaghetti westerns of the day. Many were school dropouts, and they were open to the criticisms of the education (q.v.) system of the First Republic (q.v.) and of the regime itself that were put forward by such opposition figures as Manandafy Rakotonirina (q.v.). In their politicized form they were rebaptized ZOAM, Zatovo Orin'asa Anivon'ny Madagasikara, or "the young unemployed of Madagascar." They were active in the meetings that preceded the May 1972 Revolution (q.v.) and in the revolution itself. The succeeding Ramanantsoa regime (q.v.) was unable to satisfy their hopes for education or for employment, and many were drawn to the radical populism of Richard Ratsimandrava (q.v.). With the formation of the Democratic Republic of Madagascar, some ZOAM were recruited into the Tanora Tonga Saina (q.v.).

BIBLIOGRAPHY

Madagascar has inspired an abundance of literature, both by the Malagasy themselves and by foreign observers, with the bulk of the easily accessible material written in French. Although this abundance is an advantage for researchers, it creates problems for the bibliographer, and imposes some criteria of selection. I have been particularly selective in my selection of materials written before 1960 (the Grandidier volume for the period from 1933 to 1956 has over 20,000 entries). I have included only a selection of important articles dealing with topics—such as the origins of the Malagasy—discussed in the body of the Dictionary. I have also tried to include a reference to each of the important writers on Madagascar during this period and to cite the important works of participants in Malagasy politics, like the poet-politician Jacques Rabemananjara.

I have also been selective in covering the period since 1960. I have included most articles from the major Malagasy journals of history and geography: *Omaly sy anio, Taloha, Tantara,* and *Madagascar:Revue de Géographie.* Other periodicals published in Madagascar, which usually publish in French and sometimes in English, are listed in the Bibliography with their dates of publication. I have excluded articles in Malagasy on the grounds that anyone who had already acquired a knowledge of the language must be at an advanced stage of learning about the island. I have been less restrictive in listing articles on the modern politics and economics of Madagascar, since there is much less available material. In this section, I have tried to include all articles and books of importance. Entries under a given author are listed chronologically.

Overviews of various periods of Malagasy history, in English, are to be found in the volumes of the Cambridge *History of Africa* and the more recent UNESCO *General History of Africa.* Yearly reviews of Malagasy politics and economics can be found in the *Annuaire des pays de l'Océan Indien (APOI* in the Bibliography).

Monthly and weekly reports can be found in *Africa Confidential, The African Research Bulletin* (political and economic issues), and *Lettre de l'Océan Indien/Indian Ocean Newsletter. Africa South of the Sahara* has a general overview of Malagasy history, politics, and economy, with annual updates.

The organization of the Bibliography is as follows:

1. Journals
2. Bibligraphies
3. Works Published before 1896
4. Works published between 1896 and 1960
   A. History and Anthropology
   B. Contemporary Politics and Economics
5. Works Published After 1960
   A. History and Ethnography
   B. Politics and Economics
   C. Geography and Resources
6. Language, Literature, and the Arts (All Periods)

1. Journals

Dates of publication are given for Malagasy journals. Abbreviations for journals used throughout this Bibliography are indicated in parentheses. For a complete list of Malagasy newspapers, periodicals, and journals, see *Geographical Index to Periodicals.*

Africa Confidential.

Africa Research Bulletin.

Afrique-Asie.

Afrique contemporaine.

Ambario: revue d'animation culturelle et scientifique 1978–.

Annales Malgaches (Université de Madagascar).

Série Droit (Faculté de Droit et des Sciences Économiques) 1963–.

Série Lettres (Faculté des Lettres et Sciences Humaines) 1963–.

Annuaire du monde politique, diplomatique et de la presse de Madagascar 1959–1978.

Annuaire du monde politique, administratif et diplomatique de Madagascar 1978–. (Antananarivo: Madprint, 1982) (Guide permanent de l'administration des pays de l'Océan Indien).

Annuaire des Pays de l'Océan Indien (APOI).

Antananarivo Annual 1875–1900.

Archipel.

Arts malgaches 1965–.

Asie du Sud-Est et Monde Insulindien (ASEMI).

Bulletin de l'Académie Malgache 1902–.

Bulletin de Madagascar 1950–.

Bulletin du Comité de Madagascar (Paris) 1895–1899.

Bulletin économique de Madagascar 1901–1932.

Cahiers du Centre d'Etudes des Coutumes (Université de Madagascar. Centre d'Etudes des Coutumes) 1966–1975.

Cahiers d'Histoire Juridique et Politique 1975– (follows *Cahiers du Centre d'Etudes des Coutumes).*

La Capacité (Université de Madagascar. Faculté de Droit et des Sciences Economiques) 1966–.

La Chronique administrative (Université de Madagascar. Ecole Nationale de Promotion Sociale) 1970–.

Civilisation Malgache (Université de Madagascar. Faculté de Lettres et Sciences Humaines) 1964–.

Etudes malgache (Institut des Hautes Etudes) (irreg.) 1960–.

La Grande Ile Militaire 1953–1958.

Institut de Recherche Scientifique de Madagascar. Mémoires.

Série A. Biologie animalie. 1948–.
Série B. Biologie végétale. 1948–.
Série C. Sciences humaines. 1952–.
Série D. Sciences de la terre. 1949–.
Série E. Entomologie. 1952–.
Série F. Océanographie. 1957–.

Jeune Afrique.

Lakroa 1926–.

Lettre de l'Océan Indien/Indian Ocean Newsletter.

Le lien: organe mensuel des protestantes de langue française de l'Océan Indien 1935–1966.

Linguistique et enseignement (Université de Madagascar. Institut de Linguistique Appliqué) 1971–.

Lumière 1935–1975.

Madagascar. Bulletin économique 1903–1933.

Madagascar Miscellanies (19 vols.) London: London Missionary Society (articles published at various times and in various locations, collected by J. Sibree).

Madagascar: Revue de géographie (Université de Madagascar. Laboratoire de Géographie) 1962–.

Mémoires de l'Académie malgache (irreg.) 1926–.

Musée d'art et d'archéologie, Université de Madagascar. *Travaux et Documents* (irreg.)

Le naturaliste Malgache 1949–1962.

Notes, Reconnaissances, et Explorations 1897–1900.

Nouvelles malgaches.

Océan indien actuel 1977–.

Omaly sy anio (Hier et Aujourd'hui (Université de Madagascar. Département d'Histoire) 1975–.

Revue d'agriculture et d'élevage à Madagascar 1933–.

Revue de Géographie (Université de Madagascar) 1970–.

Revue de Madagascar (1) 1899–1911, Comité de Madagascar; (2) 1933–1969, Government of Madagascar.

Revue économique de Madagascar (Université de Madagascar. Faculté de Droit et des Sciences Économiques) 1966–.

Taloha (Université de Madagascar. Musée d'Art et d'Archéologie) 1965–.

Tantara (Société d' Histoire de Madagascar) 1974–.

Tany Malagasy/Terre malgache (Université de Madagascar. Ecole Nationale Supérieure Agronomique) 1966–.

2. Bibliographies

Andriamirado, C., ed. *Répertoire des thèses et mémoires soutenus devant l'Université de Madagascar, mars 1977–mars 1979.* Antananarivo: Université de Madagascar, Rectorat, 1979.

AUPELF (Association des Universités Partiellement ou Entièrement de Langue Française) *Archives africaines.* Paris.

Bibliographie nationale de Madagascar. Tananarive: Université de Madagascar, 1964–.

Bibliographie des travaux en langue française sur l'Afrique au Sud du Sahara. Paris: Ecole des Hautes Etudes en Sciences Sociales, Centre d' Etudes Africaines.

Conover, H. F. *Madagascar: A Selected List of References.* Washington, D.C.: Library of Congress, 1942.

Coulanges, P., and Coulanges, M. ''Bibliographie analytique des travaux de l'Institut Pasteur de Madagascar, 1898–1978.'' Archives de l'Institut Pasteur de Madagascar, 1979.

Domenichini, J.-P., and Domenichini-Ramiaramanana, B. ''La récherche en sciences humaines à Madagascar (1974–1978).'' *ASEMI* 9 (1978): 41–50.

Domenichini-Ramiaramanana, B. ''Bibliography des publications sur la langue et la littérature malgaches (1974–1978).'' *ASEMI* 9 (1978): 51–70.

Donque, G. ''Bilan de dix-sept années de récherches au Laboratoire de Géographie de l'Université de Madagascar.'' *Madagascar: Revue de Géographie* 32 (January–June 1978): 99–114.

———. ''Etudes de géographie malgache dans le cadre de mémoires de maîtrise.'' *Madagascar: Revue de Géographie* 40 (January–June 1982): 99–111.

Duignan, P. *Madagascar (the Malagasy Republic): A List of Materials in the African Collections of Stanford University and the Hoover Institution on War, Revolution, and Peace.* Stanford: Hoover Institution, 1962.

Faublée, J. ''Dictionnaires malgaches.'' *Journal de la Société des Africanistes* 13 (1943): 213–215.

Feuer, G. ''Madagascar: état des travaux.'' *Review française de science politique* 12 (1962): 920–962.

Fonteville, J. *Bibliographie nationale de Madagascar, 1956–1963.* Tananarive: Université de Madagascar, 1971.

Grandidier, A., and Grandidier, G. *Bibliographie de Madagascar.* Paris, 1905 (covers period 1500–1903), 1933, 1956.

Hommes et destins: dictionnaire biographique d'Outre- Mer, vol. III: *Madagascar.* Paris: Académie des Sciences d'Outre-Mer, 1979.

Jaegle, C.-E. *Essai de bibliographie: Madagascar et dépendances (1905–1927).* Tananarive: Gouvernement Général, 1929.

Jones, R. *Africa Bibliography Series: South-East Central Africa and Madagascar.* London: International Africa Institute, 1961.

Madagascar et Réunion, vol. 1: *Madagascar.* Paris: Encyclopédie de l'Empire Français, 1947.

Miège, J. L. ''La récherche sur l'Océan Indien à l'Institut d'Histoire des Pays d'Outre-Mer (IPHOM-Aix).'' *APOI* 2 (1975, published 1977): 443–448.

Molet, L. ''Bibliographie critique récente sur Madagascar.'' *Canadian Journal of African Studies* 1 (1967): 51–63.

Platt, E. T. ''Madagascar, Great Isle, Red Isle: A Bibliographical Survey.'' *Geographical Review* 27 (1937): 301–309.

Poitelon, J.-P., et al. *Périodiques malgaches de la Bibliothèque Nationale.* Paris: Bibliothèque Nationale, 1970.

Rabearamana, G. "Les récherches dans la géographie malgache: bilan, problèmes et perspectives." *Récherche, Pédagogie et Culture* 9 (1981): 24–29.

Radimilahy, M., and Rasamuel, D. *Contribution bibliographique en archéologie.* Tananarive: Université de Madagascar, Musée d'Art et d'Archéologie, 1982.

Raison-Jourde, F. "Bibliographie des publications sur l'histoire et l'anthropologie de Madagascar (1974–1978)." *ASEMI* 9 (1978): 71–98.

Rantoandro, G. "La récherche au Département d'histoire de la Faculté des Lettres de Tananarive." *Archipel* 11 (1977): 37–42.

Razafintsalama, G. *Périodiques malgaches: liste provisoire des collections conservées à la Bibliothèque Nationale, 1866–1960.* Paris: Bibliothèque Nationale, 1964.

La récherche française en afrique tropicale et à Madagascar. Paris: Académie des Sciences d'Outre-Mer, 1984.

Sibree, J. *Madagascar Bibliography, Including Publications in the Malagasy Language and a List of Maps of Madagascar.* London: Trubner, 1885.

Situation de la récherche en 1984, perspectives 1985–1987. République Démocratique de Madagascar. Ministère de la Récherche Scientifique et Technologique pour le Développement. Direction de la Planification et de la Coordination, 1985.

Witherell, J. W. *Madagascar and Adjacent Islands: A Guide to Official Publications.* Washington, D.C.: Library of Congress, 1965.

Works Published Before 1896

Abinal, A. *Vingt ans à Madagascar: colonisation, traditions historiques, moeurs et croyances.* Paris: n.p., 1885.

Benyowski, M. A. *Memoirs and Travels.* London: n.p., 1790.

Besson, L. *Voyage au pays des Tanala indépendants de la region d'Ikongo.* Paris: n.p., 1894.

Brunet, L. *La France à Madagascar, 1815–1895.* Paris: Hachette, 1895.

———. *L'oeuvre de la France à Madagascar: La conquête, l'organisation, le général Gallieni.* Paris: A. Challamel, 1903.

Cameron, J. *Recollections of Missionary Life in Madagascar.* 1874.

Carol, J. *Chez les Hova, au pays rouge.* Paris: P. Ollendorf, 1898.

Castonnet des Fosse, H. *Madagascar.* Paris: La Société Bibliographique, 1884.

Catat, L. *Voyage à Madagascar, 1889–90.* Paris: Hachette, 1895

Cazeneuve, M. *A la Cour de Madagascar. Magie et diplomatie.* Paris: Delagrave, 1896.

Copland, S. *A History of the Island of Madagascar.* London: n.p., 1822.

Cousins, W. E. *Madagascar of Today: A Sketch of the Island.* London: London Missionary Society, 1895.

Cowan, W. D. *The Bara Land.* London: London Missionary Society, 1881.

———. ''Geographical Excursions in the Betsileo, Tanala and Bara Countries.'' *Proceedings of the Royal Geographical Society* 4 (1882): 521–537.

de Lavaissière, C. *Histoire de Madagascar, ses habitants et ses missionaires.* 2 vols. Paris: V. Lecoffre, 1884.

Drury, R. *Madagascar; or, Robert Drury's Journal During Fifteen Years Captivity on That Island.* London, 1729. See also *Madagascar ou le journal de Robert Drury pendant ses quinze ans de captivite,* in vol. 4 (1906) of A. Grandidier, *Collection des Ouvrages Anciens Concernant Madagascar.*

Duchesne, J. *L'expédition de Madagascar.* Paris: Lavauzelle, 1896.

Ellis, W. *History of Madagascar.* London: Fisher and Son, 1838.

———. *Three Visits to Madagascar.* London: John Murray, 1859.

———. *Madagascar Revisited.* London: John Murray, 1867.

———. *The Martyr Church: A Narrative of the Introduction, Progress, and Triumph of Christianity in Madagascar.* London: n.p., 1870.

Ferrand, G. *Contes populaires malgaches.* Paris: E. Leroux, 1893. Reissued in microfiche by Association des Universitiés Partiallement ou Entièrement de Langue Française, Archives Africaines, 1977.

Flacourt, Etienne de. *Histoire de la grande île de Madagascar* Paris, 1658. *See also* A. Grandidier, *Collection des Ouvrages Anciens Concernant Madagascar (COACM)* 8 (1913).

———. *Rélation de ce qui s'est passé en ile de Madagascar depuis l'année 1642 jusqu'en 1660.* Paris: Pierre Bienfait, 1661. See also *COACM* 9 (1920).

Fleury, T. ''Quelques notes sur le nord de Madagascar.'' *Bulletin de la Société de Géographie Commerciale de Bordeaux* (1886): 194–209, 226–245, 257–282, 290–312.

Froberville, E. de. ''Aperçu sur la langue malgache et récherches sur la race qui habitait l'île de Madagascar avant l'arrivée des Malais.'' *Bulletin de la Société de Géographie de Paris* 11 (1839): 29–46, 257–274.

———. ''Historique des invasions madécasses aux îles comores et à la côte orientale d'Afrique.'' *Annuaire des voyages et de la géographie* 2 (1845): 194–208.

Guillain, C. H. *Documents sur l'histoire, la géographie, et le commerce de la partie occidentale de Madagascar.* Paris: Imprimerie Royale, 1845.

Hanotaux, G. *L'affaire de Madagascar.* Paris: n.p., 1896.

Humbert, G. *Madagascar. I. L'île et ses habitants. II. La dernière guerre franco-hova (1883–85).* Paris: Berger-Lévrault, 1895.

Jully, A. ''Funerailles, tombeaux et honneurs rendus aux morts à Madagascar.'' *L'Anthropologie* (1887): 385–401.

Knight, E. F. *Madagascar in War Time.* London: Longmans, 1896.

Last, J. T. ''Notes on the Languages Spoken in Madagascar.'' *Journal of the Anthropological Institute* 25 (1896): 46–71.

Leclerc, M. ''Les peuplades de Madagascar.'' *Revue d'éthnographie* (1886): 397–432; (1887): 1–32.

Leguevel de Lacombe, B.-F. *Voyage à Madagascar et aux Iles Comores (1823 à 1830).* Paris: 1840; reissued, Geneva: Slatkine, 1980.

Le Myre de Vilers, C. M. ''Le traité hova.'' *Revue de Paris* (November 15, 1895): 225–241.

McLeod, L. *Madagascar and Its People.* London: Longmans, 1865.

Madagascar, Past and Present, by a Resident. London: Bentley, 1847.

Martin, F. *Memoire concernant l'îlede Madagascar, 1665–1668.* Paris: see also *COACM* 9 (1920).

Matthews, T. T. *Thirty Years in Madagascar.* London: Religious Tract Society, 1904.

Mullens, J. "On the Origin and Progress of the People of Madagascar." *Journal of the Anthropological Institute* 5 (1876): 181–196.

Oliver, S. P. *Madagascar and the Malagasy, with Sketches in the Provinces of Tamatave, Betanimena, and Ankova.* London: Day, 1863.

Parker, G. W. "On Systems of Land Tenure in Madagascar." *Journal of the Anthropological Institute* 12 (1883): 277–280.

———. "New Code of Laws for the Hova Kingdom of Madagascar, Promulgated at Antananarivo on March 29th, 1881." *Journal of the Anthropological Institute* 12 (1883): 306–318.

Pfeiffer, I. *The Last Travels of Ida Pfeiffer.* London: 1881.

Phelps, J. W. *The Island of Madagascar.* New York: J. B. Alden, 1885.

Piolet, J.-B. *Madagascar et les Hova.* Paris: C. Delagrave, 1895.

Richemont, ?. *Documents sur la Compagnie de Madagascar.* Paris, 1897.

Routier, G. *Les droits de la France sur Madagascar.* Paris: H. Le Soudier, 1895.

Saillens, R. *Nos droits sur Madagascar et nos griefs contre les Hova, examinés impartialement.* Paris: P. Monnerat, 1885.

Shaw, G. A. *Madagascar and France.* London: Religious Tract Society, 1885.

Sibree, J. ''Curious Words and Customs Connected with Chieftanship and Royalty Among the Malagasy.'' *Journal of the Anthropological Institute* 21 (1892): 215–229.

———. Decorative Carvings on Wood, Especially on the Burial Memorials, by the Betsileo/Malagasy.'' *Journal of the Anthropological Institute* 21 (1892): 230–244.

———. *Fifty Years in Madagascar.* London: Allen and Unwin, 1924.

———. *Madagascar Before the Conquest.* London: Allen and Unwin, 1896.

———. *Madagascar, the Great African Island.* London: Trubner, 1880.

———. *Madagascar and Its People.* London: Religious Tract Society, 1870.

———. ''Relationships and the Names Used for Them Among the Peoples of Madagascar, Chiefly the Hovas; Together with Observations upon Marriage Customs and Morals Among the Malagasy.'' *Journal of the Anthropological Institute* 9 (1880): 35–49.

———. ''Relics of the Sign and Gesture Language Among the Malagasy.'' *Journal of the Anthropological Institute* 13 (1884): 208–214.

Wake, C. S. ''Notes on the Origin of the Malagasy.'' *Journal of the Anthropological Institute* 11 (1882): 21–31.

4. Works Published Between 1896 and 1960

A. History and Anthropology

Andriamanjato, R. *Le tsiny et le tody dans la pensée malgache.* Paris: Présence Africaine, 1957.

———.''La culture malgache.'' *Présence africaine* 22 (1958): 58–62.

Arbousset, F. *Le fokonolona à Madagascar.* Paris: Domat-Montchrestien, 1950.

———. ''Le fokonolona à Madagascar.'' *Revue juridique et politique de l'Union française* (1950): 472–498.

Ardent du Picq, C. P. *L'influence islamique sur une population malayo-polynesienne de Madagascar.* Paris: Lavauzelle, 1933.

Auber, J. *Français, Malgaches, Bantous, Arabes, Turcs, Chinois, Canaques: parlons-nous une même langue? Essai de sémantique comparée.* Tananarive: Imprimerie Officielle, 1958.

Bernard-Thierry, S. ''Les perles magiques à Madagascar.'' *Journal de la Société des Africanistes* 29 (1959): 33–90.

Berthier, H. *Notes et impressions sur les moeurs et coutumes du peuple malgache.* Tananarive: Imprimerie Officielle, 1933.

Birkeli, E. *Marques de boeufs et traditions de race.* Oslo: Documents sur l'Ethnographie de la Côte Occidentale de Madagascar, 1926.

Bouchereau, A. ''Note sur l'anthropologie de Madagascar, des Iles Comores, et de la côte orientale d'Afrique.'' *L'Anthropologie* 8 (1897): 149–164.

Boudou, A. *Les Jesuites à Madagascar au XIXe siècle.* 2 vols. Paris: Beauchesne, 1942.

Cahuzac, A. *Essai sur les institutions et le droit malgache.* Paris: Chevalier, Maresq et cie., 1900.

Cailliet, E. *Essai sur la psychologie Hova.* Paris: Presses Universitaires Françaises, 1926.

———. *La foi des ancêtres: essai sur les représentations collectives des vieux malgaches.* Paris: Annales de l'Académie des Sciences Coloniales, 1930.

Callet, F. *Tantaran'ny andriana eto Madagascar.* 2 vols. Tananarive: Imprimerie Officielle, 1908. Translated into French by G. S. Chapus and E. Ratsimba (q.v.).

Camboue, P. "Notes sur quelques moeurs et coutumes malgaches." *Anthropos* 2 (1907): 981–989.

———. "Les dix premiers ans d'enfance chez les malgaches: circoncision, nom, éducation." *Anthropos* 6 (1909):375–386.

———. "Jeux des enfants malgaches." *Anthropos* 6 (1911): 665–683.

Chamla, M. C. *Récherches anthropologiques sur l'origine des malgaches.* Paris: Mémoires du Muséum, 1958.

Champion, P. "La tache pigmentaire congénitale à Madagascar et aux Comores." *Journal de la Société des Africanistes* 7 (1937): 79–92.

Chapus, G. S., and Mondain, G. *L'action protestante à Madagascar.* Tananarive: London Missionary Society, 1937.

———. *Un homme d'état malgache, Rainilaiarivony.* Paris: Editions de l'Outremer, 1953.

———, and Ratsimba, E. *Histoire des rois d'Imerina.* Tananarive: Académie Malgache, vol. 1, 1953; vol. 2, 1956;

vols. 3 and 4, 1958. Translation of Callet, *Tantaran'ny Andriana* (q.v.).

Charbonneau, J. *Gallieni à Madagascar.* Paris: Nouvelles Editions Latines, 1950.

Chauvin, J. *Jean Laborde.* Tananarive: Imprimerie Moderne de l'Emyrne, 1939.

———. ''Le prince Ramahatra.'' *Revue d'histoire des colonies* 27 (1939): 33–46.

Clark, H. E. *The Story of the Friends' Foreign Missions in Madagascar.* London, 1902.

Colin, P. ''Les Tanouses: étude d'une mentalité primitive [Antanosy emigrés].'' *Ethnographie* 41 (1943): 23–71.

———. *Aspects de l'âme malgache.* Paris: Editions de l'Orante, 1959.

Condominas, G. *Fokonolona et collectivités rurales en Imerina.* Paris: Berger-Lévrault, 1960.

Cotte, V. *Regardons vivre une tribu malgache. Les Betsimisaraka.* Paris: La Nouvelle Edition, 1947.

Dahl, O. C. ''Le systeme phonologique du proto-malgache.'' *Norsk Tidsskrift for Sprogvidenskap* 10 (1938): 189–235.

———. ''Etudes de phonologie et de phonétique malgaches.'' *Norsk Tidsskrift for Sprogvidenskap* 26 (1951): 148–200.

———. *Malgache et Maanjan, une comparaison linguistique.* Oslo, 1951.

Dama-Ntosha. *Le Buddhisme malgache.* Tananarive: Imprimerie Antananarivo, 1938.

———. *Les temps nouveaux.* Tananarive: Imprimerie de Tananarive, 1945.

———. *Histoire politique et réligieuse des malgaches depuis les origines jusqu'à nos jours.* Tananarive: Librarie Mixte, 1952.

———. *La technique de la conception de la vie chez les malgaches révélée par leurs proverbes.* Tananarive: Imprimerie Masoandro, 1953.

Dandouau, A. "Coutumes sakalava: le sikidi." *Anthropos* 9 (1914): 546–568, 833–872.

———. *Contes populaires des Sakalava et des Tsimihety de la région d'Analalava.* Algiers: Carbonel, 1922.

———. "Ody et fanafody: charmes et rémèdes [sakalava et tsimihety]." *Revue d'ethnographie et des traditions populaires* 2 (1922): 111–128.

———. "Enigmes et dévinettes sakalava et tsimihety." *Revue d'ethnographie et des traditions populaires* 6 (1925): 1–26.

———. and Chapus, G. S. *Histoire des populations de Madagascar.* Paris: Larose, 1952.

Danielli, M. "The Witches of Madagascar: A Theory of the Function of Witches and of Their Organization Based on Observations of an Existing Cult [Merina and Betsileo]." *Folklore* 58 (1947): 261–276.

———. "The State Concept of Imerina, Compared with Theories Found in Certain Scandinavian and Chinese texts." *Folklore* 61 (1950): 186–202.

Darcy, J. *Cent années de rivalité coloniale, l'affaire de Madagascar.* Paris, 1908.

David, R. ''Le problème anthropobiologique malgache: nouvelles observations sur les Mahafali du sud-ouest de Madagascar.'' *Journal de la Société des Africanistes* 9 (1939): 119–152.

David-Bernard, E. *La conquête de Madagascar.* Paris: P. Sorlot, 1944.

Decary, R. ''L'industrie chez les Antandroy de Madagascar.'' *Revue d'ethnographie et de traditions populaires* 7 (1926): 38–52.

———. *L'Androy (extrème sud de Madagascar): Essai de monographie régionale.* Paris: SEGMC, vol. I, 1930; vol. II, 1933.

———. ''Les tatouages chez les indigènes de Madagascar.'' *Journal de la Société des Africanistes* 5 (1935): 1–39.

———. L'Etablissment de Sainte-Marie de Madagascar sous la Restauration et le rôle de Sylvain Roux. Paris: SEGMC, 1937.

———. ''La chasse et le piégeage chez les indigènes de Madagascar.'' *Journal de la Société des Africanistes* 9 (1939): 3–41.

———. *La faune malgache, son rôle dans les croyances et les usages des indigènes.* Paris: Payot, 1950.

———. *Moeurs et coutumes des malgaches.* Paris: Payot, 1951.

———. ''La protection des plantes et la conservation des récoltes à Madagascar.'' *Journal de la Société des Africanistes* 29 (1959): 193–216.

———. *Les ordalie et sacrifices rituels chez les anciens malgaches.* Pau: Imprimerie Marripouey, 1959.

———. *L'Ile Nosy Be de Madagascar: Histoire d'une colonisation.* Paris: Société d'Editions Maritimes et d'Outre–Mer, 1960.

Delteil, P. *Le fokon'olona (commune malgache) et les conventions de fokon'olona.* Paris: F. Loviton, 1931.

De Martonne, E. "Psychologie du peuple malgache." *Revue de la psychologie des peuples* 3 (1948): 40–43, 166–210.

Deschamps, H. *Madagascar.* Paris: Berger- Lévrault, 1947.

———. *Les pirates à Madagascar aux XVIIe et XVIIIe siècles.* Paris: Berger-Lévrault, 1949.

———. *Les migrations intérieures passées et présentes à Madagascar.* Paris: Berger-Lévrault, 1959.

———. *Histoire de Madagascar.* Paris: Berger-Lévrault, 1960.

———. "Conceptions, problèmes et sources de l'histoire de Madagascar." *Journal of African History* (1960): 249–56.

———. and Chauvet, P. *Gallieni Pacificateur.* Paris: Presses Universitaires Françaises, 1949.

———. and Vianes, S. *Les malgaches du sud-est.* Paris: PUF pour l'Institut International Africain, 1959.

Dez, J. "Le retournement des morts chez les Betsileo." *Ethnographie* 51 (1956): 115–122.

———. "Chez les Betsimisaraka de la région de Nosy Varika: les Tangalamena." *Journal de la Société des Africanistes* 29 (1959): 229–238.

Dubois, H.-M. "Les origines des malgaches." *Anthropos* 21 (1926): 72–126; 22 (1927): 80–124.

———. "Le sambatra ou la circoncision chez les Antambahoaka, tribu de la côte est de Madagascar (Mananjary)." *Anthropos* 22 (1927): 741–764.

———. "L'idée de Dieu chez les anciens malgaches." *Anthropos* 24 (1929): 281–311; 29 (1934): 757–774.

———. "Etude sur les fady (tabous malgaches)." *Bibliotheca africana* 3 (1929): 117–134; 4 (1930): 327–341.

———. "Le caractère des Betsileo." *Anthropos* 25 (1930): 209–237.

———. *Monographie des Betsileo.* Paris: Institut d'Ethnologie, 1938.

———. "Le fait central des funerailles au Betsileo." *Annales Lateranensi* 2 (1938): 73–145.

Engelvin, A. *Les vezo ou enfants de la mer: monographie d'une sous-tribu sakalava.* Paris: Librairie Vincentienne et Missionnaire, 1937.

———. *La belle vie vécue par un missionnaire lazariste à Madagascar de 1911 à 1954.* Paris: Les Missions Lazaristes, 1955.

Escande, E. *La Bible à Madagascar.* Paris: Société des Missions Evangeliques, 1923.

Falk, K. "L'ancien village au Vakinankaratra." *Historisk-Antikvarisk Rekke* 4 (1958): 1–27.

Faublée, J. "L'elevage chez les Bara de Madagascar." *Journal de la Société des Africanistes* 11 (1941): 115–124.

———. "Dans le sud de Madagascar: deux ans chez les Bara." *Comptes rendus de l'Académie des Sciences Coloniales* 7 (1941): 115–124.

———. "L'alimentation des Bara." *Journal de la Société des Africanistes* 12 (1942): 157–201.

———. "Demographie de Madagascar." *Journal de la Société des Africanistes* 13 (1943): 209–213.

———. "*L'ethnographie de Madagascar.* Paris: Nouvelle Edition, 1946.

———. *Récits Bara.* Paris: Institut d'Ethnologie, 1947.

———. "A Madagascar: Les villages Bara, site, migration, évolution." *Revue de géographie humaine et d'ethnologie* 1 (1948): 36–53.

———. "L'équilibre d'une société malgache traditionnelle: les Bara." *Cahiers Charles Foucauld* (1950): 373–383.

———. "Techniques divinatoires et magiques chez les Bara de Madagascar." Journal de la Société des Africanistes 21 (1951): 127–138.

———. *La cohésion des sociétés Bara.* Paris: Presses Universitaires Françaises, 1954.

———. *Les esprits de vie à Madagascar.* Paris: Presses Universitaires Françaises, 1954.

Faublée, M., and Faublée, J. "Pirogues et navigation chez les Vezo du sud-ouest de Madagascar." *Anthropologie* 54 (1950): 532–554.

Ferard, R. L. *Benyowski gentilhomme et roi de fortune.* Paris: Larose, 1931.

Ferrand, G. "Notes sur la région entre Mananjary et Iavibola." *Bulletin de la Société de Géographie* (1896): 5–25.

———. *Les musulmans à Madagascar et aux Comores.* 3 vols. Paris: Leroux, 1891–1902.

———. *Contes populaires malgaches.* Paris: Leroux, 1893.

———. ''L'élément arabe et souahili en malgache ancien et moderne.'' *Journal asiatique* 6 (1903): 451–485.

———. ''Un texte arabico-malgache du XVIe siècle.'' *Notices et extraits de la Bibliothèque Nationale* 38 (1903): 449–576.

———. ''Un chapitre d'astrologie arabico-malgache d'après le manuscrit 8 du fonds arabico-malgache de la Bibliothèque Nationale.'' *Journal asiatique* 8 (1905): 193–273.

———. ''Les migrations musulmanes et juives à Madagascar.'' *Annales du Musée Guimet, Revue de l'Histoire des Religions* 52 (1905): 381–417.

———. ''Les Iles Ramny Lamery, Wakwak, Komor des géographes arabes, et Madagascar.'' *Journal asiatique* 10 (1907): 433–566.

———. *Essai de phonétique comparée du malais et des dialectes malgaches.* Paris: Geuthner, 1909.

———. ''Note sur l'alphabet arabico-malgache.'' *Anthropos* 4 (1909): 190–206.

———. ''Les voyages des javanais à Madagascar.'' *Journal asiatique,* 10th ser., 15 (1910): 281–330.

Finbert, E.-J. *Le livre de la sagesse malgache.* Paris: Robert Lafont, 1946.

Foury, B. *Maudave et la colonisation de Madagascar.* Paris: Société de l'Histoire des Colonies Françaises, 1956.

Frère, S. *Madagascar. Panorama de l'Androy.* Paris: Aframpe, 1958.

Froidevaux, H. ''Les préludes de l'intervention française à Madagascar au XVIIe siècle, navigateurs, géographie et commerçants français de 1504 à 1640.'' *Revue des questions historiques* 86 (1909): 436–479.

———. *Madagascar.* Vol. 6 in G. Hanotaux, ed. *Histoire des colonies françaises et de l'expansion de la France dans le monde.* Paris: Société d'Histoire Nationale, 1933.

Gautier, E.-F. ''Les Hovas sont-ils des malais?'' *Journal asiatique* (1900): 278–296.

———. *Notes sur l'écriture antaimoro.* Paris: Leroux, 1902.

———. ''Le calendrier malgache.'' *Journal asiatique* (1911): 97–117.

Gayet, G. ''Immigrations asiatiques à Madagascar.'' *Civilisation* 5 (1955): 54–65.

Gourou, P. ''Gallieni.'' In *Les techniciens de la colonisation,* ed. C. A. André, Paris: PUF, 1947.

———. ''Milieu local et colonisation réunionnaise sur les plateaux de la Sakay.'' *Cahiers d'Outre-Mer* 9 (1956): 36–57.

Grandidier, A., and Grandidier, G. *Collection des ouvrages anciens concernant Madagascar.* 9 vols. Paris: Comité de Madagascar et Union Coloniale, 1903–1920.

Grandidier, G. *Le Myre de Vilers, Duchesne, Gallieni: quarante ans d'histoire de Madagascar 1880–1920.* Paris: SEGMC, 1923.

———. ''A Madagascar: anciennes croyances et coutumes.'' *Journal de la Société des Africanistes* 2 (1932): 153–207.

Gravier, G. *Madagascar: les malgaches, origines de la colonisation française, la conquête.* Paris: C. Delagrave, 1904.

Harry, Miriam. *Radame, premier roi de Madagascar.* Paris: Ferenczi, 1949.

Hayes, E. H. *David Jones: Dauntless Pioneer.* London: Teachers and Taught, 1923.

Hellot, F. *La Pacification de Madagascar.* Paris: Berger-Lévrault, 1900.

Hornell, J. ''Les pirogues à balancier de Madagascar et de l'Afrique orientale.'' *Géographie* 34 (1920): 1–23.

Houlder, J A. *Among the Malagasy.* London: J. Clarke, 1912.

Hyet, E. L. *Tragédie malgache? Reportage social sur la region Merina (Hauts plateaux de Madagascar).* Paris: Imprimerie de la Renaissance, 1936.

Joleaud, L. ''Le boeuf de Madagascar, son origine, son rôle dans les coutumes sakalavas.'' *Anthropologie* 34 (1924): 102–107.

Julien, G. *Institutions politiques et sociales de Madagascar.* 2 vols. Paris: Guilmoto, 1908–1909.

———. ''Le culte du boeuf à Madagascar.'' *Revue d'éthnographie et de traditions populaires* 19 (1924): 246–268.

———. ''Langage cérémonial chez les malgaches.'' *Anthropologie* 36 (1926): 312–314.

———. *Pages arabico-madécasses.* 3 vols. Paris: SEGMC, 1929, 1933.

———. ''L'habitation indigène dans les possessions françaises—Madagascar.'' *La terre et la vie* (1931): 100–111; 160–173.

Launois, P. *L'état malgache et ses transformations avant le regime français.* Paris: Domat-Montchrestien, 1932.

———. *Madagascar, hier et aujourd'hui.* Paris: Editions Alsatia, 1947.

Le Barbier, C. "Contes et légendes du pays des Bara." *Revue d'ethnographie et des traditions populaires* 6 (1921): 119–137.

———. "Contribution à l'étude des Bara- Imamono de Madagascar." *Anthropologie* 31 (1921): 69–93, 319–328, 495–517.

Lebon, André. *La pacification de Madagascar, 1896–1898.* Paris: Plon, 1928.

Lieb, A. "Mystical Significance of Colours Among the Natives of Madagascar." *African Studies* 6 (1947): 77–81.

Lhande, P. *Madagascar, 1832–1932. Notre épopée missionaire.* Paris: Plon, 1932.

Linton, R. "Culture Areas in Madagascar." *American Anthropologist* 30 (1928): 363–390.

———. *The Tanala, a Hill Tribe of Madagascar.* Chicago: Field Museum of Natural History, 1933.

———. "The Tanala of Madagascar." In *The Individual and His Society,* ed. A. Kardiner. New York: Columbia University Press, 1939.

Lyautey, P. *Gallieni.* Paris: Gallimard, 1959.

Malzac, V. *Histoire du royaume hova depuis ses origines jusqu'à sa fin.* Tananarive: Imprimerie Catholique, 1912.

Mannoni, O. *Prospero and Caliban: The Psychology of Colonization.* Metuchen, N.J., and London: Scarecrow, 1956.

Mellis, J. V. *Nord et nord-ouest de Madagascar. Volamena et Volafotsy, suivi d'un vocabulaire du nord-ouest expliqué, commenté et comparé au Merina.* Tananarive: Imprimerie Moderne de l'Emyrne, 1938.

Michel, L. *La réligion des anciens Merina.* Aix-en-Provence: La Pensée Universitaire, 1958.

Molet, L. *Le bain royal à Madagascar.* Tananarive: Imprimerie Lutherienne, 1956.

———. "Consécration d'un charme contre la grêle près de Tananarive." *Le monde non-chrétien* 40 (1957): 314–325.

———. "Le cérémonie d'intronisation à Madagascar et ses implications economiques." *Cahiers internationaux de sociologie* 5 (1958): 80–87.

———. "Les principales populations malgaches." *Revue de la psychologie des peuples* 14 (1959): 41–48.

Mondain, G. *Les idées réligieuses des Hovas avant l'introduction du christianisme.* Cahors: Couselant, 1904.

———. *L'histoire des tribus d'Imoro au XVIIe siècle, d'après un manuscrit arabico-malgache.* Paris: Leroux, 1910.

———. *Raketaka: tableau de moeurs feminines malgaches, dressé à l'aide de proverbes et de fady.* Paris: Publications de la Faculté des Lettres d'Alger, 1925.

———. *Un siècle de mission à Madagascar.* Paris: n.p., 1948.

Nooteboom, C. "De betrellingen tusssen Madagascar en Indonesie." *Zaire* 3 (1949): 881–894.

Orlova, A. S. "The Village Community of Feudal Madagascar." *Kratkiye Soobshcheniya* 29 (1958): 117–124.

Paulhan, J. "Les hain-teny merinas." *Journal asiatique* (1912): 133–162.

———. *Les hain-teny merinas: poésies populaires malgaches [texte malgache et traduction].* Paris: Geuthner, 1913.

———. *Les hain-teny [traduction].* Paris: Gallimard, 1939; reprint, 1960.

Perrier de la Bathie, H. *La biogéographie des plantes de Madagascar.* Paris: SEGMC, 1939.

Radaody-Ralarosy, E. P. "Le costume malgache: le lamba." *Rythmes du monde* 4 (1946): 41–50.

Rakoto-Ratsimamanga, A. "Tache pigmentaire heréditaire et l'origine des malgaches." *Revue anthropologique* 50 (1940): 5–119.

Ramandraivonona, D. *Le malgache; sa langue, sa réligion.* Paris: Présence Africaine, 1959.

Ranaivo, C. "Les experiences de fokonolona à Madagascar." *Le monde non-chrétien* (1949): 133–148.

Ranaivo, F. "Le folklore malgache." *Présence africaine* 14/15 (1957): 155–164.

Randrianarisoa, P. *Madagascar et les croyances et coutumes malgaches.* Caen: Caron, 1959.

Razafimino, C. *La signification réligieuse du fandroana ou de la fête du nouvel an en Imerina.* Tananarive: Imprimerie FMA, 1924.

Razafy-Andriamihaingo, S. "The Position of Women in Madagascar." *African Women* 3 (1959): 29–33.

Renel, C. *Le folklore de Madagascar. 1. Contes merveilleux. 2. Fables et fabliaux, lexique.* Paris: E. Leroux, 1910.

Ribard, M. E. "Contribution à l'étude des aloalo malgaches (monuments commemoratifs)." *Anthropologie* 34 (1924): 91–102.

Rusillon, H. *Un culte dynastique avec évocation des morts chez les Sakalaves de Madagascar: le tromba.* Paris: A. Picard, 1912.

———. *Au pays Tsimihety: feuilles de route d'un missionnaire.* Paris: Société des Missions Evangeliques, 1923.

———. *Un petit continent: Madagascar.* Paris: Société des Missions Evangeliques, 1933.

Sachs, C. *Les instruments de musique à Madagascar.* Paris: Université de Paris, Institut d'Ethnologie, 1938.

Soury-Lavergne, P., and De la Dévèze, R. P. ''La fête de la circoncision en Imerina: autrefois et aujourd'hui.'' *Anthropos* 7 (1912): 336–371, 627–633.

———. ''La fête nationale du fandroana en Imerina.'' *Anthropos* 8 (1913): 306–324, 779–800.

———. ''Destinées et astrologues en Imerina.'' *Anthropos* 12/13 (1917–1918): 395–418, 818–851; 16/18 (1921–1922): 890–912.

Suau, P. *La France à Madagascar, histoire politique et religieuse d'une colonisation.* Paris: Perrin, 1909.

Tastevin, C. ''D'où viennent les noirs malgaches? Ou l'émigration des noirs d'Afrique à Madagascar avant l'arrivée des Hovas.'' *Ethnographie* 39 (1941): 19–32.

———. ''Zimbabue, preuve de l'origine africaine des noirs de Madagascar et de la langue malgache.'' *Ethnographie* 41 (1943): 379–391; 43 (1945): 51–70.

———. ''De l'Africanité de quelques phonèmes auxiliares considerés à tort comme préfixes en malgache.'' *Ethnographie* 45 (1947–1950): 178–202.

Thebault, E.-P. *Traité de droit civil malgache.* 3 vols. Paris: Jouve, 1951–1953.

Thiout, M. *Madagascar et l'âme malgache.* Paris: Horizons de France, 1961.

Thonet, A. "Etude des peuplades antaimoro." *Annales de l'Association des Naturalistes de Levallois-Perret* 22 (1935–1936): 39–56.

Trautmann, R. *La divination à la Côte des Esclaves et à Madagascar.* Paris: Larose, 1939.

Van Gennep, A. *Tabou et totemisme à Madagascar.* Paris: E. Leroux, 1904.

Wastell, R. E. P. *British Imperial Policy in Relation to Madagascar, 1810–1896.* Ph.D. thesis, University of London, 1944.

You, André. *Madagascar, colonie française 1896–1930.* Paris: SEGMC, 1931.

B. Contemporary Politics and Economics

Anthouard, A. F. I. D' *L'expédition de Madagascar en 1895.* Paris: SEGMC, 1930.

Augagneur, V. *Erreurs et brutalités coloniales.* Paris: Editions Montaigne, 1927.

Baron, R. "L'immigration karany ou indo-pakistanaise à Madagascar." *L'Afrique et l'Asie* (1954): 47–54.

Boiteau, P. *L'affaire de Madagascar.* Paris: Comité Franco-Malgache, 1949.

———. *Contribution à l'histoire de la nation malgache.* Paris, 1958.

Boudry, R. ''Le problème malgache.'' *Esprit* (February 1948): 189–220.

———. ''J'ai témoigné au procès de Madagascar.'' *Esprit* (January 1949): 125–140.

———. ''Decolonisation à Madagascar.'' *Pensée* 78 (1958): 43–65.

Bourgeois-Gavardin, M.-J. ''L'application de la loi-cadre et la réorganisation politique et administrative de Madagascar.'' *Nouvelle revue française d'outre- mer* 49 (1957): 149–166.

Boussenot, G. ''Le drame malgache.'' *Revue politique et parlementaire* (May 1947): 109–128.

Cahiers Charles de Foucault (1950) [special number on Madagascar].

Casseville, H. *L'ile ensanglantée.* Paris: Fasquelle, 1948.

Chevalier, L. *Madagascar, Populations et ressources.* Paris: PUF, 1952.

Chévigné, P. de ''Je reviens de Madagascar, la rébellion malgache et ses enseignments.'' *Les Annales Conferencia* (February 1951): 25–31.

Coppet, M. de, ed. *Madagascar* Paris: Encyclopédie de l'Empire Français, 1947.

———. ''Le problème de la main-d'oeuvre à Madagascar et ses nouveaux aspects.'' *Revue international de travail* 3 (1949): 273–293.

Darsac, R. ''Contradictions et partis malgaches.'' *Revue de l'Action populaire* 20 (1958): 836–849.

Debousset, O. *L'organisation municipale à Madagascar.* Paris: Recueil Sirey, 1942.

Délélée-Desloges, J. G. *Madagascar et dépendances.* Paris: SEGMC, 1931.

D'Esmé, J. *L'ile rouge.* Paris: Plon, 1928.

Dumont, R. *Evolution des campagnes malgaches.* Tananarive: Imprimerie Officielle, 1959.

Fenard, G. *Les indigènes fonctionnaires à Madagascar.* Paris: Domat-Montchrestien, 1939.

Gallichet, H. *La guerre à Madagascar: historie anecdotique des expéditions françaises de 1885 à 1895.* Paris: Garnier, 1897.

Gallieni, J. S. *Neuf ans à Madagascar.* Paris: Hachette, 1908.

———. *Lettres de Madagascar, 1896–1905.* Paris: SEGMC, 1928.

Gaudemet, P. M. "La provincialisation à Madagascar." *Revue juridique et politique de l'Union Française* 12 (1958): 295–311.

Grosclaude, E. *Un Parisien à Madagascar: aventures et impressions de voyage.* Paris: Hachette, 1898.

Hance, W. A. "Transportation in Madagascar." *Geographical Review* (1958): 45–68.

Hardyman, J. T. *Madagascar on the Move.* London: Livingstone Press, 1950.

Hatzfeld, O. *Madagascar.* Paris: PUF, 1952.

Isnard, H. "La vie rurale à Madagascar." *Cahiers d'Outre-Mer* 4 (1951): 39–60.

———. "La colonisation agricole à Madagascar." *Revue de géographie alpine* 39 (1951): 97–125.

———. "Les bases geographiques de la monarchie Hova." *Etudes d'Outre-Mer* (1954): 165–175.

———. *Madagascar* Paris: A. Colin, 1955.

———. "Les plaines de Tananarive." *Cahiers d'Outre-Mer* 8 (1955): 5–29.

———. "Nouvelle orientation de la modernisation du paysannat malgache." *Cahiers d'Outre-Mer* 10 (1957): 367–372.

Ivry, H. "Le mouvement national malgache." *Esprit* (February 1948): 221–238.

Jacquier, L. *La main-d'oeuvre locale à Madagascar.* Paris: Henri Jouve, 1904.

Jumeaux, R. "Essai d'analyse du nationalisme malgache." *Afrique et Asie* (1957): 31–42.

Keller, K. *Madagascar, Mauritius and the Other East-African Islands.* London: Sonnenschein, 1901.

Lapalud, M. *L'Administrateur colonial à Madagascar, ses attributions.* Paris: A. Colin, 1903.

Leblond, M. *Madagascar, creation française.* Paris: Plon, 1934.

Lyautey, L. H. G. *Dans le sud de Madagascar; pénétration militaire, situation politique et économique, 1900–1902.* Paris: Lavauzelle, 1903.

———. *Lettres du Tonkin et de Madagascar (1894–1899).* Paris: A. Colin, n.d.

———. *Paroles d'action, Madagascar-Sud-Oranais-Oran-Maroc (1900–1926).* Paris: A. Colin, 1927.

———. *Lettres du sud de Madagascar, 1900–1902.* Paris: A. Colin, 1935.

Mace, R. *L'évolution du régime foncier à Madagascar.* Paris: Larose, 1936.

Minelle, J. *L'agriculture à Madagascar.* Paris: Marcel Rivière, 1959.

Olivier, M. *Six ans de politique sociale à Madagascar.* Paris: B. Grasset, 1931.

Rabemananjara, J. "Les fondements culturels du nationalisme malgache." *Présence africaine* (February-May 1958): 125–142.

———. "L'indépendance de Madagascar." *Présence africaine* (June-July 1958): 120–124.

———. *Nationalisme et problèmes malgaches.* Paris: Présence Africaine, 1958.

Rabemananjara, R. *Madagascar: Histoire de la Nation malgache.* Paris: Lachaud, 1952.

———. *Madagascar sous la Rénovation malgache.* Paris: Lachaud, 1953.

Rallion, P. H. *Les fonctionnaires à Madagascar.* Tananarive: Imprimerie du Progrès de Madagascar, 1909.

Robequain, C. "Une capitale montagnard en pays tropicale: Tananarive." *Revue de géographie alpine* 37 (1949): 3–60.

———. *Madagascar et les bases dispersées de l'Union française.* Paris: PUF, 1958.

Sabatier, F. *Le problème de la main-d'oeuvre à Madagascar.* Toulon: Librairie Maritime, 1903.

Stephane, R. "Le procès de Tananarive." *Temps modernes* (1948): 698–709.

Stibbe, P. *Justice pour les malgaches.* Paris: Editions du Seuil, 1954.

Vaude, M. ''L'Affaire malgache.'' *Revue de troupes coloniales* (January 1948): 3–15.

5. Works Published Since 1960

A. History and Ethnography

Abé, Y. ''Ancien mode de subsistance pratiqué sur les hautes terres centrales de Madagascar.'' *ASEMI* 8 (1977): 79–98.

———. *Le riz et la riziculture à Madagascar: une étude sur le complexe rizicole d'Imerina.* Paris: CNRS, 1984.

''Actes du Colloque de Majunga (13–18 avril 1981): Histoire et civilisation du Nord-Ouest malgache.'' *Omaly sy anio* 17–21 (1983–1984) [special issue].

Adam, P. ''Le peuplement de Madagascar et le problème des grandes migrations maritimes.'' In *Movements de populations dans l'Océan Indien.* Paris: H. Champion, 1979.

Althabe, G. ''Progrès et ostentation économiques: problèmes socio-économiques des communautés villageoises de la côte orientale malgache.'' *Revue Tiers-Monde* 9 (1968): 128–160.

———. *Oppression et libération dans l'imaginaire.* Paris: Maspero, 1969.

———. *Anthropologie de la Mananano.* Tananarive: ORSTOM, 1970.

Archdeacon, S. ''Erotic Grave Sculpture of the Sakalava and Vezo.'' *Transition* 12 (1964): 43–47.

Association des Géographes de Madagascar. *Atlas de Madagascar.* Tananarive: Le Bureau pour le Développement de la Production Agricole et le Centre de l'Institut Géographique National, 1970.

Augustins, G. ''Tombeaux, alliance matrimoniale et droits d'usage sur les rizières en Imamo (hauts plateaux de Madagascar).'' *Ethnographie* 80 (1979): 69–83.

Ayache, S. ''Esquisse pour le portrait d'une Reine: Ranavalona I.'' *Omaly sy anio* 1–2 (1975): 251–270.

———. ''Un intellecteuel malgache devant la culture européenne.'' *Archipel* 12 (1976): 95–119.

———. *Raombana l'historien, introduction à son oeuvre.* Fianarantsoa: Librarie Ambozontany, 1976.

———. ''Jean Laborde, vu par les témoins malgaches.'' *Omaly sy anio* 5–6 (1977): 191–222.

———. ''De la tradition orale a l'histoire écrite: l'oeuvre de Raombana.'' *Omaly sy anio* 12 (July-December 1980): 77–104.

———. ''Pouvoir central et provinces sous la monarchie merina au XIXe siècle.'' In *Le sol, la parole, et l'écrit: 2000 ans d'histoire africaine.* Paris: Société Française d'historie d'Outre-Mer, 1981

———. and Richard, C. ''Une dissidence protestante malgache: l'Église Tranozozoro.'' *Omaly sy anio* 7–8 (1978): 133–182.

Bardonnet, D. ''Les minorités asiatiques à Madagascar.'' *Annuaire française de droit internationnel* (1964): 126–224.

Baré, J. F. ''Successions politiques et légitimité: l'exemple sakalava du Nord (1700–1800).'' *ASEMI* 4 (1973): 85–97.

———. ''La terminologie de parenté sakalava du Nord (Madagascar).'' *L'Homme* 14 (1974): 5–41.

———. *Pouvoir des vivants, langage des morts.* Paris: Maspero, 1977.

———. *Sable rouge. Une monarchie de nord-ouest malgache dans l'histoire.* Paris: L'Harmattan, 1980.

Battistini, R. *L'Extreme Sud. Essai de Géographie physique.* Paris: Cujas, 1963.

———. *Géographie humaine de la plaine côtière mahafaly.* Paris: Cujas, 1964.

———. *L'Afrique australe et Madagascar.* Paris: PUF, 1968.

———, and Vérin, P. ''Ecologic changes in protohistoric Madagascar. In *Pleistocene Extinctions: The Search for a Cause,* ed. P. S. Martin and H. E. Wright. New Haven: Yale University Press, 1967.

———. ''Témoignages archéologiques sur la Côte vezo de l'embouchure de l'Onilahy à la Baie des Assassins.'' *Taloha* 4 (1971): 51–63.

Bauberot, J. ''L'antiprotestantisme politique à la fin du XIXe siècle. 1. Les débuts de l'antiprotestantisme et la question de Madagascar.'' *Revue d'histoire et de philosophie religieuse* 52 (1972): 449–484.

Beaujard, P. ''La lutte pour l'hégémonie du royaume à travers deux variants d'un même mythe: le Serpent-à-sept-têtes.'' *ASEMI* 8 (1977): 151–204.

———. ''Hiérarchie végétale et hiérarchie sociale à Madagascar: la place symbolique des tubercules et du riz et leurs origines à travers les mythes et les contes.'' *ASEMI* 12 (1981): 157–191.

———. *Princes et paysans, les tanala de l'Ikongo: un espace social du sud-est de Madagascar.* Paris: L'Harmattan, 1983.

———. "D'une princesse morte au miel de la vie." *Cahiers de la littérature orale* 18 (1985): 89–108.

———. "Riz du ciel, riz de la terre: idéologie, système politique et riziculture dans les royaumes tanala de l'Ikongo (côte sud-est de Madagascar) du XVIIIe au XIXe siècle." *Etudes rurales* 99–100 (1985): 389–402.

Belrose-Huyghues, V. "Un exemple de syncrétisme esthétique au XIXe siècle: le rova de Tananarive d'Andrianjaka à Radama I." *Omaly sy anio* 1–2 (1975): 173–210.

———. "Considérations sur l'introduction de l'imprimerie à Madagascar." *Omaly sy anio* 5–6 (1977): 89–105.

———. "Le contact missionnaire au féminin: Madagascar et la L. M. S." *Omaly sy anio* 7–8 (1978): 83–131.

———. "La pénétration protestante à Madagascar jusqu'en 1827: du nonconformisme atlantique à la première mission de Tananarive." *Bulletin de la Société de l'Histoire du Protestantisme Français* 127 (1981): 349–362.

———, tr. "L'itinéraire de Frère Gaspar de San Bernardino: une visite portugaise à la Côte Ouest de Madagascar en 1606." *Taloha* 9 (1982): 39–87.

———. "La pénétration chrétienne du Sud." *Etudes Océan Indien* 4 (1984): 236–255.

Berg, G. "The Myth of Racial Strife and Merina King Lists." *History in Africa* 4 (1977): 1–30.

———. "Riziculture and the Founding of the Monarchy in Imerina." *Journal of African History* 22 (1981): 289–308.

Bernard, A. *Essai sur la transition de la société Mahafaly vers les rapports marchands.* Paris: Editions de l'ORSTOM, 1978.

Bernard-Thierry, S. ''Les pélérinages dans les Haut-Plateaux malgaches.'' In *Les pélérinages.* Paris: Seuil, 1960.

———. ''Les perles magiques à Madagascar.'' *Journal de la Société des Africanistes* 29 (1960): 33–90.

Besy, A. ''Origine des malgaches.'' *Tantara* 6 (1977): 82–91.

Binoche, J. ''Le rôle des parlementaires d'outre-mer dans la conquête de Madagascar.'' *Revue d'histoire moderne et contemporaine* 22 (1975): 416–432.

Blanc-Pamard, C. ''Du paddy pour les porcs. Dérives d'une société rizicole. L'exemple des Hautes Terres centrales de Madagascar.'' *Etudes rurales* 99–100 (1985): 327–345.

———. ''Communautés rurales des Hautes Terres malgaches et gestion de l'eau.'' In *Les politiques de l'eau en Afrique,* ed. G. Conac. Paris: Economica, 1985.

Bloch, M. ''Astrology and Writing in Madagascar.'' In *Literacy in Traditional Societies,* ed. J. Goody. Cambridge: Cambridge University Press, 1968.

———. ''Tombs and Conservatism Among the Merina of Madagascar.'' *Man* (1968): 94–104.

———. *Placing the Dead.* London: Seminar Press, 1971.

———. ''The Implications of Marriage Rules and Descent Categories for Merina Social Structure.'' *American Anthropologist* 73 (1971): 164–178.

———. ''Decision-making in Councils Among the Merina of Madagascar.'' In *Councils in Action,* ed. A. I. Richards and A Kuper. Cambridge Papers in Social Anthropology, no. 6, 1971.

———. ''Property and the End of Affinity.'' In *Marxist Analyses and Social Anthropology,* ed. M. Bloch. London: Malaby Press, 1975.

———. ''The Disconnection Between Rank and Power as a Process.'' *Annales Européennes de Sociologie* 18 (1977): 107–148.

———. ''Marriage Amongst Equals: An Analysis of the Marriage Ceremony of the Merina of Madagascar.'' *Man* 13 (1978): 21–33.

———. ''Slavery and Mode of Production in Madagascar: Two Case Studies.'' In *Asian and African Systems of Slavery,* ed. J. L. Watson. Berkeley: University of California Press, 1979.

———. ''Hierarchy and Equality in Merina Kinship.'' *Ethnos* (1981): 5–18.

———. ''*From Blessing to Violence: History and Ideology in the Circumcision Ritual of the Merina of Madagascar.* Cambridge: Cambridge University Press, 1986.

———. *Ritual, History and Power: Selected Papers in Anthropology.* London: Athlone Press, 1989.

Boismery, H.; Ottino, P.; and Roche, D. R. ''Le blanc, le jeûne et le calendrier (étude de rélations sémantiques de terme malais, malgaches et swahilis).''*Etudes sur l'Océan Indien* 1 (1984): 236–255.

Boiteau, P. ''Edouard Planque et le mouvement national malgache.'' *Cahiers de l'Institut Maurice Thorez* 28 (1972): 69–78.

———. ''Les droits sur la terre dans la société malgache précoloniale.'' In CERM, *Sur le mode de production asiatique.* Paris: Editions Sociales, 1969.

———. "Quelques éléments pour l'histoire des organisations syndicales à Madagascar." *Cahiers d'Histoire de l'Institut Maurice Thorez* 14 (1980): 145–156.

Bouillon, A. *Madagascar: le colonisé et son "âme": essai sur le discours psychologique colonial.* Paris: L'Harmattan, 1981.

Boulfroy, N. "Vers l'art funéraire mahafaly." *Objets et mondes* 16 (1976): 95–116.

Boutonne, J. "L'expérience de la colonisation militaire à Madagascar au temps de Gallieni." *Omaly sy anio* 12 (July-December 1980): 7–13.

Brown, M. *Madagascar Rediscovered: A History from Early Times to Independence.* London: Tunnacliff, 1978.

Cabanes, R. "Le nord-est de Madagascar." In *Essais sur la réproduction de formations sociales dominées.* Paris: ORSTOM, 1977.

———. "Guerre lignagère et guerre de traite sur la côte nord-est de Madagascar aux XVIIe et XVIIIe siècles." In *Guerres de lignages et guerres d'États en Afrique,* ed. J. Bazin. Paris: Editions des Archives Contemporaines, 1982.

Cabot, J., and Hoerner, J.-M. "Les sociétés rurales du Sud-Ouest malgache face à l'aménagement." *Les Cahiers d'Outre-Mer* 34 (1981): 305–320.

Cahiers du CACID 1 (1979): "1947—Madagascar" [special number].

Campbell, G. "Labour and the Transport Problem in Imperial Madagascar, 1810–1895." *Journal of African History* 21 (1980): 341–356.

———. "Madagascar and the Slave Trade, 1810–1895." *Journal of African History* 22 (1981): 203–227.

———. ''The Adoption of Autarky in Imperial Madagascar, 1820–1835.'' *Journal of African History* 28 (1987): 395–412.

———. ''Currency Crisis, Missionaries, and the French Takeover in Madagascar, 1861–1895.'' *International Journal of African Historical Studies* 21 (1988): 273–289.

———. ''Gold Mining and the French Takeover of Madagascar.'' *African Economic History* 17 (1988): 99–126.

———. ''Slavery and Fanampoana: The Structure of Forced Labour in Imerina (Madagascar).'' *Journal of African History* 29 (1988): 463–486.

———. ''An Industrial Experiment in Pre-colonial Africa: The Case of Imperial Madagascar, 1825–1861.'' *Journal of Southern African Studies* 17 (1991): 525–560.

———. ''Disease, Cattle, and Slaves: The Development of Trade Between Natal and Madagascar, 1875–1904.'' *African Economic History* 19 (1990–1991): 105–135.

———. ''The State and Precolonial Demographic History: The Case of Nineteenth Century Madagascar.'' *Journal of African History* 32 (1991): 415–445.

———. ''The Menalamba Revolt and Brigandry in Imperial Madagascar, 1820–1897.'' *International Journal of African Historical Studies* 24 (1991): 259–291.

Cellier, A. ''Notes sur les populations de la rive droite du Bas-Mangoky en 1906.'' *Taloha* 4 (1971): 99–110.

Chandon-Moet, B. *Vohimasina, village malgache.* Paris: Nouvelles Editions Latines, 1972.

Chapus, G., and Ratsimba, E. *Traduction du Tantaran'ny Andriana—Histoire des Rois, du R. P. Callet.* Académie Malgache et Université de Nice, 1978.

———. *Index des Tantaran'ny Andriana eto Madagasikara—Histoire des Rois.* Tananarive: Académie Malgache, 1978.

Charmes, J. "La monographie villageoise comme démarche totalisante: application à la paysannerie des hauts plateaux malgaches." *Revue Tiers-Monde* 14 (1973): 639–652.

———. "Constitution de la rente foncière au lac Alaotra à Madagascar. Première vague consécutive à l'abolition de l'esclavage." *Cahiers ORSTOM,* série sciences humaines, 14 (1977): 59–69.

———. "Les blocages socio-culturels du développement en tant que manifestations des rapports de domination (Madagascar)." *Monde du développement* 24 (1978): 877–908.

Chazan, S. *La Société Sakalave.* Paris: Karthala, 1991.

Chéminements: écrits offerts à Georges Condominas. ASEMI 11 (1980) [special number].

Comarmond, P. de "Ampandraofana. Le village et l'histoire (Madagascar)." *Cahiers ORSTOM,* série sciences humaines, 14 (1976): 323–342.

Condominas, G. *Fokon'olona et collectivités rurales en Imerina.* Paris: Berger-Lévrault, 1960.

———. "La situation coloniale à Madagascar (La société Merina)." *Cahiers internationaux de sociologie* 30 (1961): 67–74.

Cornevin, R. "Le 15 septembre 1777, le Français Nicolas Mayeur entrait à Tananarive." *L'Afrique littéraire et artistique* 56 (1980): 70–89.

Cornu, H. *Paris et Bourbon, La politique française dans l'Océan Indien.* Paris: Académie des Sciences d'Outre-Mer, 1984.

Coulaud, D. *Les Zafimaniry: un groupe éthnique de Madagascar à la récherche de la forêt.* Tananarive: Imprimerie Fanontam-Boky Malagasy, 1973.

———. ''Les forgerons à la lisière forestière du Nord-Betsileo.'' *Journal de la Société des Africanistes* 43 (1973): 235–242.

———. ''Réflexions sur la notion d'éthnie à Madagascar: l'exemple du Nord des pays tanala et betsileo.'' *Taloha* 6 (1974): 89–116.

Crouzet, M. ''Madagascar vu par Flacourt.'' *Mondes et cultures* 40 (1980): 463–472.

Dahl, O. *Contes malgaches en dialecte sakalava.* Oslo: Universitetsforlaget, 1968.

———. ''Un cockney parlant malgache vers 1710'' [Robert Drury]. *Norsk Tideskrift for Sprogvidenskap* 24 (1971): 83–162.

Decary, R. *La mort et les coutumes funéraires à Madagascar.* Paris: Larose, 1962.

———. *Coutumes guerrières et organisation militaire chez les anciens malgaches.* Paris: Editions Maritimes et d'Outre-Mer, 1966.

———. *La divination malgache par le sikidy.* Paris: Imprimerie Nationale, 1970.

Délivré, A. *L'Histoire des rois d'Imerina. Interprétation d'une tradition orale.* Paris: Klincksieck, 1974.

Delval, R. *Radama II, prince de la Renaissance malgache.* Paris: L'Ecole, 1972.

———. ''The Indians in Madagascar.'' *Kroniek van Afrika* 3 (1975): 250–257.

———. "Les activités économiques de Majunga des origines à 1869" In *Les ports de l'Océan Indien aux XIXe et XXe siècles.* Aix-en- Provence: Université de Provence, 1982.

Deschamps, H. "Andrianampoinimerina ou la raison d'Etat au service de l'unité malgache." *Les Africains,* vol. 2. Paris: Editions Jeune Afrique, 1977.

———. "Rainilaiarivony, l'homme d'Etat malgache époux de trois Reines." In *Les Africains,* vol. 5. Paris: Editions Jeune Afrique, 1977.

Desjeux, D. *La question agraire à Madagascar: administration et paysannat de 1985 à nos jours.* Paris: L'Harmattan, 1979.

———. "Réforme foncière et civilisation agraire à Madagascar." *Le mois en Afrique,* no. 184 (1981): 55–61.

Devalière, F. "Madagascar: l'histoire nouvelle explore ses royaumes." *Cahiers d'études africaines* 24 (1984): 505–509.

Dez, J. "La lecture des documents arabico-malgaches." *ASEMI* 8 (1977): 3–44.

———. "L'illusion de la non-violence dans la société traditionnelle malgache." *Droit et cultures* 2 (1981): 21–44.

———. "Essai sur le calendrier arabico-malgache." In *Etudes sur l'Océan Indien* (1984): 58–119.

Domenichini, J.-P. "Jean Ralaimongo (1884–1943) ou Madagascar au seuil du nationalism." *Revue française d'histoire d'outre-mer* 56 (1969): 236–287.

———. "Une tradition orale: l'histoire de Ranoro." *ASEMI* 8 (1977): 99–150.

———. "L'écuelle de Milangana (XVème siècle)." *Ambario* 1–2 (1978): 127–131.

———. ''Problématiques passées et présentes de l'archéologie à Madagascar.'' *Récherche, pédagogie et culture* 9 (1981): 10–15.

———. ''Le souvenir des princes et de leurs peuples.'' *Etudes Océan Indien* 4 (1984): 63–80.

———. *Les dieux au service des rois: histoire orale des Sampin'Andriana ou palladiums royaux de Madagascar.* Paris: CNRS, 1985.

Domenichini-Ramiaramana, B. ''Qu'est-ce qu'un hain-teny?'' In *Colloque sur la traduction poétique,* ed. R. Etiemble. Paris: Gallimard, 1978.

———. ''Littérature orale et histoire: un itinéraire passant par la domaine malgache.'' *ASEMI* 12 (1981): 133–155.

———. *Du Ohabolana au Hainteny: langue, littérature et politique à Madagascar.* Paris: Karthhala, 1982.

———, and Domenichini, J.-P. ''La tradition malgache, une source pour l'histoire de l'Océan Indien.'' *Taloha* 8 (1979): 57–81.

———. ''Regards croisés sur les Grands Sycamores, ou l'armée noire des anciens princes d'Imerina.'' *ASEMI* 11 (1980): 55–95.

———. ''Aspects de l'esclavage sours la monarchie Merina d'après les textes législatifs et réglementaires.'' *Omaly sy anio* 15 (1982): 52–98.

Donque, G. ''Les minorités chinoise et indienne à Madagascar.'' *Revue française d'études politiques africaines* (February 1968): 85–103.

———. ''Tananarive.'' *Revue française d'etudes politiques africaines* (July 1971): 29–40.

Drysdale, H. *Dancing with the Dead: A Journey Through Zanzibar and Madagascar.* London: Hamish Hamilton, 1991.

Dublis, R. *Olombelona: essai sur l'existence personnelle et collective à Madagascar.* Paris: L'Harmattan, 1979.

Dumon, F. *La communauté franco-malgache.* Brussels: Institut de Sociologie Solvay, 1960.

Duran, P. "La consommation ostentatoire en milieu rural à Madagascar." *L'Homme* 7 (1967): 30–47.

Ellis, S. D. K. "The Political Elite of Tananarive and the Revolt of the Menalamba: The Creation of a Colonial Myth in Madagascar, 1895–1898." *Journal of African History* 21 (1980): 219–234.

———. *The Rising of the Red Shawls: A Revolt in Madagascar, 1895–1899.* Cambridge: Cambridge University Press, 1985.

———. "The Merina Background, from Andrianampoinimerina to the French Conquest." in *Norwegian Missions in South Africa and Madagascar,* ed. J. Simensen and F. Fluglestadt. Oslo: Norwegian Universities Press, 1986.

———. *Un complot colonial à Madagascar: L'affaire Rainandriamampandry.* Paris: Karthala, 1990.

Emphoux, J.-P. "Archéologie de l'Androy: deux sites importants: Andranosoa et la manda de Ramananga." *Omaly sy anio* 13–14 (1981): 89–97.

Esoavelomandroso, F. "Les Sadiavahe. Essai d'interprétation d'une révolte dans le Sud (1915–1917)." *Omaly sy anio* 1–2 (1975): 139–171.

———. "Langue, culture et colonisation à Madagascar: malgache et français dans l'enseignement officiel (1916–1940)." *Omaly sy anio* 3–4 (1976): 105–163.

———. ''Commerçants malgaches de nationalité française à Tananarive, de 1910 aux années 30.'' *Omaly sy anio* 15 (1982): 171–183.

Esoavelomandroso, M. ''Notes sur l'enseignement sous Ranavalona Ier: l'instruction reservée a l'élite.'' *Ambario* 1–2 (1978): 283–290.

———. ''Permanence de l'histoire malgache. L'unité dans la diversité.'' *Aujourd'hui l'Afrique* 11–12 (1978): 2–6.

———. *La province maritime orientale du ''Royaume de Madagascar'' à la fin du XIXe siècle (1882–1895).* Antananarivo: Imprimerie FTM, 1979.

———. ''Les Créoles malgaches de Tamatave au XIXe siècle.'' *Diogène* 111 (1980): 55–69.

———. ''A propos des groupes paysans en Imerina, 1794–1810.'' *Omaly sy anio* 15 (1982): 171–183.

———. ''Un marchand de produits à Tananarive dans les années 1930.'' In *Entreprises et entrepreneurs en Afrique, XIXe et XXe siècles.* Paris: L'Harmattan, 1983.

Estrade, J.-M. ''Un culte de possession: le tromba.'' *Mondes et cultures* 39 (1979): 763–772.

———. *Un culte de possession à Madagascar: le tromba.* Paris: L'Harmattan, 1985.

Fagereng, E. *Une famille de dynasties malgaches.* Oslo: Universitetsforlaget, 1971.

———. ''Origine des dynasties ayant regné dans le Sud et l'Ouest de Madagascar.'' *Omaly sy anio* 13–14 (1981): 125–140.

Fanony, F. ''La riziculture sur brulis (tavy) et les rituels agraires dans la région de Mananara Nord.'' *Terre malgache/Tany malagasy* 17 (1975): 29–48.

———, and Gueunier, N. J. ''Le mouvement de conversion à l'Islam et le rôle des confréries musulmanes dans le Nord de Madagascar.'' *ASEMI* 11 (1980): 151–168.

———. ''Deux documents sur l'insurrection malgache de 1947.'' *Etudes Océan Indien* 3 (1983): 113–156.

Faublée, J. ''Anciennes influences islamiques à Madagascar.'' In *Sociétés africaines, monde arabe et culture islamique.* Paris: Université de la Sorbonne Nouvelle, 1979.

Fauroux, E. *La formation sakalava, ou l'histoire d'une articulation ratée.* Paris: ORSTOM, 1975.

———. ''La formation Sakalava dans les rapports marchands: pour l'introduction de la dimension historique dans les études d'anthropologie économique.'' *Cahiers ORSTOM,* série sciences humaines, 14 (1977): 71–81.

———. ''Boeufs et pouvoirs: les éleveurs du sud-ouest malgache.'' *Politique Africaine* 34 (1989): 63–73.

Feeley-Harnik, G. ''Divine Kingship and the Meaning of History Among the Sakalava of Madagascar.'' *Man* 13 (1978): 402–417.

———. ''The Sakalava House.'' *Anthropos* 75 (1979): 559–585.

———. ''The King's Men in Madagascar: Slavery and Kingship in Sakalava Monarchy.'' *Africa* 52 (1982); 31–50.

———. ''The Political Economy of Death: Communication and Change in Malagasy Colonial History.'' *American Ethnologist* 11 (1984): 1–19.

———. *A Green Estate: Restoring Independence in Madagascar.* Washington, D.C.: Smithsonian Institution Press, 1991.

Filesi, T. ''La mediazione italiana nel conflitto franco-malgache del 1883–1885.'' *Rivista de studi politici internazionali* 40 (1973): 275–324.

Filliot, J. M. *La traite des esclaves vers les Mascareignes au 18e siècle.* Paris: ORSTOM, 1974.

Fluglestadt, F. ''Tompontany and tompon-drano in the History of Western and Central Madagascar.'' *History in Africa* 9 (1982): 61–76.

———, and Simensen, J., eds. *Norwegian Missions in African History. II. Madagascar.* Oxford: Oxford University Press, 1986.

Forman, C. W. ''A Study in the Self-Propagating Church: Madagascar.'' In *Frontiers of the Christian World Mission Since 1938,* ed. W. C. Horr. New York: Harper, 1962.

Fremigacci, J. ''Mis en valeur coloniale et travail forcé: la construction du chemin de fer Tananarive-Antisirabe (1911–1923).'' *Omaly sy anio* 1–2 (1975): 75–138.

———. ''La colonisation à Vatomandry-Mahanoro. Espérances et désillusions.'' *Omaly sy anio* 3–4 (1976): 167–250.

———. ''Ordre économique colonial et exploitation de l'indigène: petits colons et forgerons betsileo 1900–1923.'' *Archipel* 11 (1978): 177–223.

———. ''Protectorat intérieur et administration directe dans la province de Tulear (1904–1924).'' *Revue française de l'histoire d'outre-mer* 68 (1981): 359–379.

Gardiner, W. ''Witchcraft, Sorcery and Cattle Herding Among the Sakalava of West Madagascar.'' *World Review of Animal Production* 14 (1978): 57–61.

———. ''Sakalava Divination.'' in *Festschrift in Honor of Edward Norbeck,* ed. Christine M. Drake. Houston: Rice University Studies, 1979.

Gontard, M. "La politique réligieuse de Gallieni à Madagascar pendant les premières années de l'occupation française." *Revue française d'histoire d'outre- mer* 58 (1971): 183–214.

———. "La situation réligieuse à Madagascar à la veille de la seconde Guerre mondiale." *Revue française d'histoire d'outre-mer* 60 (1973): 408–421.

Gow, B. A. "The Backgrounds of the British Protestant Missionaries of Madagascar, 1861–1895." *Histoire sociale/Social History* 8 (1975): 314–327.

———. "The Attitude of the British Protestant Missionaries Towards the Malagasy People, 1861–1895." *Kenya Historical Review* 3 (1975): 15–26.

———. "Tranobiriky: An Independent Merina Church." *Transafrican Journal of History* 5 (1976): 84–111.

———. *Madagascar and the Protestant Impact: The Work of the British Missions, 1818–1895.* London: Longmans, 1979.

Guerin, M. *Le défi. L'Androy et l'appel à la vie.* Fianarantsoa: Librairie Ambozontany, 1977.

Gueunier, N. J. "Le thème de la sorcellerie maléfique dans la littérature populaire écrite à Madagascar." *ASEMI* 6 (1975): 71–84.

———. "Sculpture et gravure sur bois chez les Betsileo (Madagascar)." *Ethnographie* 71 (1976): 5–22.

———. *Les monuments funéraires et commémoratifs de bois sculptés betsileo.* Tulear: Publications du Centre Universitaire, 1978.

Hardyman, M. "Church and Sorcery in Madagascar." In *African Initiations in Religion,* ed. D. Barrett. Nairobi: East African Publishing House, 1971.

Hébert, J.-C. "Analyse structurale des géomancies comoriennes, malgaches, et africaines." *Journal de la Société des Africanistes* 31 (1961): 115–208.

———. "Filan'ampela, ou propos gallants des Sakalava." *Journal de la Société des Africanistes* 34 (1964): 227–253.

———. "Les rites de l'enjambement à Madagascar (Le Mandika)." *ASEMI* 8 (1977): 1–23.

———. "Notes sur Madagascar (côte est et Imerina) du traitant Jacques de la Salle, recueillies par l'Unienville en 1816." *Omaly sy anio* 12 (July-Decenber 1980): 129–175.

Heurtebize, G., and Verin, P. "Premières decouvertes sur l'ancienne culture de l'Androy (Madagascar). Archéologie de la vallée du Lambomety sur la Haute Manambovo." *Journal de la Société des Africanistes* 44 (1974): 113–121.

———. "La tranovato de l'Anosy. Première construction érigée par des Européens à Madagascar." *Taloha* 6 (1974): 117–142.

———. "Les progressions démographique et spatiale chez les Antandroy vues à travers le clan des Afomarolahy." *Omaly sy anio* 13–14 (1981): 113–121.

Hugon, P. "Aperçus historiques de l'enseignement à Madagascar." *APOI* 2 (1975): 79–101.

Huntington, W. R. "Death and the Social Order: Bara Funeral Customs (Madagascar)." *African Studies* 32 (1973): 65–84.

———. "Bara Endogamy and Incest Prohibition." *Bijdragen Tot de Taal-, Land-, en Volkenkunde* 134 (1978): 30–62.

———. *Gender and Social Structure in Madagascar.* Bloomington: Indiana University Press, 1988.

Jacob, G. ''Léon Suberbie et les rélations franco-malgaches de 1882 à 1887.'' *Revue française d'histoire d'outre-mer* 52 (1965): 315–351.

———. ''Les intérêts économiques lyonnais à Madagascar de la conquête à la première guerre mondiale.'' *Bulletin du centre d'histoire économique et sociale de la région lyonnaise* (1971): 1–18.

———. ''Influences occidentales en Imerina et deséquilibres économiques avant la conquête française.'' *Omaly sy anio* 5–6 (1977): 223–244.

———. ''Sur les origines de l'insurrection du Sud-Est de Madagascar (novembre-décembre 1904).'' *Omaly sy anio* 13–14 (1981): 249–261.

———, and Koerner, F. ''Economie de traite et bluff colonial: la Compagnie Occidentale de Madagascar (1895–1934).'' *Revue des questions historiques* (1972): 333–366.

Janvier, Y. ''La géographie gréco-romaine a-t-elle connu Madagascar?'' *Omaly sy anio* 1–2 (1975): 11–41.

Joubert, J.-L. ''Une île imaginaire, Madagascar vu par les européens.'' *L'Afrique littéraire et artistique* 34 (1975): 2–13.

Joussaume, R., and Ramarijaona, V. '' Sépultures mégalithiques à Madagascar.'' *Bulletin de la Société Préhistorique Française* 82 (1985): 534–551.

Kadima-Nzuji, M. *Jacques Rabemananjara: l'homme et l'oeuvre.* Paris: Présence Africaine, 1981.

Keenan, E. O. ''A Sliding Sense of Obligatoriness: The Polystructure of Malagasy Oratory.'' *Language in Society* 2 (1973): 225–243.

———. ''Norm-makers, Norm-breakers: Uses of Speech by Men and Women in a Malagasy Community.'' In *Explorations in the Ethnography of Speaking,* ed. R. Bauman and J. Sherzer. New York: Cambridge University Press, 1974.

Kent, R. K. ''Madagascar and Africa: The Problem of the Bara.'' *Journal of African History* 9 (1968): 387–408.

———. ''Madagascar and Africa: The Sakalava, Maroserana, Dady and Trumba Before 1700.'' *Journal of African History* 9 (1968): 517–546.

———. ''The Sakalava: Origins of the First Malgasy Empire.'' *Revue française d'histoire d'outre–mer* 55 (1968): 145–189.

———. ''Madagascar and Africa: The Anteimoro, a Theocracy in Southeastern Madagascar.'' *Journal of African History* 10 (1969): 45–65.

———. ''How the French Acquired Madagascar, 1642–1896.'' *Tarikh* 3 (1969): 14–22.

———. *Early Kingdoms in Madagascar, 1500–1700.* New York: Holt, Rinehart and Winston, 1970.

———. *Madagascar in History: Essays from the 1970s.* Albany, Calif., 1979.

———. ''Possibilité de colonies indonésiennes en Afrique avec référence speciale à Madagascar.'' *Omaly sy anio* 9 (January-June 1979): 129–150.

Koechlin, B. ''Notes sur les implications de l'emploi primaire de l'organe de la vue chez les Vezo et Mikea du sud-ouest de Madagascar.'' *Archipel* 1 (1971): 123–139.

———. ''Quelques exemples de communications avec la surnature chez les Vezo du sud-ouest de Madagascar.'' *ASEMI* 4 (1973): 85–132.

———. *Les Vezo du sud-ouest de Madagascar.* Paris: Mouton, 1975.

———: Dez, J.; and Ottino, P. ''Madagascar, échantillon de l'Atlas éthnolinguistique sur l'Asie du sud-est et le Monde insulindien.'' *ASEMI* 3 (1972): 71–83.

Koerner, F. ''L'échec de l'éthiopianisme dans les églises protestantes malgaches.'' *Revue française d'histoire d'outre-mer* 58 (1971): 215–238.

———. ''Les évènements de 1947 à Madagascar.'' *Esprit* (September 1971): 315–326.

——— ''Le Front Populaire et la question coloniale à Madagascar, le climat politique en 1936.'' *Revue française d'histoire d'outre-mer* 61 (1974): 436–454.

Kottak, C. P. ''Cultural Adaptation, Kinship and Descent in Madagascar.'' *Southwestern Journal of Anthropology* 27 (1971): 129–147.

———. ''Social Groups and Kinship Calculation Among the Southern Betsileo.'' *American Anthropologist* 73 (1971): 178–193.

———. ''A Cultural Adaptive Approach to Malagasy Political Organization.'' In *Social Exchange and Interaction,* ed. E. Wilmsen. Ann Arbor: Anthropological Papers of the Museum of Anthropology, University of Michigan, 1972.

———. ''The Process of State Formation in Madagascar.'' *American Ethnologist* 4 (1977): 136–155.

———. *The Past in the Present: History, Ecology, and Cultural Adaptation in Highland Madagascar.* Ann Arbor: University of Michigan Press, 1980.

———, et al., eds. *Madagascar: Society and History.* Durham, N.C.: Carolina Academic Press, 1986.

Lahady, P. *Le culte betsimisaraka et son système symbolique.* Fianarantsoa: Librairie Ambozontany, 1979.

Lapierre, J. W. "Problèmes socio-culturels de la nation malgache." *Cahiers internationaux de sociologie* 40 (1966): 57–72.

———. "Tradition et modernité à Madagascar." *Esprit,* no. 367 (1968): 57–68.

Lavondès, H. *Bekoropoka. Quelques aspects de la vie familiale et sociale d'un village malgache.* Paris: Mouton, 1967.

———. "Pouvoirs traditionnels dans un royaume du Sud-Ouest malgache (nord du Fiherenana)." *Omaly sy anio* 13–14 (1981): 193–207.

Lejamble, G. *Le fokonolona et le pouvoir.* Tananarive: Centre de Droit Publique et de Science Politique, 1963.

———. "Quelques directions de récherche pour une archéologie des Vazimba de l'Imerina." *Taloha* 7 (1978): 93–104.

Lombard, J. *La royauté sakalava: formation, développement et éffondrement du XVII au XXe siècle. Essai d'analyse d'un système politique.* Tananarive: ORSTOM, 1973.

———. "Notes prises de Moroundava à Tsimanandrafouza—na. Cahier no. 13 des notes manuscrites d'A. Grandidier." *ASEMI* 7 (1976): 63–100.

———. "Le royauté sakalava—Menabe—Resultats d'une enquête et présentation d'un corpus de traditions orales et de littérature." *Cashiers ORSTOM,* série sciences humaines, 13 (1976): 173–202.

Lombard-Jourdan, A. "Des malgaches à Paris sous Louis XIV." *Archipel* 9 (1975): 79–92.

Lugozi, G. ''Le cas de l'état merina de Madagascar précolonial.'' In *Folklore in Africa Today.* Budapest: Artes Populares, 1984.

Lupo, P. *Eglise et décolonisation a Madagascar.* Fianarantsoa: Ambozontany, 1975.

———. ''Catholicisme et civilisation malgache à la fin du XIXeme siècle (pistes de récherche).'' *Omaly sy anio* 5–6 (1977): 313–334.

———. ''La communauté catholique d'Antananarivo entre 1883 et 1885: documents pour l'histoire réligieuse de Madagascar.'' *Omaly sy anio* 7–8 (1978): 317–354.

———. ''Gallieni et la laïcisation de l'école à Madagascar.'' *Omaly sy anio* 16 (1982): 69–99.

———. *Une église des laïcs à Madagascar: les Catholiques pendant la guerre coloniale de 1894–5.* Paris: Presse du Centre National de Récherche Scientifique, 1990.

Macau, J. *La Suède et le Madagascar au debut du XVIIIe siècle.* Aix-Marseille: IPHOM, 1974.

Mack, J. *Madagascar: Island of the Ancestors.* London: British Museum, 1986.

''Madagascar et l'Europe'' *Revue française d'histoire d'outre-mer* 73 nos. 1 and 2 (1986), [special issues].

Mangalaza, E. ''Ngatra et razana chez les Betsimisaraka.'' *Cahiers éthnologiques* n.s. 1 (1980): 45–64.

———, and Meriot, C. ''Un angano betsimisaraka: Tsy ambara valy (Ce qu'on ne montre pas à son beau-frère).'' *Cahiers éthnologiques* 4 (1983): 86–154.

Manoro, R. ''Terminologies de parenté et formes d'adresse chez les Tsimihety.'' *Cahiers éthnologiques* 4 (1983): 63–85.

Maron, C. ''Un organe de presse confessionel: l'hébdomadaire *Lumière* de 1965 à 1972.'' *Kroniek van Afrika* 3 (1974): 283–298.

———. *L'hébdomadaire ''Lumière'' à Madagascar, de 1935 à 1972*. Aix-en-Provence: Presses Universitaires d'Aix-Marseilles, 1977.

Massiot, M. *L'administration publique à Madagascar: Evolution de l'organisation administrative territoriale de Madagascar de 1896 à la proclamation de la République Malgache.* Paris: Librairie Générale de Droit et de Jurisprudence, 1971.

Mauny, R. ''The Wakwak and the Indonesian Invasion of East Africa in 945 A.D.'' *Studia* (Lisbon, 1965): 7–16.

Michel, L., and Delval, R. ''La langue peut-elle indiquer l'origine des peuplements malgaches?'' *Mondes et cultures* 39 (1979): 427–443.

Molet, L. ''Cadres pour une éthnopsychiatrie de Madagascar.'' *L'Homme* 7 (1967): 5–29.

———. ''Les monnaies à Madagascar.'' *Cahiers Vilfredo Pareto* 21 (1971): 203–234.

———. ''Origine et sens du nom des Sakalava de Madagascar.'' In *Etudes de géographie tropicale offertes à Pierre Gourou.* Paris: Mouton, 1972.

———. ''L'origine chinoise possible de quelques animaux fantastiques malgaches.'' *Journal de la Société des Africanistes* 45 (1975): 123–138.

———. ''Conception, naissance et circoncision à Madagascar.'' *L'Homme* 16 (1976): 33–64.

———. *La conception malgache du monde, du surnaturel et de l'homme en Imerina.* Paris: L'Harmattan, 1979.

Mollat du Jourdin, M. "La mer et Madagascar." *Omaly sy anio* 5–6 (1977): 27–54.

Munthe, L. "La tradition écrite arabico-malgache: un aperçu sur les manuscrits existants." *Bulletin of the School of Oriental and African Studies* 40 (1977): 96–109.

———; Ayache, S.; and Ravoajanahary, C. "Radama Ier et les anglais: les négotiations de 1817 d'après les sources malgaches." *Omaly sy anio* 3–4 (1976): 9–104.

Mutibwa, P. M. "Patterns of Trade and Economic Development in Nineteenth Century Madagascar." *Transafrican Journal of History* 2 (1972): 33–63.

———. "Britain's Abandonment of Madagascar: The Anglo-French Convention of August 1890." *Transafrican Journal of History* 3 (1973): 96–111.

———. "Social and Political Organisation of Malagasy Society in the First Half of the Nineteenth Century." *Tarikh* 4 (1973): 31–41.

———. *The Malagasy and the Europeans: Madagascar Foreign Relations, 1861–1895.* London: Longmans, 1974.

Nicolai, A. "Electricité et Eaux de Madagascar: un service publique dans un contexte colonial au service d'une entreprise." In *Entreprises et entrepreneurs en Afrique, XIXe et XXe siècles.* Paris: L'Harmattan, 1983.

Oberle, P. *Tananarive et l'Imerina.* Tananarive: Société Malgache d'Edition, 1976.

Ottino, P. *Les économies paysannes malgaches du Bas Mangoky.* Paris: Berger-Lévrault, 1963.

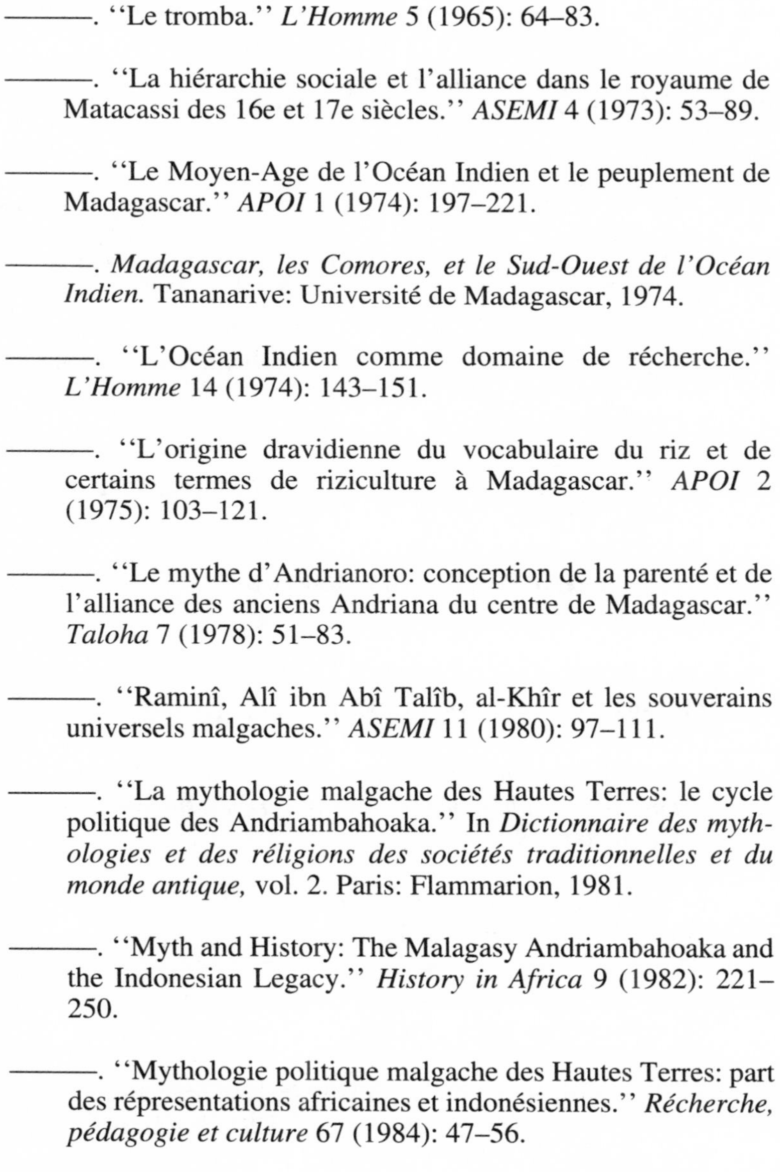

———. "Le tromba." *L'Homme* 5 (1965): 64–83.

———. "La hiérarchie sociale et l'alliance dans le royaume de Matacassi des 16e et 17e siècles." *ASEMI* 4 (1973): 53–89.

———. "Le Moyen-Age de l'Océan Indien et le peuplement de Madagascar." *APOI* 1 (1974): 197–221.

———. *Madagascar, les Comores, et le Sud-Ouest de l'Océan Indien.* Tananarive: Université de Madagascar, 1974.

———. "L'Océan Indien comme domaine de récherche." *L'Homme* 14 (1974): 143–151.

———. "L'origine dravidienne du vocabulaire du riz et de certains termes de riziculture à Madagascar." *APOI* 2 (1975): 103–121.

———. "Le mythe d'Andrianoro: conception de la parenté et de l'alliance des anciens Andriana du centre de Madagascar." *Taloha* 7 (1978): 51–83.

———. "Raminî, Alî ibn Abî Talîb, al-Khîr et les souverains universels malgaches." *ASEMI* 11 (1980): 97–111.

———. "La mythologie malgache des Hautes Terres: le cycle politique des Andriambahoaka." In *Dictionnaire des mythologies et des réligions des sociétés traditionnelles et du monde antique,* vol. 2. Paris: Flammarion, 1981.

———. "Myth and History: The Malagasy Andriambahoaka and the Indonesian Legacy." *History in Africa* 9 (1982): 221–250.

———. "Mythologie politique malgache des Hautes Terres: part des répresentations africaines et indonésiennes." *Récherche, pédagogie et culture* 67 (1984): 47–56.

Paillard, Y.-G. "Visions mythiques d'une Afrique colonisable: Madagascar et les fantasmes européens à la fin du XIXe siècle.'' *Revue française d'histoire d'outre-mer* 77 (1990): 159–176.

———. *Les incertitudes du colonialisme: Jean Carol à Madagascar.* Paris: L'Harmattan, 1990.

———. ''Domination coloniale et récupération des traditions autochtones, le cas de Madagascar de 1896 à 1914.'' *Revue d'histoire moderne et contemporaine* 38 (1991): 73–104.

———, and Boutonne, J. ''Espoirs et déboires de l'immigration européenne à Madagascar sous Gallieni: l'expérience de colonisation militaire.'' *Revue française d'histoire d'outre-mer* 65 (1978): 333–351.

Pannetier, J. ''Archéologie des pays antambahoaka et antaimoro.'' *Taloha* 6 (1974): 53–71.

Paulhan, J. F. *Jean Paulhan et Madagascar, 1908–1910.* Paris: Gallimard, 1982.

Pavageau, J. ''Rapports de parenté et développement capitaliste à Madagascar.'' *Economie* (1979): 111–131.

———. *Jeunes paysans sans terres: l'exemple malgache: une communauté villageoise en période révolutionnaire.* Paris: L'Harmattan, 1981.

———. ''Culture villageoise et idéologies dominantes à Madagascar.'' *Economie* (1981): 109–124.

Payrot, A. ''Action missionnaire de l'Eglise malgache.'' *Journal des missions évangéliques* (March-April 1964): 51–63.

Perspectives nouvelles sur le passé de l'Afrique noire et de Madagascar: mélanges offerts à Hubert Deschamps. Paris: Publications de la Sorbonne, 1974.

Pesquidoux, A. de. ''Le Gascon Jean Laborde, conquérant pacifique de Madagascar.'' *Bulletin de l'Académie des Sciences et Lettres de Montpellier* 14 (1983): 3–15.

Poirier, J. *Etudes de Droit africaine et de Droit malgache.* Paris: Cujas, 1965.

——— ''Aspects de l'urbanisation à Madagascar: les villes malgaches et la population urbaine.'' *Civilisations* 18 (1968): 80–109.

———. ''Les villages fortifiés bezanozano.'' *Taloha* 4 (1971): 127–152.

———. ''L'adoption en ancien droit coutumier bezanozano.'' In *L'autre et l'ailleurs: Hommage à Roger Bastide.* Paris: Berger-Lévrault, 1976.

———. ''Problèmes de la mise en place des couches éthniques et des couches culturelles à Madagascar.'' In *Mouvements de populations dans l'Océan Indien.* Paris: H. Champion, 1980.

———, and Dez, J. ''Glottochronologie et histoire culturelle malgache.'' *Taloha* 9 (1982): 97–120.

———, and Rabenoro, A. *Tradition et dynamique sociale à Madagascar.* Nice: Institut d'Etudes et de Récherche Interéthniques et Interculturelles, 1978.

———. ''Tromba et Ambalavelona chez les Bezanozano. Aspects des phénomènes de possession à Madagascar.'' In *Ethnologiques. Hommages à Marcel Griaule,* ed. Solanges de Ganay et al. Paris: Hermann, 1987.

Prats, Y. *Le développement communautaire à Madagascar.* Paris: L.G.D.J., 1972.

Rabearimanana, L. ''Presse et luttes politiques à Madagascar.'' *Aujord'hui l'Afrique* 11–12 (1978): 74–77.

———. ''Un grand journal d'opinion malgache: *Ny Fandrosoam-Baovono* (1931–1959).'' *Omaly sy anio* 11 (January-June 1980): 7–48.

———. *La presse d'opinion à Madagascar de 1947 à 1956: contribution à l'histoire du nationalisme malgache du lendemain de l'insurrection de 1947 à la veille du loi-cadre.* Antananarivo: Librairie Mixte, 1980.

———. ''La presse d'opinion et luttes politiques à Madagascar de 1945 à 1956.'' *Revue française d'histoire d'outre-mer* 67 (1980): 99–122.

———. ''Le Sud et la presse malgache des années soixante.'' *Omaly sy anio* 13–14 (1981): 293–303.

———''Les journalistes autonomistes tananariviens de 1945 à 1956.'' *Omaly sy anio* 15 (1982): 185–200.

———''Une expérience de développement rural dans les années 1950: les collectivités de Vakinakaratra.'' *Omaly sy anio* 16 (1982): 101–121.

———. ''Une entreprise coloniale d'après la Seconde Guerre mondiale à Madagascar: la société sucrière de la Mahavavy.'' In *Enterprises et entrepreneurs en Afrique, XIXe et XXe siècles.* Paris: L'Harmattan, 1983.

———''La promotion de la caféiculture sur la côte est de Madagascar dans les années 1950. Résultats économiques et répercussions sur le niveau de vie du petit planteur malgache.'' *Revue française d'histoire d'outre-mer* 74 (1987): 55–70.

Rabedimy, J.-F, ''Contribution de l'ombiasa à la formation du royaume Menabe, le togny.'' *ASEMI* 7 (1976): 255–270.

———. *Pratiques de divination à Madagascar. Téchnique du sikidy en pays sakalava Menabe.* Paris: ORSTOM, 1976.

———. ''Essai sur l'idéologie de la mort à Madagascar.'' In *Les hommes et la mort: rituels funéraires à travers le monde,* ed. J. Guiart. Paris: Le Sycomore, 1979.

———. ''Pages de texte sacrés extraits des arts de divination dit 'sikidy.' '' *ASEMI* 11 (1980): 431–436.

Rabemananjara, J. ''Le peuplement de Madagascar: thèses en présence.'' In *Rélations historiques à travers l'Océan Indien.* Paris: UNESCO, 1980.

Rabenoro, A. ''Trois générations de Malgaches en France: trois formes d'adoptions? (1930–45, 1945–60, 1960 . . .).'' *Cahiers d'anthropologie* 2 (1975): 23–33.

Radaody, F. ''Pouvoir colonial, associations et syndicats à Madagascar.'' In *Villes et sociétés urbaines en Afrique noire. Vol. 1: Les villes pré-coloniales.* Paris: Laboratoire ''Conaissance du Tiers-Monde,'' 1981.

Radimilahy, C. ''Archéologie de l'Androy.'' *Récherche, pédagogie et culture* 55 (1981): 62–65.

———. ''Migrations anciennes dans l'Androy.'' *Omaly sy anio* 13–14 (1981): 99–111.

Rahamefy, H. ''L'Eglise du Palais à Madagascar.'' *Le monde non-chrétien* 22 (1959): 381–422.

Raherisoanjato, D. ''Les rites réligieux dans le Betsileo, leurs supports matériels et leur contenu historique, l'exemple du 'Tafotona.' '' *Cahiers éthnologiques* 4 (1983): 45–62.

Raison-Jourde, F. ''Le catholicisme malgache: passé et présent.'' *Revue française d'études politiques africaines* (1970): 78–99.

———''Spiritualité et ecclésiologie protestantes en Imerina sous la colonisation.'' *Revue d'histoire de la spiritualité* 49 (1973): 165–197.

———. ''L'acculturation par l'Ecriture Sainte à Madagascar. Une réligion de l'Ecriture dans une civilisation orale.'' In *Histoire du texte. Récherche sur la place du livre dans le christianisme.* Paris: La Bussière, 1974.

———. ''Les Ramanenjana, une mise en cause populaire du christianisme en Imerina.'' *ASEMI* 7 (1976): 271–293.

———. ''Radama II ou le conflit du réel et de l'imaginaire dans la royauté merina.'' In *Les Africains,* vol. 8. Paris: Editions Jeune Afrique, 1977.

———. ''L'échange inégale de la langue. L'introduction des téchniques linguistiques dans une civilisation de l'oral (Imerina au XIXe siècle.).'' *Annales. Economies, Sociétés, Civilisations* 32 (1977): 639–669.

———''Ethnographie missionnaire et fait réligieux au XIXe siècle: le cas de Madagascar.'' *Revue française de sociologie* 19 (1978): 525–549.

———. ''A Madagascar: le temps comme enjeu politique.'' *Annales. Economies, Sociétés, Civilisations* 36 (1981): 143–161.

———. ''Le travail missionnaire sur les formes de la culture orale à Madagascar entre 1820 et 1886.'' *Omaly sy anio* 15 (1982): 33–52.

———, ed. *Les Souverains de Madagascar: l'histoire royale et ses résurgences contemporaines.* Paris: Karthala, 1983.

———. ''Mission LMS et Mission jésuite face aux communautés villageoises Merina: fondation et fonctionnement des paroisses entre 1869 et 1876.'' *Africa* 53 (1983): 55–72.

———. ''Le travail et l'échange dans le discours d'Andrianampoinimerina (Madagascar, XVIIIe siècle).'' In *Le travail et ses réprésentations,* ed. M. Cartier. Paris: Archives Contemporaines, 1984.

———. "Les élites malgaches, ou comment changer pour mieux conserver?" *Labour, Capital and Society/Travail, capital et sociétés* 17 (1984): 174–194.

———. "Une rébellion en quête d'un statut: 1947 à Madagascar." *Revue de la Bibliothèque Nationale* 34 (1989): 24–32.

Raison, J.-P. "Immigration in the Sakay District, Madagascar." In *Population Growth and Economic Development in Africa,* ed. S. H. Ominde et al. London: Heinnemann, 1972.

———. "Utilisation du sol et organisation de l'espace en Imerina ancien." In *Etudes de géographie tropicale offertes à Pierre Gourou.* Paris: n.p., 1972.

———. "Perception et réalisation de l'espace dans la société merina." *Annales. Economies, Sociétés, Civilisations* 32 (1977): 412–429.

———. "Discours scientifique et manipulation politique: les Européens face aux Merina et à l'Imerina de la fin du XVIIIe siècle aux lendemains de la conquête." In *Science de l'homme et conquête coloniale: constitution et usages des sciences humaines en Afrique (XIXe et XXe siècles),* ed. D. Nordman and J.-P. Raison. Paris: Presses de l'Ecole Normale Supérieure, 1980.

———. *Les Hautes terres de Madagascar et leurs confins occidentaux: enracinement et mobilité des sociétés rurales.* Paris: Karthala, 1984.

———. "Madagascar, dans le Sud-Ouest de l'Océan Indien." *Herodote* 37–38 (1985): 211–235.

Rajaona, A. "Le dinam-pokonolona, mythe, mystique ou mystification?" *APOI* 7 (1980): 145–167.

Rajaonah, V. "La chasse et le piégeage à Madagascar: téchniques et traditions." *Présence africaine* 96 (1975): 527–557.

Rajaonarimanana, N. ''Notes sur la site d'Anjorodalana (canton d'Ambatomarina, sous-préfecture d'Ambositra).'' *Taloha* 7 (1978): 5–18.

———. ''Achèvement des funérailles et offrande de linceuls: rites funéraires et commémoratifs des Betsileo du Manandriana.'' In *Les Hommes et la mort: rituels funéraires à travers le monde,* ed. J. Guiart, Paris: Le Sycomore, 1979.

———. ''Le manuscrit arabico-malgache inédit de Mosa Mahefamanana.'' *Etudes Océan Indien* 2 (1983): 73–93.

———. ''Traité sur les djinns d'après le manuscrit arabico-malgache du Musée des arts africains et océaniens, Paris,'' *Etudes Océan Indien* 6 (1985): 125–150.

Rajaonarison, E. ''Mythe sur l'origine des Mahafaly et de la dynastie Maroserana (Sud-Ouest de Madagascar).'' *ASEMI* 8 (1977): 87–117.

Rakoto, G. ''Les récherches démographiques à Madagascar.'' *Demographie africaine* 48-49 (1985): 39–43.

Rakoto, I. ''L'esclavage dans l'ancien Madagascar.'' *Tantara* 4-5 (1976): 125–137.

Rakotoarisoa, J. A. ''Notes archéologiques sur les forts des régions de Tamatave et de Fenerive.'' *Taloha* 6 (1974): 15–38.

———, and Heurtebize, G. ''Note sur la confection des tissus du type Ikat à Madagascar. Les Laimasaka de la région de Kandreho et d'Anbatomainty.'' *Archipel* 8 (1974): 67–81.

Rakotonirina, M. ''Ostentation économique et dynamique villageoise à Madagascar.'' *Economie et sociétés* 2 (1968): 833–846.

Rakotondrabe, T. ''Tamatave, ville portuaire du 'royaume de Madagascar' au XIXe siècle.'' In *Villes et sociétés urbaines en Afrique noire. Vol. 1: Les villes pré-coloniales.* Paris: Laboratoire ''Connaissance du Tiers- Monde,'' 1981.

Rakotosamimanana, B. R. ''Cercles de mariages dans la caste hova et la caste mainty de l'ancienne région d'Ambodirano (Tananarive) et résultants anthropologiques à partir de quelques paramètres.'' *Anthropologie* 80 (1976): 491–508.

Ralaikoa, A. ''Problèmes de démographie historique dans le Sud-Betsileo (Madagascar).'' In *Histoire démographique, concept d'éthnie,* ed. C. Coquery-Vidrovitch. Paris: L'Harmattan, 1985.

Ralaimihoatra, E. *Histoire de Madagascar.* Antananarivo: Hachette, 1969.

Ralaimihoatra, G. ''L'ancien site fortifié de Kilonjy.'' *Taloha* 4 (1971): 153–165.

Ramiandrisoa, F. ''Les Wak-Wak, entité géographique ou éthnolinguistique?'' *Tantara* 1 (1974): 1–29.

Raminosoa, N. ''Rapport de mission: récherche sur l'organisation sociale des Vakinakaratra.'' *ASEMI* 7 (1976): 197–202.

Randriamandimby, B. ''Le concept de hiérarchie en Imerina historique.'' *ASEMI* 4 (1973): 3–16.

Randriamandimby Ravoahangy-Andrianavalona, J. *La VVS, Vy, Vato, Sakelika (Fer, Pierre, Ramification). Contribution à l'étude sur l'origine du Nationalisme malgache.* Paris: n.p., 1978.

Randrianarisoa, P. *La diplomatie face à la politique des grandes puissances, 1882-1895.* Tananarive: Trano Printy Loterana, 1970.

Rantoandro, G. ''Contribution à l'étude d'un groupe social peu connu du XIXe siècle: les maromita.' *Omaly sy anio* 16 (1982): 41–60.

Raoul, Y., and Raoul, S. "Culte dynastique et possession: le tromba de Madagascar." *L'évolution psychiatrique* 47 (1982): 975–984.

Rasamuel, D. "Une fouille à Ambohitrikanjaka en 1979." *Taloha* 9 (1982): 7–24.

———. "Des déportés en Imerina au XIXe siècle." *Omaly sy anio* 15 (1982): 99–116.

——— "Les anciens sites d'habitat à Madagascar: les Hautes Terres et le Sud." *Omaly sy anio* 16 (1982): 125–139.

———. "Alimentation et téchniques anciens dans le Sud malgache à travers une fosse à ordures du XIe siècle." *Etudes Océan Indien* 4 (1984): 81–109.

———. "Culture materielle ancienne à Madagascar: contribution des pays riverains de l'Océan Indien dans le mouvement des idées dans l'Océan Indien occidental." In *Actes de la Table Ronde de Saint-Denis.* Saint-Denis, Réunion, 1985.

———. *Fanongoavana, site ancien des Hautes Terres.* Paris: Karthala, 1986.

Ratsivalaka, G. "La traite européenne des esclaves en Imerina au debut du XIXe siècle." *Tantara* 7–8 (1979): 113–135.

Ravoaianahary, C. "Le peuplement de Madagascar: tentatives d'approche." In *Rélations historiques à travers l'Océan Indien.* Paris: UNESCO, 1980.

Razafiangy Dina, J. *Etrangers et malgaches dans le sud-ouest sakalava (1845–1904).* Aix-en-Provence: Université de Provence, 1982.

Razafindranoro, C. "Les contradictions sociales au sein de la paysannerie 'Merina.' " *Terre malgache/Tany malagasy* 16 (1974): 173–190.

Razafindratovo, J. *Etude du village d'Ilafy.* Tananarive: ORSTOM, 1965.

Razafintsalama, A. "Histoire et tradition chez les Tsimahafotsy." *ASEMI* 4 (1973): 17–33.

———. *Les Tsimahafotsy d'Ambohimanga: organisation familiale et sociale en Imerina (Madagascar).* Paris: Société d'Etudes Linguistiques et Anthropologiques de France, 1981.

Récherches, pédagogie et culture 9, no. 50 (1981): special number, "Regards sur l'histoire de Madagascar."

Robert, M. "Les musulmans à Madagascar et dans les Mascareignes." *Revue française d'études politiques africaines* 12 (1977): 46–71.

Rolland, D. "Introduction à une anthropologie de la basse Matitanana." *Taloha* 6 (1974): 39–52.

Rossi, G, "Une ville de colonisation française dans l'Océan Indien: Diégo-Suarez." *Cahiers d'Outre-Mer* 26 (1973): 410–426.

———. *L'Extrème-Nord de Madagascar.* Aix-en-Provence: EDISUD, 1980.

Rouhette, A. "Aspects historico-juridiques du tombeau merina." *Droit et cultures* 2 (1981): 5–20.

———. "L'évolution des communautés rurales à Madagascar: le Fokonolona." In *Les communautés rurales. lère partie: Sociétés sans écriture (Afrique, Amérique, Europe).* Paris: Dessain et Tolra, 1983.

———. "La polygynie dans la société traditionnelle de Madagascar." *Droit et culture* 6 (1983): 35–65.

Rousseau, A. ''Le fokonolona, collectivité locale malgache.'' *Revue juridique et politique, indépendance et coopération* (1968): 263–284.

Roux, J.-C. ''Caractères démographiques des migrations spontanées dans une zone de terre neuve du Nord-Ouest malgache.'' In *African Historical Demography,* vol. 2. Edinburgh: Centre of African Studies, University of Edinburgh, 1981.

Ruud, J. *Taboo: A Study of Malagasy Customs and Beliefs.* 1st ed., Oslo, 1960; Tananarive: Trano Printy Loterana, 1970.

Sabeau-Jouannet, L. ''Essai de psychologie transculturelle appliquée au groupe éthnique merina.'' *Confrontation psychiatrique* 14 (1976): 5–54.

Scarpa, A. ''Le reveil des médecins traditionnels: l'intérêt et les perspectives de la médecine traditionnelle à Madagascar.'' *Curare* 3 (1980); 31–44.

Schlemmer, B. ''Communautés paysannes et cadre politique: les Sakalaves du Menabe.'' In *Communautés rurales et paysanneries tropicales.* Paris: ORSTOM, 1976.

———. ''Les Sakalava du Menabe et la colonisation de la vallée de Tsiribihina.'' In *Essais sur la réproduction de formations sociales dominées.* Paris: ORSTOM, 1977.

———. *Le Menabe de 1897 à 1947: cinquante ans d'une colonisation.* Paris: ORSTOM, 1980.

———. ''Ethnologie et colonisation. Le moment de la conquête et le moment da la gestion. Eléments de réflexion à partir du cas du Menabe.'' In *Sciences de l'homme et conquête coloniale: constitution et usages des sciences humaines in Afrique (XIXe et XXe siècles),* ed. D. Nordman and J.-P. Raison. Paris: Presses de l'Ecole Normale Supérieure, 1980.

Schmidt, M. E. "Prelude to Intervention: Madagascar and the Failure of Anglo-German Diplomacy, 1890–1895." *Historical Journal* 15 (1972): 715–730.

Seagre, D. A. "Madagascar: An Example of Indigenous Modernization of a Traditional Society in the Nineteenth Century." *St. Anthony's Papers* 21 (1969): 67–91.

Secord, A. W. *Robert Drury's Journal and Other Studies.* Urbana: University of Illinois Press, 1961.

Serre-Ratsimandisa, G. "Théorie et pratique du 'Fokonolona' moderne à Madagascar." *Canadian Journal of African Studies* 12 (1978): 37–58.

Simon, P. "Au sujet de l'unité culturelle malgache." *L'Afrique et l'Asie modernes,* no. 103 (1974): 32–45.

Slawecki, L. *French Policy Towards the Chinese in Madagascar.* Hamden, Conn.: Shoestring Press, 1971.

Southall, A. "Ideology and Group Composition in Madagascar." *American Anthropologist* 73 (1971): 144–164.

———. "Ecology and Social Change in Madagascar: Linton's Hypothesis on the Tanala and Betsileo." *American Anthropologist* 77 (1975): 603–609.

Stiles, D. "Tubers and Tenrecs: The Mikea of Southwestern Madagascar." *Ethnology* 30 (1991): 251–263.

Stratton, A. *The Great Red Island.* New York: Scribner, 1964.

Thiout, M. *Madagascar et l'âme malgache.* Paris: Horizons de France, 1961.

Thompson, A. "The Role of Firearms and the Development of Military Technology in Merina Warfare c. 1785–1828." *Revue française de l'histoire d'outre-mer* 61 (1974): 417–435.

Toussaint, A. *Histoire des îles Mascareignes.* Paris: Berger-Lévrault, 1972.

Tronchon, J. *L'insurrection malgache de 1947: essai d'interprétation historique.* Paris: Maspero, 1974.

———. "Ravoahangy, conscience du patriotisme malgache." In *Les Africains,* vol. 1. Paris: Editions Jeune Afrique, 1977.

Tsien Tche-Hao. "La vie sociale des chinois à Madagascar." *Comparative Studies in Society and History* 3 (1961): 170–181.

Urbain-Faublée, M., and Faublée, J. "Charmes magiques malgaches." *Journal de la Société des Africanistes* 39 (1969): 139–149.

Valette, J. *Les rélations extérieures de Madagascar au XIX siècle.* Tananarive: Imprimerie Nationale, 1960.

———. *Etudes sur le règne de Radama Ier.* Tananarive: Imprimerie Nationale, 1962.

———. "Le traité conclu entre Radama I et Lesage le 4 février 1817." *Revue française d' histoire d'outre-mer* 62 (1974): 572–578.

———. "Aux origines de l'évangelisation de Madagascar: les débuts de l'apostolat de Jones (1818–1819)." *Revue française d'histoire d'outre-mer* 65 (1977): 376–392.

Verin, P. *Arabes et islamisés à Madagascar et dans l'Océan Indien.* Tananarive: Imprimerie Nationale, 1967.

———. *Les échelles anciennes du commerce sur les côtes nord de Madagascar.* Lille: Université de Lille, Service de Diffusion des Thèses, 1975.

———. "The African Element in Madagascar." *Azania* 11 (1976): 135–151.

———. ''Migrations et contacts entre Madagascar et l'outre-mer jusqu'au XVIIIe siècle.'' *APOI* 3 (1976): 73–82.

———. ''Aspects de la civilisation des échelles anciennes du Nord de Madagascar.'' In *Mouvements de populations dans l'Océan Indien.* Paris: H. Champion, 1979.

———. ''Le problème des origines malgaches.'' *Taloha* 8 (1979): 7–28.

———. ''Les apports culturels et la contribution africaine au peuplement de Madagascar.'' In *Rélations historiques à travers l'Océan Indien.* Paris: UNESCO, 1980.

———. *The History of Civilization in Northern Madagascar.* Rotterdam: Balkema, 1986.

———; Kottak, C. P.; and Gorlin, P. ''The Glottochronology of Malagasy Speech Communities.'' *Oceanic Linguistics* 8 (1970): 26–83.

Vernier, E. *Index des Tantaran'ny Andriana eto Madagascar. Histoire des Rois.* Paris: Musée de l'Homme, 1978.

———, and Millot, J. *Archéologie Malgache.* Paris: Catalogues du Musée de l'Homme, 1971.

Vidal, H. *La séparation des églises et de l'Etat à Madagascar, 1861–1968.* Paris: n.p., 1970.

Vig, L. *Charmes. Spécimens de magie malgache.* Oslo: Universitetsforlaget, 1969.

———. *Croyances et moeurs des Malgaches.* Antananarivo: Trano Printy Loterana, 1977.

Vogel, C. ''Stratégies d'équilibre et d'expansion dans une population d'Imerina.'' *ASEMI* 4 (1973): 35–51.

———. *Les quatre-mères d'Ambohibaho: études d'une population régionale d'Imerina (Madagascar).* Paris: SELAF, 1982.

White, W. M. *Friends in Madagascar, 1867–1967.* London: Friends' Service Council, 1967.

Wilson, P. "Tsimihety Kinship and Descent." *Africa* 37 (1967): 133–153.

———. "Sentimental Structure: Tsimihety Migration and Descent." *American Anthropologist* 73 (1971): 193–208.

———. "The Problem with Simple Folk." *Natural History* 86 (1977): 26–32.

Wright, H. T., and Kus, S. "Reconnaissances archéologiques dans le Centre d'Imerina." *Taloha* 7 (1978): 27–45.

B. Politics and Economics

Albafouille, F.; Raymond, J.; and Gianucci, J. "Aspects financiers de la gestion communale à Madagascar." *Revue juridique et politique, indépendance et coopération* 22 (1968): 285–292.

Allen, P. "Madagascar: The Authenticity of Recovery." In *The Politics of the Indian Ocean Islands,* ed. J. M. Ostheimer. New York: Praeger, 1975.

———. *Security and Nationalism in the Indian Ocean: Lessons from the Latin Quarter Islands.* Boulder, Colo.: Westview Press, 1987.

Althabe, G. "Les manifestations paysans d'avril 1971." *Revue française d'études politiques africaines* (*RFEPA*) (June 1972):71–77.

———. ''Le Monima [Mouvement National pour l'Indépendance de Madagascar].'' *RFEPA* (February 1973):71–76.

———. ''Les luttes sociales à Tananarive en 1972.'' *Cahiers d'études africaines* 20 (1980): 404–447.

Andriamirado, S. ''Heurs et malheurs des fokonolona.'' *Autogestion et socialisme* 39 (1977): 51–64.

———. *Madagascar aujourd'hui.* Paris: Editions Jeune Afrique, 1984.

Archer, R. *Madagascar depuis 1972.* Paris: L'Harmattan, 1976.

Aspects actuels et perspectives de l'économie de Madagascar. Paris: Institut de Science Economique Appliquée, 1962.

Bardonnet, D. ''La juridiction administrative à Madagascar.'' *Actualité juridique* (July–August 1962):396–408.

Baumont, J. C. ''Le diagnostique du sous-développement malgache.'' *Croissance des jeunes nations* (October 1963).

Berg, E. ''The Liberalization of Rice Marketing in Madagascar.'' *World Development* 17 (1989): 719–728.

Bezy, F. ''La transformation des structures socio-économiques à Madagascar (1960–1978).'' *Cultures et développement* 11 (1979): 83–116.

Bilbao, R. ''L'organisation judiciaire de la République malgache.'' *Recueil pénant* (1961): 47–56.

———. *Le droit malgache de la nationnalité.* Paris: Cujas, 1965.

Bilévitch, B., and Vyssotskaia, N. ''Documents-programme de la révolution malgache.'' In *Idéologie de la démocratie révolutionnaire africaine.* Moscow: Academy of Sciences, 1984.

Blanc, P. ''Les spécificités du problème économique de Madagascar.'' *Mondes et cultures* 44 (1984): 321–339.

Blardonne, G. ''Madagascar: le développement du sous-développement.'' *Croissance des jeunes nations* (December 1984): 10–13.

Boiteau, P. ''Où en est Madagascar?'' *Démocratie nouvelle* (December 1961): 62–69.

———. ''Madagascar: les raisons profondes d'un mécontentement.'' *Cahiers du communisme* (July–August 1972): 63–78.

Bouillon, A. ''Le MFM malgache.'' *Revue française d'études politiques africaines* (November 1973): 46–71.

Boussenot, G. ''Comment Madagascar devint Etat souverain.'' *Revue politique et parlementaire* (August–September 1960): 114–123.

British Overseas Board of Trade. Tropical Advisory Group. Trade Mission to the Democratic Republic of Madagascar. *Report.* London, 1984.

Cadoux, C. ''Les nouveaux aspects de l'organisation administrative locale à Madagascar.'' *Droit administratif* (1965): 76–93.

———. ''Madagascar: constitution et régime politique.'' *Bulletin de l'Institut des Hautes Etudes d'Outre-Mer* 4 (1966): 5–24.

———. *La République malgache.* Paris: Berger-Lévrault, 1969.

———. ''Les élections générales de 1982–1983 à Madagascar: des élections pour quoi faire?'' *Année africaine* 1983(published 1984): 67–85.

———. ''Madagascar depuis 1985: vers la Troisième République.'' *APOI* 11 (1986–1989): 137–172.

———. *La deuxième république malgache: extraits de l'Annuaire des pays de l'Océan indien.* Talence: CEGET, 1989.

Camacho, M. ''Bilan de la politique de coopérativisation de l'agriculture 1976–1980.'' *Terre malgache/Tany malagasy* 21 (1982): 155–180.

Chaigneau, P. ''Un mode d'orientation socialiste à la péripherie du socialisme: le cas de Madagascar.'' *Pouvoirs* 22 (1982): 109–116.

———. ''Madagascar: la crise économique face aux vicissitudes politiques.'' *L'Afrique et l'Asie modernes* 138 (1983): 12–26.

———. ''La presse à Madagascar.'' *Les cahiers de la communication* 3 (1983): 283–319.

———. ''Le système des partis à Madagascar (De la tentative d'unification au développement des scissions inter et intra-partisanes).'' *Recueil pénant* 93 (1983): 306–345.

———. ''Politique et franc-maçonnerie dans le Tiers-Monde: l'exemple de Madagascar.'' *L'Afrique et l'Asie modernes* 145 (1985): 10–18.

———. *Rivalités politiques et socialisme à Madagascar.* Paris: CHEAM, 1985.

———. ''Madagascar: les ambiguités d'une réélection.'' *L'Afrique et l'Asie modernes* 161 (1989): 51–58.

Chaleur, P. ''Révolte à Madagascar.'' *Etudes* (November 1972): 503–522.

Comte, J. *Les communes malgaches.* Tananarive: Librairie de Madagascar, 1963.

Conac, G., and Feuer, G. ''Les accords franco-malgaches.'' *Annuaire française de droit international* (1960): 859–880.

Countant, P. ‘‘Les accords de défense avec la République malgache.’’ *Revue administrative* 78 (1960): 628–629.

Covell, M. *Madagascar: Politics, Economics, Society.* London: Frances Pinter, 1987.

Delcourt, A. ‘‘Les rélations extérieures de Madagascar.’’ *Revue française d’études politiques africaines* (April 1969): 47–66.

Délépine, J. ‘‘Madagascar: vers une nouvelle indépendance.’’ *Esprit* (1971): 407–427.

Déléris, F. *Ratsiraka: socialisme et misère à Madagascar.* Paris: L’Harmattan, 1986.

Delval, R. ‘‘Le syndicalisme à Madagascar.’’ *Recueil Pénant* 75 (1965): 563–583.

———. ‘‘Les musulmans à Madagascar en 1977.’’ *L’Afrique et l’Asie modernes* 115 (1977): 28–46; 116 (1978): 5–19.

Desjeux, D. ‘‘Essai d’interprétation nouvelle de la fonction des opérations de développement à partir d’une note de lecture sur l’impérialisme chez Lénine et Rosa Luxembourg.’’ *Tany malagasy/Terre malgache* 17 (July–December 1975): 229–248.

Donque, G. ‘‘Quelques données sur l’économie malgache en 1975.’’ *Madagascar: Revue de Géographie* 33 (July–December 1978): 85–91.

‘‘Dossier des entreprises socialistes malgaches.’’ *Afrique-Asie* (October 16–29, 1978): 31–54.

‘‘Dossier Madagascar.’’ *Journal des missions évangeliques,* 1982.

Durufle, G. *L’ajustement structurel en Afrique (Sénégal, Côte d’Ivoire, Madagascar).* Paris: Karthala, 1988.

Escaro, A. ''Les militaires et le pouvoir politique à Madagascar de 1960 à 1975.'' *Le mois en Afrique* 18 (August–September 1983): 48–53.

Gaudusson, J. de. *L'adminstration malgache.* Paris: Berger-Lévrault, 1976.

———. ''La nouvelle constitution malgache du 31 décembre 1975.'' *Revue juridique et politique, indépendance et coopération* 30 (1976): 261–299.

———. ''Madagascar: révolution socialiste et réforme des structures administratives: premier bilan.'' *Année africaine* (1978): 269–285.

———. ''Propos sur les aspects idéologiques et institutionnels des récentes réformes des fokonolona: le fokonolona en question.'' *APOI* 5 (1978): 15–36.

———. ''Madagascar: des entreprises publiques aux entreprises socialistes.'' In *Les entreprises publiques en Afrique Noire.* Paris: Pédone, 1979.

———. ''Madagascar (1975–1979).'' *Annuaire de législation française et étrangère* 28 (1979–1980; published 1983): 513–529.

Gayet, G. ''Premiers bilans de la République malgache.'' *Revue de défense nationale* (October 1961): 1636–1646.

Gendarme, R. *L'économie de Madagascar, diagnostic et perspective de développement.* Paris: Cujas, 1962.

Gerard, P. ''Madagascar: les chances de la révolution socialiste.'' *Etudes* (April 1976): 499–515.

———. ''L'Eglise et les chrétiens dans le Madagascar d'aujourd'hui.'' *Pro Mundi Vita* (July–August 1978): 2–42.

GIMOI. ''Trois jours qui ebranlèrent Madagascar.'' *Revue française d'études politiques africaines* (June 1972): 44–50.

Gintzburger, A. ''Accommodation to Poverty: The Case of the Malagasy Peasant Communities.'' *Cahiers d'études africaines* 23 (1983): 419–442.

Givelet, N. ''Le fokonolona malgache ou l'expression d'une âme collective.'' *Ceres* 11 (1978): 31–37.

Goguel, A. M. ''La diplomatie malgache.'' *Revue française d'études politiques africaines* (January 1972): 78–103.

Greenaway, D., and Milner, C. ''Industrial Incentives, Domestic Resource Costs, and Resource Allocation in Madagascar.'' *Applied Economics* 22 (1990): 805–821.

Harchaoui, S. ''Recensement général de la population et des habitats de 1975 à Madagascar.'' In *Recensements africains. lére partie: monographies méthodologiques.* Paris: Groupe de Travail de Démographie Africaine, 1981.

Heseltine, N. *Madagascar.* New York: Praeger, 1971.

Hugon, P. ''L'impacte de l'aide sur le développement: le cas de Madagascar.'' *Tiers-Monde* 14 (1973): 793–824.

———. ''L'enseignement enjeu de la compétition sociale à Madagascar.'' *Tiers-Monde* 15 (1974): 491–510.

———. ''L'évolution économique de Madagascar de la lére à la seconde république.'' *Revue française d'études politiques africaines* 12 (1977): 26–57.

———. ''Madagascar: chronique économique et démographique.'' *APOI* 5 (1978): 423–433.

———. ''Le développement des petites activités à Antananarivo: L'exemple d'un procesus involutif.'' *Canadian Journal of African Studies* 16 (1982): 293–312.

Indrianazafy, G. T., and Rahetla, J. ''Les mécanismes juridiques de protection des droits de la personne en République démocratique de Madagascar.'' *Revue juridique et politique, indépendance et coopération* 36 (1982): 170–188.

Isnard, H. ''Disparités régionales et unité nationale à Madagascar.'' *Cahiers internationaux de sociologie* 32 (1962): 25–42.

Jouffrey, R. ''Didier Ratsiraka et le socialisme malgache.'' *Afrique contemporaine* 20 (May–June 1981): 6–12.

Kent, R. *From Madagascar to Malagasy Republic.* New York: Praeger, 1962.

Laforge, A. ''L'Océan Indien, zone de deséquilibre et de conflits.'' *Est et Ouest* 34 (October 31, 1982): 2–11.

Latremolière, J. ''Madagascar: une remontée économique morose.'' *Marchés tropicaux et méditerranéens* (November 9, 1984): 2731–2733.

Le Bourdiec, P. ''Economie urbaine et disparité régionale à Madagascar.'' In *Les formes de l'économie urbaine en Afrique noire et à Madagascar.* Table Ronde CEGET-CNRS. Talence: CEGET, 1983.

Lecaillon, J., and Germidis, D. *Inegalité des revenus et développement économique: Cameroun, Côte d'Ivoire Madagascar, Sénégal.* Paris: PUF, 1977.

Lefèvre, J. ''Le Parti Social-Démocrate de Madagascar.'' *Revue française d'études politiques africaines* (April 1969): 67–84.

Leisinger, K. M. ''Multinational Companies and Agricultural Development: A Case Study of Taona Zina in Madagascar.'' *Food Policy* 12 (1987): 227–241.

Léonard, W. ''Quelques réflexions sur l'expérience de Madagascar en matière de politique artisanale.'' *Tiers-Monde* 21 (1980): 337–351.

Lettre de l'Océan Indien. *Madagascar: secteurs clés de l'économie.* Paris: Lettre de l'Océan Indien, 1986.

Leymarie, P. ''Les accords de coopération franco-malgaches.'' *Revue française d'études politiques africaines* (*RFEPA*) (June 1972): 55–60.

———. ''Madagascar: l'heure de verité [nouvelle politique après mai 1972].'' *RFEPA* (September 1972): 22–24.

———. ''La malgachisation en question.'' *RFEPA* (January 1973): 28–32.

———. ''La nouvelle diplomatie malgache.'' *RFEPA* (January 1974): 29–33.

———. ''L'AKFM malgache.'' *RFEPA* (November 1974): 46–60.

———. ''Le fokonolona: la voie malgache vers le socialisme?'' *RFEPA* (April 1975): 42–67.

———. ''L'armée malgache dans l'attente (1960–1972).'' *RFEPA* 12 (1977): 50–64.

———. ''Madagascar: L'an III de la révolution.'' *Spéciale Afrique-Asie* (February 6, 1978).

———. ''Le Parti du Congrès pour l'indépendance de Madagascar (AKFM).'' *RFEPA* (April 1979): 44–59.

———. ''Madagascar: la course de vitesse des socialistes.'' *Le monde diplomatique* (July 1982): 16–19.

Madagascar. Paris: Jeune Afrique, 1979.

''Madagascar: Charte du mouvement coopératif socialiste.'' *Revue des études coopératives* 57 (1978): 153–154.

"Madagascar (dossier)." *Le Courrier: Afrique-Caraïbes-Pacifique-Communauté européene* 80 (July–August 1983): 7–26.

"Madagascar: sept ans de révolution." *Océan Indien actuel* 8 (1978): 19–35.

"Madagascar, une touche de l'Asie au large de l'Afrique." *Sudestasie* 26 (1982): 19–45.

Mafrezi, A., and Randretsa, I. "Evolution et structure de la population de Madagascar." *Démographie africaine: bulletin de liaison* 48–49 (1985): 51–60.

Maynard, P. "Le president Philibert Tsiranana par lui-même." *Revue française d'études politiques africaines* (June 1972): 104–114.

Mitchell, B., and Rakotonirina, X. *Impacte de la route Andapa-Sambava: étude socio-économique de la cuvette d'Andapa, Madagascar.* Washington, D.C.: World Bank, 1977.

Moine, J. "Madagascar: les militaires s'accrochent au pouvoir." *L'Afrique et l'Asie modernes* 105 (1975) 56–62.

———. "Océan indien et progressisme." *L'Afrique et l'Asie modernes* 121 (1979): 3–23.

———. "Madagascar: difficultés pour le President Ratsiraka." *L'Afrique et l'Asie modernes* 129 (1981): 42–52.

Molet, L. "Madagascar depuis 1972 (critique)." *L'Afrique et l'Asie modernes* 113 (1977): 96–109.

Mounier, B. "Le caractère des institutions malgaches." *Revue juridique et politique d'outre-mer* (July–September 1960): 317–333.

———. "Le parlement de la République malgache." *Revue*

juridique et politique d'outre-mer (October–December 1960): 489–550.

Mukonoweshuro, E. G. "State Resilience and Chronic Political Instability in Madagascar." *Canadian Journal of African Studies* 24 (1990): 376–399.

Nelson, H. D. *Area Handbook for the Malagasy Republic.* Washington, D.C.: American University, 1973.

Les options fondamentales pour la planification socialiste. Antananarivo: République Démocratique de Madagascar, 1978.

Oraison, A. "A propos du différend franco-malgache sur les îles éparses du canal de Mozambique (La succession d'états sur les îles Glorieuses, Juan de Nova, Europa et Bassas de India)." *Revue générale de droit international publique* 85 (1981): 465–513.

Pascal, R. *La République malgache: Pacifique indépendance.* Paris: Berger-Lévrault, 1965.

Pascual, P. "Madagascar." *Annuaire de législation française et etrangère* (1981–1982; published 1984): 507–524.

Petitjean, B. *Le système agro-industriel et les pays du Tiers-Monde. Le cas de Madagascar.* Special issue of *Terre malgache* 18 (1976, 1977), 2 vols.

Pidoux, E. *Madagascar, Maître à son bord.* Lausanne: Editions Sociales, 1962.

"Le plan malgache 1978–1980: développement de l'industrialisation dans une structure socialiste renforcée et contribution plus importante du financement interne." *Industries et travaux d'outre-mer* 27 (1979): 269–272.

Prats, Y. *Le développement communautaire à Madagascar.* Paris: Librairie Générale de Droit et de Jurisprudence, 1972.

———. ''Les nouvelles institutions socialistes du développement économique en République démocratique malgache.'' *APOI* 4 (1977): 15–23.

''Le problème du riz à Madagascar.'' *Revue française d'études politiques africaines* (January 1974): 65–74.

Rabemora, F. ''Dix années de socialisme à Madagascar.'' *Etudes* (May 1985): 581–591.

Rabenoro, C. *Les rélations extérieures de Madagascar de 1960 à 1972*. Paris: L'Harmattan, 1986.

Rabesahala, G. ''Madagascar Revolutionary Democrats.'' *World Marxist Review* 15 (1972): 119–125.

———. ''Madagascar Looks Ahead.'' *World Marxist Review* 17 (1974): 121–126.

Rabevazaha, C. ''La maîtrise populaire de développement: planification régionale et besoins essentiels à Madagascar.'' *Revue internationale du travail* 120 (1981): 469–483.

Rabotovao, S. ''Le cas de la République démocratique de Madagascar.'' *Annuaire du Tiers-Monde* 8 (1982–1983; published 1984): 173–180.

Racine, A. ''The Democratic Republic of Madagascar.'' In *The New Communist Third World: An Essay in Political Economy,* ed. P. J. Wiles. London: Croom Helm, 1982.

Rajoelina, P. *Quarante années de vie politique de Madagascar, 1947–1987*. Paris: L'Harmattan, 1988.

Rakoto, G. ''Evolution des politiques de population à Madagascar.'' *Démographie africaine: bulletin de liaison 48–49* (1984): 45–49.

Rakoto, H. ''L'économie malgache, ou quatre ans d'exécution du premier plan quinquénnal.'' *Revue française d'études politiques africaines* (May 1969): 66–105.

Rakoto, J. ''La crise de l'enseignement supérieur à Madagascar.'' *Revue française d'études politiques africaines* (November 1971): 53–79.

Rakoto-Ramiarantsoa, H. ''Développement à contre-sens: un aménagement hydro-agricole qui n'a pas donné les résultats escomptés.'' in *Les politiques de l'eau en Afrique,* ed. G. Conac et al. Paris: Economica, 1985.

Rakotovao, J. D. ''Jeunesse malgache et déchristianisation.'' *Soritra-Perspectives* 1 (1978): 233–251.

Ramahatra, O. *Madagascar: une économie en phase d'ajustement.* Paris: L'Harmattan, 1989.

Ramaholimihaso, A. *Madagascar: terre d'énigme.* Antananarivo: Société Malgache d'Editions, 1983.

Ramangosoavina, A. ''La justice dans les pays en voie de développement.'' *Revue juridique et politique, indépendance et coopération* 19 (1965): 503–520.

———. ''La commune malgache devant les problèmes sociologiques du développement.'' *Revue juridique et politique, indépendance et coopération* 2 (1968): 189–204.

Ramanitra, V., and Rasoanaivo, C. ''Coup d'état manqué, riche d'enseignements pour la République démocratique de Madagascar.'' *Revue juridique et politique, indépendance et coopération* 37 (1983): 194–212.

Ramamonjisoa, J. ''Le sisal à Madagascar.'' *Madagascar: Revue de Géographie* 31 (July–December 1977): 87–117.

———. ''Le Centre Economique et Téchnique de l'Artisanat.'' *Madagascar: Revue de Géographie* 32 (January–June 1978): 55–83.

———. ''Les expériences malgaches dans la domaine des aménagements rizicoles.'' In *Les politiques de l'eau en Afrique,* ed. G. Conac et al. Paris: Economica, 1985.

Ramaro, A. ''Donnez-nous quinze ans.'' *L'économiste du Tiers-Monde* (November 1980): 24–27.

Ramarolanto-Ratiary. ''L'entreprise socialiste à Madagascar.'' *Revue internationale de droit comparé* 36 (1984): 541–587.

Randrianahinoro, S. ''La jurisprudence de la Cour Suprême de Madagascar en matière de vol de boeufs.'' *Recueil pénant* 94 (1984): 5–15.

———. ''La justice civile rendue par les Fokonolona à Madagascar.'' *Recueil pénant* 101 (1991): 181–189.

Randrianamana, G. ''L'apprivoisement de la main-d'oeuvre de la zone périphérique de la ville de Tananarive: le phenomène du Toby.'' *Tany malagasy/Terre malgache* 17 (July–December 1975): 49–64.

Ranivoharison, J. *Législation et administration scolaires à Madagascar.* Antananarivo: Librairie Mixte, 1981.

Ranjeva, R. ''Aspects juridiques originaux de la commune malgache.'' *Revue juridique et politique, indépendance et coopération* 22 (1968): 249–262.

———. ''Les propositions de Madagascar à la 3e Conférence des Nations-Unies sur le droit de la mer.'' *Afrique contemporaine* 16, 93 (September 1977): 1–8.

Ratsimbazafy, A. ''Autopsie de la crise de Madagascar.'' *Rémarques africaines* (July 10, 1972): 4–7.

Ratsiraka, D. ''Le Boky Mena [Red Book] Charte de la révolution malgache.'' Tananarive, 1975. See *Afrique-Asie* 156, 157, 159 (March 6, March 20, April 17, 1975).

———. *Stratégies pour l'An 2000.* Paris: Editions Afrique, Asie, Amérique Latine, 1983.

Ravaloson, J. "Madagascar: le socialisme aux calendes grècques." *Le mois en Afrique,* 19 (215–216 Jan 1984): 139–144.

Ravel, J.-L. *L'assistance téchnique à Madagascar: approche psycho-sociologique de la rélation de coopération.* Paris: Ministère des Rélations Extérieures, Coopération et Développement, 1983.

Ravelojaona, B. "Madagascar: la logique de crise." *Année Africaine* (1990–1991): 301–325.

Razakarivony, B. "Le fokonolona et le développement économique." *Tantara* 3 (1975): 3–51.

Robert, M. "Les musulmans à Madagascar et dans les Mascareignes." *Revue française d'études politiques africaines* (June–July 1977): 46–71.

Roux, C. "Le récentrage et la réstructuration de l'économie malgache depuis 1974." *Le mois en Afrique* 15 (176–177 August–September 1980): 81–97.

Sauvy, A. "La République de Madagascar: population, économie, et perspectives de développement." *Populations* 17 (1962): 443–458.

Serre, G., and Rasoarahona, C. "Organisation militaire et révolution à Madagascar." In *La politique de Mars: Les procesus politiques dans les partis militaires,* ed. A. Roquie. Paris: Le Sycomore, 1979.

Shuttleworth, G. "Policies in Transition: Lessons from Madagascar." *World Development* 17 (1989): 397–408.

Société Malgache d'Etudes Juridiques. "La vocation de la commune malgache et le développement." *Revue juridique et politique, indépendance et coopération* 22 (1968): 205–248.

Spacensky, A. ''Regards sur l'évolution politique malgache.'' *Revue française de science politique* (1967): 263–285, 668–688.

———. *Madagascar. 50 ans de vie politique.* Paris: Nouvelles Editions Latines, 1970.

———. ''Dix ans de rapports franco-malgaches (1960–1970).'' *Revue française d'études politiques africaines* (December 1970): 77–92.

Textes rélatifs à l'élection du Président de la République démocratique de Madagascar. Antananarivo: Imprimerie Nationale, 1982.

Thierry, S. *Madagascar.* Paris: Seuil, 1961.

Thompson, V., and Adloff, R. *The Malagasy Republic.* Stanford: Stanford University Press, 1965.

Trigon, M. ''Madagascar: un combat difficile pour construire le bonheur et la liberté.'' *Les cahiers du communisme* 60 (January 1984): 78–81.

Trappe, P. *Soziale Breitenwirkung einer Entwicklungs-intervention. ''Lac Alaotra—grenier de Madagascar.''* Basel: Social Strategies Publishers, 1987.

Valette, J. ''La parti social-démocrate de Madagascar.'' *RFEPA* (September 1969): 73–83.

———. ''Les groupes éthniques à Madagascar.'' *RFEPA* (April 1974): 31–40.

Vérin, P. ''Coopération et francophonie dans les pays de l'Océan Indien.'' *Mondes et cultures* 42 (1982): 163–172.

Veyrier, M. ''La Réunion, Madagascar: le droit des peuples.'' *Les cahiers du communisme* (1976): 81–91.

Vinet, J.-M. "Les orientations nouvelles de l'économie malgache." *Afrique contemporaine* 84 (March–April 1976): 12–16.

"La Voix de l'Eglise à Madagascar." *Etudes* (May 1985): 593–601.

World Bank. *Madagascar: Recent Economic Developments and Future Prospects.* Washington, D.C.: World Bank, 1979.

Y.T. "De la déontologie des avocats du barreau de Madagascar." *Recueil pénant* 85 (1977): 441–449.

C. Geography and Resources

Battistini, R. *L'extrème sud de Madagascar. Etude de geomorphologie.* Paris: Cujas, 1964.

———. *Géographie humaine de la plaine côtière mahafaly.* Paris: Cujas, 1964.

———. "Villes et régions malgaches." *Acta geographica* 3 (1977): 36–38.

———, and Vindard, G., eds. *Biogeography and Ecology in Madagascar.* The Hague: Junk, 1972.

Boulanger, J.-C. "Développement, aménagement linguistique et terminologie: un mythe? L'exemple de la malgachisation." *Language Problems and Language Planning* 13 (1989): 243–263.

Cabanes, R. "Histoire d'un développement réussi: le nord-est de Madagascar." *Tiers-Monde* 23 (1982): 325–329.

Chatel, M.; Dechanet, R.; and Notteghem, R. "Amelioration variétale du riz pluvial à Madagascar." *Agronomie tropicale* 36 (1981): 253–265.

Dequire, J. ''L'amélioration du vanillier à Madagascar.'' *Journal de l'agriculture tropicale et de botanique appliquée* 23 (1976): 139–158.

Donque, G. *Contribution geographique à l'étude du climat de Madagascar.* Tananarive: La Librairie de Madagascar, 1977.

Douessin, R. *Géographie agraire des plaines de Tananarive.* Tananarive: Association des Géographes de Madagascar, 1977.

———. ''L'industrie dans les regions du Sud et du Sud-Ouest de Madagascar.'' *Omaly sy anio* 13–14 (1981): 357–374.

Gori, G., and Trama, P. *Types d'élevage et de vie rurale à Madagascar.* Bordeaux: Centre d'Etudes de Géographie Tropicale, 1979.

Hance, W. A. ''The Economic Geography of Madagascar.'' *Tijdschrift voor Economische en Sociale Geografie* 48 (1957): 161–172.

Hoerner, J.-M. ''L'agriculture et l'économie de marché dans le Sud-Ouest de Madagascar.'' *Omaly sy anio* 13–14 (1981): 337–348.

———. ''Tulear et le Sud-Ouest de Madagascar: approche démographique.'' *Madagascar: Revue de Géographie* 39 (July–December 1981): 9–49.

———. ''L'évolution des stratégies paysannes des originaires tompontany du Sud-Ouest de Madagascar.'' *Madagascar: Revue de Géographie* 42 (January–June 1983): 59–78.

———, and Cabot, J. ''Les industries de Toliara (Tulear), stagnation et mutation.'' *Les Cahiers d'Outre-Mer* 36 (1983): 75–85.

———. ''Les vols de boeufs dans le Sud malgache.'' *Madagascar: Revue de Géographie* 41 (July–December 1982): 85–105.

Keraudren-Aymonin, M. ''La flore malgache: un joyau à sauvegarder.'' *Science et nature,* no. 106 (1971): 5–14.

Lapaire, J.-P. ''L'évolution récente des baiboho du nord-ouest (region de Mampikony-Port Berge).'' *Madagascar: Revue de Géographie* 29 (1976): 117–154.

Le Bourdiec, F. ''L'évolution de la riziculture dans l'Ouest malgache.'' *Madagascar: Revue de Géographie* 30 (January–June 1977): 9–32.

———. ''Géographie historique de la riziculture malgache.'' *Madagascar: Revue de Géographie* 31 (July–December 1977): 11–72.

———. ''Aspects des relations villes-espace nationale: l'exemple de Madagascar.'' *Société languedocienne de géographie: bulletin trimestrielle* 16 (January–June 1982): 29–36.

Mondeil, R. ''Association agriculture-élevage dans le Moyen-Ouest: étude de cas d'une Coopérative socialiste de production.'' *Terre malgache/Tany malagasy* 21 (1982): 81–124.

Neuvy, G. ''Le réseau routier, facteur de développement à Madagascar: évolution économique de la région d'Andapa.'' *Madagascar: Revue de Géographie* 36 (January–June 1980): 21–62.

———. ''Mise en valeur des terres à Madagascar: la plaine agricole de Mahabo-Morondava.'' *Terre malgache/Tany malagasy* 21 (1982): 137–154.

Oberle, P., ed. *Madagascar: un sanctuaire de la nature.* Paris: Diffusions Lechevalier, 1981.

ORSTOM. Collection *Atlas des structures agraires à Madagascar* [several volumes].

Oxby, C. ''L'agriculture en forêt: transformation de l'utilisation des terres et de la société dans l'Est de Madagascar.'' *Unasylvia,* no. 148 (1985): 42–51.

Perrier de la Bathie, H. *La biogéographie des plantes de Madagascar.* Paris: SEGMC, 1963.

Petitjean, B. ''Le système agro-industriel et les pays du Tiers-Monde: le cas de Madagascar.'' *Revue juridique et politique, indépendance et coopération* 30 (1976): 177–203.

Rabetsitonta, T. A. ''Madagascar.'' In *L'évolution des éffectifs de la population des pays africains.* Paris: Groupe de Démographie Africaine, 1982.

Rakotoarisoa, J. A. *La région de Didy: économie, sociétés culture.* Tananarive: Musée de l'Université de Madagascar, Travaux et Documents, 1983.

Randrianarison, J. ''Le boeuf dans l'économie rurale de Madagascar.'' *Madagascar: Revue de Géographie* 31 (July–December 1977): 9–81.

Ratsimandratra, C. ''La dynamique urbaine de Tsiroanomandidy, capitale du Bongolava.'' *Madagascar: Revue de Géographie* 41 (July–December 1982): 41–84.

Ratsimbazafy, E. ''Terre des hauts-plateaux et perspectives de réstructuration.'' *Terre malgache/Tany malagasy* 16 (1974): 153–172.

Ravotoson, C. ''Les problèmes du tavy sur la côte est malgache et les solutions possibles.'' *Madagascar: Revue de Géographie* 35 (July–December 1979): 141–163.

Rechenmann, J. *Gravimétrie de Madagascar: interprétation et rélations avec la géologie.* Paris: ORSTOM, 1982.

Rossi, G. ''L'érosion a Madagascar: l'importance des facteurs humains.'' *Les Cahiers d'Outre-Mer* 32 (1979): 355–370.

———. *L'extrème-nord de Madagascar: étude de géographie physique.* Aix-en-Provence: EDISUD, 1979.

Rouvéyran, J.-C. *La logique des agricultures de transition: l'exemple des sociétés paysannes malgaches.* Paris: Maisonneuve et Larose, 1972.

Salomon, J.-N. "Tulear: un exemple de croissance et de structure urbaine en milieu tropicale." *Madagascar: Revue de Géographie* 30 (January–June 1977): 33–62.

———. "Une culture semi-industrielle à Madagascar: les plantes à parfum." *Les Cahiers d'Outre-Mer* 32 (1979): 158–178.

———. "Les vignobles et les vins de Madagascar." *Les Cahiers d'Outre-Mer* 33 (1980): 335–362.

———. "Problèmes de communication sur la Côte Est malgache: une réhabilitation du Canal des Pangalanes." *Les Cahiers d'Outre-Mer* 35 (1982): 63–76.

Singer, R.; Budtz-Olsen, O. E.; Brain, P.; and Saugrin, J. "Physical Features, Sickling, and Serology of the Malagasy of Madagascar." *American Journal of Physical Anthropology* 15 (1957): 91–124.

6. Language, Literature, and the Arts (All Periods)

Andriantsilaniarivo, E. "Le théâtre malgache." *Culture française,* no. 3–4 (1982) and no. 1 (1983): 91–98.

Bemananjara, Z. "La malgachisation. Aperçu sur les problèmes rélatifs à l'enseignement du française à Madagascar." In *Les rélations entre les langues négro-africaines et la langue française.* Paris: Conseil International de la Langue Française, 1977.

———. "Linguistique et révolution." *Soritra-Perspectives* 1 (1978): 39–50.

———. ''Madagascar.'' In *Inventaire des études linguistiques sur l'Afrique d'expression française et sur Madagascar.* Paris: Conseil International de la Langue Française, 1978.

———. *Contes malgaches.* [Malagasy texts and French translation]. Paris: Conseil International de la Langue Française, 1979.

Beaujard, P. ''Histoires des trois fils du roi et des soeurs ainées jalouses de leur cadette: étude d'un conte de Madagascar.'' *ASEMI* 10 (1979): 181–245.

———. ''Un conte malgache: des 'Enfants chez l'ogre.' '' *Cahiers de littérature orale* 12 (1982): 39–81.

Bourjea, S. ''J. Rabemanajara à la croisée du cri et du silence.'' In *Six conférences sur la littérature africaine d'expression française,* ed. W. Leiner. Tübingen: Attempo, 1981.

———. *Les débuts de l'orthographe malgache.* Oslo: Universitetsforlaget, 1966.

———. *Contes malgaches en dialecte sakalava. Textes, traduction, grammaire et lexique.* Oslo: Universitetsforlaget, 1968.

———. ''La subdivision de la famille Barito et la place du malgache.'' *Acta orientalia* 38 (1977): 77–134.

Dandouau, A. *Contes populaires des Sakalava et des Tsimihety de la région d'Analalalava.* Algiers: Carbonnel, 1922.

Decary, R. *Contes et légendes du sud-ouest de Madagascar.* Paris: Larose, 1964.

Delval, R., et al. ''L'évolution des sciences humaines à Madagascar.'' *Mondes et cultures* 49 (1989): 435–503.

Deschamps, H. *Le dialecte Antaisaka.* Tananarive: Pitot de la Beaujardière, 1936.

Dez, J. ''Le malgache.'' In *Inventaire des études linguistiques sur l'Afrique d'expression française et sur Madagascar.* Paris: Conseil International de la Langue Française, 1978.

———. *Structures de la langue malgache: éléments de grammaire à l'usage des francophones.* Paris: Publications des Orientalistes de France, 1980.

———. *Vocabulaire pour servir au déchiffrement de documents arabico-malgaches.* Paris: Université de Paris VII, Département de Récherches Linguistiques, 1981.

Domenichini-Ramiaramanana, B. *Hainteny d'autrefois,* édition bilingue. Tananarive: Imprimerie Centrale, 1968.

———. *Le malgache: essai de description sommaire.* Paris: Société d'Etudes Linguistiques et Anthropologiques de France, 1976.

Dubois, H. *Essai de dictionnaire Betsileo.* Tananarive: Imprimerie Officielle, 1917.

Faublée, J. *Introduction au malgache.* Paris: Librairie Orientale et Américaine, 1946.

———. *Récits Bara.* Paris: Institut d'Ethnologie, 1947.

———. ''Les variations linguistiques à Madagascar.'' *Comptes rendus trimestriels des séances de l'Académie des Sciences d'Outre-Mer* 19 (1959): 256–266.

———. ''Le premier colloque international sur la linguistique malgache.'' *Comptes rendus trimestriels des séances de l'Académie des Sciences d'Outre-Mer* 37 (1977): 725–727.

———. ''Les études littéraires malgaches de Jean Paulhan.'' *Journal de la Société des Africanistes* 54 (1984): 79–93.

Ferrand, G. *Contes populaires malgaches.* Paris: Leroux, 1893.

———. *Essai de phonétique comparée du malais et des dialectes malgaches.* Paris: Geuthner, 1909.

Hugon, P. *Economie et enseignement à Madagascar.* Paris: Institut International de Planification de l'Enseignement, 1977.

Jully, A. *Manuel des dialectes malgaches.* Paris: André, 1901.

Koechlin, B. "Un conte malgache en langue sakalava-vezo, Vuru-be." *L'Homme* 11 (1971): 31–61.

Koenig, J.-P. "Rabemananjara et les différentes influences de la littérature française." *Présence francophone* 15 (1977): 47–55.

Lévi-Strauss, C. "Chanson madécasse." In *Orients: pour Georges Condominas.* Paris: Sudasie, 1981.

Longchamps, J. de. *Contes malgaches.* Paris: Erasme, 1955.

Lormian, H. *L'Art malgache.* Paris: De Boccard, 1932.

Mack, J. "Malagasy Art in Its Contexts." *Africa* 43 (1988): 481–490.

Malzac, V. *Vocabulaire français-malgache. Nouvelle édition . . . augmentée d'un précis de grammaire malgache.* 1st ed., 1896. Paris: SEGMC, 1946.

———. *Grammaire malgache.* 1st ed., 1908. Paris: SEGMC, 1951.

———. *Dictionnaire français-malgache.* Paris: SEGMC, 1956.

———, and Malzac, V. *Dictionnaire malgache-français.* 1st ed., 1888. Paris: SEGMC, 1955.

Marre, A. *Grammaire malgache: fondée sur les principes de la grammaire javanaise.* 1st ed., 1876. Paris: AUPELF, 1976 [microfiche].

———. *Vocabulaire des principales racines malaises et javanaises de la langue malgache.* 1st ed., 1896. Paris: AUPELF, 1976 [microfiche].

Meritens, G., and Veyriéres, P. de. *Le livre de la sagesse malgache.* Paris: Editions Maritimes et d'Outre-Mer, 1967.

Montagne, L. *Essai de grammaire malgache.* Paris: SEGMC, 1931.

Oberle, P. ''Aux origines de l'art malgache.'' *L'Afrique littéraire et artistique* 51 (1979): 75–81.

Ottino, P. ''Le thème du monstre dévorant dans les domaines malgache et bantou.'' *ASEMI* 8 (1977): 205–251.

Rabearison. *Contes et légendes de Madagascar.* Tananarive: Imprimerie Protestante, 1964.

Rabenalisoa Ravalitera, J. ''1972–1982: une décennie de chansons populaires à Madagascar.'' *Modes populaires d'action politique* 3 (1984): 124–145.

Rabenilaina, R. B. *Morpho-syntaxe du malgache: description structurale du dialecte bara.* Paris: SELAF, 1983.

Rabenoro, C. ''L'Académie malgache.'' *Comptes rendus trimestriels des séances de l'Académie des Sciences d'Outre-Mer* 37 (1977): 483–498.

Rahaingoson, H. ''La malgachisation de l'enseignement: considérations générales.'' In *Les rélations entre les langues negro-africaines et la langue française.* Paris: CILF, 1977.

Rajhonson, R., and Ratsima, M. ''L'enseignement de la langue malgache au niveau de l'enseignement de base.'' *Linguistique et enseignement* 3 (1977): 39–72.

Rakotofiringa, H. *Etude de phonétique expérimentale: l'accent et les unités phonétiques élémentaires de base en malgache-merina.* Lille: Atelier de Reproduction des Thèses, 1982.

———. ''Les emprunts révélateurs de la structure syllabique du malgache-merina.'' *Bulletin de l'Institut de Phonétique de Grenoble* 13 (1984): 131–152.

Rakotomalala, M. ''Le hiran-tsakalava du Vonizongo: chants populaires malgaches.'' *ASEMI* 11 (1980): 483–490.

Ramamonjisoa, S.; Schrive, M.; and Raharinjanahary, S. *Femmes et monstres: tradition orale malgache.* Paris: CILF, 1981.

Randiamampita. M. ''Bilan sur le statut des langues dans l'enseignement à Madagascar.'' *Linguistique et enseignement* 3 (1977): 10–38.

Ribard, M. ''Contribution à l'étude des aloalo malgaches.'' *L'Anthropologie* 34 (1924): 91–102.

Richardson, J. *A New Malagasy-English Dictionary.* 1st ed., 1885. Farnborough, Hants, 1967.

Sachs, C. *Les instruments de musique à Madagascar.* Paris: Institut d'Ethnologie, 1938.

Thomas-Fattier, D. *Le dialecte sakalava du Nord-Ouest de Madagascar: phonologie, grammaire, lexique.* Paris: SELAF, 1982.

Turcotte, D. ''La planification linguistique à Madagascar: réaménager les rapports entre les langues françaises et malgaches.'' *International Journal of the Sociology of Language* 32 (1981): 5–25.

———. *La politique linguistique en Afrique francophone: Une étude comparative de la Côte d'Ivoire et de Madagascar.* Quebec: Centre Internationale de Récherche sur le Bilinguisme, 1981.

Urbain-Faublée, M. *L'Art malgache.* Paris: Presses Universitaires Françaises, 1963.

Webber, J. *Dictionnaire malgache-français redigé selon l'ordre des racines par les missionnaires catholiques de Madagascar et adapté aux dialectes de toutes les provinces.* Ile Bourbon (Réunion): Imprimerie Catholique de Notre-Dame de la Ressource, 1853.

———. *Dictionnaire français-malgache.* Ile Bourbon (Réunion): Imprimerie Catholique de Notre-Dame de la Ressource, 1855.

Zefaniasy Rafaralahy, B. ''La situation linguistique à Madagascar.'' *Cahiers de CACID* 2 (1982): 156–182.

ABOUT THE AUTHOR

Maureen Covell is a professor of Political Science at Simon Fraser University in Burnaby, British Columbia, Canada. She wrote her doctoral dissertation on local politics in Madagascar, a research undertaking that involved an extensive stay on the island. In particular, she lived for several months in Antananarivo, Fianarantsoa, and Toliara. Among her acquaintances at the time were several people who were subsequently active in the politics of the Second Republic.

Dr. Covell is the author of *Madagascar: Politics, Economics, and Society,* and of articles on Malagasy local government and foreign policy.